This publication was donated by

West Central Maryland Chapter No. 92

in the interest of
furthering professionalism in
the field of Real Estate Management

IREM

For a catalog of publications and educational programs
available through the **Institute of Real Estate Management**
of the NATIONAL ASSOCIATION OF REALTORS®,
write to: IREM
   430 N. Michigan Ave.
   Chicago, IL 60611

The Practice of Real Estate Management

MONTGOMERY COUNTY BOARD OF REALTORS, INC.
3809 Farragut Avenue, P.O. Box 270
Kensington, Maryland 20895

Nancye J. Kirk, Project Editor

The Practice of Real Estate Management

for the Experienced Property Manager

William Walters Jr., CPM®

Institute of Real Estate Management
of the NATIONAL ASSOCIATION OF REALTORS®
430 N. Michigan Avenue, Chicago, Illinois 60611

AAW 1274

ACKNOWLEDGMENTS

Bliss, Edwin C. *Getting Things Done.* Copyright © 1976 by Charles Scribner's Sons.

Drucker, Peter. *The Effective Executive.* Copyright © 1977 by Peter F. Drucker. *Management: Tasks, Responsibilities, and Practices.* Copyright © 1973, 1974 by Peter F. Drucker. *The Practice of Management.* Copyright © 1954 by Peter F. Drucker. Reprinted by permission of Harper & Row, Inc.

Gellerman, Saul W. *Management by Motivation.* Copyright © 1968 by American Management Association, Inc. All rights reserved. Reprinted by permission of the publisher.

Kellogg, Marion S. *What To Do About Performance Appraisal.* (Rev. ed.) Copyright © 1975 by AMACOM, a division of American Management Associations. All rights reserved. Reprinted by permission of the publisher.

Mackenzie, R. Alec. *The Time Trap.* Copyright © 1972 by AMACOM, a division of American Management Associations.

Mazirow, Arthur and Arthur Bowman. *Advanced Legal Aspects of Real Estate for the California Broker.* 1976. Reprinted by permission of the authors.

McKay, Edward S. *The Marketing Mystique.* Copyright © 1972 by American Management Association, Inc. All rights reserved. Reprinted by permission of the publisher.

The publisher also is grateful to A. Alexander Bul, CPM®, of Henry S. Miller Management Corporation, Dallas, Texas; Gary R. Holme, CPM®, of The Beaumont Company, Los Angeles, California; and E. Robert Miller, CPM®, of The Robert A. McNeil Corporation, San Mateo, California, who reviewed the manuscript prior to publication.

Throughout this publication, masculine pronouns have been used to refer to individual property managers, executive officers, resident managers, applicants, occupants, prospects, tenants, etc., regardless of whether they are men or women. This was done for the sake of convenience and does not imply that any or all of these persons are or should be men.

International Standard Book Number: 0–912104–37–6
Library of Congress Catalog Number: 79–84053
Printed in the United States of America

A Note of Appreciation

This book was not a natural or easy assignment for the author. It has taken approximately 600 hours during a three-year time span to complete. A good deal of assistance for ideas and experience came from friends and associates who are members of the Institute of Real Estate Management.

Special contributions to this book were made by: Lee Carlson, CPA, controller for the William Walters Company, who assisted with the trust-fund accounting chapter; Elaine Zuicker, my secretary, who prepared the manuscript; and Beverly Dordick, librarian of the NATIONAL ASSOCIATION OF REALTORS®, for her guidance and assistance in gathering resources for the historical section of this book.

Finally, a very special note of gratitude to an exceedingly talented and persevering young lady, Nancye Kirk, who is responsible for the editing and rewriting of my manuscript. Her constant challenges for improvement and her outstanding organizational skills are significantly responsible for whatever success this book may enjoy.

William Walters Jr., CPM®

Foreword

THE INSTITUTE OF REAL ESTATE MANAGEMENT of the NATIONAL ASSOCIATION OF REALTORS® is an organization of professional property managers who have distinguished themselves in the areas of education, experience, and ethical conduct. IREM offers property managers and the public an expansive program of educational courses and seminars, textbooks, and audiovisual programs. *The Practice of Real Estate Management for the Experienced Property Manager* has been prepared as part of this professional program.

About the Author

William Walters Jr., CERTIFIED PROPERTY MANAGER® (CPM®), is president of William Walters Company, a real estate management firm headquartered in Los Angeles, California. Walters joined the family-owned company in 1949 upon graduation from the University of Southern California. Thirteen years later he acquired full ownership of the firm and expanded the base of its real estate service activities. His innovative thinking has been responsible for the company's extraordinary growth, its management portfolio having tripled in size since he joined the firm. The company now has offices in Los Angeles, Orange County, and San Diego, California, and in Phoenix, Arizona, and employs a staff of 60 persons, including 10 CPMs®. Its portfolio represents more than $300 million in real estate assets, including approximately 11,000 apartment units, 4,000 condominium units, and one million square feet of office space.

In addition to its pure management activity, William Walters Company has a management consulting division that provides marketing, operating, and financial management expertise to investors who have special real estate problem situations. The firm also is involved in the sale and acquisition of investment properties, and it has been successful in numerous real estate rehabilitation efforts. Another important element of the company's activity in the management of real estate assets is its role as general partner of a number of limited partnerships, providing the financial and executive management capabilities that limited partners seek.

The author has generously shared his knowledge and experience through active participation in the Institute of Real Estate Management. Walters's involvement in the Institute began in 1953, when he received the CPM® designation, and it culminated with his election as the 1971 national IREM president. In the interim, he served as a regional vice president and president of the Los Angeles IREM Chapter, was an instructor in several IREM educational courses, and was instrumental in the development of courses focused on the leasing and management of office buildings and the management of the real estate management office. Walters continues to be involved in IREM's educational program, specifically in the development of an advanced educational program for CPMs®. In 1977, Walters was the recipient of the highest honor bestowed by the Institute—the J. Wallace Paletou Award, presented annually to the individual who has made the most significant contribution to the professional of real estate management.

Walters's other business affiliations, past and present, include: director of the former Mission National Bank in Los Angeles, trustee for a real estate investment trust, general partner for publicly held limited partnerships, and developer of office buildings and apartment houses and a mobile home park.

Contents

ix

Part III   The Acquisition of Business

t V   The Management Office

Preface

THE PRACTICE OF REAL ESTATE MANAGEMENT *for the Experienced Property Manager* is for and about the professional who manages income property and the business enterprise that supports that professional. Together, the property manager and the management company provide the professional service known as the practice of real estate management.

The role of the property manager is discussed in terms of scientific management skills and what a manager should understand about decision making, innovating, planning, organizing, coordinating, controlling, and directing work. The assumption is that the reader is an experienced property manager who has mastered the techniques of operating real estate. Consequently, this text does not discuss management's operational tasks, such as collecting rent, preparing a maintenance schedule, or marketing space. Those fundamentals are explained at length in real estate management courses conducted by the Institute of Real Estate Management and textbooks that deal with the practical, day-to-day aspects of managing property. Rather, the focus here is on encouraging the property manager to understand that he is in a rapidly changing industry, one that affords great opportunity for the professional who possesses or can acquire the insight and understanding of scientific management in order that his performance might produce greater economic results. The introduction reviews the evolution of scientific management and the skills required of the modern manager.

Part I, The Property Manager, provides a critical examination of the practice of property management and the attributes of a professional property manager. Its theme is that the practitioner who knows only the operational skills and techniques of managing property but has no understanding of the discipline of management is not a professional property manager. At best, he is a property supervisor.

The successful practice of real estate management requires that a professional property manager be supported by an efficient and enterprising organization which assists in achieving the investment goals of the clients. Equally important, a property management firm must be capable of achieving its own business objectives. Part II, The Company Plan, discusses at length the fundamentals of long-range and short-range planning and techniques for creating the strategic plan for a property management company and establishing an organizational structure to sustain that plan.

As with undoubtedly all professional service firms, the person at the top of a management firm is the key to a successful organization. An entrepreneurial chief executive is the innovative force that utilizes the total resources of the enterprise in order to realize long-term growth and profitability. Achieving an acceptable growth level is dependent upon obtaining new business. Part III, The Acquisition of Business, looks at the role of the property manager in acquiring new business and subsequently incorporating that business into the management firm's operations.

Inasmuch as a significant portion of a property manager's time is spent with his subordinates, it is imperative that he is able to establish good working relationships with his employees. Part IV, Managing People, concentrates on employment policies and selection, training and development, performance appraisal, and systems of motivation.

A property management firm will not be successful in meeting its corporate objectives without an efficient, effective central management office. Part V, The Management Office, describes the work that must be accomplished in order that the office might function as the nerve center of the organization. Attention is focused on the overall operation of the management office, the trust accounting function, and the insurance and legal considerations about which the experienced property management must be knowledgeable.

A cardinal purpose of this book is to outline the tasks and responsibilities of today's property manager and real estate organization and identify the opportunities that await the management profession. By reviewing the development of the field of property management, the real estate manager can examine his own concepts and qualifications and determine if they are based on current standards that will enable him to grasp new opportunities or if he is operating on standards that are no longer applicable. The conclusion of this text reviews the historical evolution of real estate management, providing the framework upon which the property manager may perform this self-evaluation.

Introduction

FOR THE EXPERIENCED PROPERTY MANAGER to take full advantage of existing opportunities in the real estate industry, a knowledge of the industry's origins and evolution is essential. Certain significant developments have greatly altered the direction of property management. The most recent of these occurred in the early 1970s, a period of double-digit inflation and tremendous oversupply in the real estate market.

There were several sources of economic difficulty during this time. One of them involved real estate investment trusts (REITs), which piled huge debts on thin foundations of equity capital. Material shortages delayed construction of many projects, and developers, many of whom had borrowed from REITs, ran out of funds before their buildings were completed. To avoid foreclosure, new loans were advanced. Unfortunately, the REITs often pumped in so much money that the projects could not be economic. This unhealthy financial situation was brought to the public's attention when the principal of one of the largest apartment developers in the nation filed for protection from his creditors under the bankruptcy act. It later was learned that about 20 REITs had made loans, many of them substantial, to this developer.

Meanwhile, numerous other real estate ventures were failing, and lenders were taking over the distressed properties. Professional property management burst into public awareness as it was faced with the challenge of salvaging these properties. The need for a new kind of property manager arose. Property management was

5

forced toward a level of maturity that put the accent on professionalism, thoroughness, and training. In consequence, the scope of
the professional property manager today extends beyond merely
supervising the operations of properties. It encompasses the basic
management tasks of planning, organizing, motivating, and coordinating. Not only must fundamental property management skills be
mastered, but the discipline of scientific management also must be
conquered if effective organizational leadership is to be exhibited.

Scientific Management and Industrialization

As the twentieth century opened, the United States was experiencing
general prosperity, growing industrialism, and significant social
change. The 1900 census put the population at 76,212,168, an increase
of almost 21 percent over the population of 1890. Fifty cities had
populations of more than 100,000, three had populations exceeding
1,000,000, and more than one-third of the nation's people lived in
urban areas—evidence of the shift from an agrarian to an urban
society.

Not only were cities growing, but business was growing as well.
At the turn of the century, hardly a dozen American corporations,
other than railroads, were capitalized at more than $10 million.
Six years later, the number of such corporations rose to 300, approximately 50 of which were capitalized at more than $50 million. In
addition, tremendous strides were being made in the field of scientific
invention—above all, in the use of electricity. Although the typical
American's daily life was changed by electricity, the most far-reaching
application was in industry. By 1914, 30 percent of the American
factory capacity was electrified. With this new source of energy, factories could locate near sources of raw materials and labor and in
market and port cities rather than near coalfields and river valleys,
which formerly were needed to provide the required energy.

As inventions were introduced, their impact on business became
evident: Growth was inevitable. With strides being made in the
various industries, business management had to grow to meet society's demands. The first significant book on the subject of management, written by Frederick W. Taylor and published in 1911,
was appropriately entitled *Scientific Management*. Taylor, one of
the first people to study the nature of work, espoused the basic theory
of scientific management: Business managers have a responsibility
to eliminate waste and improve efficiency in industry while simul-

taneously relieving the worker from back-breaking toil. Taylor's philosophy was that efficiency is highly desirable for both workers and managers: Workers earn higher wages, and managers experience lower costs. He theorized that, in an efficient organization, the manager properly defines the worker's task, selects the right worker for the right job, and motivates the worker to a higher level of performance.

These ideas do not sound particularly startling to the contemporary mind; however, at the turn of the century, they were revolutionary and aroused a great deal of controversy. Prior to this, management's efforts were largely in the direction of trying to persuade workers to produce more, without having any clear idea of how much they should or could produce. Taylor believed this common practice to be nothing less than a defection on the part of management. Over a period of years, he worked out three techniques to relieve this situation: (1) Prescribe the exact order and method of work; (2) describe the tools and equipment to be used; and (3) establish the time in which the task is to be accomplished. The first two requirements Taylor accomplished through the use of motion studies, the last through a time study. The latter, which became identified with scientific management and was the center of much controversy, involved watching a good worker use prescribed methods and equipment in order to determine the time in which that task should be performed.

Considered characteristic of a "first-class worker" was willingness to accomplish the amount of work that management established as proper. This willingness, wrote Taylor, comes if an appropriate incentive is offered. Taylor proposed a merit payment plan that rewarded poorly for below-standard performance and handsomely for above-standard performance.

At the same time in France, Henri Fayol was making some profound contributions to management thinking. Fayol was concerned with efficiency at the organizational level rather than at the task level, with overall control rather than details of operations. Pointing out that tasks at successively higher levels become less technical and more managerial, he developed the concept that is now called administration. Fayol's contribution to management theory was unique and valuable. He was ahead of his time in proclaiming the significance of planning, organizing, directing, and controlling in the management discipline. Furthermore, he was author of the organizational chart, job specifications, and the concept of management education.

The general feeling of stagnation that was prevalent between the two world wars encouraged little advancement in the field of management during the 1920s and 1930s. The period, however, did produce three innovative thinkers: General Robert E. Wood, who headed Sears, Roebuck and Company; Pierre S. DuPont of DuPont and Company; and Alfred P. Sloan Jr. of General Motors. Wood's contribution involved analyzing the growing urban market and expanding Sears's emphasis to include not only that of a mail-order plant serving farmers but also that of a retail store equipped to serve a more sophisticated city population. He instituted a series of merchandizing innovations to accomplish this goal; these included designing products, developing manufacturers who could produce large quantities of these products, and building numerous retail outlets to merchandise the products. DuPont's and Sloan's contributions revolved around the big-business principle known as decentralization, or the reorganization of a company into numerous autonomous companies that remain under central control. DuPont crudely applied this theory in 1920, when he divided his family-owned company, and Sloan refined it when he decentralized GM's operations in 1921 and 1922. Sloan also developed systematic approaches to business objectives, business strategy, and strategic planning.

Also during the period following World War I and well into the thirties, management became more conscious of its human relations problems. Society in general, and lawmakers in particular, recognized that big business was exploiting labor and the consumer. Laws were enacted to stop child labor abuse, compensate workers who were injured in industrial accidents, improve working conditions, and safeguard employee health. Labor unions gained large memberships, whose voices were being heard on wages, hours, and working conditions. Psychology was an advancing science, and its applications to work and everyday life were receiving added emphasis. Management began to appoint specialists known as personnel managers to handle the problems of human relations, and labor relations was becoming part of the management discipline.

Property Supervision and Urbanization

While the application of management theory and practice reached the factories that were dominating city life, it was slower to break into other institutions, specifically property management. As the urban shift was taking place, the means for handling the ever-increasing numbers of city dwellers began to change. At the end of the nineteenth century, multifamily dwellings were of four and six units, small retail stores were built along principal boulevards, and businesses were housed in small structures. As the cities grew, density increased progressively. Larger buildings—office buildings, commercial structures, and apartments—became necessary. Owners usually managed their own real estate; however, sometimes local brokers provided caretaker services or acted as buffers between tenant and owners. Property management involved little more than keeping an eye on a property, basically providing nursemaid service. The practice of property management was lagging far behind the technical developments of the new industrial era. Managerial actions frequently were improvised to meet problems as they arose, the manager or owner relying upon intuition and rule-of-thumb procedures and policies.

To understand clearly the role of property management during the period from 1900 to 1920, consider what W.W. Hannan, president of the National Association of Real Estate Exchanges, said in 1913:

> Management is what I consider the most important phase of apartment house investment. The manager of the building must see to it that the halls are kept clean, that the employees about the building are kind and courteous and that dozens of other details are not neglected, or the tenants will move out. They will go where there is proper management. Your manager should be a man of strong character and business ability. He should stand in the same relation to his apartment house as a conductor does to his train or a captain to his ship. He should be in absolute control. He should not permit the manifold suggestions and complaints of his tenants to sway him from the proper course.

But the role of management was beginning to change. E. Orris Hart, in an address delivered before the Chicago Real Estate Board in 1921, had this to say about managers: "It is a mistake for a broker, capable of doing a large personal business in sales and leasing, to accept the agency and management of property with the view of giving it his personal attention." A 1917 article in the *National Real Estate Journal* written by John A. Carroll supported the changing nature of property management:

> Good rent men are in demand, probably because renting is a business, or especially, is new and sufficient time has not been had to develop specialists in this line. All real estate men of 10 or 15 years experience know when the renting department was an unimportant part of the

real estate office and this class of work was delegated to clerks.

The situation has changed. A few years ago almost all renting and managing was done by owners themselves. To own a home or business place was the rule. Probably 75 percent of the population of any city was represented by owners and 25 percent by tenants. In 20 years the ratio has reversed; 75 percent are tenants and 25 percent are owners. This accounts for the development of rent as a separate and important branch of the real estate business. Business, although large and important, has developed much faster than have the men who make renting and managing a speciality.

Property Management and Professionalism

The real estate boom that occurred in the 1920s formed the foundation for the second phase of development of the real estate management industry. Public confidence in real estate as an investment was at an all-time high. New sources of financing allowed for unprecedented building activity in principal cities. While apartment houses of more than 100 units were still rare, multifamily dwellings were being built in great numbers. New office buildings were being developed in downtown areas. Likewise, there was much development of retail stores in both cities and outlying areas.

By the 1920s, the National Association of Real Estate Boards (NAREB), originally founded in 1909 as the National Association of Real Estate Exchanges and today the NATIONAL ASSOCIATION OF REALTORS®, began to mention property management at some of its national meetings. The focus was on cooperative apartments, business property rentals, chain store leasing, operating rental agencies, and the operation and maintenance of apartments. As a consequence of this interest, NAREB created a Property Management Division, which held its first organizational meeting in 1923. Some 250 NAREB members registered for membership.

In 1924, with construction of apartment buildings reaching unprecedented highs, NAREB's Property Management Division conducted a building survey. It revealed the danger of developing or investing in buildings "where there is a likelihood they will not pay a reasonable return." The purpose of this survey was to indicate the importance of advance management planning and analysis to determine the earning power of a projected real estate development or building. Thus, the scope of property management was changing dramatically. The property manager was no longer merely a caretaker or rent man. His duties were being expanded to include performing market analyses, budgeting, and handling public relations.

In a 1926 article, "Analyzing the Property Manager's Job," published in the *National Real Estate Journal,* Carlton Schultz, Chairman of the Property Management Division of NAREB, listed these "things a property manager must do":

1. Determine the possible and probable gross income.
2. Budget the expense.
3. Determine the rental policies.
4. Secure the tenants.
5. Maintain the mechanical condition of the building.
6. Maintain the physical condition of the building.
7. Make the building look attractive.
8. Keep the building clean.
9. Keep the building in repair.
10. Act as accountant for the building.
11. Collect the rents.
12. Pay the bills.
13. Buy all materials.
14. Supervise all alterations.
15. Pay taxes and secure tax adjustments.
16. Keep the building insured.
17. See that damage suits are avoided.
18. Follow up civic matters which may have a bearing on the future income or expense of the building.

The Depression for real estate started in 1928 when the supply of new income properties exceeded tenant demand. During the next five years, most of the apartment houses and office buildings built during the twenties fell into the hands of their primary lenders— banks, insurance companies, savings and loan associations, and bond holder committees. Ironically, this depressed situation proved to be a boon to the property management business. Great concentrations of property were in the hands of former lenders. Since little proven real estate management experience was available, these lenders-turned-owners created their own management capability. A handful of real estate practitioners identified themselves with this new field of property management, and it was a few of these people who gathered during the depths of the Depression and founded the Institute of Real Estate Management (IREM).

The Institute's first meeting was held on October 5, 1933, in Chicago with eight people in attendance. The corporate charter was received from the state of Illinois less than a year later. The primary concern of IREM's founding fathers was financial responsibility of the practitioners in the business of managing real estate for others. Originally, management firms, not individual property managers, were eligible to become members of IREM. Each firm was required to have one representative who was a member of NAREB and to follow certain ethical standards of practice. Specifically, a member firm was required to avoid commingling of funds, carry a fidelity bond on all employees who handled money, and refrain from reaping financial benefit from the use of a client's funds without full disclosure.

Shortly after IREM's formation, the first efforts toward improving the competence of the membership were made. These efforts focused on national meetings (which offered discussions on subjects of importance), publication of the *Journal of Real Estate Management* (later the *Journal of Property Management*), and development of an educational program. The first course offered emphasized the basics of property management, including the renting of space, a major problem during the Depression. Other subjects were maintenance and repair, purchasing, real estate taxes, collections, accounting, reporting to owners, insurance, legal aspects of the landlord-tenant relationship, and property analysis. Out of the 62-hour course, however, only one hour was spent on a subject called executive control of the management business, and but two hours were devoted to personnel matters.

By the mid-1930s, property management had attracted a great deal of attention and interest. Like scientific management two decades earlier, it began to think about efficiency in operation. Management was becoming cost conscious, with stress on reducing overhead and operating costs. Howard Haney pointed out in a 1934 article in the *Journal of Real Estate Management* the necessity for identification of qualified real estate managers:

> Property management isn't the collection of rentals any more. It's a scientific business that is just in its infancy and can grow to enormous proportions. . . . We in the real estate management field, and especially those engaged in the handling of apartment property, are just waking up to the value of cooperation to the extent of exchanging experiences as to our various problems.

One of the most innovative theories to come out of the property management industry during this period was expressed by James C. Downs Jr., who was among the founders of IREM. In an article entitled "The Management Program" that appeared in the *Journal of Real Estate Management* in 1938, Downs recognized management as being a practice that requires planning and analysis. The management program (now usually referred to as the management plan) was proposed as a short-term plan wherein the manager analyzed the market, the neighborhood, and the property before making recommendations as to what should be done with the property:

> To the average person who thinks of a ship at sea, completely surrounded by hundreds of miles of water, the compass and sextant loom up as the blessed instruments by which a successful voyage is made possible. As a matter of fact, a sea captain, no matter how skilled in the art of instruments, cannot complete a successful voyage without a map showing the position of his destination. Knowing how to navigate is one thing; knowing your destination is another. After learning something of the mechanics of navigating a property management problem, the next step involves the process of property management mapmaking—the process of determining your destination—the management program.

The Management Boom

The professional manager as a dynamic, decision-making force came into focus during the 25 years following World War II. The Great Depression—which fostered a change in the economic philosophy wherein the government thought its spending programs assured national prosperity—and World War II—which brought about increased mass production and amazing growth in the size of companies—had dramatic effects on all segments of United States society. The country became a conglomerate of big institutions—industry, associations, labor unions, governments, retail stores, universities, farms, and financial institutions. Indeed, almost everything became bigger and bigger. Bigness cried out for the professional manager who could assume responsibility for the performance of these institutions. Terms like strategic planning, missions, methods analysis, computer programs, management by objectives, and asset management grew in acceptance. These concepts gave a new definition to management and the role of the manager.

In 1954, Peter Drucker published *The Practice of Management,* a book that has become required reading for every student of management. In it he discussed the importance of the seven foundations of management: scientific management, decentralization, personnel management, manager development, managerial accounting, marketing, and long-range planning.

• Scientific management is an objective method of solving problems. First, the problem is identified; next, information is collected, classified, and analyzed; finally, plans are formulated to determine the usefulness and validity of the objective.

- Decentralization is the principle of establishing a business where it is most appropriate. The idea that a business must be located in a specific city, state, or even country, or that it must operate in only one location, was rejected. A business should locate were productive resources, workers, market opportunities, transportation facilities, and financial resources are available.
- Personnel management involves recruiting, selecting, training, supervising, and motivating employees. Drucker considered job descriptions, appraisals, wage and salary administration, and human relations programs as helpful in learning ways to fit people into organizational structures in orderly fashions.
- Manager development refers to the constant challenge to learn the skills needed to become effective in the future.
- Managerial accounting recognizes the use of information and analysis as the foundation for managerial decision making. (The computer, with its programs and management information systems, has broadly expanded this ability.)
- Marketing, according to Drucker, is one of the basic functions of management, inasmuch as the purpose of a business is to create a customer. Too often the concept of marketing is inaccurately limited to the sole endeavor of selling. Yet in addition, marketing requires defining the market area, researching the needs and wants of customers, developing a service to meet that demand, recruiting and selecting and training manpower to deliver that service, and developing the sales approach and advertising support.
- Long-range planning is needed in order to fully utilize available resources, take advantage of all opportunities, and optimize long-term growth and profitability. Economic, political, and social situations can change the nature of a business. Managers, as the leaders of industry, must recognize and plan for change. A long-range plan, either formally written or informally understood, attempts to help an enterprise focus on market needs and marshall the necessary resources to meet them.

Management education in business schools and universities proliferated during this boom in the field of management. Before World War II, only Harvard University taught management. By the late sixties, the number of such schools numbered well into the hundreds, and graduate programs in schools of business were available throughout the country. The management explosion also fostered the founding of societies dedicated to specialized aspects of management, such as marketing, advertising, packaging, office work, computerization, industrial relations, and scores of others, all adding to the growing body of knowledge available to managers. The most important of these was the American Management Association, founded in 1923 as an outgrowth of several organizations. After a struggle for survival during the Great Depression, it became a large and successful organization that today provides training in various aspects of management.

The management boom in American business and industry ended in the late 1960s. By that time, management had identified the essential functions of organizing work for productivity, recognized the responsibility of management for producing economic results, and learned a great deal about leading the worker toward productivity and achievement.

The mystique of management was gone. It had matured and become a fully taught and universally practiced discipline. But another lesson was yet to be learned. The dollar crisis of 1971 proved that management is not infallible. This was shown by some major business debacles, notably the failures of Penn Central and Lockheed Aircraft. These failures made professional management appear something less than competent and professional. Thus, management passed its period of innocence.

Management Theory in Property Management Thought

The period following World War II was characterized by a major real estate shortage and a consequent demand for all types of rental space. Vacancies were few, which meant there was little apparent need for the services of property management. The profession continued to take the direction originated by Downs and developed further by H.P. Holmes. In his 1949 article entitled "The Fundamentals of Real Estate Management," Holmes elaborated on the management program concept:

> Having carefully analyzed the situation relative to a particular parcel of real estate, the property manager is now in a position to formulate and recommend to the owner a definite management program. In developing this program, the following should be kept in mind: (1) the purpose of the program; (2) what it includes; and (3) how its requirements can be fulfilled.

It has been said that the purpose of a management program is to assist in preserving the owner's investment, to present him with a steady and satisfactory return on his investment, to enhance the value of the property, and to shield the owner from the cares and worries incidental to ownership.

The management program is a statement of facts, objectives, and policies to be followed in a definite plan of action. To obtain the whole-hearted approval and support of the owner, this program should include:

1. An analysis of the property.
2. An analysis of the neighborhood.
3. An estimate of value based upon earnings.
4. A statement of the financial situation.
5. An estimate of the highest and best use to which the property may be put.
6. The development of a possible rental schedule.
7. The preparation of a budget of operations.
8. A plan for securing proper tenantry.
9. A calendar of maintenance, rehabilitation and modernization.
10. A calendar of purchases, including specifications.
11. A plan for adequate operating personnel.
12. A plan for keeping records and furnishing reports.
13. A plan for administering the program.

If a management program properly fulfills its requirements, it will aid in obtaining the highest possible gross income, as well as exercising an efficient control over operating costs.

Let us now consider the detailed information about the property which must be gathered in order to formulate the most successful management program. This information has to come from the property manager's personal fund of knowledge obtained through study and experience. In other words, such a program is a balanced combination of the facts concerning the property, plus what the property manager has found out through personal experience, plus what he has learned through observation and study.

In the late 1950s and early 1960s, real estate supply began to catch up with demand. When the tide finally turned and vacancies began to appear, property owners again realized the need for the services of professional management.

The real estate management industry, as most service industries, gave little thought to the concept of management until the late sixties. Prior to that time, real estate management was still a task-oriented activity. The business by and large was concerned only with improving techniques of production and observing how the government affected opportunities. Property managers were concerned with renting apartments rather than marketing programs, cutting operating costs rather than long-range planning, and income and expense statements rather than cost accounting analysis.

This changed in the late 1960s and early 1970s, during which time a tremendous amount of income property was developed. At the close of the third quarter (1968–1975), real estate experienced its greatest commitment of new capital for the development of income-producing properties. Apartment projects containing from 100 to 500 units began to replace smaller apartment houses. Office buildings developed in the 1950s had 10,000 to 15,000 square feet per floor; during the sixties and early seventies, they were often designed with 30,000 square feet per floor. Shopping centers had not one department store but oftentimes as many as five major retail businesses. Furthermore, for the first time since the twenties, ownership was in the portfolio of the public through interests in REITs and large limited partnerships. Real estate had a need for the professional manager, a need commercial and industrial institutions recognized during the 1950s and 1960s.

The property management industry now has some large companies that provide all types of management services. Companies with more than 50 employees are not uncommon. The people who run these enterprises have become committed to mastering the management discipline. Chief executive officers realize they must be opportunity-focused, not simply problem-focused, if they are to be prepared to meet the challenges of the future.

No less important is application of the principles of management to small businesses. In many respects, management is even more important to a small business, which must compete with larger firms but cannot afford to make the same mistakes. It must carefully identify its competitive strengths and plan its activity. Furthermore, a smaller company provides less opportunity for specialization. The executive officer must perform widely varied management tasks, since his business probably does not justify full-time specialists in, say, strategic planning or marketing or the management of people.

Currently a new dimension—social responsibility—is being added to the scope of management. Public opinion, employee pressures, and legislative requirements are making it clear that society expects more from management than goods, services, and profits. The big challenge for real estate management in the coming decades, then, will not be for technological innovations but for social innovations. As urban areas continue to grow in population and age physically, the challenge will be to improve the housing needs of people, business, and industry; respond to environmental considerations; and make all resources more productive.

I
The Property Manager

1

Profile of a Property Manager

PROPERTY MANAGEMENT HAS A DEFINITE MEANING within the real estate industry. The term "property management" refers to situations in which someone other than the owner oversees the operation of a property. Although a landholder may manage his property, he technically is not a property manager. The property manager acts as an agent to exercise executive supervision over a piece of real estate for an owner in exchange for a fee.

Scope of Property Management

In the capacity of agent, a property manager is concerned primarily with income-producing property, i.e., property that is leased or rented. Consequently, the manager's typical primary purpose is to maximize net income over the economic life of the property. However, not all real estate investors have the same ownership goals and objectives.

Consider the well-to-do retired investor who has made a sizeable investment in a well-located downtown office building: His investment goal is to have a continuous flow of spendable income for many years to come with a minimal amount of responsibility on his part. The classic definition of producing the highest possible net income over the economic life of the property aptly describes what property management means to this investor. However, consider property management from the point of view of the high-income corporate executive who has made a major investment in a highly-leveraged apartment house: His investment goal is to maximize the available tax shelter oportunities and have the property appreciate in value so that it can be disposed of in five years when the depreciation advantages wane. His interest is not with the economic life of the property but rather with a particular five-year period. Similarly, other property owners have other objectives, among them pride of ownership, protection from inflation, and safety of principal.

Essentially, property management is a professional activity that assists owners in achieving their investment objectives through quality services. In consequence, the scope of the property manager's duties is wide. Some act as consultants, recommending ways of remodeling a property or changing its use in order to maximize income. Others become experts in the tax aspects of real estate investing or financing techniques. In addition, property managers often specialize in the management of a specific type of property, such as multifamily housing, office buildings, shopping centers, or mobile home parks. In general, the principal duties of a property manager are these: marketing and leasing space in the building under management; operating and maintaining the property; and collecting rents and keeping records. The property manager performs whatever administrative tasks are needed to relieve the owner of the responsibility of managing the property himself.

Property management is a relatively new and evolving development within the real estate industry. The duties connected with it have changed as economic and social situations have changed. From approximately 1900 to 1925, the property manager performed a caretaker function. He did little more than collect rents, pay bills, perform maintenance chores, and report unusual operating problems to owners. The Great Depression altered this situation. Subsequent to the Stock Market Crash of 1929, a significant number of unprofitable income properties came under the ownership of private and institutional investors. Consequently, an economic need for a higher level of competency in property management was realized. Through the Institute of Real Estate Management, designated in 1933 as part of the National Association of Real Estate Boards (now the NATIONAL ASSOCIATION OF REALTORS®), individuals could become CERTIFIED PROPERTY MANAGERS® upon completion of a course of study and proof of experience, and organizations could achieve similar recognition as ACCREDITED MANAGEMENT ORGANIZATIONS®.

The demand for property management decreased during the

post-World War II housing shortage, when attracting and accommodating tenants was no problem. During this time property management continued to gain technical knowledge and experience; still, the manager's skills remained limited in scope. Few properties had sufficient employees to offer an opportunity to become proficient in managing people, and few managers were involved with the financial aspects of management programs.

Noticeable changes in the property management industry began to occur in the 1960s, several factors having an impact. One was a shift from single-family residences to large, usually high-rise, multifamily structures as popular alternate means of fulfilling housing needs. Apartment complexes of from 100 to 500 units were replacing smaller ones, and condominiums began to grow in acceptance and number. Other new construction—of office buildings and shopping centers especially—likewise was on a grander scale. All of these new, larger properties called for management assistance. Second, the sixties saw a sharp increase in the supply of available mortgage money, an added impetus to real estate development. Third, and very important, ownership was again, for the first time since the 1920s, in the portfolio of the public through ownership interests in real estate investment trusts (REITs) and large limited partnerships.

The result of these dramatic changes was the appearance of new opportunities for property management and the demand for a higher level and different kind of property management service than had been required previously. The business of managing income properties began to call for the property manager who could organize, operate, and assume the risk of the total business venture, i.e., the asset manager. Real estate had discovered the need for professional management—a need commercial and industrial institutions had discovered a decade earlier during the management boom of the 1950s.

The Property Management Firm

The real estate management industry continues to undergo change, and its future has not yet been fully defined in terms of expectations and level of professional performance. Change, especially when it involves something as large as a national industry, is slow moving. Managers whose foresight and experience help them attain a pinnacle of achievement will recognize opportunity and prepare themselves to be asset managers.

Traditionally, the property management function was regarded as a relatively insignificant department of a real estate firm. Recent interest in the role management can play in the success of major real estate investment decisions has led to a reevaluation of this archaic attitude. As a consequence, agency property management firms are growing in number and importance. Understanding the different kinds of property management companies and the levels of service they provide may be helpful in preparing to meet the opportunities of the future.

One kind of company is strictly a service organization, providing maintenance and accounting services and responding to tenant grievances but not performing renting or leasing activity. Firms of this type manage condominiums, cooperatives, industrial parks, or office buildings that are fully leased with long-term tenancies. A second kind of property management company is responsible for the day-to-day operation of rental income property, i.e., handling the leasing function and maintaining property. Concern for the property's performance, however, usually ends with net operating income, and the owner continues to make most management decisions. For example, the owner retains the authority to set the level of maintenance and rehabilitation funds that can be expended, decide what types of employees the manager shall hire and set their pay scale, and establish policies that affect tenants.

These two kinds of property management company, however, are not prominent. Most professional property management companies are asset management firms. The asset management company performs a total management function, assuming responsibility for the economic performance of a property. Its concern extends beyond net operating income, recommending how income from the property can be invested most effectively. Obviously, the managerial talents required by the asset management firm are considerably more demanding than those required by the two other kinds of firms. Consequently, the characteristics and goals of this property manager will be different as well.

The Property Manager and the Property Supervisor

The terms "property manager" and "property supervisor" are appropriate for differentiating between the two levels of practitioner who may be found in the industry. The difference between the two lies in the way given individuals consider their jobs, the way they operate, the way they make decisions, and the way they measure their success. A person's title within a property management company is irrelevant within this discussion. What is relevant is the scope of assigned duties and attitude toward those duties.

Effectiveness and Efficiency

When a property manager is given an existing building to manage, he receives an ongoing business: The facilities and equipment are in place; the building has employees who have specific jobs to perform. The manager's administrative responsibility is to utilize these resources to produce the optimum investment yield. Economists consider this to be efficiency—doing what has already been done only doing it better and focusing on costs. There is, however, another approach—focusing on effectiveness. This requires concentrating on opportunities to provide revenue, creating new markets, or changing the economic characteristics of existing markets. According to Peter Drucker, management consultant, author, and professor, "Efficiency is concerned with doing things right. Effectiveness is doing the right things." (*Management: Tasks, Responsibilities, and Practices* [New York: Harper & Row, Inc., 1974]) While efficiency is a requisite for survival, effectiveness forms the groundwork for success.

A difference between a property manager and property supervisor is whether the approach to solving operating problems ends with efficient solutions or effective ones. A property supervisor, being efficient, seeks solutions. A property manager, being effective, seeks understanding. The good property supervisor is knowledgeable and efficient in hiring and supervising employees. He understands maintenance and repair and purchasing procedures. He knows what to do with the parts of a building that wear and where to get good buys on appliances, equipment, and supplies. He is proficient at collecting rents and knowledgeable about state laws concerning enforcement of tenant contracts. Given an apartment complex to manage, the property supervisor maintains the structure, collects rents and enforces lease agreements, buys efficiently and approves contracts, hires and supervises the resident manager, and takes care of tenant grievances. He does all of this efficiently, having learned given solutions to given problems.

A property manager, on the other hand, is effective. The way he manages a property increases its value. His thinking is not, Can I buy it cheaper? but, rather, What can I do to increase value? He seeks understanding of a problem, not merely a solution; he wants to know why something happens, pursuing techniques that may be used to handle future problems.

To point out this difference between a property supervisor and a property manager, an examination of how each would deal with a hypothetical operating problem—five apartments that become vacant on the first of the month—is illustrative.

The efficient supervisor inspects the apartments prior to the first day of the month of their vacancy to determine if any improvements will be needed after the tenants vacate. His examination indicates that some painting is necessary. Consequently, he places an order for the painter to begin work the day after the apartments become vacant. His inspection also reveals that the carpets and draperies need to be cleaned, and he gives approval to the resident manager to have this done as soon as the painting is completed. Since five apartments will be vacant at the same time, he decides to advertise in the local newspaper; he writes a classified ad and orders that it start seven days before the end of the month. The efficient property supervisor thus examines the problem, determines the amount of rehabilitation necessary to ready the apartments for renting, and expands his possibilities of attracting prospects by advertising in the newspaper.

The effective property manager does these things; he, however, goes a step further, seeking an understanding of the situation. He questions the rental price and market conditions. He contemplates changes in lease terms. He asks himself: Is this the time to test the market for a longer commitment in lease term? Are these five vacancies at one time indicative of a change that's going on in the neighborhood? Is the competition becoming more severe?

Action and Reaction

Another key difference between a property manager and a property supervisor lies in the fact that a property manager makes things happen while a property supervisor merely responds to problems. The property manager is an active force; the supervisor is reactive.

The previous illustration may be expanded to illustrate this difference in attitude and method of operating. Assume that the five vacant apartments were rerented in eight days. To the property supervisor, the problem is solved. The property manager, however, still has questions: Why did the units rent so fast? Where did the prospects come from? How did they get there? Did changes in policy cause a faster rental? Is the market stronger than anticipated?

A situation in which an apartment building's keys were stolen also may be cited in order to illustrate the difference between the active property manager and the reactive property supervisor. When the keys were taken, fear of lack of security immediately swept the residents. Some began to withhold their rents. A property supervisor responded to the immediate problem by replacing all of the building's locks and reacting to complaining tenants on an individual basis. The property manager developed a more far-reaching plan. It included not only replacing the locks but also instilling in the tenants a renewed sense of security and dealing with those tenants who were illegally withholding their rental payments according to company policy. His actions created a positive atmosphere and eliminated irresponsible behavior.

Still another example between property management and supervision can be drawn from a situation involving a vacant apartment in need of rehabilitation. The supervisor inspected the unit and determined that it needed new carpeting, window shades, stove, and refrigerator. The manager examined the apartment and agreed that it could not be rerented with the existing carpeting, shades, and appliances. However, before reaching a decision concerning the replacements, he asked himself these questions: If carpeting is necessary, how can I improve the rental value by recarpeting? What colors and styles are in decorating vogue today? Rather than replacing the window shades, what are the economics of using drapes as an alternative? Can they support a higher rental value? Can I attract a more stable, longer-term tenant by these improvements? Can I rent the apartment without providing a stove or refrigerator? Is there an economic limit to what this neighborhood will support? His curiosity is endless.

In summary, then, a manager asks the question: What action can I take—what changes in this product, its services, and the market can I make—that would improve the economic performance of the property?

Authority and Responsibility

In order to function as a property manager, a person must have the guarantee of an authority structure. He has to know which decisions are his to make and which are reserved for a different or higher authority. It is the task of the property management company and the property owner to define their performance objectives and assign the property manager his area of responsibility for the performance of the property. That responsibility then must be accompanied by the authority necessary to meet those objectives.

Organizational authority is the right of one person to require another person to fulfill specific duties because of rank and position within the organization. Responsibility is the quality of being accountable for the performance of delegated duties; it implies trustworthy performance without guidance. No one can motivate the responsible property manager; he has to motivate himself. No one can direct him; he has to direct himself. Above all, no one can supervise him; he establishes his own standards, his own performance, and his own objectives. He can be productive only if he is responsible for his own job.

Persons in the management business all too often experience difficulty dealing with clients who hold management responsible for the performance of their properties yet withhold the authority required to make management programs viable. For example, in order to effectively manage an income property, a property manager must have absolute authority for the hiring and firing of on-site staff. He cannot be responsible for the results by on-site management if he does not have the authority to direct its activities. If the owner reserves the right to make final judgments on directives to the on-site staff, he effectively is assuming responsibility for their activities. Without authority, the property manager is nothing more than a property supervisor who assists the owner in the management of the property. On the other hand, a property manager who has authority must be accountable for results. All too often, managers blame poor results on the action of their subordinates. This is a denial of the authority structure. The excuse that others are at fault may be legitimate a first time and acceptable a second time, but it is inexcusable a third time.

Another difference, then, between a property manager and a property supervisor lies in the degree of responsibility with which each is charged and, more importantly, whether the necessary level of authority accompanies that responsibility. The property manager takes the responsibility for his job from the management agreement between the owner and the property management company and, subsequently, the company delegates the necessary authority to him. He realistically cannot be held responsible for the performance of a property if he is not granted the authority that likewise makes him accountable for it.

Property Manager Behavioral Characteristics

Associated with every field of endeavor is a set of human characteristics. A person who possesses the characteristics that correspond with a given endeavor is more likely to succeed in that effort than the person who lacks them. Thus, behavioral characteristics may be considered in determining an individual's compatibility with a given line of work and, subsequently, his success in that work. Unless there is a matching of job characteristics and human personality, there is little chance for career advancement. For instance, selling life insurance demands an aggressive, outgoing personality, the ability to meet strangers easily, and the persistence not to readily take no for an answer. An introvert selling life insurance probably would find little success because his personality would conflict with the behavioral pattern required by the job. Similarly, a person making a career commitment to property management would do well to examine those behavioral characteristics conducive to becoming a successful professional manager.

Sociability

Property management is a people-oriented business, and a property manager is able to get along with people. He has good relations with those to whom he reports (property owners, his superior), his staff subordinates, and tenants. While a manager is not necessarily a naturally gregarious person, he is able to work effectively with others and displays a level of confidence when dealing with other businessmen.

Attentiveness to Detail

Likewise, property management is a detail-oriented business, and a manager is capable of supervising the details of operation. This means closely inspecting invoices, regularly visiting vacant apartments or offices to verify that they are in proper renting order, responding to the petty problems of resident managers and bookkeepers, seeing to it that tenant grievances are fairly disposed of, making close and careful inspection of monthly operating reports, etc. The property manager who ignores the details of an income property's operation will not be successful in the business.

Ability To Overcome Resistance

A successful property manager has a competitive attitude that enables him to overcome resistance and be a firm negotiator when the situation calls for one. This characteristic will be called upon whether negotiating with an owner or prospective owner, tenant, supplier, or subordinate employee.

The following situation illustrates the need to be able to overcome resistance when dealing with a prospective tenant, in this case of an office building: The prospect has an interior decorator with luxurious, over-budget ideas for the space. The decorator must be dealt with politely but firmly. On the one hand, the manager must plan a space that is both functional and attractive, keeping in mind that the cost of remodeling is a crucial factor. On the other hand, he runs the risk of losing the tenant if he cannot provide the space the tenant—and the decorator—wants. The astute property manager is able to overcome the resistance introduced in the form of the interior decorator while maintaining the tenant's commitment to lease the space.

Assertiveness

Assertiveness is a desirable characteristic in a property manager. He needs to be self-assured and have a determined attitude toward getting results by personally initiating action and following through. However, his assertiveness preferably lies in solving problems rather than in dealings with people.

Ability To Work Within an Organizational Structure

In agency real estate management, a company may have numerous clients with a great number of buildings, thousands of tenants, and hundreds of employees working on the properties. It is extremely important that the company operates in a structured atmosphere and that the property manager sees himself as a team player.

The key to a property management company's operational structure is its manual of standard operating procedures. The company cannot afford a property manager who belittles the importance of these procedures and bypasses them. If he fails to function within the structure of the procedures, a breakdown in communications occurs and the team spirit evaporates.

Energy

A property manager is energetic. Property management is a fast-paced activity, and the practitioner is able to handle a variety of tasks simultaneously and make decisions quickly. His confidence and determination that result from his high energy level contribute heavily to his overall effectiveness.

Decisiveness

Being a manager means making decisions. Often, a property manager is required to make policies or judgments that are unpopular with tenants or employees. Employees and tenants alike are entitled to prompt answers to questions or decisions on their problems, even though such answers or decisions may be met with disfavor.

Indecisiveness leads to a waste of valuable time. Before arriving at a decision, many managers vacillate and procrastinate. Their fear of making a wrong or unpopular decision squanders time and, consequently, money and causes needless worry. For instance, most property managers have been faced with the difficult decision-making situation of possibly having to terminate an employee. If the employee is an on-site manager of a sizeable apartment complex and his ineffectiveness is causing the property to experience lower income and higher operating costs, indecision can be very expensive for both the property owner and the management company. In addition to the obvious loss of income, the management company experiences waste if other employees must spend an inordinate amount of time covering for the deficiencies of the on-site manager. Postponing the decision indefinitely may result in the loss of the management account. Such a grim outcome may be prevented if the property manager has the fortitude to make a difficult decision and immediately implement it.

Of course, not all problems facing property managers are as clearcut as this. Take, for example, a situation in which 20 tenants of an 84-unit luxury apartment building sign a petition asking for a daytime security guard in response to a series of recent apartment break-ins. A manager's first step in deciding how to handle this problem is to gather the facts. Some of the information needed is: the experience of other neighbors and the past history of daytime robbery problems; whether this is a temporary police problem or a long-term security problem; the cost of daytime guards; the cost of alternate security measures; opinions of the other tenants as to the seriousness of the problem and their feelings about it. The second step in decision making is to examine the various courses of action that may be available. In this example, these include: hiring a security guard; hiring a security guard but passing the cost on to the tenants through increased rents; installing other security devices; gaining police assistance in solving the problem; making better use of building employees during daytime hours.

In any decision making, all alternatives are considered carefully. Most decisions come out as compromises. Recognizing this, the decision maker ascertains which compromise appears to satisfy the main requirements. The property manager should look upon decision making not as a problem but as an opportunity. The process challenges his skills in the balancing of values, teaches him the art of effective compromise, and resolves problems so that the business can go forward.

Entrepreneurship

Another characteristic is needed to rise to the executive level. That key ingredient is entrepreneurship. An entrepreneur is an innovator, a person who makes things happen and assumes the consequent risks.

Interestingly, an entrepreneur's behavioral characteristics may be incompatible with those listed previously as desirable in a property manager. For instance, an entrepreneur usually is more aggressive than would be preferred, and his independent attitude may not be conducive to working well in a structured environment. However, the entrepreneur is a mover who has the charisma to sell ideas; he's a risk taker, a thinker. The management boom of the fifties produced new definitions of the term "manager," one of which was offered by Drucker: ". . . the first criterion in identifying those people within an organization who have management responsibility, is not command over people. It is the responsibility for contribution." *(Management: Tasks, Responsibilities, and Practices* [New York: Harper & Row, Inc., 1974])

French economist J.B. Say (1767–1832) defined an entrepreneur as one who directs resources toward more productive investments, thus creating wealth. The entrepreneurial property manager takes the initiative to organize and manage an enterprise and creates new business and markets. He usually assumes a substantial portion of risks, losses, and profits. The profits—not wages—become his reward for taking the risks. In addition, the entrepreneurial property manager is recognized by his tendency to solve problems himself rather than have someone solve them for him.

Commitment to Continued Education

Important to a property manager's ability to achieve is a commitment to continued learning. Formalized education at the university and college level and through the Institute of Real Estate Management is the scaffolding on which the education of daily experience is built. Yet even as experience is gained, knowledge is refreshed through attendance at special seminars and courses available to the property manager. Similarly, reading the multiplicity of printed materials broadens a basic education. Without continued exposure to new ideas and practices, the manager becomes obsolete. The basics of management knowledge may not change drastically; however, never-ending study in economics, accounting, laws, technical improvements, and social change is a necessity for anyone who wants to grow in his profession.

Integrity

The final proof of a manager and the final demand on management is integrity, a moral soundness in business dealings that tests steadfastness to truth, purpose, responsibility, and trust. Managers cannot compromise when it comes to demanding integrity from their superiors, their subordinates, or themselves. No matter how knowledgeable or experienced the manager may be, if he lacks integrity he destroys himself, other people, and, in the long run, his organization. He corrupts the purpose of the organization and destroys its spirit. Integrity cannot be taught or demanded, but it is an absolute requisite for a professional property manager and one quality he must carry with him to the organization.

In recognition of the importance of integrity to the professional property manager, the Institute of Real Estate Management adopted a Code of Professional Ethics for CERTIFIED PROPERTY MANAGERS®. The objective of the code is

> To establish and maintain public confidence in the honesty, integrity, professionalism and ability of the professional property manager. . . . This Code and performance pursuant to its provisions will be beneficial to the general public and contribute to the continued development of a mutually beneficial relationship among CERTIFIED PROPERTY MANAGERS®, REALTORS®, clients, employers and the public.

(The code appears in its entirety as figure A.1 in the appendix of this text.)

Job Descriptions

A wide range of abilities and experience exists among the practitioners in the field of real estate management. For lack of qualitative job descriptions, most of these people call themselves property managers. This is a misnomer. A proper job description might identify, within a larger management organization, varying levels of responsibility ranging from the chief executive officer of the company down to an administrative assistant, all of whom are regularly involved in managing real estate. In a smaller firm the property manager role may operate through a single person. Indeed, the property owner may retain part of the property manager's responsibilities for himself and participate in the management of the building. Job descriptions follow of four of the most common principal positions within the property management profession and may erase some of the confusion.

Chief Executive Officer

The chief executive of the property management organization needs to be, above all else, an entrepreneur. He is the major producer of new business for the organization, as well as its chief administrative officer. It is his job to optimize the economic results of the operation through effective management of its opportunities and resources. He spends as much as 25 percent of his time in planning for the operation and the growth of the company. He also has the responsibility of supervising property managers and aiding them in their professional growth. In some large companies, the tasks typically assumed by the chief executive are divided among several individuals. In very large companies, for instance, the president is the chief executive officer. His responsibilities include developing business, planning, and establishing policy. Vice presidents are responsible for the supervision, development, and growth of other property managers. The chief operating officer has a great need to execute organizational structure. In addition, he must be sensitive to people, willing to exhibit leadership and sublimate his own ego to see others grow. Not all operating officers are good property managers; conversely, successful property managers may not be good operating officers.

Job Description
Chief Executive Officer

The chief executive officer is, in the final analysis, responsible for the results of the enterprise. His duties and responsibilities vary widely from company to company depending upon its size, its problems and opportunities, and the talents of the team of people he has assembled. This list of tasks represents those typically performed by the chief executive officer in a real estate management organization.

Plans
1. Sets the mission statement for the company. Responsible for identifying the company philosophy.
2. Establishes the company objectives.
3. Initiates the long and short term company plan.

Organizes
1. Determines the organizational structure.
2. Recruits and selects the personnel who are responsible for any operational function under his supervision.

Directs and Motivates
1. Provides leadership toward achieving company objectives.
2. Develops people and counsels with them.
3. Maintains motivation of employees and high morale.

Controls
1. Evaluates company's performance.
2. Supervises costs of operations.

Operational Responsibilities (Usually Cannot Be Delegated)
1. Develops new business.
2. Deals with clients.
3. Develops and maintains company's public relations program.

Property Manager

A property manager is a knowledgeable professional who has the experience and skills to operate real estate and also understands the fundamentals of business management. He is able to qualify for the designation of CERTIFIED PROPERTY MANAGER®. In addition, a property manager usually is charged with assisting the company in the development of new business and recognition of new business opportunities.

Job Description
Property Manager

Objective
To acquire, service, and maintain property management accounts for company income and profit.

Goals
1. Assist owners in achieving their investment objectives through quality professional property management services.
2. Provide these services through methods and procedures established by company policy and programs.
3. Make recommendations to improve the profit and productivity of the company.
4. Identify and develop new business opportunities for the company.
5. Develop professional abilities.

Basic Responsibilities for Achieving Goals
1. Toward servicing property management accounts:
   a. The property manager is responsible for all actions that involve or influence the properties he manages.
   b. He is accountable to the owner, the company, and the state in which he operates.
   c. He fully understands and carries out all company policies in dealing with properties, owners, and tenants.
   d. When managing property, he is responsible for the following:
      1) Planning. Creates an innovative management plan that describes the anticipated operation of the property during the next year.

    2) Organizing. Organizes the operation of the property to produce expected results. Establishes performance goals for the on-site managers and other supervisory personnel so that each job is directed, with teamwork, toward the objectives of the management plan.

    3) Staffing. Selects, trains, and motivates on-site personnel.

    4) Directing. Provides administrative support to on-site personnel who have the responsibility for the day-to-day operation of the property.

    5) Controlling. Oversees collection of income and the management of expenses so as to produce the maximum economic benefit to the property.

    6) Operating. Administers day-to-day implementation of a standard operating procedural manual.

    7) Analyzing. Analyzes the operating results of the property in relationship to its plan. Makes recommendations for adjustments to the plan as needed.

    8) Communicating. Keeps owners and/or corporate officers advised of significant operational problems and deviations from the management plan.

2. Toward identifying and developing new business opportunities for the company:

    a. The property manager shall solicit new property management accounts for the company.

        1) His primary area of concern for new business is the same geographical area in which he currently manages properties.

        2) He needs to identify and become familiar with all owners of properties that qualify as potential property management accounts in his geographical area.

        3) Using the company's new business program, he initiates and supervises the solicitation of new business from these owners.

    b. The property manager may participate in other commissionable services provided to clients by the company.

        1) In addition to property management, the company provides services for buying, selling, refinancing, leasing, and consulting as a part of its asset management program. The property manager can assist in providing these services.

        2) The property manager shall continue to improve his knowledge in areas of asset management in order to qualify for these assignments.

3. Toward developing his professional abilities (primarily accomplished during nonbusiness hours):

    a. Attends and passes advanced educational courses and seminars.

    b. Obtains a broker's license.

    c. Teaches a real estate class in local college or university.

    d. Actively participates in local chapter of IREM.

    e. Writes articles for publication on subjects related to the industry.

    f.   Accepts speaking engagements before local audiences.

    g.   Participates in company educational offerings.

Minimum Qualifications

1. Has four years full-time experience managing properties, three of which have been with the company.
2. Holds the designation of CERTIFIED PROPERTY MANAGER®.
3. Has demonstrated ability in preparing management plans and servicing property management accounts.
4. Has successfully managed properties with significant operational problems.
5. Demonstrates a professional attitude in every aspect of his work, a positive and enthusiastic attitude being a hallmark of a successful property manager.

Compensation

1. Salary.
2. Commissions for assistance and participation in fees earned for real estate services other than property management.
3. Local and national dues paid for membership in Realty Board and Institute of Real Estate Management.
4. Upon proving enterpreneurial abilities, eligibility to become a partner, participating in the profits of the firm.

Property Supervisor

Most practitioners in the field of real estate management are property supervisors. They are efficient in supervising the operation of a property. They are service oriented. They tend to manage by crisis. Property supervisors spend little time planning, either for themselves of for the property they manage. If asked how they intend to reach personal long-range goals, they probably do not have plans. A property supervisor usually has no contact with clients; however, as a service-oriented individual, he relates well with property employees. He is detail-oriented and particularly skilled at taking care of the great number of minor matters that are collectively important to the performance of a property. He needs a great deal of supervision but follows instructions well.

Job Description
Property Supervisor

The property supervisor reports to and is accountable to the department manager.

Basic Responsibility

Responsible for the performance of the personnel and the maintenance of the physical properties on projects under his supervision in accordance with established company policies and procedures.

Specific Responsibilities

1. Ensures that on-site personnel comply with all published policies and procedures established for the project.

2. Personally inspects exterior and interior of each assigned project at least once a month, using approved checklist; prepares written recommendations for physical repairs and/or replacements as required in coordination with supervisor.
3. Reviews all delinquent accounts and determines action required; assists resident manager or control clerk in collection of delinquencies and returned checks.
4. Ensures that all funds collected are transmitted immediately so that excess funds are not retained on premises.
5. Periodically audits petty cash fund.
6. Spot checks new leases for accuracy and completeness.
7. Compares lease information with monthly rent roll for proper security deposits, starting date, etc.
8. Inspects vacancy report status to ensure report is accurate and up to date.
9. Inspects vacancies ready to show and analyzes those not ready to show.
10. Checks work order forms for those completed and those outstanding; determines age of incomplete work orders and reasons for being incomplete.
11. Reviews with resident manager status of operating budget; determines necessary reductions or increases in allocations and has those changes approved by supervisor.
12. Schedules unannounced observation and performance evaluation of on-site personnel on all properties.
13. Inspects and inventories supplies in storeroom prior to approving any purchase order. (If a card file inventory system is maintained, information should be available immediately, including type of material, cost and other specifics, right in the office.)
14. Reviews in detail all purchase orders prepared by the project to ensure clarity and justification of requirement.
15. Prepares detailed list of capital replacements required or anticipated, when applicable, and submits these recommendations to his supervisor.
16. Inspects pool condition and equipment spring, summer, and fall for proper maintenance, when applicable.
17. Prepares preventive maintenance checklist by day, week, or month for maintenance personnel to perform. (This includes, but is not limited to, air conditioning, heating, hot water heaters, air handling units, filters, etc. If property supervisor is not capable of preparing a checklist or of determining the calibre of maintenance performed, an experienced consultant firm should be used in establishing maintenance program and preparing appropriate checklists. The property supervisor should receive guidelines and instructions in reviewing work performance.)
18. Does not approve expenditures exceeding the proposed budget without the approval of his supervisor. This does not include emergencies.
19. Approves normal advertisements; special display ads requiring an unusual expenditure should be discussed with supervisor.

20. Makes recommendations for increases or reductions in rental schedule, with complete justification, and seeks approval from supervisor.
21. Ensures compliance with Federal Wage and Hour Act, all state and local laws, OSHA, Workmen's Compensation Act. (In this connection, the property supervisor reviews resident managers' work schedules to ensure compliance with Federal Wage and Hour Act.) Prepares and obtains signatures on all salaried employee employment contracts.
22. Ensures that properly executed releases are obtained prior to employment of any minor.
23. Furnishes property management department with valid copies of workmen's compensation and liability coverage for any contractor prior to engaging same to perform work for any property managed by the company.
24. Reviews, approves, and submits employee time sheets to central office on due date.
25. Approves all invoices for payment as soon as they are presented and returns same to accounting for payment. (Any invoice not approved for payment is presented to supervisor for disposition.) Reviews all unpaid purchase orders that are outstanding over 45 days to determine status and makes decision on disposition.
26. Meets with supervisor biweekly to discuss projects, rentals and vacancies, budgets, personnel, and any other problems.
27. Obtains written approval from owner for all proposed expenditures not included in monthly operating budget prior to commencement of work. (Written approval will include manner of payment to managing company or contractor. Management contract should provide a dollar amount that cannot be exceeded for nonbudgeted expenditures. Competitive bids should be obtained on large expenditures.)
28. Interviews and hires both the resident manager and the engineer. (All other employees of the property should be hired by the resident manager.)
29. Reviews leasing procedures with resident manager and on-site office personnel.
30. Shops competition every three months to remain aware of market.
31. Prepares annual budgets for each project with the assistance of supervisor and submits to the owner for approval. (Format in preparing next year's projection should include current and past year's operating statistics for each reference. Budget comparisons and previous year comparisons with comments should be provided in order that the financial status of the project may be easily analyzed.)
32. Reviews monthly income and expense statements and reports any problem areas to supervisor.
33. Projects employee evaluation. (An evaluation form should be completed annually on each employee by the resident manager. The completed evaluation should be reviewed with the property supervisor. The two jointly discuss the evaluation with the employee and note the employee's comments.)
34. Provides tenant comment and evaluation form to each resident annually and to all vacating tenants. (The results and conclusions

should be reviewed by the property supervisor with the department head and owner.)

35. Annually reviews all insurance coverage to determine if adequate coverage is provided at the most economical premium obtainable.
36. Annually reviews all contractual services.
37. Is encouraged to attend trade association meetings and seminars to keep up to date on trends and changing conditions.
38. Implements controls, policies, and procedures to conserve utilities. (Monthly records should be kept on consumption of units used for fuel, electricity, gas and water. This information should be available to supervisor.)
39. Arranges for the completion of acquisition and termination forms on properties. (The forms should be forwarded to the supervisor for management file and to other departments.)
40. Is responsible for downtime on units that become vacant; inspects vacant unit prior to occupancy by new tenant to determine condition of unit and confirm that tenant has not obtained possession early.
41. Is responsible for current posting of all licenses, permits, notices, and occupancy permits required by federal, state, and local jurisdictions.
42. Supports a methodical system of procedures and/or formats established for all branches. (This includes the area of filing systems, business correspondence, purchase order procedures, rent collections, property maintenance, personnel requirements, etc.).

Administrative Assistant

Some organizations use administrative assistants to assist property managers in performing their responsibilities. An administrative assistant assumes responsibility for the time-consuming details necessary for the effective operation of a property. An understanding of and preferably some experience in bookkeeping is needed, inasmuch as this is an area that will demand a considerable amount of time. An administrative assistant also has some authority with which to respond to the needs of on-site managers.

Job Description
Administrative Assistant

The administrative assistant reports to and is accountable to either a property manager or property supervisor.

Basic Responsibility
Assists one of the above-named positions in the performance of his operational tasks. The tasks assigned to the administrative assistant will, of course, greatly depend upon the needs of his superior. However, most typically these would include the more routine and detailed tasks such as follows:

1. Oversees rental collection and delinquent rents.

2. Approves payment of bills.
3. Visits properties on a weekly basis to assist on-site managers in their needs.
4. Inspects all vacancies and notices to vacate and reports findings to his superior.
5. Reviews all reports produced by bookkeeping department for accuracy and clarity.
6. Resolves minor tenant grievances.
7. Prepares routine leases.
8. Places advertising when needed.
9. Conducts preliminary employee interviews.
10. Audits payroll to ensure it does not exceed budget without approval of superior.
11. Shops competing buildings from time to time to assist superior in establishing rents.

Career Development

These job descriptions point to a definite career ladder. Traditionally, the concept for advancement for the property manager begins with managing small buildings and graduates to managing larger, more complex properties. Upon achieving a level of proficiency, the property manager stops taking care of buildings and becomes a manager of managers. He steps out of the day-to-day operations of properties and supervises people who would carry on those chores.

This concept of advancement is erroneous and unhealthy, both for the property manager and the company. Like research scientists or doctors or lawyers, property managers must be recognized as specialists whose income, public recognition, and professional standing are based upon the application of knowledge and the production of visible results.

The concept that one must supervise other professionals in order to climb the career ladder of success is no longer true. In fact, only a small percentage of good property managers have the ability to lead and supervise others. Managing other professionals is very different from managing property. People should be rewarded for the knowledge they possess and the subsequent results they can achieve, not merely their ability to supervise others. Many property managers simply are not characteristically suited to be people managers. The manager of people must be constantly prepared to subordinate his ego to the egos of the people who work for him. The successful property manager who exhibits signs of assertiveness, ability to overcome resistance, and entrepreneurship seldom is compatible with this role.

If a company's top management hopes to retain top quality

property managers, it must realize the worth of those property managers and learn to recognize them for the real estate specialists they have become, not reward them by making them the people managers they aren't. As expertise grows, the property manager should be rewarded by being assigned the management of larger and more complex properties. He should be recognized as the valuable resource that he is. Property management is a professional service, and the necessary resource is the ability to manage property. What property management companies must have are producers who can assume responsibilities for the management of large, complex properties. They do not need office managers. Managing other property managers or property supervisors is not more important than managing real estate.

The property manager career ladder begins with understanding the differences between being a property manager and a property supervisor, between being efficient and being effective. It requires study and knowledge about the principles and practices of professional scientific management. A property manager has the technical knowledge to operate real estate, an ever-changing profession affected by the national economy, tax laws, insurance requirements, landlord-tenant relationships, energy conservation techniques, utility rates, and society. He is an entrepreneur and shares in responsibility of the performance of the company. The property manager ascends this career ladder through gaining experience, since ultimately it takes experience to qualify for assuming greater responsibility in the management of real estate assets.

2

The Management Function

THE PROPERTY MANAGER WHO BECOMES a moving force within his organization is able to perform certain tasks and assume certain obligations with which management in general is charged. The experienced
real estate manager is knowledgeable about the basic skills of
management and able to apply these skills as he supervises the operations of properties. Only when these management skills are sharpened
can the property manager become the "dynamic, life-giving element"
described by Peter Drucker. According to Drucker:

> In a competitive economy, above all, the quality of performance of
> managers determines the success of a business, indeed, they determine its
> survival. For the quality and performance of its members is the only
> effective advantage an enterprise in a competitive economy can have.
> (*The Practice of Management* [New York: Harper & Row, Inc., 1959])

Obligations of Management

The realm of responsibility of a property manager at the executive
level extends far beyond the day-to-day operations of properties under
his stewardship. As a key member of the management team, adopting
a specific course of executive action is mandatory. Certain obligations
await executive attention. These obligations revolve around economic
performance, employee performance, society, time, administration,
and innovation.

Economic Performance

The foremost obligation of management is to economic performance.
Consequently, the primary goal of a property manager is the sound

economic performance not only of a property but of the total asset. If this goal is not met and the service expected is not provided, the management account will be withdrawn. Should this occur on a continual basis, the future of the property firm itself will be in serious jeopardy.

The most common method of upgrading the economic performance of a real estate investment is by increasing income (raising rents) or reducing operating costs, or both. However, improved economic performance can be affected in other ways. For instance, an owner's investment yield may be measured in terms of appreciation in value, accomplished through refinancing and achieving a lower loan constant. Or, a property may appreciate in market value if an effective management program leads to a greater stability in the quality of the investment and its tenancy, thus lowering the capitalization rate. Other alternatives also are available. For instance, occasionally the tax-free exchange of one asset for another with greater possibilities is a measure of improved economic performance. Likewise, tax shelter opportunities may be optimized in order to improve economic performance. (With the passage of the Tax Reform Act of 1976, the importance of real estate as a tax shelter has grown even greater. While the act dealt fatal or near-fatal blows to numerous other forms of tax shelter, real estate escaped relatively unscathed. As a result, one of the major attractions of investing in real estate remains the tax benefits that can be realized.)

Employee Performance

A second obligation of management is toward employee effectiveness and achievement. Organization of work must be accomplished in such a way that it can be performed efficiently and effectively while being satisfying to the persons who perform it.

Probably one of the greatest challenges is to meet this obligation as it relates to on-site managers. It is not uncommon for an on-site manager of an apartment complex to be a housewife whose children have grown or one who has found it necessary to supplement her family income, someone who is young and just starting a career, or someone making a mid-life career change. Each may lack experience and skill in the industry yet be talented in terms of ability to relate to people and display the proclivity to make common-sense decisions on day-to-day problems. Each needs assistance in organizing his work so that he may become an effective buffer between residents who want well-maintained and safe housing at the lowest possible rent and an owner whose goal is to obtain the highest possible return on his investment. The manager's duty is to plan and organize the on-site manager's responsibilities so they can be met effectively. Simultaneously, the work must be made satisfying if it is to be personally fulfilling and challenging and offer opportunity of advancement. Jobs made interesting and meaningful lead to employees who have a sense of personal achievement and consequently perform at a high level.

Society

"The third task of management," according to Drucker, "is managing the social impacts and the social responsibilities of the enterprise." (*Management: Tasks, Responsibilities, and Practices* [New York: Harper & Row, Inc., 1974]) A real estate service firm, as any other enterprise, does not exist in isolation. It affects many people—the people who work for it, the people who work in the office buildings or live in the apartments it manages, and the people who live in the communities in which managed properties are located. An inherent quality of business is that it will have an impact on people. The business can be justified only if it exercises positive control over this impact.

By at least four methods a real estate management firm may manage, in a positive way, the impacts it has on people and neighborhoods. First, it may be a source of meaningful and productive jobs. Second, it may provide good and safe housing for residents and office space for businesses. Third, it may improve the quality of life. For instance, it may upgrade the aesthetic value of properties under its management, conserve utilities, or limit the use of pollutants. Fourth, it may conduct its business relationship with the public according to high ethical and professional standards.

Time

The fourth obligation management has is to the element of time. Management must remain ever conscious of the future as well as the present, of the long-term impact as well as the short-term one. The property manager acts in the present, but actions must be tempered with a concern for the future.

A property manager, for example, plans for the present and the future of a property through preparation of a management plan for its operation. However, this plan never is seen as a static entity but rather is constantly updated. If it is to produce long-run profits, management periodically must reappraise the situation and possibly restructure the program to fit the current economic environment and business trends. Similarly, realization of immediate profits should not be seen as the solution to a management problem if the long-term healthy operation of a property is endangered by short-term crisis responses.

The selection of an on-site staff also calls for an awareness of the element of time. A principal objective of a property manager is to develop an outstanding team of on-site employees for each property under his stewardship. This requires considerable effort and time. Settling for mediocrity in team capability and performance in order to shorten the time requirement scuttles long-range goals. The manager cannot compromise by retaining an unsatisfactory—albeit trained—employee in order to avoid the trial of recruiting, selecting, and training a new person who can properly meet the challenges of the particular job description.

Similarly, management must realize the importance of the element of time in implementation of the corporate plan. Every project within the organization requires that a time frame be constructed. This time frame must include a final completion date with intermittent deadlines at which times performance may be checked. Thus, realistic scheduling becomes one of the means by which management can achieve its obligation to time.

Administration and Innovation

Management has a fourth obligation, this one dual in nature: It is an administrator over the existing resources and an innovator of new resources for the future. Thus, the astute manager goes beyond what exists to that which could exist.

It is not enough for the manager of an apartment complex simply to perform a market survey of his competition once or twice a year in order to learn market rates and then adjust his rents to meet that market. The innovative manager attempts to anticipate changes in the rental market. He understands the economic forces of supply and demand, demographics, employment, and neighborhood values —all of which affect rental markets. Through constant research, study, and awareness, he makes judgments as to when these forces will create change and acts immediately on his informed opinion, not waiting to join others in reacting. If a property manager is an innovator, he is not satisfied with what already is known. He creates, through innovation and marketing, new values.

A situation involving a 20-year-old apartment building in a

suburban neighborhood that experienced the migration of several large companies from the downtown area of a major city illustrates the thinking of the innovative manager. The apartment building, composed primarily of moderately priced, medium-sized, one-bedroom apartments, had experienced 93 percent occupancy during the previous two years prior to the influx of new industry. The obvious prediction was that the vacancy would disappear as numerous new jobs were placed in the neighborhood. In fact, the manager realistically could predict that he would be in a position to increase rental rates. Typically what happens is that the manager waits for the vacancy to disappear before testing the rental market via small rent increases on future vacancies. After 12 or more months, he makes a rental adjustment to existing tenants, the newer tenants having proven a change in the market through their willingness to pay higher rentals.

The innovative manager, however, makes an in-depth study of changing economic factors and immediately responds based on his judgment of how the rental market will be affected. The increase in new jobs in the neighborhood, the compatibility of the apartment building's size, the rental price to new tenants, the level of rent people will pay to live closer to their work, the supply of available apartments—these and other factors are considered before the manager establishes new rates. Subsequently, the innovator closely follows the market's reaction to his analysis. When he determines that his thinking is correct, he immediately raises all rents to meet new market conditions.

Roles of Management

Meeting the obligations of management requires the performance of five distinct roles. The first is planning—determining the objectives of the enterprise, outlining the goals for each set of objectives, and deciding what must be done to reach them. The second role is as an organizer. Having analyzed the objectives to be reached, the work that must be performed is defined and divided into manageable functions. Third, a manager is a communicator. He makes the organizational objectives effective by constantly relaying them and their status to the people whose performance is needed and conversely receiving information from these sources. Fourth, a manager is a controller. He establishes standards of measurement then applies them as he analyzes, appraises, and interprets the performance of those who are assigned to certain tasks. The final role is as a developer of people, building a profitable organization through quality programs of selection, training, and motivation.

Planner

The property manager's role as a planner relates primarily to his responsibility for preparing management plans for the operation of investment properties. Preparing a management plan requires input from both the property owner and the managing agent. The property owner first states his purpose in owning the property and sets his long-range objectives; the property manager is involved in the establishment of goals, programs, and strategy needed to meet these objectives. When formulating a plan, it is well for the manager to remember three rules:

1. Short-term and long-term objectives are interrelated. They tend to compete for allocation of resources; there is a dangerous tendency to sacrifice long-term results for short-term gains. The two, however, must be compatible. For example, renting to marginal tenants might produce income in the present yet result in problems in the future. It is always difficult, frequently impossible, to achieve the longer term results unless short-term goals have been established and are accomplished along the way.

2. All categories of organizational objectives, including financial, marketing, and personnel, are interrelated. They too tend to compete for allocation of resources. Furthermore, there is a tendency to give a higher priority to financial rather than to personnel management, to recruiting rather than to training, to quantity rather than to quality, to tangible matters rather than to intangible matters. For optimum results, all objectives must be compatible and mutually beneficial; the objectives of each category must support the objectives of the other categories.

3. Meeting objectives requires that resources be provided in the right quantity, quality, time, and place. An objective without essential resources is not an objective; it is a delusion. An objective, then, requires a willing expenditure of resources.

Organizer

The organization of work is usually the task that determines the performance and success of a business program. This calls for establishment of a logical structure that encourages people to work together productively. Organizing means assigning responsibility and authority and developing the right team of workers to ensure that work is accomplished effectively with the best use of time, energy, and money. While there are many systems for effective management organization, one of the most viable approaches is a system called Management by Objectives, generally known as MBO. Essentially, MBO is a system whereby work is organized and objectives are set in an attempt to motivate workers to a level of more effective performance.

The initial step in MBO requires that the goals of the business organization be identified by the executive echelon. These goals are communicated downward to the managers, who are asked what they can do to achieve them. Based upon their responses, the individual managers of the business are assigned various responsibilities in such a way that their combined effort equals the overall organizational goals and is directed towards achieving them. MBO assumes that managers are more effective when they have a voice in setting the individual goals toward which they and their departments will be working and against which their performance will be monitored. A byproduct of the system is a set of written objectives—sort of a performance contract—to which both the superior and the subordinate can agree.

The objectives stated in the performance contract must have several characteristics if they are to be useful in organizing work. For one thing, they are in writing to reduce the chance of misunderstanding. The objectives are measurable, or at least verifiable. They specify quantity, quality, costs, and/or return. The objectives include a time period for their accomplishment. Objectives are challenging; businesses do not advance if targets are too easily reached. Likewise, objectives are attainable; unattainable objectives are frustrating and demotivating. Thus, the performance contract consists of written statements of objectives that are measurable, give a time period, and are challenging but attainable.

As an example, consider a property manager who works with his superior to outline a performance contract for the coming year. It covers the usual areas for which property managers are held accountable—leasing programs, operating costs, tenant relations. It also contains objectives concerned with development of on-site managers, including this one: "Conduct training sessions for resident managers in the techniques of improving tenant relations." Obviously, this isn't sufficient. The statement lacks the qualitative and quantitative indicators and a timetable that would make it challenging and measurable. How many resident managers are to be trained? By when? How many training sessions will be required? Suppose, instead, the objective reads something like this: "Beginning January 1, conduct training sessions for three resident managers each month in the techniques of improving tenant relations so that all nine resident managers are coached by April 1." This is much more appropriate. The objective now is measurable, involves a time period, and is challenging yet attainable. More importantly, it is stated specifically and clearly enough for the superior to know what to expect from the property manager and for the property manager to know what is expected of him and how his performance with respect to this one objective will be evaluated.

While the basic process of MBO sounds simple, if not properly administered, it may end in failure. To succeed, a commitment comes from all persons involved. There is a follow-up program to re-evaluate the viability of the objectives and measure performance. The objectives include the input of employees. Coaching and assistance is available at all times. The objectives and the time schedules are realistic yet challenging. Furthermore, no employee is given an objective that is out of his control to accomplish. No supervisory or managerial job exists independently of other jobs. A property manager depends on the bookkeeping department, the maintenance crews, and others to accomplish the operating objectives for a property. Likewise, property managers within the company must cooperate and depend on one another if company goals are to be accomplished. The wise MBO manager knows this and ensures that objectives are not agreed to until all of the involved or affected parties are consulted.

MBO is not a way of circumventing managerial judgment. Specific, clearly stated objectives are beneficial in evaluating performance but are no substitute for management judgment. MBO is not a solution to managerial problems but is an effective system by which work may be organized.

Communicator

A property manager will not be an effective manager until he learns and executes good communication skills. Managerial communications is a reciprocal process that includes not only sending information but also receiving it. Without both input and output, the communications network does not function.

The MBO system, in itself, is a form of communication. The success of MBO depends in large part on a superior properly relaying to his employee what his specific objectives are. Through organizing the missions and goals of the enterprise into missions and goals of individual managers, there is a written understanding of what everyone is trying to achieve and how they plan to achieve it.

The importance of stating specifically what is wanted should never be ignored. Numerous examples of how property managers can cause problems through poor communications could be cited. A typical example involves adding a new employee to a property payroll. The property manager tells the payroll bookkeeper, "Add John Smith to the payroll at the 624 Building at $1,000 per month starting the first of next month." His oral instruction leaves out hourly rate, number of hours per week, eligibility for health plan, paid holidays and vacations, job classification for the monthly operating report, etc. The payroll clerk may make the wrong assumption on any one of these categories and cause an error that may become time consuming, irritating, and costly to correct. What the property manager should have done is instruct payroll bookkeeping in writing.

Similarly, poor verbal communication with maintenance employees may lead to expensive lost time and higher repair bills. Or a property manager may tell a resident manager to "Give that tenant legal notice to pay his rent." The resident manager who follows this direction and gives the usual notice to pay or quit automatically voids the tenant's future lease obligations. The responsibility for bridging such potentially dangerous communication gaps rests with the manager.

Inherent in the verbal communication system are three possible sources of misunderstanding. One source is background noises that mask or distort oral messages or typographical errors and misprints that creep into written communications. The second is the lack of clarity in the way a message is framed. Ambiguity can be caused by poor handwriting or bad diction, but more often it is a matter of poor choice of words. If sentences are wordy and difficult to understand, the intent may be lost. For instance, ambiguity can come about from the use of jargon. Every business and profession has its own terminology—even property management, with such terms as graduated rent, unit mix, hold harmless, and death clause. The more people there are who understand the meanings of certain words, the better the network of communications will be. Unfortunately, jargon may be a confusing rather than a clarifying device. While a code of terms provides clarity and accuracy to a conversation among people who understand the code, the terms cause misunderstandings among those who lack this knowledge The third source of possible communications breakdown is faulty reception on the part of the listener. To paraphrase Drucker, communication occurs when the listener receives the message. Until this happens, there is only noise.

Crucial to a strong line of communication, then, is listening. How does a person recognize if he has weak listening skills, and what can be done about it? To respond to the first question, there are several signs of poor listening. One is impatience or even contemptuousness of the speaker, possibly because the message is too dull or too wordy. Another is an inability to repeat what has just been said because the listener is engrossed in his own thoughts or is framing a reply to something said earlier. Another sign is the listener prematurely thinking that he understands the speaker because he recognizes the background and operating style. Conversely, a sign may be that the listener cannot follow the speaker because his experience or point of view is not relevant to the situation. A fifth sign of poor listening involves the listener giving an irrelevant reply to the speaker. A sixth is learning that a third party's interpretation of what was said is very different from the listener's interpretation.

The presence of any of these signs calls for strengthening of listening and concentrative skills, eliminating the barriers that are getting in the way of effective listening. The three most common barriers include, first, a speaker who turns the listener off. Maybe his style is uncomfortable, or he's a whiner or complainer or constant braggadocio. An irritating style may interfere with concentration to the message. Second, the subject matter may turn the listener off. Understanding a troublesome subject is corrected by taking the time to master it. Third, a pressing matter on the listener's mind may interfere with concentrative and listening powers. The need to solve one problem intrudes with the ability to concentrate on another.

A manager, in his role as a decision maker, relies on information from others; therefore, he must not allow these barriers to impede his reception of information. However, once the barriers are eliminated and information is forthcoming, the job is not done. It is then incumbent upon a manager to verify the authenticity of the sources of all information and of the information gathered.

Since subordinates are oftentimes key sources of information, a rapport that hinges on trust and confidence must be developed. This means treating people with openness and showing respect for their knowledge and expertise; it does not mean being dictatorial and abrupt. The manager is alert to minor discrepancies, small gaps or omissions, or minute ambiguities in the information he is given. His eyes and ears are open. He listens to all sources, suspending his biases and preconceptions, matching input against input, holding fragmentary bits and pieces of data for later confirmation, building a mental picture of a situation he must assess through second-hand information. He is sensitive to communicative pitches that are too pat, which may mean they have been manipulated for the sake of consistency. He begins to identify the subordinates who may be trying to create illusions for him, as well as the ones who communicate honestly and directly.

Controller

A control system, while needed to operate, regulate, and guide a business enterprise, does not ensure success. Rather, such a system serves as the rein that keeps business activities from wandering from their intended path and the means by which managers stay informed of the performance of properties. As a controller, a manager's job is to evaluate, appraise, examine, and investigate. All of these steps are necessary for ascertaining whether or not plans and objectives are being achieved. Control, then, involves checking to make certain that everything is proceeding as intended.

An effective control system meets five requirements: (1) It is based upon agreed-to standards. Most often this involves a comparison of planned versus actual for the measurable quantities of the project at hand. (2) It is timely. Reports are made at regular intervals, and data is available in time to take corrective action if necessary. (3) It is as quantitative as possible in order to avoid inclination toward subjective interpretation. (4) It is focused on elements that are important, not minutiae. (5) It is focused on results, not effort.

The central control systems used by a property manager are comparison of the operating statement with the budget, employee evaluations, vacancy reports, delinquent rent reports, and wage and hour controls. With the computer, persons involved in real estate management have acquired great capacity to design controls for processing and analyzing large amounts of data in a very brief time. The advent of these management information and control systems is the primary reason for the new-found ability to grow while not losing an awareness of what's happening at various managed properties.

In addition to these general company controls, each manager is responsible for establishing and maintaining the supplementary controls needed to assume successful completion of the tasks within his scope of responsibility. If, for example, the manager of an office building is responsible for the suite development of space for a new tenant, he needs to plan for and establish budgets and time schedules and arrange for allocation of resources of money and building employees in order to complete the job. Subsequently, these controls are essential in measuring the progress of the project vis-a-vis his plan.

Developer of Human Resources

The fifth responsibility of the property manager is to professionally develop the people who work for him. It falls to the manager to select, train, and motivate his staff and create a team whose aim is to meet the objectives of the organization. (The role of the manager as a developer of human resources is so crucial that three chapters of this text, chapters 13, 14, and 15, have been devoted to this topic.)

3

Managerial Performance
and Compensation

AN ABLE, COMPETENT PROPERTY MANAGER is a real estate management
firm's most valuable resource. Many years and much effort are needed
to build a strong management team, but it can be disbanded in a
very short time if not properly directed. A formal program of continuously measuring the performance of property managers and,
based upon the appraisal, rewarding them for their achievements
and efforts can help to keep the team intact.

Performance Appraisal

Property managers at the professional level—especially those who are
achievement oriented—need feedback regarding their performance
level. Consequently, establishment and application of standards of
measurement for property managers are important to a firm's operation. The principal tool for developing and rewarding managers
is a performance appraisal, an exercise that carefully tests the performance of each individual manager. The results of the appraisal,
which are reviewed with the subject, determine not only the property
manager's salary recommendation but also whether or not he is to
be given more challenging assignments and added responsibility.

Job evaluations revolve around two variables: What is to be
measured, and how the measurement is to be made. A job description is a guide in determining what is to be measured. However, in
addition to judging fulfillment of specific tasks, overall professional

performance—a reflection of company standards—needs to be evaluated. To ensure good company health, the performance demand level is high. This does not mean success at fulfilling every assignment every time, but rather consistency in performance over an extended period of time. Any performance record includes a few mistakes. The true measure of quality lies in ability to achieve effective results in a variety of assignments over a long time.

At its best, a performance appraisal depends heavily on subjective judgment. It hinges on the quality, relevance, accuracy, and completeness of the information gathered and the opinion of the appraiser. Even if the purpose of and factors to be considered in an appraisal are agreed upon, the results may vary according to who is performing the appraisal. Obviously, one appraiser has different priorities and rates certain factors higher or lower than his associates. Appraising human performance is a subject of considerable research by social scientists. Still, it is extremely important that the subject views the appraisal as fair and knows why he is being judged. He needs to know, for instance, that the appraisal expresses the values and beliefs of the organization and his relation to those values and beliefs. Likewise, he needs to know what goes into the judgment and how that judgment will be applied.

Respect for the appraisal and the people who prepare and administer it is critical to the success of the evaluation process. Unless the manager is receptive to the feedback it offers, wants to improve, and feels some desire for personal growth, any effort to counsel him is unlikely to be successful. The purpose of an appraisal is to strengthen the organization by improving each individual property manager's ability to perform. Thus, its focus is based upon opportunities rather than problems. The attitude of the appraisal interview must be one of searching together for solutions to opportunities rather than one-sided sermonizing on the principles of good management. The interview should end with both parties agreeing to a short-range plan that outlines how the manager can improve his professional abilities through the opportunities available to him. The effective short-range plan is in writing and includes quantitative objectives and definitive programs for achieving them.

A performance appraisal should eliminate, as much as possible, the influence of subjectivity and be designed to meet the organization's particular needs. The evaluation form in figure 3.1 represents one tried and tested method of monitoring a property manager's performance and is recommended for use by real estate service firms. This formal appraisal plan becomes a means of objectively con-

Property Manager Performance Appraisal

Policy

It is company policy to conduct a performance appraisal of each property manager by a vice president at least twice annually. These reviews are intended to serve two primary functions: (1) increase the effectiveness of the property manager, the vice president, and the company; and (2) establish a uniform and equitable method of measuring the property manager's performance for annual compensation review.

Procedure

The vice president is to complete this form and review it with the applicable property manager. The completed and signed form is to be kept in the property manager's personnel file.

Category	Point Value	X	Grade (10 Highest)	=	Total Points
1. Adherence to Job Description	10		____		____
2. Quality of Management Plan	10		____		____
3. Organization of Property Operations	10		____		____
4. Implementation of Management Plan	10		____		____
5. Analysis and Communication	10		____		____
6. Owner Satisfaction	10		____		____
7. On-Site Critiques	10		____		____
8. Completion of Company Assignments	7		____		____
9. Adherence to Company Policies	6		____		____
10. Supervision Time	6		____		____
11. Relationship with Other Personnel	6		____		____
12. Professional Growth	5		____		____
Total	100	X	____	=	____

Vice President_____
Property Manager_____   Date_____

Figure 3.1. Form for appraising performance of a property manager.

sidering concrete data that indicate managerial performance. The underlying assumption is that both parties are aware of the work level expected. The appraisal is based on actual ability to achieve this work level.

Performance appraisal methods vary considerably, and no consensus has been reached as to the single most effective approach. A ranking system, for instance, compares the overall performance of one manager against the performance of other managers within the organization. A point system identifies the components of a job and assigns a point value to each component. A separate evaluation is performed for each element; the points then are added to determine the comprehensive evaluation.

The appraisal form illustrated in figure 3.1 utilizes a point value system with weights for each factor. As can be seen, the evaluation is based on performance in 12 categories. The first seven categories relate to the manager's ability to oversee the operations of income property, the latter five relate to company responsibilities. A description of these 12 categories follows.

Adherence to Job Description

A typical job description assigns parameters of responsibility and authority and lists regular and ongoing tasks that are to be performed by the person occupying the position. This description may be used as a checklist to ascertain if the subject of the appraisal is doing what is expected of him.

The difficulty in responding to this section of the performance appraisal lies in the fact that many executive jobs cannot be described with the same degree of exactitude as other jobs. The duties listed on the job description may not be detailed; rather, it may cover broad areas of responsibility, scope of authority, and relationships within the organization. Still, the property manager's job description can be used to ascertain if the subject has the skills to fulfill his job obligations and has assumed the necessary accountability.

Quality of Management Plan

A management plan is the fundamental document for the operation of a property. It is a written program that details how a property is to be managed during the coming year and includes the property's annual budget. Ability to create a quality, operable management plan, judged in terms of the degree of knowledgeable, professional analysis that goes into it, is rated. Also evaluated are the accuracies and foresight exhibited in the design of the previous year's plans.

Organization of Property Operations

A function of the property manager is to organize work connected with a property in such a way that it produces the desired results as outlined in the management plan. Important to the evaluation is a judgment as to the manager's ability to establish performance objectives for on-site managers and other supervisory personnel so that each job is directed, with teamwork, toward the overall objectives of the management plan.

Implementation of Management Plan

A management plan is worthless if it is not properly implemented. A manager's ability to do this is a critical part of his performance appraisal. This category of evaluation encompasses the staffing, directing, controlling, and operating responsibilities of the property manager as listed in the job description. In performing the appraisal, primary emphasis is on ability to select, train, and supervise on-site personnel effectively while controlling total operating costs.

Analysis and Communication

As a year progresses and social and economic conditions change, it may be necessary to make adjustments to the management plan. It is extremely important for managers to be able to identify changes in markets as they occur, analyze them, put them in the perspective of a property being managed, and make recommendations for adjustments to the management plan based upon this analysis.

Subsequently, sound ongoing communication is needed to keep the on-site staff, supervisor, and property owner informed of the property's operational status. If a line of communication is maintained throughout, should any significant operational problems occur, the property manager is in a position to easily communicate these problems and his solutions to his supervisor and the property owner.

Owner Satisfaction

Maintaining a viable relationship with a property owner often is as challenging as managing a property. Therefore, evaluating a property manager on his ability to satisfy clients is important in the overall appraisal process. Many times this part of the evaluation calls for the input from the owner. A responsibility of the corporate officer performing the evaluation, therefore, is to discuss the operation of a property with the owner from time to time and determine his degree of satisfaction with the performance of the property manager assigned to that account.

On-Site Critiques

Typically, an executive officer routinely visits all properties overseen by property managers under his supervision. On these visits he judges how well the property is maintained, the condition and rentability of vacant space, the appearance and attitude of employees, the thoroughness and effectiveness of the marketing program, etc. The findings of these critiques then are summarized and incorporated into the performance appraisal.

Completion of Company Assignments

From time to time, assignments other than those specifically listed in the job descriptions are given to property managers. These special assignments often are directed toward assisting the management team in developing new procedures or uncovering necessary information. For example, a property manager may be asked to review and update a vendor list so that all managers are aware of the best sources for buying products and services, or he may be requested to provide data for a study on electricity costs or some other operating expense. In this segment of the performance appraisal, the manager is rated on his performance in completing special assignments fully and on time and the quality of information received.

Adherence to Company Policies

A property management company functions as a team with established sets of rules, policies, and procedures for handling operating situations. To be an effective team, all participants must operate within these guidelines. This portion of the evaluation calls for a rating as to the manager's ability to perform within the structure of the standard operating policies and procedures.

Supervision Time

Typically each property manager comes under the responsibility of one of the company officers. That officer will need to devote time to training, supervising, and motivating the property manager. However, as a knowledgeable professional, the manager is expected to be able to carry on in many areas without ongoing assistance and supervision. The manager is graded down in this portion of the appraisal if he requires an inordinate amount of support time.

Relationship with Other Personnel

The property manager who does not meet his responsibilities is a burden to the staffs of other departments, especially the bookkeeping department. The unfortunate result of an ineffective manager may be that other supervisory personnel find themselves faced with morale problems. In this category, the property manager is rated as to how well he assumes his obligations so that he does not cause extra work for the supportive office staff. Similarly, his personality and its effect on his relationships and compatibility with colleagues within the firm are considered.

Professional Growth

Both the effort toward developing professional growth and the results of that effort are worthy of being judged. Professional growth is gained through attending continuing education programs, offered both by trade associations and colleges and universities, and reading and studying a great deal. True professionals spend several hours weekly digesting information on the many areas of knowledge that apply to their work. Periodicals, journals, books, lectures, seminars, courses—all are key sources of expanding one's professional realization. Likewise, teaching and writing are viable methods of increasing knowledge, there being some truth in the adage that the teacher is the one who learns the most.

Management Compensation

In designing a financial compensation program for property managers, the objectives of the program first must be defined. Chief among these is to attract and motivate the professionals without whom the business could not achieve its company goals. Furthermore, the pay system should be designed to encourage and reward exceptional performance; i.e., a merit plan may be considered. Because the typical real estate management enterprise spends a major portion of its gross income on people-related expenses, it is crucial that the compensation program be designed in such a way that each dollar produces the maximum employee motivation.

Some behavioral scientists claim that money does not lead to improved performance. However, failure to establish proper levels of pay has decidedly debilitating effects. If wages are adequate, other needs become important; if wages are considered inadequate, they are rated first in importance. A compensation system is viewed as a method of determining one's place with a group. The amount paid becomes a measuring stick as to how a property manager relates to and compares with others, especially his peers. Furthermore, when wage levels are tied to performance and compensation is viewed as a form of recognition, the compensation program leads to improved property manager performance. Figure 3.2 is a representation of how a sampling of 14 property managers ranked the importance of the various types of rewards available to them.

In adopting a property manager compensation package, certain basic considerations should be weighed. Any fair compensation system recognizes the need to have a reasonable degree of stability in one's standard of living. Furthermore, some provision should be made that will, at the minimum, offer protection against catastrophic expenses. Generally, a property manager compensation package includes a base salary, competitive with salaries paid by other companies for similar positions, and benefits that would cover major personal expenses. Such benefits are designed to motivate a property manager to continue to be productive without adding financial worries to the concerns that would be caused if, for example, a member of his family became seriously ill.

In addition to providing a comfortable standard of living and a sense of security for a property manager and his family, an appropriate compensation plan leaves room for the manager to be continually motivated to achieve a higher performance level. To this end, the compensation package generally includes the possibility of receiving some form of supplementary reward. Indeed, most of the increase in total managerial compensation since the end of World War II has been in the form of supplements to base salaries. There is an ongoing search for the ideal compensation plan that both continues to motivate and appropriately rewards the manager. The most common form of extra compensation is commissions, based

Means of Reward	Rating														Average
Salary	1	1	1	1	1	1	1	2	2	3	3	5	6		2.07
Bonus	1	1	2	2	2	2	3	3	3	4	4	5	5	6	3.07
Title and Responsibilities	1	2	2	2	2	3	3	3	4	4	6	8	8		3.64
Rewarding Assignments	1	2	2	3	3	3	3	4	5	5	5	5	6	7	4.57
Security within Company	1	1	2	3	4	4	4	5	6	8	8	8	8	9	5.07
Fringe Benefits	2	3	4	5	5	6	6	6	6	6	6	6	7	9	5.93
Prestige of Work Environment	4	4	4	5	5	6	7	7	7	7	7	8	8	9	6.28
Special Recognition	4	4	5	6	7	7	7	7	8	8	8	9	9	9	6.64
Company Sponsorship of Outside Activity	4	5	6	7	7	8	8	8	9	9	9	9	9	9	7.64

Figure 3.2. Representation of how a sampling of 14 property managers ranked the importance of types of reward.

on the principle of profit sharing. Other kinds of extra compensation are bonuses, deferred compensation, stock options, or extraordinary benefits. Utilizing these compensation methods, various compensation packages are available: straight commission, no guarantees, small guarantees plus commission, straight salary, good salary plus commissions, good salary plus bonus plan, minimum salary plus profit sharing. Regardless of the type of package offered, however, the following policy guidelines are worthy of adoption:

1. Managers should be discouraged from discussing their compensation plans with their colleagues. This should serve to eliminate the problem of one manager feeling he is receiving less recognition or status because his compensation package is different from someone else's. Every effort must be made to treat all equitably and fairly. However, top management is the judge of each manager's relative merits to the team and is the final judge as to the dimension of responsibilities and performance.

2. In order to attract and retain quality property managers, they must be well compensated, both in terms of paycheck and recognition. Those individuals who are able to qualify as entrepreneurial managers receive compensation that is consistent with the highest in the industry.

3. A commission business requires production. Managers may receive salaries that are less than the guarantee they could receive elsewhere, but, by generous participation in profits, their opportunities for increased compensation may be very high.

4. A basic property manager benefit package may be minimal; however, extraordinary insurance benefits should be available to individuals who require them for peace of mind and security. The extra cost of higher benefits then could be subtracted from participants' ability to participate in profits.

5. Until an individual acquires the skills and attitude to fully fit the job description of a property manager, his compensation should be straight salary plus minimal benefits. He should not have the opportunity to participate in the bonus plan or profit-sharing plan.

Commissions

A continuing challenge is to determine a fair way to share the gains from higher productivity in such a way that managers will be interested in improving their own performance and the productivity of the organization as a whole. Measuring a property manager's productivity level is difficult. One measurement is the total management fees attributable to the properties under his stewardship. A commission system offers a wage incentive based upon these fees. Typically, a property manager on commission is paid a base salary against a percentage of these fees. This provides a simple method of directly rewarding the manager for the amount of responsibility he is assuming and his level of productivity. Furthermore, financial risks for the company practically are eliminated.

For example, assume that Joe Cornell, CPM®, is a property manager with the City Management Company. Joe manages eight apartment buildings containing 1,400 units and has a base salary (plus auto and medical benefits) of $2,000 per month against 22 percent of the gross fees earned. Last month the management fees were $12,200. Therefore, Joe's current compensation is 22 percent of $12,200, or $2,684 per month. Assume also that part of Joe's management portfolio was two buildings, owned by a single owner, totalling 400 units; the monthly management fee was $3,500 of the $12,200 total. If this owner decides to sell his buildings to new owners who will provide their own management, Joe is left with a portfolio of 1,000 units representing monthly fees of $8,700. Twenty-two percent of $8,700 is $1,914, or less than his minimum guarantee. The company, however, continues to pay Joe $2,000 per month. Everyone is motivated to actively strive to build up Joe's management portfolio.

Simple as it sounds, the commission system is not without pitfalls. The primary problem lies in trying to assign a fair value to the manager's time and, at the same time, not put undue risk upon the company. The company, in establishing a percentage of the gross, has the problem of comparably weighing the relative abilities and merits of each of its property managers. There is also the problem of assigning too low or too high a percentage value in relation to the effort that is required to manage a property. For example, a property manager managing several small, widely scattered properties needs to receive a higher percentage of the gross income than the property manager who has two very large complexes in the same neighborhood. The latter is not faced with the problem of travel time nor dealing with less efficient on-site employees. Another problem involves peer recognition. If one property manager, for just cause, receives a higher percentage commission than other managers, it is sometimes difficult to explain the reasoning for this to his peers.

In this instance, the compensation plan would not motivate but would have a definite demotivating effect.

Bonuses

Effective bonus plans are designed with two objectives in mind. One, the bonus relates to individual performance; hence, compensation to property managers within a company may vary based on performance levels. Two, the bonus relates to company profits. One obligation of management is to economic performance, the fundamental mission of a real estate management company being realization of a profit. Any bonus plan should be mathematically related to the executive-level property manager's ability to contribute to the company profit. Hence, the fund from which bonuses are paid usually is a predetermined portion of the company profits. The share of the fund distributed to each manager is based upon individual performance, salary level, or both.

Deferred Compensation

A deferred compensation plan provides for postponement of income to a property manager until some later time, usually upon retirement when his income is lower. Deferred income plans are offered because of their possible tax advantages to the recipients, providing a means of income averaging in order to avoid unusually high income taxes in a given period of time.

Unless very unusual circumstances exist, this form of compensation seldom applies to real estate management organizations. Those interested in this type of program probably would be wise to first investigate available retirement or pension fund plans.

Stock Options

Stock options are another kind of managerial incentive. A stock option is a right to buy a specified number of shares of company stock at a stated price within a definite period of time. They are offered primarily to the top executives of a company who are in positions to affect its profits and growth. Stock options became quite popular after the 1950 enactment of an Internal Revenue Code, which provided that gains in value between the option price and the selling price of the stock would be taxed at the capital gains rate, which is much less than the ordinary income tax rate. Subsequent changes to the Internal Revenue Code, however, made the conditions for use of stock options more stringent. Consequently, popularity for this form of compensation lessened.

Fringe Benefits

One problem with fringe benefits is that they sometimes are too costly, the expense of providing them far outstripping the advantages. The employee ends up with a small paycheck but a luxury benefit package. In industry, one-third to one-fourth of the total compensation package is expended for fringe benefits. In a typical management company, employee benefits are the second largest item of expense, ranking only after payroll. As dollars spent for this purpose increase, it becomes more and more important to the success of a business enterprise that the money be spent wisely.

Benefits are payments made by an employer on behalf of an employee that accrue to the benefit of the employee but are not direct cash remuneration. Some benefits provide protection from hardship; others are in the form of time off or paid-for pleasantries. Some benefits—specifically workmen's compensation, social security, and unemployment insurance—are required by law. Optional benefits include medical, hospital, dental, life, and disability insurance; defrayment of costs for attending educational courses and payment of professional dues; company automobiles; luxury travel; private club memberships; employee dining rooms; and paid time off for vacations, sick leave, holidays, birthdays, and serious illness or death of a family member.

Some basic rules should be kept in mind when establishing a fringe benefit program. First and most important, benefits need to be structured so as to give the beneficiary the most for the money. For example, a medical plan essentially needs to protect against catastrophic illness. Few employees can afford to be insured for the risk of small medical bills, but, with soaring medical care costs, they do need unlimited protection for major medical problems.

A second rule is recognition that the benefit needs of individuals are different. Viable benefit plans are adaptable to each individual property manager's needs. This is far preferable to having one plan forced upon the group collectively. The need for term life insurance and the need for protection against interruption of income provide good examples. The loss of income to an employee because of his disability or the loss of income to his family because of his death can be much more significant to a manager with a large family or who has limited resources than to a manager with no family or who has considerable capital resources. Individual needs should be provided for as long as they are not met at the expense of those who do not have the same needs.

A third rule concerning benefits is that reimbursement for business expenses be fair but frugal. If the real estate management business is to show a profit, there is no room for lavish expense accounts or unrealistic transportation allowances. If these benefits are important to the property manager for social or income tax reasons, they must be considered as part of his total compensation and a downward adjustment made either to his base salary or bonus compensation. This is not to say that the manager should not be given an allowance for reasonable expenses. The emphasis, however, should be on reasonable, the nature of management assignments dictating the amount of the allowance. When the property manager's assignments require that he travel out of the city, he is of course entitled to be reimbursed, this becoming a regular operating expense of the management business. To the contrary, little need exists for property managers to entertain clients, vendors, or employees. A written policy that dictates under what conditions a manager may be entitled to reimbursement for these activities avoids problems arising in this area.

A small benefit many firms give to property managers is paying their dues for belonging to real estate associations and professional organizations. Likewise, many forward-thinking companies also have policies related to paying for the cost of educational courses and seminars attended by a manager.

4

Time Management

A MANAGER'S FUNDAMENTAL RESOURCES are knowledge, people, capital, and time. Knowledge can be continually expanded through study and experience. There is an almost inexhaustible supply of people. In this economy, capital is available to a manager if he can prove that an economic opportunity exists. Time, however, is a finite resource. The supply of time is totally inelastic. Each day has 24 hours, no more. No matter what the demand, the supply cannot be accrued. Yesterday's time and wasted time are gone forever and cannot be replaced.

A successful, professional manager makes good use of all the resources available to him, including time. Most people take time for granted, giving it little consideration except when it is apparent that there is a lack of it. Yet of the four basic resources, time is the easiest to develop. The effective manager is distinguished by his ability to manage not only property, money, and people, but time as well.

Obstructions to Effective Time Utilization

Property managers are beset by several problems that lead to an ineffective use of time. The first revolves around constant pressure to participate in unproductive and time-wasting situations. Pressures might come from unsolicited phone calls from vendors or tradesmen, people seeking free information on how to buy or operate real estate, and meetings or ceremonies that are unrelated to productive activity.

The second fundamental problem in managing time is that most people think they use their time more wisely than they do. Few people can rely on memory to tell them how they spend their time. Studies have revealed that when executives are asked to estimate how they spend their time and then follow that estimate with an actual time log, little resemblance is found between the supposed and the actual time usage. As proof of this, 17 property managers were asked to estimate how they used their time. After submitting their estimates, they were asked to keep a time log for four consecutive weeks. The results of this experience provided some startling revelations:

Task	Hours Per Week	
	Estimate	Actual
Recruiting and selecting employees	1.0	.4
Training employees	2.2	1.0
Supervising employees	6.1	8.6
Accounting functions	7.4	5.1
With owners	3.1	2.6
Solving building problems	9.6	12.4
Meeting with supervisor	2.1	.9
Travel	4.1	4.8
Mail	2.0	.9
Planning and budgeting	2.1	4.5
Other: Company operations	1.8	1.2
Other fee business	1.2	.7
New business	2.0	.8
Personal	0	.3
Average work week	44.8	44.2

A third time management problem is constant interruptions while attempting to work. Preparing an annual budget for a property, for instance, requires a minimum of six to eight hours of intense analysis and numerous calculations. To allow interruptions from phone calls, the office staff, or even so-called emergency situations while attempting to prepare a budget reduces time to sheer waste. To be effective, every property manager needs to dispose of time in fairly large segments. The manager can work for long hours but not reach an acceptable level of accomplishment if his hours are divided into bits and pieces. This is particularly true in the routine supervision of a building and its on-site management staff. A visit to a building by a property manager usually results in irrelevant gossip concerning tenants, tradespeople, or neighbors, none of which has anything to do with the building's management. A primary purpose of a property visit is to audit the management program to be sure it is being implemented in a satisfactory manner and to see if any changes are called for. The manager should be available to help the on-site management in resolving its problems. The irrelevant discussion in no way contributes to—in fact detracts from—accomplishing this purpose. Furthermore, an on-site visit represents wasted time unless sufficient time is scheduled to do a thorough job. It is much more effective to schedule fewer visits to a property but, while there, spend the time necessary to do a complete job. This is far preferable to stopping by briefly every few days to respond to a problem or check on a situation.

The fourth time management problem for a property manager is the mixing of personal relationships with business relationships. Managers are in the business of dealing with people. To give a hurried response to a question or to stifle discussion may cause ill feelings, yet long conversations can produce tremendous inefficiency in the use of time. The one-on-one personal relation is one dimension of the problem. Another occurs in large offices in which appreciable amounts of time are wasted because of the socializing relationships that evolve. The more people are together, the more they socialize; consequently, the time available for work, accomplishment, and results diminishes.

Once a property manager has identified the problems that make time management difficult, he is in a position to remedy the situation through a time management plan.

The process of managing time requires three steps: (1) recording time; (2) managing time; (3) organizing time. The first step involves finding out where time actually goes, followed by step two, making effective use of time and cutting out unproductive demands on it. Once accomplished, the manager can consolidate his productive hours into the largest possible continuing segments.

Recording Time

The first step in the program of improving the effectiveness of time use is to diagnose how it is spent. An astute manager begins the solution of his time management problem by studying his work habits and time usage.

Industry, with its constant effort to increase productivity, is conscious of how the time of industrial labor is used, and it was in industry that time studies first became commonplace. It is noteworthy that while much research has been done on time effectiveness and its impact on industry, in service professions—such as real estate management—very little educational effort has been devoted to how practitioners can increase their productivity through better time management. People in a service business are really selling their time. They have different incomes because of their varying capabilities to produce commissions and fees. While a part of this compensation is based upon ability, another part is based on how much can be accomplished in a given period of time or in a day's work. The result is production; the formula for production is ability plus use of time. The property manager's income is dependent upon his level of managerial ability and the amount of work he can accomplish in a given period of time. Consequently, successful managers are those who derive maximum benefit from a minimum investment of time.

In *The Effective Executive* (New York: Harper & Row, Inc., 1966), Peter Drucker says, "One has to record time before one can know where it goes and before, in turn, one can attempt to manage it. The first step toward executive effectiveness is therefore to record actual time use." A time inventory or log is necessary in recording and subsequently studying habits and uses of time. Experts on time management have suggested all kinds of time logs that can be applied to the process of recording daily work habits and uses of time. Probably the best log is one that is devised by the manager to meet his own needs. An example of a time log appears as figure 4.1.

In designing a time log, several factors should be considered. One requirement is that it be a written record, the memory, as cited earlier, not being an accurate recorder of how time is used. The log should facilitate the recording of uses of time in 15-minute periods. Proof of habits that only take a few minutes at a time but are repeated many times during the day can make the manager well aware of ineffective use of time. For example, one poor work habit was brought to the attention of a manager while logging his time: People were bringing him checks to sign throughout the day. These constant interruptions were disruptive and unnecessary not only to the manager but also wasted the time of the bookkeepers, who had to constantly interrupt their work in order to get the checks signed. A simple program of accumulating checks for signing at one time was

Time Log

Activity	First Week					Second Week					Third Week					Fourth Week				
	M	T	W	T	F	M	T	W	T	F	M	T	W	T	F	M	T	W	T	F
Recruiting/Selecting Employees																				
Training Employees																				
Supervising Employees																				
Accounting																				
With Owners																				
Solving Building Problems																				
Meeting with Supervisors																				
Travel During Working Hours																				
Mail																				
Planning and Budgeting																				
Other (Describe on Other Side)																				
Personal																				

Instructions: Record time by quarter hours. Account for all working hours every day.

Figure 4.1. Time log for maintaining record of property manager's business time usage.

initiated. This eliminated interruptions while still providing for getting the checks signed and mailed on time.

To ensure accuracy, time usage should be recorded in the log several times daily. Furthermore, in order to get a fair sample of actual time use, the first log should be kept for a period of at least three or four weeks. After two or three weeks' experience in keeping track of time, time usage can be categorized and headings created for the time log that more appropriately describe actual activities.

The use of time logs by property managers is not restricted to this first-time analysis. Rather, they should be used systematically to re-evaluate how time is being spent and what work habits are being established, perhaps unknowingly. Only by constant effort at managing time can drifting into poor work habits be prevented. Some executives keep a continuous log and review it monthly. Others use it several times yearly for stretches of two to four weeks; after each inventory, time schedules can be reworked based on actual performance.

Managing Time

After completion of an initial time log, the systematic management of time, based upon study of the actual use of time, is called for. The manager identifies the time-wasting, nonproductive activities. He analyzes his time log to become aware of both good and bad work habits. He studies how he misuses his time by not delegating work, not scheduling work, not making decisions, not establishing priorities, and not setting good work patterns. Subsequently, a program is adopted that rectifies his ineffectiveness.

Delegating

The term "delegation" needs some defining. Essentially, it means giving someone something to do. However, there is an added dimension: It also means giving comparable responsibility along with the task that has been delegated. Delegation does not mean getting someone else to do part of a job. Giving a subordinate a distasteful job that nobody wants is not delegating—it's assigning. To effectively delegate, a manager asks himself: Which of my activities could be done by someone else just as well, if not better?

For example, the whole process of taking legal action for nonpayment of rent is a task performed by many property managers that easily could be delegated to others. A manager's secretary, for instance, could be given this responsibility. Of course, successful delegation requires preparation. In this case, the manager first must thoroughly explain to his secretary all of the legal aspects, procedures, and reasons for initiating action against a tenant. Guidelines about proceeding with legal action and/or accepting settlement must be established. The pertinent legal forms or lawyers to be used when necessary should be specified, and the secretary advised on the fee structure for those legal costs. After the secretary fully understands the proper legal procedures for pursuing action against delinquent tenants, the property manager is in a position to properly delegate the responsibility for pursuing such action. As a control, a once-a-month reviewing process might be established, at which time the manager would examine the rent roll reports and the status of each delinquency.

Delegating with strings attached is self-defeating. If, for example, the manager asks the secretary to handle legal matters regarding nonpayment of rent but then asks to see daily reports, be informed of all conversations with the attorney, approve legal fees, and review all correspondence with tenants prior to mailing, he has not delegated responsibility. He has simply assigned his secretary a series of tasks to assist him in carrying out this responsibility. People do a better job, and take more pride in it, if they can make some decisions themselves. The key to delegation is entrusting. When delegating, the entire matter, along with sufficient authority to make necessary decisions, must be entrusted to the subordinate. This is quite different from saying, "Just do what I tell you to do." At the same time, of course, delegation does not mean abdication of accountability. It is not an escape from responsibility. Ultimate accountability remains within the domain of the manager.

Although delegation is one of the principal means of managing time, few managers use this tool to its fullest. This is largely due to the number of obstacles that stand in the way of delegation. Lack of confidence in subordinates is, of course, one of the primary problems. However, few managers realize that their lack of confidence lies in their own managerial skills. An obligation of management is to select a competent staff and subsequently train people to accept responsibility. If confidence in subordinates is lacking, this basic obligation has not been met. Furthermore, as long as subordinates are denied responsibility, they will never have the opportunity to prove that they warrant confidence.

Other obstacles also get in the way of delegation. One is the "I can do it better myself" attitude adopted by many managers who have not learned to accept the fact that their subordinates also may be capable of producing quality work. Additional obstacles include inexperience in delegating, lack of skill in balancing workloads and establishing priorities, and fear of being resented by subordinates to whom work is delegated.

Stopping Interruptions

One of the greatest yet most deceptive time wasters is interruptions. Many interruptions occur under the guise of emergencies or a subordinate's "need to know" before he can take action on a problem. What often is discovered is that no emergency existed or the subordinate did not need the information immediately in order to proceed toward the solution to his problem. It is surprisingly interesting to analyze how interruptions are allowed to disturb work. How much time is wasted because phone calls are accepted in the middle of conversations with others or while performing important work? How much time is lost if attention is diverted from the job at hand to study a newly arrived piece of mail or a message?

Interruptions cannot be eliminated. Many are simply requests to do what is expected. But interruptions can be minimized, and this is important, because an hour of concentrated effort is worth more than two hours composed of 10- or 15-minute segments. It takes time to mentally adjust after an interruption. The goal should be to eliminate wasted transition time by minimizing interruptions.

Interestingly, the telephone, which can be the business world's greatest time saver, can instead, if used improperly, be the biggest time waster. One way of avoiding this is to exercise more control over telephone usage. The first step in this control is to log incoming calls for a period of one month and then analyze them. Is there a particular resident manager who is calling an unusual number of times and, if so, is it because he lacks direction or is incompetent? Are there frequent calls that should be referred to other people? Perhaps better instructions to the switchboard operator or receptionist can cut down on this kind of interruption. Are calls coming from vendors who are seeking payment of invoices? If a vendor's inquiry is legitimate and a reasonable length of time has passed since he rendered his statement, this may be a signal that the bookkeeping department requires direction. On the other hand, many vendors repeatedly ask for payment before a reasonable period of time has elapsed. Possibly the manager should reconsider doing business with these vendors. The price for the service or product may be reasonable, but the overall cost may be expensive if there is an excess of annoying and unnecessary telephone calls.

A telephone management program is a solution to these problems. For instance, a manager may consider setting aside a time for phone calls. If a schedule is established as to when a manager is available for calls or short meetings, coworkers and subordinates will adjust to that routine and feel comfortable in knowing that he definitely can be reached during those hours. A particularly good time to be available is during the first hours of the working day. Generally, it is too early to visit properties. Furthermore, persons who need to be reached by phone are usually more available during early working hours as well. Establishing a schedule and letting everyone know about it can decrease interruptions.

Most property managers run into the problem of being constantly interrupted by owners of properties they manage. These clients can be terrible time wasters. They call repeatedly, seeking information or status of some insignificant situation. They think nothing of interrupting work or causing an inconvenience. They are concerned about their investment, and the property manager is their pacifier.

One property management executive found an interesting solution to this problem: The president of a successful marketing organization made his first major real estate investment when he purchased a large suburban office building. Shortly after assigning the management account, telephone calls to the property manager in charge began. The owner called five and six times a day inquiring about all kinds of details. He had made a major financial commitment in a new business venture, and it was clear he was insecure about the operation of that business. After several weeks and hundreds of calls, the property manager said, "Look, Bob, all of these calls you're making to me are wasting a lot of our time. Why don't we solve this problem by my agreeing to call you every day at noon. You can accumulate a list of all the questions that you want answered, and we can handle this in one phone call a day." It was agreed, and the daily calls were initiated. Because the client was forced to list his questions and think about them, the lists began to grow smaller. Soon it was agreed that daily calls were not necessary. In a short time, biweekly calls solved the problem. The point of this example is to emphasize the need to establish some mutually agreeable system of communication with the client to increase his comfort level and, above all, reduce interruptions.

Furthermore, when phone calls are answered or when personal meetings are held with visitors to the office, a manager can increase efficiency by setting the tone of the conversation at the onset. Each person has his own conversational style. A conversation that starts with an inquiry such as, "What can I do for you?" will get to the point much more quickly than a conversation that starts, "Hi, how are you? How are things going?"

Making Decisions

The two chief time consumers in decision making are perfectionism and procrastination. The manager who strives for the perfect solution has set a goal that is not only unobtainable but frustrating and wasteful. Likewise, those who vacillate or refuse to arrive at a point of decision not only waste time but also create extra problems caused by worrying. Worry is a destructive force that greatly reduces performance ability.

A manager plagued with indecisiveness may examine some simple guidelines that will improve his ability to handle decisions. For one thing, decisions should be timely. From an objective point of view, postponing a decision may be the worst alternative a manager could choose in terms of his company's or a property's welfare. Sometimes any decision is better than no decision. Experts say that in 80 percent of the situations requiring decisions, time is the most important ingredient. The first question the manager should analyze when presented with a problem requiring a decision, then, is the time factor: Will delay be the most costly decision?

Second, fear should be eliminated from decision making. Oftentimes, a decision is postponed out of fear of making a mistake, there being a lack of confidence in ability to arrive at the proper answer. If the fear could be relieved by gathering more facts or getting outside consultation, a manager should proceed immediately to do whatever needs to be done in order to provide confidence in making a decision. Anxiety over the consequences of an erroneous decision is not an attribute of a quality manager. Gamble is implicit in all decisions. There are no riskless decisions, nor will an executive ever have all the facts. Decision must be reached without all the facts and the risk accepted. Those who try to escape the risk of decision making by procrastination not only fail to measure up as managers but waste enormous amounts of valuable time.

Third, personal deadlines for making decisions should be imposed and adhered to. Likewise, when delegating a task or scheduling the steps to be taken toward an objective, deadlines for all persons involved should be established. These deadlines, of course, must be realistic. Not allowing enough time can be a thief of time as well, there being some truth to the adage that haste breeds waste.

Establishing Sound Work Habits

Increasing productivity through better management of time involves habits. An analysis of work patterns can identify those work habits that need to be changed. A habit is an action that has become permanent by custom or persistent repetition. The greater the number of details of daily life that can be handed over to effortless automatic practice, the more the mind is set free for more important work.

Psychologists have done considerable study on the subject of developing good habits and breaking bad ones. Essentially, it has been learned that three conditions are necessary for making a new habit. One is motivation. It is not necessary to conduct laboratory experiments to show the importance of motivation in the learning of a new habit. The close relationship between motivation and learning is apparent on ordinary observation. The second condition rests on the principle of immediate rewards or, conversely, punishment. The sooner a reward follows the desired act, the greater the tendency of that act to be repeated the next time. Conversely, the sooner an incorrect act is punished, the greater the tendency to not do that act again. Third is interest. The more interesting the habit, the more easily it will be learned. If the newly desired work habit is important toward attaining one of the manager's primary goals, he probably will find that he learns it quickly and painlessly.

Because people have different behavioral characteristics, the types of habits that are easily formed for one person may be very difficult for another. Similarly, people have different goals and ambitions. It is easier to establish a new habit or break an old one if it helps to attain a high priority objective or goal. Conversely, it is difficult to break habits that are compatible with basic behavioral characteristics, even though they may be great wasters of time. Procrastination is probably one of the chief examples of a time wasting habit. Many managers put off doing unpleasant tasks, procrastinate when unsure of themselves, or try to ignore difficult jobs. R. Alec Mackenzie in his book, *The Time Trap* (New York: AMACOM, a division of American Management Associations, 1972), says, "Countering these habits requires self-discipline and persever-ance." Norman Vincent Peale described how he faced up to the bad habit of procrastination by adopting the following system: picking one area of procrastination and conquering it; learning to set priori-ties and focusing on one problem at a time; setting deadlines and letting them be known; not avoiding the most difficult problems; and not being paralyzed by perfectionism.

Similar plans can be outlined for breaking other bad habits. The habits of a lifetime are not easily shaken off, but the undesirable ones can be broken by following five simple rules:

1. Lose a bad habit by replacing it with a good one. It's hard merely to keep from doing something, but it is often easy to do some-thing else in its stead. For example, if a property manager is impatient with detail (in a business filled with details) and tends to make hasty decisions in order to avoid detail, he could create a new habit of taking the time to do something right and saving the time of doing it over.

2. Grasp every opportunity to use the new habit; practice makes perfect. Perhaps by nature a manager is a very outgoing and loquacious person who enjoys socializing. This can be an ex-pensive time waster during business hours. A new habit would be to socialize elsewhere: He can meet visitors outside of the office or conduct conferences standing up, using every opportun-ity to establish this new habit during business hours.

3. Burn bridges; make it impossible to retreat. By telling friends and coworkers what he intends to do, inviting them to point it out if he fails, a manager is asking for their help in breaking old habits and establishing new ones.

4. Permit no exceptions. With each failure, the manager goes back nearly to where he started. Good habits cannot be learned on the exception basis. An effort must be made to make no excep-tions.

5. Practice as much as possible. Over-practiced learning is retained longer. A desired action practiced but a few times will never become a habit.

For example, most property managers spend several hours a week traveling in an automobile. This usually wasted time can be-come very productive if the manager commits to forming a habit that would make constructive use of commuting time. He might keep a small pad and pencil in the glove compartment so that key words can be jotted down as reminders of ideas he has. While driving, for instance, he may think about the problem of replacing a resident manager at a sizeable apartment complex. How will this be accomplished? Are there any people in the organization who should be contacted? Will an ad need to be run? If so, when, and what should it say? If notes are made of these thoughts, the actual decision making that comes later will be facilitated.

Increasing Communication

A good deal of managerial time is spent in communicating with subordinates. This time can be maximized if the manager realizes that poor communication is a thief of time. Communication relies upon how the subordinate receives a message as well as how it is delivered. Improving communications with subordinates begins with listening to their perspective.

The first step is to determine the subordinate's understanding of the job, problem, or situation and his objectives in solving that problem. For example, when a manager continually finds that the vacant apartments at a property are not ready to rent, the solution is to sit down with the resident manager and have him establish what he thinks his responsibilities are in solving this problem. It well may be that he assumes it is someone else's job to make apartments ready to rent. Or he may feel it's the property manager's responsibility to see that the painter, cleaning crew, etc., do their jobs. After this discussion, the property manager can point out the exact nature of the resident manager's responsibility. Much time is saved if communications are clear and no assumptions are made.

Establishing Sound Nonwork Habits

In the final analysis, the management of time gets down to the management of self. One way the effectiveness of working hours can be improved is to improve habits of living during nonbusiness hours.

Exercise, for instance, can lead to increased efficiency. As John F. Kennedy said:

> Physical fitness is not only one of the most important keys to a healthy body, it is the basis of dynamic and creative intellectual activity. The relationship between the soundness of the body and the activities of the mind is subtle and complex. Much is not yet understood. But we do know what the Greeks knew: That intelligence and skill can only function at the peak of their capacity when the body is healthy and strong; that hardy spirits and tough minds usually inhabit sound bodies.

Common sense says that a person in good physical condition increases the effectiveness of his working hours through increased energy. The degree of aggressiveness with which he performs tasks throughout the day will be in direct relation to his physical health.

Getting the proper amount of sleep likewise can be important to maintaining a high level of effectiveness. However, not everyone needs eight hours sleep each night. Some people need eight, others more, but most can effectively get along with less. According to specialists who have studied the subject of sleep and sleep habits, adults sleep an average of 7 to 7½ hours per night; however, for many, fewer hours of sleep may be sufficient. More sleep than is needed wastes time, has no apparent health benefit, and might even be harmful. The manager who can feel rested with six hours of sleep a night, instead of the eight hours he may be getting, increases his weekday productivity by two hours a day, or 40 hours per month. Getting enough rest is an important rule, but wasting time through poor sleep habits likewise should be considered.

Because the field of real estate management is dynamic and ever changing, property managers must continually spend time expanding their realm of knowledge. One of the best means of doing this is through reading, yet this is a very time-consuming task. A way to combat this dilemma is to take a course in speed reading to increase reading rate and comprehension.

In addition, selectivity in reading is advised. Most books and magazines have only a few ideas to offer; the goal should be to find these ideas as quickly as possible. Scanning a table of contents for pertinent subjects saves time, as does reading the first few paragraphs of an article before making the commitment to study the complete text.

Organizing Time

Having identified the ways efficiency is lost through improper use of time and methods of solving those problems, a manager is ready to examine how he can organize his time and gain more hours for productive work or leisure.

"Effective, successful people are people who get the maximum benefit from a minimum investment of time. They are aware that it must be used with the utmost discretion," according to Edwin C. Bliss in his book, *Getting Things Done* (New York: Charles Scribner's Sons, 1976). Being effective always starts with planning. This thesis is so basic, so elementary, yet few property management executives take the time to plan time-consuming activities. Hours are devoted to attending to the chores of operating a property, designing forms, and attending meetings, yet not even 10 minutes a day is spent planning how to make time more efficient.

One of the biggest time wasters is trying to decide what to do next. The very nature of the real estate management business is detail. Property managers at any given moment have an enormous number of details to attend to, as well as the need for creative thinking or planning of management programs. It is very easy to waste a great amount of time by simply trying to decide what to do next. Waste can be minimized by organizing a daily work schedule, creating a daily list of tasks that need attention. This list should not be partly in one's head or on scraps of paper but organized in writing on one page. The next step is to spend 10 minutes every day planning priorities. One way to establish priorities is to divide the list into three parts: Items that are the most important and need attention first are given priority one classification, the next in importance are priority two, the least important are priority three.

Having assigned priorities to the tasks, some questions about the work to be accomplished should be asked: Have I a clear idea of what I want to accomplish this week? Have I set my priorities according to importance rather than urgency? Of the tasks listed here, which should be performed in the office during normal business hours? Are there tasks here that can be better performed working in a quiet atmosphere at home, commuting, etc.? Are there tasks listed here that can be delegated or assigned and better performed by someone else? Which of these tasks can be handled by telephone rather than written communication? What deadlines do I need to set for myself to make decisions on any of these matters? What will happen if I don't do one of the tasks? (If the answer is nothing, don't do it.) Am I yielding to the temptation to clean up insignificant items first rather than focusing on the more important ones?

Another idea for scheduling time involves communication with others. Every property manager has certain people he talks with every week. Because the memory is a poor reminder, a list of these people's names should be maintained. When something comes up that should be discussed with one of them, a note of it is made next to the appropriate name. Reminders then are available on all subjects that need to be discussed. This informal written agenda will save time when the meeting is held.

Time is the scarcest resource, and, unless it is properly managed, nothing else can be managed. The property manager, by analyzing his use of time, systematically establishes a means of improving productivity through eliminating time wasters, organizing work, establishing objectives, and planning for goals. He is on the road toward contribution and effectiveness.

II

The Property Management
Company Plan

5

Legal Organizational Forms

IN ESTABLISHING A PROPERTY MANAGEMENT FIRM—a business enterprise as opposed to an investment vehicle—the ownership is faced with determining a legal form of business organization. This process calls for serious thought. A number of factors must be taken into consideration, including the number of people involved in the ownership of the enterprise, income tax considerations, the extent and probability of exposure to liability, and respective individual goals. Furthermore, no decision should be made on this matter without advice from legal counsel specializing in business law and a certified public accountant qualified to advise on income tax considerations. Nonetheless, the ownership can be aware of the considerations that will affect the decision.

The most common forms of organization are the sole proprietorship, partnership, and corporation. Each has both advantages and disadvantages, and none is necessarily preferable to the other two. Essentially, the owners must focus on what is important to them. Figure 5.1 visually deferentiates between the characteristics of the forms of organization. A more thorough explanation of each follows.

Sole Proprietorship

The sole proprietorship is the oldest form of business organization. Under it, an enterprise is owned and managed by a single individual.

The primary advantage of this form of ownership lies in its simplicity. In most states, a property manager may form a proprietorship merely by showing evidence of a valid state real estate broker's license and a business license from the city or municipality in which business is conducted.

Likewise, the income tax considerations are simple. The business and its owner are considered as a single taxable entity. All of the income and tax attributes of the proprietorship are reflected directly in the owner's individual income tax statement. The applicable tax rate is the same as the personal income tax rate.

The sole proprietorship also offers great flexibility in its operation. Should the owner want to transfer the ownership of the enterprise, free transferability is permitted. In addition, the sole proprietorship enjoys a minimum amount of restrictions and regulations.

Characteristics	Sole Proprietorship	General Partnership	Corporation
Personal Liability	Yes.	Yes.	Under some circumstances may be limited to amount of investment.
Continuity	Business dissolved at death of sole proprietor.	May be dissolved at withdrawal or death of general partner.	Continuity unaffected by death or withdrawal of shareholder, officer, or director.
Transferability of Ownership	No restrictions.	All general partners usually must consent to transfer.	Transferable by selling shares, subject to previously agreed upon restrictions.
Management	Proprietor manages with minimum formal regulation.	Usually ruled by majority vote.	In control of a board of directors elected by the shareholders.
Taxation of Equity	Entity in effect nonexistent; all tax attributes of proprietor reflected directly on individual income tax.	Entity not taxed; each partner reflects his pro rata share of partnership income or loss, whether or not actually distributed.	Entity pays tax on its income; stockholders pay additional tax on corporate dividend distribution.
Tax Rates	Investor taxed at ordinary individual income tax rates on net income from proprietorship.	Partner taxed on his share of partnership taxable income.	Shareholders taxed on dividend distributions to the extent they derive from accumulated or current earnings and profits.

Figure 5.1. Characteristics of legal organizational forms.

While it is regulated by the applicable state real estate laws and all federal and state laws governing employees, taxation, etc., it does not have imposed on it the extra layer of regulations that are placed upon corporations and partnerships.

This form of ownership, however, is not without drawbacks, all of which rest on the fact that a sole proprietorship's life and success depend upon one individual. A sole proprietor is personally and fully responsible for the debts of the business. In addition, raising capital may be difficult. Expansion generally requires more capital than an individual possesses or can borrow. Consequently, few sole proprietorships can grow; in fact, most remain quite small.

A final disadvantage of a sole proprietorship is lack of continuity of the enterprise. In the event of the death of the proprietor, the business is dissolved.

Partnership

A general partnership is a form of business organization in which two or more persons enter a business as co-owners to share in the profits and losses. Partnerships are the most commonly adopted form of business organization in situations in which more than one individual is involved in an enterprise designed to provide professional services—such as property management. Partners collectively are called a firm; the name under which they conduct business is the firm name. The firm is not a corporation, nor is it recognized as distinct from the members composing it. Any change among the partners, therefore, destroys the identity of the firm.

Partnerships are created and formed by agreement. The agreement may be oral, but it is obviously a much better practice to have the agreement of partnership in writing. Although oftentimes partners will be quite satisfied with their working relationship and have no conflicts, problems are sure to arise under certain circumstances, such as at the death of one of the partners. Furthermore, the purpose of the partnership's business can be as wide or narrow as the partners decide; for example, a partnership need not be formed merely to perform real estate services but also might include the acquisition of income property or another business activity. The purpose can be best agreed to when it is expressed in writing.

In creating a partnership, the capital contributions made by each partner need not necessarily be the same or equal, nor is it necessary to have the profits distributed on a basis proportionate to capital contributions. For example, one partner might contribute the money, equipment, and facilities needed to conduct the management business, while the other contributes no property or capital but devotes most of his time to the firm's operations and provides its expertise. Still, they may share profits and losses either equally or in any combination agreeable to both.

For the purpose of conducting business, every partner in a general partnership is an agent of the firm and of his copartners. In lieu of an agreement to the contrary, all partners have an equal voice with respect to the management and conduct of the business affairs of the partnership. Therefore, unless specifically stated otherwise, management of a partnership usually is ruled by majority vote. Furthermore, when one partner makes a commitment in the name of the firm, the firm is bound to that commitment. To remedy what could become an unfortunate situation, the partners may have an agreement restricting the powers of any one of them to bind the firm in such a manner. When the responsibilities for management of the affairs of the partnership are stated clearly in this contract, it becomes the vehicle for spelling out each partner's rights, duties, and liabilities and the extent to which each is authorized to bind the partnership. However, the agreement limiting the binding powers of a partner is effective only if the third party with whom a partner is dealing has notice of the agreement and its content. Usually partnership agreements also provide that each partner indemnify the others for any personal liabilities reasonably incurred.

One of the major disadvantages of a general partnership revolves around the fact that the personal liability of each partner is unlimited. Legally, partners are jointly liable for the debts of the firm; a creditor suing to collect sues the partners as a group. However, any one partner is wholly liable for all of the debts of the partnership. If, for example, two out of three partners in a property management partnership are insolvent, the third is liable for all of the debts of the enterprise to the total extent of his personal assets. The extent of the firm's liability thus becomes the same as that of the individual partner.

Furthermore, the legal liability of a partnership is almost unlimited if the firm is liable for loss or injury caused to a third party or for any penalty incurred by any wrongful act by or omission of a partner acting in the ordinary course of business. A partnership also is liable to make good a loss caused if one partner, acting within his apparent authority, receives money or property from a third person and misapplies it. In addition, because the liability of the partners for debts and obligations of the firm is joint and several, a partner who retires does not cease to be liable for the debts or obligations incurred before his retirement.

An advantage of the general partnership as a business organization lies in its income tax treatment. For federal income tax purposes, a partnership itself does not receive income—or suffer losses—and thus cannot pay taxes. Rather, a partnership is a mere conduit of an entity that files, in lieu of an income tax return, a partnership information return, indicating income distribution to each partner based upon ownership or contractual agreement. Each partner, in turn, reports on his individual income tax return his share of gain or loss. Each is responsible to pay his own tax, the tax rate being the same as his personal income tax rate.

The duration of a general partnership can be for any time fixed by the partners, or, if there is no agreement as to time, it may be dissolved by any partner at any time or upon the death of a partner. The partnership agreement may provide for the continuation of the business after the death or withdrawal of a partner; however, this kind of provision presents some tax consequences that need professional counsel. If the partnership agreement specifies a fixed term, the parties may continue the business beyond that term simply by agreeing to extend the partnership. This may be accomplished either by agreeing to another fixed term or by having an agreement to continue until it is terminated by any of the partners. A partner at any time may terminate his relationship with the partnership even though he does so in breach of the partnership agreement. Though this may result in an action for damages against him by the remaining partners, the partnership is automatically dissolved.

In regard to transferability of ownership, all general partners usually must consent. Typically as well, no partner may sell his portion of ownership without the approval of the other partners.

Numerous legal and tax considerations must be weighed before ownership can realistically decide whether a partnership is the most appropriate form of business structure for its business purpose. These considerations demand explanation by competent professional counsel.

Corporation

The corporate form of organization offers businesses that deal in personal services some unique advantages not available through other forms of ownership. A corporation exists as a distinct legal entity separate and apart from the owners, who are called shareholders or stockholders. Consequently, a corporation, apart from the actual individual shareholders, may own property, incur debts and earn profits, and sue or be sued.

Unlike a proprietorship and a partnership, a corporation in the United States is created by statute law, which may vary from one state to another. In some states incorporation, or the act of forming a corporation, is quite simple; in others, it is more difficult. Typically, a corporation begins when several persons agree to purchase some of its stock and apply for a charter from the state. A typical application for a charter includes the corporation's name, purpose, intended life, and location; the amount, type, and value of stock to be issued; and names of officers and directors. Upon approval of the application and payment of all required fees, the corporation comes into existence as verified by articles of incorporation or a corporate charter.

The company organized as a corporation is limited to involvement in only those business activities that are within the scope of the powers expressed or implied in its state charter or certificate of incorporation. While it is common for attorneys to draft articles of incorporation for a newly formed company that provide for a wide range of business activities, the corporation still is restricted by these articles. To engage in other business activities not specified or enlarge its ownership requires an amendment to the articles and approval by the state regulatory body. Thus, the business freedom of a corporation is not as broad as that enjoyed by sole proprietorships and partnerships.

Neither is the management of a corporation as free-form as is that of the other forms of organization. In fact, it is quite definitive and can be somewhat cumbersome. Corporate charters usually provide that directors of the corporation are elected by majority vote of the shareholders. The board of directors, as the central authority of the corporation, manages the affairs of the corporation and acts according to the majority vote of the owners. The board is accountable and responsible to the stockholders for any acts or conduct which may be outside the scope of its charter powers or for any acts that are otherwise improper or unlawful. The board of directors elects the officers. They are charged with the operation of the company but can exercise only such authority as is delegated to them by the corporate charter or certificate of incorporation by-laws. They are answerable to the board of directors and must account to the board for their activities. The officers can bind the corporation by their conduct or acts that are within their scope of actual or apparent authority.

One of the chief advantages of the corporation is limited liability; that is, each shareholder is personally liable for the debts of the business only to the extent of his capital investment. If, for example, a shareholder buys 100 shares of a corporate property management company's stock at $20 per share and the company goes bankrupt, his loss can be no greater than $2,000. However, since the shareholders of a professional service company would, in all probability, be its officers and directors, it is wrong to assume that the corporation necessarily shields the operators of the business from all forms of legal liability. Still, the corporate structure does offer more protection from exposure to legal liability than does the sole proprietorship or partnership.

An effect of this limited liability is evidenced in another benefit of the corporation—its ability to raise much larger amounts of capital than the two other principal forms of organization. One method of doing this is through issuance and sale of either stocks or bonds. Another is by borrowing. If a lender is satisfied with the credit of the corporation, the corporation is the entity that is responsible for the obligation of the debt, not the individual shareholder. His risk is limited to the amount of his investment.

Another characteristic of a corporation revolves around transferability of ownership. This is a simple matter in many corporations, requiring little more than the sale of stocks. However, such transferability may be subject to previously agreed restrictions. Most professional service corporations, for instance, restrict the sale of stocks to outsiders.

Continuity is another advantage of the corporate form of organization. Inasmuch as a corporation exists as a separate legal entity for an indefinite period of time, it has continuity of life. There is no need to create a new or modified form of ownership to replace it upon the death, retirement, withdrawal, or proven incompetence of any— or all—of its shareholders.

Of all the characteristics of a corporation, however, probably the most notable revolves around income tax considerations. From an income tax standpoint, the corporate form of ownership offers both opportunity and restriction. Since the corporation is a legal entity that exists separate and apart from its stockholders, it is a separate taxable entity for income tax purposes. The corporation, after calculating its gross income and operating expenses, arrives at a net taxable profit against which corporate income taxes must be paid. Any distribution of the corporation's net income after taxes is a dividend to the shareholders. Each shareholder then must report his individual income from the corporation on his personal income tax statement. The effect is double taxation of the income that flows to the shareholder. On the other hand, the corporate income tax rate usually is considerably less than the individual income tax rate. As of this writing, the federal corporate income tax rate was 20 percent of the first $25,000 of corporate income, 22 percent of the next $25,000, and 48 percent of the balance. On the average, then, the corporate tax structure usually results in a lower total tax paid per owner than either of the other two forms of ownership.

Furthermore, to the extent that corporate income can be paid out in salaries to the principals, and since the amount paid in salaries is a legitimate deductible expense for a business enterprise, the double tax can be avoided. Thus, the corporate form of ownership offers the corporation a tax advantage of lower income tax rates than if the business organization was a sole proprietorship or partnership. For example, consider a married sole proprietor of a real estate management business who had a 1977 taxable income of $76,000 and paid $29,260 in federal income taxes. That individual could have formed a corporation and paid himself a salary that would have provided him with a $50,000 taxable income as an individual, leaving the corporation with a $26,000 taxable income. The combined federal income tax effect of this structure would have been $20,680 (personal income tax of $15,460, corporate tax of $5,220), or a savings of $8,580 that year. The difference becomes even more dramatic as income is higher.

Although corporate income is taxable to a corporation and not to its shareholders until it is distributed to them in the form of dividends, a corporation may be liable for an extra tax if earnings or profits are permitted to accumulate rather than being distributed to the shareholders. Income accumulating corporations may be susceptible to a corporate surtax if the accumulation of income is greater than what is permissible. Usually, however, businesses can substantiate several hundred thousand dollars in accumulation of surpluses before they are faced with the surtax problem. In order to justify such an accumulation, there must be a reasonable need for it and a plan for its use. Some acceptable uses are business expansion, acquisition of another business, retirement of debt, and working capital requirements. Among unacceptable uses are personal loans to shareholders, relatives, or friends and investments unrelated to the business. Another tax benefit of the corporate form of ownership is that officers/stockholders and employee stockholders can have a tax-favored retirement or pension plan established for them. Still a further tax advantage can be realized by a corporation if its shareholders, by unanimous consent, elect, under Subchapter S, not to pay tax at the corporate level but rather permit the net taxable income to pass through to the shareholders as personal income on a pro rata basis. Likewise, shareholders of a Subchapter S corporation are entitled to deduct their pro rata shares of any net operating loss on their individual returns.

Unlike a partnership, a Subchapter S is not a conduit; that is, individual items of income and deduction are not passed through to the shareholders to retain the same character in the hands of those shareholders as they had in the hands of the corporation. Instead, taxable income is computed at the corporate level in much the same way as it is computed for any other corporation. The shareholders then are taxed directly on this taxable income, whether or not the corporation makes any distributions to them.

The Internal Revenue Code provides that a corporation can elect Subchapter S treatment providing it qualifies as a small business corporation. The term "small business" does not refer to the amount of corporate income, nor to the corporation's assets or net worth, but instead to the number of shareholders it has. At its inception, the corporation may have no more than 10 shareholders, and at no time may the number of shareholders exceed 15. (It is interesting to note that prior to the death of millionaire recluse Howard Hughes, the Summa Corporation elected Subchapter S treatment, thus becoming the largest "small business" corporation in the United States.) In order to qualify for Subchapter S treatment a corporation must meet certain requirements:

1. It must be a domestic corporation incorporated in the United States.
2. All the shareholders must be individuals, estates, or special types of trusts.
3. None of the shareholders may be a nonresident alien.
4. Only one class of stock may exist.
5. No more than 80 percent of the corporation's gross receipts may come from sources outside the United States.
6. No more than 20 percent of the corporation's gross receipts may

be derived from passive investment income; this includes, among other incomes, rental income for ordinary residential and commercial properties.

Subchapter S elections can be terminated; indeed, there are provisions, in some instances, for automatic termination. The Subchapter S treatment may be voluntarily revoked at any time after it has been in effect for one taxable year if all of the stockholders consent. In addition, the election is terminated automatically when a new stockholder refuses to consent to the election within 60 days of becoming a stockholder. If he does not affirmatively refuse to give his consent within the 60-day period, he is deemed to consent to the election. The election also is terminated automatically if there is any change in status that would have prevented the corporation from making the election in the first place. Once the election is terminated or revoked, the corporation may not make a new Subchapter S election until the fifth year after the year in which the termination or revocation first was effective.

Selection of Organizational Form

There is no one best form of organization for real estate management businesses. The structure chosen should not be predicated upon the type of business activity but rather upon the personal and financial goals of the individuals involved. The most important conclusion to be drawn from this cursory look at the advantages and disadvantages of the three most common legal organizational forms is that a professional real estate management business can provide increased economic opportunity via the organizational structure that is chosen.

An example of the impact that the organizational structure may have can be shown by examining the situation of a real estate agent who enters real estate management as a part-time activity to his general real estate brokerage business. After a few years, when his management business has grown into an activity that occupies the time of several full-time employees, he incorporates in order to limit his liability and acquire capital through reduced income tax rates. Twenty years later the management corporation has considerable net worth that has been invested in income property. The agent decides that he does not want to accumulate additional capital in the corporation and prepares to have all of its taxable income paid to him without the burden of double taxation. He then elects the Subchapter S status.

6

The Strategic Company Plan

LYING AT THE VERY HEART of the management discipline are the functions of decision making, evaluating information, motivating employees, innovating, and, above all, planning. The professional property manager performs these functions in order to effectively utilize the resources of his enterprise and take advantage of all opportunities. Because business is affected by economic, political, and social conditions, executive-level planning is of utmost importance. Astute managers are able to recognize changing conditions and plan for them in order to optimize long-term growth and profitability. This calls for preparation of a long-range plan for the enterprise.

Reasons for Planning

Real estate management firms, for the most part, begin as one-man operations. The business is established by an entrepreneur who has the ability not only to manage properties but also obtain new business. As the number of management accounts grows, helpers are hired to assist in managing properties. But the time comes when the owner must change from hiring helpers to hiring managers, and the move from a simplified business structure to a more complex one becomes inevitable. The entrepreneur who does not recognize when he passes the point at which he cannot operate effectively without additional property managers becomes frustrated and demoralized. One of the most effective tools for recognizing this turning point is a company plan.

A plan also provides a device for measuring company performance. The firm that has a well-calculated plan will learn from its mistakes as well as its successes; the firm without a plan may never learn why things went right or wrong. Furthermore, a plan can help in recognizing those areas of activity that should be forsaken, the systematic abandonment of incompatible or unprofitable activities being as important as the undertaking of new ones.

Planning reduces the risk that is inherent in taking advantage of opportunities. In making progressive corporate strides, a company will fall behind if it waits until its competitors have anticipated and adapted to change and then adjusts to the competition. Planning creates confidence to pioneer changes that will be advantageous to business in the long run. To gain respect as a leader in the industry, execution and implementation of a well-constructed plan is mandatory. Many times, however, predicting the effects of change and acting on that prediction involve considerable gamble. A well-developed plan outlines possible and probable results and thus enables management to minimize risk and improve the probability of success. The operator who continually uses the seat-of-the-pants approach does not begin to reach his potential and assumes unnecessary risks.

Planning also increases efficiency. A plan outlines what is to be done; therefore, it provides the structure for implementing a program with the least amount of time, work, and capital resources. With its goals, targets, benchmarks, timetables, tactics, strategies, programs, and policies, a plan describes a path to follow through a period of growth.

Planning provides leadership, giving direction so that all members of a company can work together toward the realization of common objectives and goals. Planning also helps develop managerial skills. Preparing a plan requires a manager to organize his thinking toward identifying competitive and marketing opportunities, financial needs, and staffing and payroll requirements, and predicting problems and solutions.

Planning also acts as a means of communicating. A plan tells the members of the management team what to do and why, the objectives of their work, and how their work is to be executed. By outlining assignments, a plan can be used as the means of ensuring that the necessary people are included in a given business program.

Above all, planning enables an organization to effectively focus on innovation. Most management discussions in company meetings stress the administrative function of management. Such concern is with improving what is already known and, largely, continuing to do what is being done. The anticipated outcome of these meetings is improvement, not innovation. The participants look elsewhere for innovation, waiting until creative changes are proven successful by others before giving them serious consideration.

Innovation in Planning

The opportunity for innovative thinking in the real estate industry is unlimited. By housing the nation's people, commerce, and industry, real estate is a reflection of current conditions. No other industry offers more opportunity for the entrepreneur with innovative ideas than real estate. In order for the property manager to understand the truth of this concept, he need only review the markets for his services that were created from 1968 to 1978.

In some instances entrepreneural thinkers identified the market oportunity for small investors to invest in real estate income property and began forming large, publicly held, limited partnerships to invest in such properties. The objectives of the partnerships were to provide the small investor with an annual cash return, realize appreciation in capital, and reap the tax benefits that accrue to owners of income properties. These management companies realized a continuing income from the property management services they provided for the partnerships. Other companies identified a different market for highly qualified management skills, i.e., operating subsidiaries of major corporations and overseeing pension funds that had committed enormous amounts of capital to real estate only to run into financial problems.

For a company to effectively focus on innovation, it needs to understand the meaning of innovation and some of its characteristics. Innovation, for the property manager, means identifying ongoing changes in the business environment and, based on these changes, doing something to create value. The innovative business enterprise is market focused; it continually searches for future markets for its services in order to keep pace with the changes in society. An important area for innovative opportunity, for instance, revolves around demographic developments, or the social statistics of a population. Changing patterns in the number of people, marital status and family size, and income level affect the nature and stability of a neighborhood. Taking advantage of demographic changes after they occur but before the full impact is fully realized is an innovative action.

A professional manager might consider the innovative opportunity that exists when there is a glaring disparity between the supply and demand levels of a market or economy. In the 10-year period from 1968 to 1978, the real estate management industry probably was provided more new-business opportunity for this reason than at any other time. In a few short years, many sections of the country went from shortage to tremendous oversupply and then back to shortage. At the same time, the economy was undergoing enormous inflation. As a hedge against inflation, people who normally would have rented wanted to own a piece of real estate. The consequence was the condominium boom. Innovative property managers realized the changes in supply and demand and in public attitude and provided a service that was needed—condominium management—in order to move them into leadership roles within the industry.

The innovative company continually asks itself: What is the business, and what should it be? While the first mission of a business is to optimize those business opportunities that already exist, likewise needed is constant examination of the changes taking place in the business environment. The innovative firm watches for new opportunities that are worth exploring and examines the aging process of its existing lines of service and markets. As Peter Drucker says in *Management: Tasks, Responsibilities, and Practices* (New York: Harper & Row, Inc., 1974):

> The foundation of innovative strategy is planned and systematic sloughing off of the old, the dying, the obsolete. Innovative organizations spend neither time nor resources defending yesterday. Systematic abandonment of yesterday alone can free the resources, and especially the scarcest resource of all, capable people, for work on the new.

An entrepreneurial property manager incorporates this critical element of innovation into the company plan.

Development of the Plan

Every business organization operates on a plan, whether that plan is formally written or informally understood. The quality plan, however, is a written formal statement designed to help focus on market needs and marshall the necessary resources to meet those needs.

A plan is a detailed program worked out beforehand for the accomplishment of an objective. It begins with a mission, or statement of purpose, giving the reason for the existence of the organization. Having established the mission, the plan then describes the long-range objectives for desirable future results. In order to achieve these objectives, the plan outlines some short-term goals. A plan also needs policies, broad statements of general intent that tell what is permitted or expected; procedures, more specific instructions that tell how things are to be done; and programs and projects, courses of action that must be carried out to achieve the objectives that are deemed desirable. The compatible combination of policies, objectives, and programs is strategy, designed to enable the manager to accomplish optimum results under the circumstances he believes will prevail. All of this rests on an educated assumption of an important development that cannot be accurately predicted but will have a major impact on future activities and results. In summary, then, to plan is to make an educated assumption, decide what is to be done, establish the necessary objectives and goals, then devise strategies, both long-term and short-term, for achieving them.

Companies usually talk of long-range, or strategic, planning, and short-term, or operational, planning. The property manager needs to be skilled in both. This terminology frequently is laced with confusion. Some of the misunderstanding revolves around the amount of time required to carry out each. Is a plan short-term because it takes only two months to implement? Is a decision long-range if it takes two years to carry it out? The real crux of the matter is not in the actual length of time required to complete an action but in the span of time over which that action will be effective.

To further clarify the two types of plans, a more complete comparison is necessary. Long-range planning is the process of determining how a business may make the best possible use of its resources in the future; short-term planning concentrates on making the best use of current resources. Long-range planning focuses on ways in which resources can be changed gradually to permit an enterprise to enjoy success in the future; short-term planning looks for action in a determinable period of time, usually one year or less. Long-range planning, though far from precise, does give direction; in short-term planning, the pertinent factors are well known, the variables are minimal, and the objectives are specific. While the long-range and short-term plans must be complementary—the achievement of the objectives of one being dependent on the achievement of the objectives of the other—the company plan is a long-range plan.

The purpose of long-range planning is to prevent today's managers from passing on their mistakes into tomorrow's decision making, from assuming that current services and markets will necessarily be the services and markets needed in the future.

Personal Objectives

Prior to preparing any company plan, it is imperative that the owner (or owners, shareholders, or partners) of a company decide their personal objectives, for it is these personal objectives that determine the direction the company will take. The typical owner of a property management business is motivated by one or all of three stimuli: profit, reputation, and enjoyment in work. Since most people are in the real estate management business because it provides economic opportunity, the owner needs to set objectives regarding expected levels and stability of income and goals for accumulating capital. The second motivating force is reputation. Professionals are motivated to earn recognition in the business community. As successful businessmen, they seek social stature and acceptance. If reputation in the community has a high priority among an individual's personal objectives, proper commitments and allocations of time, programs, and money are needed in order to attain this esteem. The third stimuli is enjoyment in work. Many managers place neither title nor pay as their highest priority. Of greater importance is the enjoyment received from work—an objective often found among young professionals who are much more socially conscious than their predecessors whose formative years coincided with the Great Depression. The manager whose business career began after World War II has lived through a stable financial period characterized by a relatively minor risk of unemployment and an abundance of opportunity. For this reason, he typically focuses more attention on improving the quality of life than do managers whose careers began during the 1930s and who underwent an entirely different business experience. For these people, the main objective is economic survival; a job is highly valued regardless of its social stature or level of enjoyment. Thus, business motives may be based on the conditioning of experiences as well as other factors.

Statement of Mission

A clear definition of the company mission—its purpose—is needed to establish a foundation on which the rest of the plan can be built.

The statement of mission is the starting point for all future programs, giving direction to strategic planning of the business's key activities. A mission statement should be designed to answer several critical questions that must be asked about the enterprise: What is the business? What should the business be? Who is the customer? These questions should not be answered without a great deal of serious thought; they should not be oversimplified. Such responses as: The business is real estate management, the business should be the management of income properties, and the customer is the owner of income properties, are indicative of the thinking of a property supervisor, not a property manager. They reflect a lack of innovative thinking. A professional entrepreneurial property manager does not try to answer the first two questions until he has asked and answered the third: Who is the customer?

Major changes have occurred recently in the ownership of income property in the United States, and these changes are reflected in a new definition of property management's customer. More and more property is being held by partnerships. While just a few years ago property management's focus was on income and operating expenses, the new customer wants someone to manage the total asset. Since managing real estate assets requires a commitment of longer term than managing property, and because it offers greater financial reward, a company may choose to focus its resources in this direction. The astute manager then asks himself: Who is the customer? The partnership. What should the business be? The management of real estate assets. Similarly, as condominiums become popular alternatives to apartment renting and single-family home ownership, the property manager asks: Who is the customer? The homeowners' association. What should the business be? The management of condominiums and their associations.

This is not to say that a company must focus on only one type of customer. A property management firm may successfully handle several kinds of customers who require unrelated services. For example, a company could manage apartment complexes for limited partnerships and condominiums for homeowners' associations. Although each kind of property management demands unique abilities, it is possible that these varied abilities can be combined in one management company. However, the more diversified the company becomes in the services it offers, the greater its need to have a plan—especially a plan for selecting and developing the people capable of providing different kinds of management service.

In defining the customer and examining what the business should become, an estimate of how fast a new market will develop should be made. Also, possible significant changes in customers, market structure, technology, or population dynamics that will affect the kind of business for which to program should be examined. In the past, the real estate management industry experienced dynamic growth during periods of economic adversity; conversely, growth was slow during times of low vacancy factors coupled with high reproduction costs or when properties were under federal or state rent control. Factors such as these must be considered when the mission statement is being drafted, and their impact should be incorporated into the statement.

Company Objectives

Having expressed the company's mission, the company planner is ready to develop the company's long-range objectives. How the resources of the enterprise are used is determined by the objectives established and the priorities set. Essentially, an objective is a statement of results to be achieved. It sets the stage for future action and therefore must be defined quantitatively in terms of time and money. It becomes a measuring device that tells management how the company is doing.

Setting objectives is a crucial management task. The responsibility for this phase of the plan rests with the chief executive officer. Sometimes goals will have to be based on hypothesis as well as fact. This requires business foresight, expertise, and concentrated effort from the company's most valuable resource, its executives.

In its plan, the company's strengths and weaknesses should be identified. Objectives should be written in favor of the competitive advantage, but an honest appraisal of weaknesses is just as important. It is, after all, important to plan for retrenchment as well as expansion; unplanned cutbacks do not save money, they waste it.

Objectives should be realistic and attainable. Unattainable objectives only frustrate and discourage. The company plan is the document by which the team's performance is to be judged. If objectives are unrealistic, the purpose of the plan is negated. The team develops a losing attitude because objectives are not attained. The plan becomes a piece of paper that is ridiculed and joked about rather than being a positive means of defining and measuring the team's successes.

The number of objectives should be limited. Company plans are written in order to provide an intelligent direction of work. A realistic appraisal needs to be made of how much can actually be accomplished. It is far more important to establish fewer objectives and accomplish them rather than have partial success on a much longer list of objectives.

When writing an objective, it should be kept short and simple and spell out what specifically is to be accomplished and when. Neither a long-range nor a short-term plan needs to explain how objectives and goals are going to be accomplished. Programs that detail the "how to" will be developed to implement the plan. There is a formula for writing a viable objective. In general, it starts with the word "to" and includes an action verb, such as increase, improve, complete, build, reduce, develop, reach, etc. Subsequently, the objective identifies a single major result and establishes a target date and a cost basis analysis or benefit, when applicable. Thus, it defines the what and when—but not the how and why. Based upon this formula, a company objective might read: "To obtain the management of an additional 1,000 apartment units with fees of not less than $9,000 per month during the next two years."

Since not all goals are of equal importance and only a finite number of programs can be accomplished in a given period of time, priorities should be determined. No rules are available for establishing the priorities of a plan. In the final analysis, it is a judgment reached after investigating the options and deciding what is first in importance, second, and so on. Objectives need to be established in eight key areas: marketing, innovation, organization of people, financial resources, office administration, productivity, social responsibility, and profit.

Objectives are not unalterable. As new developments occur, objectives may require change. While recommendations regarding changes to objectives require input from all staff levels, ultimate responsibility remains with the executive level. Regular evaluation of company objectives by top management is suggested to avoid stagnation.

Strategy

A complete plan requires that strategy for meeting the company's objectives be outlined. Setting strategy requires anticipating the future. The business world is not static. The executive who intends to extend current products and services into the future and does not anticipate change eventually will be out of business. Management planners must study what the industry is to become and plan for it. Some developments can be anticipated in the near future and become part of the short-term strategy; others will occur more gradually and can be incorporated into the long-term plan.

Strategic planning is concerned with identifying new and different business activities the company should try to pursue on a long-term basis. Strategic planning is not simply forecasting the future through extension of the past but rather is a combination of thought, ideas, analysis, and judgment of tomorrow's business opportunities.

Inherently, activities based on an attempt to predict the future require risk taking. Planning minimizes the risk. The organization of programs for implementation and controls for systematic feedback of information is critical. Strategic planning is concerned with specification of programs for attaining the desired objectives. When drafting programs, obsolete nonproductive practices of the past should be abandoned in favor of new and different ways to meet the objectives of the future.

Finally, the strategic plan is implemented by consigning the necessary resources to it. Putting the plan into action requires a commitment from the company's most talented people to work at specific tasks.

As an example of strategy setting—and using the advantage of hindsight—consider the strategic plan for the hypothetical Arizona Real Estate Management Company. Assume that when the plan was being devised, the company was a rapidly growing firm with two experienced property managers as partners. The partners realized they had the individual capability to expand their business beyond the market area of Phoenix and decided to examine other locales for decentralization of the business. After studying all cities within a 300-mile radius (one hour of flying time), it was decided that Las Vegas appeared to offer the greatest opportunity. At that time, Las Vegas did not have an established real estate management company. Its population increase was a result of expansion of the tourist business. Even though tenants of apartment buildings had a high level of mobility, the major hotels were planning enormous expansion of facilities. Many publicly owned developers were building new apartment and retail projects. Based upon the absence of competition, evidence of major construction, and the need for competent management to manage properties with transient tenancies, the strategic long-range planning decision was made to enter the Las Vegas market.

The partners recognized the need, when operating at a distance, to have a strong system of controls. A budget commitment of $45,000 was made to develop a computer program to track accounting and provide management information. A final commitment was for one of the partners to assume responsibility for the Las Vegas operation and be relieved of his tasks in Phoenix.

The planners anticipated the future, defined the risk that was present, studied the organization concept, provided proper controls, and, finally, committed their resources to the program.

Participative Planning

The greater the number of knowledgeable people who are involved in preparing a company plan, the greater will be its chance of success when management goes forward with it.

Planning meetings provide forums for people to express ideas and can go far toward guaranteeing that input is received from all pertinent parties. However, they can become expensive communications tools. A great deal of discretion should be used in determining how often and for what purpose planning meetings are held, and care should be exercised in conducting them.

Proof that a meeting can be expensive was evidenced by a planning committee in one management firm. The committee decided it needed to create a new job description for senior property managers, a description that would create new avenues of opportunity for certain qualifying people. A four-man executive committee collectively spent about 140 hours developing the job description. It then was presented to 12 persons who would qualify for that description. This presentation took another four hours. Upon conclusion of the project, 188 total hours had been spent in meeting time developing an acceptable job description. If a price tag of $30 per hour (not an unreasonable estimate of a property manager's hourly rate) could be put on that time, approximately $3,000 had been spent on the project. The investment proved to be a good one, inasmuch as three property managers qualified for the job description and gained renewed interest, enthusiasm, and productivity.

Unfortunately, this is more idealistic than realistic. By contrast, at the same firm a committee of 17 property managers, meeting to design a new month-to-month lease, argued varying philosophies and opinions as to what the form should include. Ten meeting hours—or 170 collective hours—or $5,100 at $30 an hour—were spent on this project, the value of that time far exceeding the benefits produced. The underlying rule, then, is to convene meetings only when management is certain to get a fair return on its investment of time and money. The purpose of a planning meeting must be of significant importance that the sum of the value of the time of those attending will at least equal the benefit of the meeting's outcome.

Other common problems that revolve around planning meetings are these: too many people in attendance, no agenda, not starting the meeting on time, a chairman who lacks authority and control, and poorly prepared attendees. All of these problems add up to inefficiency and undoubtedly lead to meetings that lack productivity. The solution is obvious. An agenda should be carefully prepared that outlines the purpose of the meeting and the subjects to be discussed; it should be distributed to all participants prior to the meeting date. The number of participants should be limited to no more than 12. The chairman should be prepared to control the session, bringing the group together to openly discuss the subject at hand yet reach an ultimate conclusion. Participants should be encouraged to contribute to a meeting's effectiveness by speaking freely yet listening to others, questioning unsupported ideas yet not raising needless questions, and keeping speeches to a reasonable length of time and on the subject at hand.

Because a number of allied business activities go hand-in-hand with property management, one growth opportunity available to property management companies is diversification. Diversification may include providing insurance brokerage services, performing consulting for real estate investors, developing an energy conservation consulting service, forming a janitorial maintenance company, or establishing a company that provides maintenance services to property owners. When diversification is considered, an extremely thorough analysis of all aspects of the new venture first must be made. This analysis requires total involvement from all staff levels. The following case study shows how all members of a company can be utilized in developing a new-business plan directed toward diversification.

Subject: The management company's executive committee is considering diversifying and forming a maintenance company subsidiary. The mission of the new company has been identified as follows:

1. To provide certain quality maintenance services to owners of property it manages at competitive prices.
2. Through the maintenance company's capabilities, to delegate much of the maintenance responsibilities from the property

managers to the maintenance company, thereby making the property manager's time more valuable to the management company.

3. To earn a profit.

The executive committee meets on the subject. Its agenda is as follows:

1. The controller will present his ideas on capital requirements, volume of business, operating costs, potential profit, etc.
2. The president, concerned about a conflict of interest problem, will voice his concerns and parameters.
3. A vice president will discuss the need for quality of workmanship.

Meanwhile, the company's property managers meet and are concerned with:

1. The availability of servicemen when needed.
2. Sources of employees for the new maintenance company.
3. The kinds of equipment and supplies that will be needed.
4. Their degree of authority in ordering and supervising the maintenance people.
5. The kind of skills that would be helpful to them.

A group of building managers also meets. They discuss these matters:

1. Areas in which they are not being well serviced.
2. Areas in which they have problems in getting work done in a timely manner.
3. Existing staff and services they would not want changed.
4. Concerns about availability of space for storing supplies.

Once the information provided by and the attitudes and opinions of the building managers, property managers, controller, and company officers are made available, management is in a much better position to decide whether forming a new maintenance company should become part of the firm's long-range plan. After an analysis of all data, it can answer the question: Is this the kind of growth that is desirable and the kind of diversity that strengthens the business?

Control of the Plan

Having established a plan that states an objective and devised a program to achieve that objective, it is important to have controls that will monitor the plan. Controlling is the process of being informed of progress, providing direction, measuring and interpreting trends and results, and knowing where, when, and how to initiate corrective action. Planning and control should go hand in hand. Failure to install controls allows people to go off in unsupervised directions; the result is that goals are not achieved.

The purpose of control is to ensure the ultimate success of a planned activity. When properly implemented, controls not only permit the early discovery of problems or deviations from the plan, but they also provide sufficient information to permit analysis of the cause of these problems or deviations. When controls are properly designed, they permit quick assessment of a troublesome situation and suggest corrective measures. If objectives are based on time limits, the control is the passing of time. Other controls may be based on cost, ratio, quantity, or even opinions, such as in employee attitude surveys.

The importance of adequate controls may be illustrated by the hypothetical company that has in its long-range plan this objective: To obtain the management of an additional 1,000 apartment units during the next two years with fees of not less than $9,000 per month. A detailed program as to how this new business is to be obtained is worked out, and the responsibility of putting the program into effect is given to one of the company officers. Controls are needed to make sure that the new-business development program is being carried out according to plan, appraise performance, detect trouble spots, and identify the unproductive elements of the program.

Unfortunately, there is no pat answer for the development of controls, since they must be tailored to each particular task. Each program must have its own set of controls if comparisons are to be made between actual situations and planned situations.

Supervision is one form of control. It includes, among other things, inspections, conferences, coaching, and checking against schedules or costs. Supervision can quickly put the spotlight on failures to comply, misunderstandings, delays, or commitments beyond authority. In fact, regularly scheduled supervision is probably the property manager's most effective means of controlling activities.

Probably the most sophisticated form of control, however, is management by exception. Under this system, the manager designs and effectively utilizes a sophisticated set of controls that identify problem areas that need his attention. As long as the work goes according to plan, the manager need not concern himself with administration. Only when there is an exception to the plan is attention warranted. With this form of control system, time and talent is not spent searching for and worrying about problems that do not exist. Rather, efforts are concentrated on known troublesome areas. Of course there is risk in this control system: If the controls are not properly designed and implemented, problems can get out of hand before the manager becomes aware that they even exist.

The Planning Process

Contrary to what usually is thought, planning is not just for large firms. In fact, small businesses have a greater need for planning than major corporations. The small firm does not have the strength to compete on all fronts, as does the larger, more diversified, multilocation real estate service firm. It must pick its competitive fights wisely. It does not have the reserve strength to survive many mistakes; hence, it must carefully calculate its moves.

The chief executive officer of a small business enterprise, faced with the problems of developing new business, managing the office, running buildings, and solving accounting problems, tends to place a low priority on long-range planning for the company. However, two basic principles should be stressed: (1) Any written planning document, no matter how brief, is better than none. (2) Getting started is the hardest part of planning; it moves more easily and surely once a beginning is made.

Planning may be procrastinated and seems unimportant only to those who have never planned. Those who have made even a small start—as long as that start reflects at least a few hours of careful thought and some effort at writing—realize the need for doing more. The principal of a small firm is advised to get started on long-range planning by following eight suggestions:

1. Write a one-page statement that lists personal goals, business goals, and competitive advantages.
2. Accept the initial responsibility of long-range planning. The planning process starts with the head of the company. The plan is a reflection of his plans, decisions, commitments, and priorities.
3. Make the plan, nevertheless, a team effort, tapping all available resources for the purpose of decision making. Bring other executives into the planning process after the chief executive officer has prepared a rough-draft outline.

4. Base plans on facts. These have more value than plans lacking
    support, research being a prerequisite to planning.
5. Set target performance specifications. These can be defined in
    terms of number of people, dollars of gross volume, branch units,
    net cash flow, or share of the market.
6. Because self-analysis often is difficult, select outsiders to critically
    review the plan in order to strengthen it. Realistic planning re-
    quires objective understanding of strengths and weaknesses.
    Outsiders often have insights that escape the chief executive and
    the staff who have close daily contact with him. Effective plan-
    ning demands creativity, new ideas: Sometimes an outsider can
    see business possibilities that insiders cannot. Naturally, long-
    range plans should be reviewed only by outsiders who can keep
    confidences, such as clients with whom there is a long and per-
    sonal relationship, property managers in other communities, or
    executives of other real estate-oriented businesses.
7. Establish controls. A plan without controls is merely wishful
    thinking. The executive who intends to achieve his plan pro-
    vides control by systematically measuring progress against his
    objectives. Reviewing the plan quarterly to determine the success
    of short-range plans and annually to gauge the level of attain-
    ment of long-range objectives helps to determine if the plans and
    objectives are unrealistic or need revision.
8. Plan in great deal of detail for one year in advance, less detail
    for two years, and even less detail for five years.

To illustrate the application of these theories to a property management company, an actual long-range plan is offered. Assume that
the company in question is an established real estate management
firm which, at the time the plan was prepared, managed approximately 10,000 apartment units, 2,000 condominium units, 1.5 million
square feet of office space, a mobile home park, two small industrial
parks, and a resort motel. The company's main office is in Los
Angeles, with satellite operations in San Diego and San Francisco,
California, and Phoenix, Arizona. The company has six officers, all of
whom share in the profits. The president and four vice presidents are
CERTIFIED PROPERTY MANAGERS®. The controller, who
heads the financial aspects of the operation, is a certified public accountant. While the main source of the company's business is from
real estate management, it also receives income from consulting serv-

ices, sale of investment properties, and leasing activities and as an insurance broker. Approximately 15 percent of the management portfolio is composed of properties of which the company is the general partner of limited partnerships. Another 20 percent of the management portfolio is under long-term contract with public partnerships, the firm serving as asset manager as well as property manager. The remainder is made up of standard management contracts terminable by either party on 30 days' notice.

On reviewing the personal goals of the principal officers of the firm, it was discovered that: (1) While growth was important, it was considered far more important to develop more stability in resources of income rather than just more income. (2) Three of the officers placed high priority on professional growth and recognition in the real estate industry. (3) The company had experienced greater than normal growth the previous year, and there was concern among all that it needed greater efficiency in its own operation. (4) Everyone was looking for more enjoyment from work; since five of the six officers had previous experience in the development of properties, it was felt that creative business activity could be more enjoyable than management activity, which typically focuses on problem property.

The next step was a meeting of property managers and officers of the company. The personal goals of the property managers were listed, and some of the obstacles in the way of achieving these were identified. It was interesting to learn that the property managers listed professional advancement as their primary goal. They wanted to improve their education and skills as managers and learn more about becoming involved in real estate activities other than management. The second goal was for more income, and the third was to be promoted in the company and gain recognition as a professional within the industry. The group listed as roadblocks in achieving goals: Getting people to follow through; finding time; retaining top on-site employees; having to do too much accounting detail.

The company president appointed a planning committee, composed of himself and three vice presidents, to be in charge of adopting the long-range plan. The committee's first task was to determine what the business should be. In order to help them in that discussion, a chart was prepared listing all of the business activities the company could pursue, an opinion of the company's abilities in each business activity, available opportunities, and the desirability of each activity in relation to the personal goals of the company officers. (Figure 6.1 shows that analysis.)

After several meetings and a great deal of discussion, the committee agreed that the company's future economic opportunity and planning should be based upon the following assumption: Even though the company had experienced unusual growth in recent years, future growth would be very difficult. The large over-supply of real estate in California and Arizona created many problem property situations that resulted in new management business. As market conditions improve and with the probability of very little new construction for the next several years, the demand for professional management services will decline. With a historical 15 percent turn-over factor, the company will need to develop a new business program in order to maintain the status quo, let alone grow.

Since high priority had been placed on stability of the manage-

Activity	Ability	Opportunity	Desirability
Management			
Apartments	Excellent.	Fair.	Yes.
Condominiums	Very good.	Excellent.	Yes; but some fee problems.
Mobile Home Parks	Very good.	Average to poor.	Yes; take advantage of all opportunities.
Office Leasing	Staff currently lacks initiative.	Average to good.	No; for now.
Sales			
Apartments	Excellent.	Poor; market is overpriced.	Yes.
Commercial	Poor; lack of experience.	Average.	No; can't compete.
Office Buildings	Average.	Average.	No; can't compete.
Condominiums	Excellent.	Very good.	Yes.
Syndication of Property	Very good.	Finding good property is difficult.	Outstanding; management business as well.

Figure 6.1. Analysis of a management firm's abilities, available opportunities, and desirabilities for preparing strategic plan.

ment accounts, the company should develop a new-business plan which would include the syndication of real estate, wherein the company would act as general partner; the development of real estate as a joint venture with more sophisticated developers; and the acquisition of other management companies that have long-term contractual arrangements either as general partners for existing limited partnerships or subsidiaries of public corporations involved in real estate development. It was agreed that the company needed to create an atmosphere where motivation existed, including a program to help property managers realize their professional goals. To this end, a program to increase capabilities and seek out and identify investment property opportunities was adopted. It was felt that since market

Activity	Ability	Opportunity	Desirability
Development of Income Property			
New Construction	Fair.	Wide range; depends on property type.	No; need more experience.
Rehabilitation	Excellent.	Limited	Yes; if opportunities can be found.
Condominium Conversion	Average.	Very good.	Outstanding; big profit potential.
Consulting Services			
Feasibility Studies	Very good.	Because of strong abilities, should develop every opportunity.	Need program to create business.
Marketing Programs	Very good.		
Management Plans	Excellent.		
Income & Expense Projections	Excellent.		
Investment Analyses	Excellent.		
Allied Business			
Insurance	Licensed; yet only used for clients.	Limited.	Maintain status quo.
Maintenance	Fair.	Very good.	Yes; improve existing programs.
Janitorial	Poor.	Very competitive.	No.

Figure 6.1 (continued)

demand for investment properties in California and Arizona was higher than had been prudently recommended to investors, new sources of business would be needed. Three potential opportunities were recognized: the purchase and rehabilitation of existing properties; condominium management; and exploration of single-family houses, mobile home parks, and motels as viable investment properties. With this information in hand, the long-range plan was drafted:

Long-Range Plan
1976–1981

Mission
To become a highly skillful, respected, profitable, and well-known real estate asset management company with operations in California and Arizona.

Goals To Be Achieved by 1981
1. Create greater stability in property management accounts by developing a new-business program that will produce long-term management contracts for at least 60 percent of total management fee income.
   Strategy
   a. Syndication of real estate: The company needs to create property acquisition capability so that it may more readily use its talents for the formation of limited partnerships. The company's role as general partner and managing agent for the partnerships will add stability to its management portfolio. The program includes hiring a director of acquisitions, who will receive a base salary and be given profit-sharing opportunity. He will be given a goal to acquire a given amount (expressed in millions of dollars) in real estate annually. It shall be the responsibility of the president to raise the equity capital needed for these acquisitions. Furthermore, the company shall endeavor to become a capital and management source in partnerships with developers.
   b. Mergers and acquisitions: The company shall seek out mergers and acquisitions of existing management companies where the acquisition candidate has a management portfolio with long-term management agreements.
2. Have the Phoenix and San Francisco offices reach a fully integrated size, i.e., become entirely self-supporting companies providing a full range of real estate services with continuity of management. A goal for monthly management fee income will be set.
   Strategy
   a. Growth begins with qualified on-site entrepreneurial management. Identify this candidate as soon as possible, then establish a business development program to expand property management fee income and local real estate acquisition capability.

b. The Phoenix acquisition program can start immediately with the recruitment of a director of acquisitions, whose sole program will be to buy houses for single-family limited partnership syndications. He shall be hired at a base salary against a commission schedule. His goal shall be to acquire seven houses per month. Equity for these partnerships will be provided through the efforts of the president and a vice president.

3. The Orange County office is to achieve a management portfolio with a stated monthly management fee income.

Strategy

a. Having identified the area manager, inaugurate an ambitious program to expand the condominium management business, inasmuch as it represents the most immediate growth opportunity.

4. Maintain a company pre-tax profit of 15 percent of gross.

5. Achieve an overall company growth rate of 13 percent per year in property management activity and 20 percent per year in brokerage services.

6. Create a given amount (expressed in millions of dollars) in equity ownership opportunities for officers and key employees of the firm.

Strategy

a. Devise a program that will provide for the creation of equity interests in lieu of fees or general partner's profit-sharing arrangements as allowed under SEC regulations and California Corporation Commission laws.

b. Create a subsidiary corporation so that capital can be accumulated at a 25 percent tax rate.

7. Continue to develop professional skills as managers of real estate assets so that each office will become recognized as a leader in its industry for that community.

Strategy

a. Increase efforts to recruit outstanding talent. Continue in-house training programs for property managers through quarterly meetings and resident managers through area training programs and other established employee educational activities.

7

The Organizational Structure

A PROPERTY MANAGEMENT COMPANY'S SUCCESS at meeting the objectives expressed in its strategic plan depends in large part on the strength of the organizational structure through which the company operates. In fact, any change in company strategy usually leads to reorganization. As new priorities are established, adjustments must be made so that the organization remains in tune with the objectives.

The small enterprise needs proper organizational structure just as much as the large firm. The small business that wants to grow needs a plan that enables it to function as a small business but posture itself for growth. No single organizational structure will fit all property management companies, but some guidelines are recommended to improve company performance. Essentially, the organizational structure must support the strategy the company wishes to pursue. This is done by identifying the activities that must be performed to achieve the company's objectives, then classifying those activities into departments. An analysis of activities therefore becomes the link between the company's objectives and the organizational structure.

Analysis of Activities

Organization starts with identifying the operational functions of the business. These basic units become the foundation of the organizational chart, such as the one in figure 7.1. The goal of the entrepreneurial property manager is to succeed. Implicit in success is

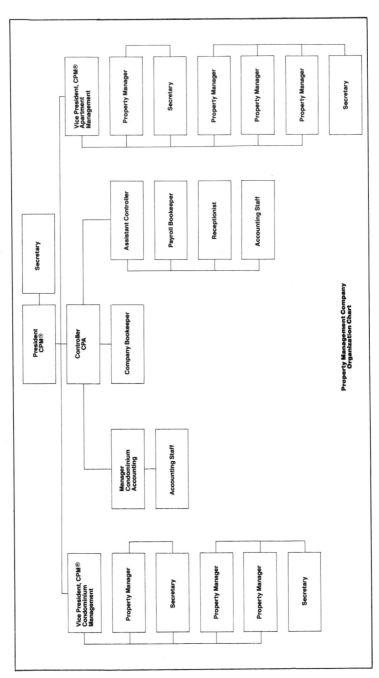

Figure 7.1. An organization chart for a typical property management company.

growth, and implicit in growth is the need for organization. Quite often companies grow from one-man operations to large enterprises because of the marketing and innovative talents of key people and without any planned organization to assist in growth. Viable organizational structures, however, do not simply evolve. Steps can be taken and rules followed to create a sound organization.

The primary requirement in creating such an organization is to identify clearly the activities that must be performed, then organize them logically into departments, each representing a specific function and responsible for performing a group of similar activities that require similar ability and experience. The activities that are identified, and, consequently, the departments that are formed, must correspond with and be in support of the objectives expressed in the company plan.

If, for example, a company's business strategy is to be a major firm in the business of managing apartments and condominiums, then two of its departments probably will be condominium management and apartment management. Furthermore, in property management, the best property manager's performance can be reduced to total incompetence if support from the accounting department fails. For this reason, the bookkeeping function cannot be ignored. This management company then will have three departments within its organizational structure—an apartment management department, a condominium management department, and a bookkeeping department.

Naturally, the basic departments needed in a company's structure will depend upon its business activity and strategic plan. In addition to the crucial bookkeeping department others may include:

Apartment Management	Janitorial Cleaning
Condominium Management	Insurance
Shopping Center Management	Residential Leasing
Office Building Management	Commercial Leasing
Mobile Home Park Management	Management Consulting
Maintenance	New-Business Development

Principles of Organization

Having identified the key activities of the company, the structure can begin to take shape. When creating the company organization, adhering to a few rules should ensure its soundness.

Define Responsibility

Every member of the management team and every employee must know exactly what is expected if overlapping of, and gaps between, responsibility are to be avoided. One method of making this delineation is to put responsibilities in writing. Not only should this eliminate duplication of work, but it also will be invaluable should a position suddenly be vacated.

A common ailment that is a result of not having clearly defined responsibilities revolves around meetings called to make decisions. Two ridiculous—but unfortunately not rare—examples are meetings to create new property management business forms or establish changes in bookkeeping procedures. Power to make such decisions should lie within someone's realm of authority, not within a meeting structure. An excess of these kinds of meetings may indicate that responsibility has not been clearly defined. The rule to follow is to minimize the need for employees to meet in order to accomplish anything.

Couple Responsibility with Authority

If a property manager is to be held responsible for the activities within his department, he must be given the full necessary authority. He must not be subject to orders from the central office that might affect his ability to successfully perform these activities. Authority must not be undermined by executives who delegate it yet continue to make decisions within the realm of that authority. A property manager, for example, should not promise a client that his building lobby will be painted within two weeks if this is within the resident manager's authority. This could upset the resident manager's arrangement with the painter to begin painting in five weeks.

Conversely, authority must be coupled with responsibility. If a property manager, through the organizational structure, is given certain authority, he must consider himself accountable for all of his actions and the actions of the department.

Delegate Decision Making

A good organization permits decisions to be made at as low a level as possible. This frees top management to concentrate on more complex matters and devote more energy to planning. The president of a real estate service company, after all, does not have to personally authorize every security deposit return or approve every secretary's salary increase. These duties can easily and efficiently be delegated to a lower level within the organization.

Minimize Organizational Levels

Too many levels within an organization are a sign of poor organization. There are numerous reasons to minimize the number of levels. For one thing, the longer the chain of command, the greater the chance of inaccuracies in communication. With each additional management level that reviews a situation, the more difficult it becomes to reach a mutual understanding. Like a rumor, by the time a communication has passed through the fifth person, it probably is not recognizable by the person who started it.

Unnecessary levels of management also encourage indecisiveness and procrastination, two enemies of good management. If a property manager who wants to spend $500 to improve a property's landscaping must check with his superior, the vice president, who must see the president of the company, who in turn needs the owner's approval, a poor organizational structure exists. Oftentimes, unnecessary decision-making levels are the fault of property owners. This problem commonly occurs in situations in which the client is a sizeable corporation with several layers of its management wanting to be involved in, yet avoid responsibility of, operating a property. By illustration, consider an office building, owned by a corporate client, for which a management company is negotiating a new 5,000-square-foot lease that calls for an approval to spend $25,000 to make modifications to the space. The property management company reports to the corporate client's controller, who doesn't feel he can grant approval. The matter then goes to the financial vice president, who wants the president to review the matter. The president isn't sophisticated in office building leasing situations, so he goes to the board of directors for approval. By the time the lease proposal is accepted, the tenant probably will have gone elsewhere. This kind of problem arises when a property management company does not reach an agreement with the owner concerning the leasing function at the time management responsibility is assumed. A full discussion on authority and responsibility at the initiation of the contract makes for a smoother organizational structure.

Furthermore, unnecessary levels of management should be eliminated because of the effect on employees. If the chief executive of the company appears remote, morale may be lowered. The objective is to build the least possible layers of management and have the shortest possible chain of command.

Limit Number of Departments

The number of functional departments should be limited to the absolute minimum required. Each function needs a leader. However, each leader can effectually coordinate only a limited number of people and groups of activities. This commonly is known as the span of control principle. The number of activities a manager can handle depends on several factors: the degree of similarity of work performed by subordinates; the complexity of the duties performed by subordinates; the actual number of immediate subordinates; the frequency with which new problems arise. The span of control, therefore, may vary from one department to another.

Furthermore, success in property management depends in large part on having as few people as possible spending time managing the office and the maximum number managing properties. It is important that growing companies do not have an overabundance of executives who sit in offices creating needless work. The business demands production, and production is managing properties. Properties cannot be managed by executive fiat from corporate offices. The executive should spend the majority of his time away from the office—managing properties, working with property managers and supervisors, and soliciting new business accounts for the company.

The author's experience indicates that a new member to the top management team generally allocates his time as follows:

- 40 percent to supervising three property managers (or property supervisors) and communicating with the clients of these properties.
- 30 percent to managing properties that are his sole responsibility.
- 20 percent to company planning and administrative functions.
- 10 percent to developing new business opportunities.

An executive who has no responsibility for direct management of properties generally allocates his time in this manner:

- 50 percent to supervising five property managers (or property supervisors) and communicating with the clients of these properties.
- 30 percent to company planning and administrative functions.
- 20 percent to developing new business opportunities.

Ignore Personal Preferences

An organization needs to be structured to support company goals, programs, and responsibilities. Then it must be fine-tuned to accommodate the talents—not the personal hang-ups—of individuals in the firm. In establishing an organizational structure, assignments cannot be made or responsibilities given in order to "make someone happy." This seriously jeopardizes the soundness of the structure. If a given individual is better qualified and more suited to assume a certain responsibility than others within the company, it should be given to him. It is not uncommon, for instance, for managers with seniority to get the most interesting assignments. This premise, however, rests on an invalid basis. Only if a senior property manager is best qualified for a particular job should he be given it.

Likewise, managers who personally prefer to avoid certain kinds of work must not be allowed to dictate to the organization. If, for example, a senior property manager in the apartment management division does not want to manage a new building account because of the kinds of tenant problems he would encounter but is willing to assume management responsibility for a luxury cooperative, it would be unwise to accommodate his personal preferences at the expense of sound organization. The organizational structure should be a true reflection of the activities performed by the company and not an attempt to accommodate a predetermined structure or personalities.

Simplify the Structure

The best organization is the simplest one that does the job. The simpler the structure, the less that can go wrong. The team concept of company officer, property manager, secretary, and bookkeeper seems to be the most effective structure for managing real property. The fewer people involved with the management of a given property, the greater the level of productivity and the greater the possibility of success in fulfilling the management plan. Management of a given property requires attention to innumerable details. The fewer people involved, the greater will be their recall of these details. Furthermore, familiarity with a property produces more efficient use of time and minimizes chance of error.

Benefits of Organization

When a property management company has built a solid organization, it will reap certain benefits that would not be evidenced if it had a poor organizational structure. Among these benefits are preparation for growth, an atmosphere of teamwork, the freeing of top management, and better communications.

Preparation for Growth

An organizational structure serves the important purpose of permitting controlled expansion. It not only divides work through specialization but likewise serves as the means of exercising control over that work. Also, by providing a logical framework within which one specialized department can be related to all others, activities can be administered in manageable units, no one individual or department being forced to bear too heavy a load.

Essentially, growth is evidenced in one of two ways—increase in size or in diversity. If top management is not freed to devote its efforts to long-range planning, there will be no effective growth. Only through an organization built on the principle of delegation of decision making will management be prepared to cope with these two forms of growth. The company's organizational structure can improve growth possibilities by making possible the training and testing of tomorrow's managers. Continuous personal development is necessary at all job levels if a company is to be positioned for expansion.

Growth is imperative to a company plan if a positive attitude is to be maintained for the people in the organization. They must feel there are opportunities for personal expansion. Each person needs a challenge that can be served through a growth posture, and organization sets this posture.

Creation of a Management Team

A company goal for growth need not be growth just for growth's sake, but rather for improved quality as well. This can be obtained through the creation of a management team, the quality of which depends on the quality of the organization.

As a company grows, the chief executive reaches a point at which there is simply more work than one person can do. He needs to manage the business through a team structure rather than continue as the sole decision maker. Upon analyzing a real estate management's growth structure, it becomes apparent that a team is needed to assist in getting business, developing management plans for properties, and overseeing property supervisors. These management team members generally come from the ranks of property managers who have displayed entrepreneurial attitudes and are adept at working with people.

Organization creates an atmosphere of team effort by increasing the feeling of cooperation and freedom. A person can work best with others when his responsibility has been clearly defined and he understands the value of cooperative relationships. A team needs structure and assignment of responsibility. Without structure, a team is a mob. Equally important, a team member does not interfere with the authority and decisions of other team members. If he feels something should be changed, he first goes to the team member who carries that responsibility; failing to persuade a change or reach a compromise, an appeal may be made to top management at the appropriate time.

It is not important that all members of the management team are close personal friends. Indeed, among competitive individuals, they may not be. Team members must, however, be supportive of one another in the operation of the company business. One should never belittle another in front of other employees or the public. At all times, the team must show an attitude of solidarity.

Freeing of Top Management

Through organization and team effort, top management is liberated from an undue amount of day-to-day functional activity and can concentrate on other responsibilities within the realm of executive control. Some of these tasks occur on a regular basis, and others need to be performed intermittently.

The first responsibility is for planning, both long range and short range. (The strategic company plan is described in detail in chapter 6.) This leads to identifying the company's mission and developing strategies. The top officer is the only person in the company who can visualize the entire business and determine the balances needed to appropriately allocate resources—people and money. As a rule of thumb, the chief executive officer should allocate up to 25 percent of his time to planning.

Another responsibility is development of new business for the company. The chief executive always will be the company's best salesman. His understanding of the management process is more convincing to property owners than is that of his associates. Furthermore, because of his position in the company, he can speak to prospective clients with more authority.

The top manager must have time for key people, both in and

out of the company. Ideally, employees' goals and aspirations as well as their capabilities and limitations are known. His responsibility extends to developing the human resources of the firm. Equally important are relationships with people outside the company. Clients, major vendors, bankers, and others in the real estate industry affect the ability of the business to perform.

The top company official sets the level of ethical and professional standards by which his company is identified. His manners, appearance, and personal habits give identity to the company. If permissive in treatment of tenants, this trait becomes part of the company image. Likewise, fair treatment of vendors, departing clients, and employees becomes part of the company's reputation. Above all, requirements for exactness, punctuality, and clarity of all fiduciary functions create public attitudes toward the professional standards practiced by the company.

Furthermore, the time of the chief officer needs to be freed because he must be available when something goes seriously wrong. It becomes his job to roll up his sleeves and solve the crisis situation. A crisis can come from any direction: It may be in the bookkeeping department, or an operational problem may arise at a property. No matter the source, he must be on hand.

The chief executive is, above all, a property manager. Involvement in the property management process is maintained by taking an active role in the creation of management plans for each property the company manages. Executive-level experience and abilities are required in developing short-term plans for properties. In addition, he may choose to assume either full or partial responsibility for supervising the management program of a new account. Since nearly all new property management assignments originate as a result of significant operating problems, executive talents may be needed in the beginning to eliminate or at least smooth out operational difficulties. A sound organizational structure ensures that time will be available to give to this function.

Improvement of Communications

An effective network of communications is crucial to the success of any enterprise. Good organization ensures the establishment of this network. The lines of authority created by the structure become the main routes used to disseminate policies and plans and make new work assignments. An organization chart, such as the one in figure 7.1, is a beneficial communications tool. The chart indicates each department's relationship within the overall structure of the firm, divides graphically the tasks to be performed, and becomes the framework for establishing both upward and downward lines of communication.

8

The Company Financial Plan

THE EXECUTIVE OF A PROPERTY MANAGEMENT COMPANY has a responsibility to see that all monetary transactions connected with the enterprise are accounted for, controlled, and interpreted. Performing these functions calls for establishment of a program of financial and managerial accounting.

Accounting is the act of classifying, recording, and summarizing financial transactions and interpreting the results. The subject can be approached from either of two directions: from the perspective of the accountant or that of the user of accounting information. The user of accounting information is more concerned with rationally and intelligently interpreting accounting data in order to make effective management decisions. This is known as managerial accounting. The accountant's primary concern is with the technical aspects of how data is collected, summarized, and reported. This is referred to as financial accounting.

Financial Accounting

The basic principles of financial accounting must be understood before accounting data can be used in the decision-making process. Financial accounting is the aspect of accounting designed to satisfy the firm's relationship with its owners and stockholders and meet the fiduciary responsibilities imposed by them. Its scope is limited to preparing historical reports which summarize the financial position of the company as a whole.

The two most important financial statements in the area of financial accounting are the balance sheet and the profit and loss statement. The former is used to determine the financial status of a property management company, and the latter's purpose is to indicate the results of its operations.

Balance Sheet

The balance sheet, which shows a company's financial position at a particular time, is presented as a statement of assets, liabilities, and owners' equity. The balance sheet equation is simply:

Assets = Liabilities + Owners' Equity

The typical balance sheet, therefore, shows the assets of the business on the left side and the liabilities and proprietorship of the business in the right column. Both sides are always in balance, thus the designation balance sheet.

Assets refer to all resources available for use by a company. They can be monetary or nonmonetary, tangible or intangible. Typical assets of a property management company are cash, money, furniture, leasehold improvements, automobiles, and equipment. Liabilities are claims of creditors against the company to whom the company owes cash or service at some future date. Owners' equity, commonly called stockholders' equity in corporations, is the balancing figure—the difference between the assets and the liabilities—and represents the claims of the owners of the business. Often this figure is referred to as net worth in proprietorships and partnerships.

A property management company's assets are divided into three subcategories: current assets, fixed assets, and other assets.

Current assets are those that easily can be converted into cash, sold, or consumed in the near future through normal business operations. Included are cash, bank deposits that are readily available, accounts and notes receivable that can be collected through the normal operating cycle, and prepaid expenses for such items as rent, insurance, and taxes.

Assets of a relatively permanent nature are fixed assets. These assets are not intended for resale in the regular operation of the enterprise. Within this category are land, property improvements, buildings, equipment, furniture, and fixtures. With the exception of land, such assets, although they may be sold when they no longer serve the purposes for which they were acquired, will be worn out through use and need to be replaced. Thus, fixed assets have a finite life. Furthermore, fixed assets generally are of a nonmonetary nature, inasmuch as the benefits from them are a result of their use rather than their conversion into cash. An office building owned by and used as the office of a management company, for instance, is a fixed asset whose value derives from its use.

Assets that fall under the "other" category are securities of one company owned by another for investment and intangible assets, such as goodwill. Goodwill is an asset that arises out of a firm's high reputation, good public relations, a favorable location, etc. Typically, however, goodwill appears as an asset only when a company has actually made a purchase; for instance, when it buys a property right.

Liabilities, which are on the credit side of the balance sheet, imply an obligation to pay money or provide services. They are the result of transactions that occurred in the past, not of ones to take place in the future. Liabilities can be divided into two categories: current liabilities and long-term liabilities.

Current liabilities are those that are expected to be satisfied within a relatively short period of time, usually one year. Essentially, current liabilities are those that will be paid from current assets; thus, a direct relationship exists between current liabilities and current assets. Among the current liabilities are notes and accounts payable, interest payable as the result of accrual, wages and salaries payable (a liability for unpaid wages in salaries when employees are paid at fixed intervals and the final pay period is not the same as the balance sheet date), and employee withholdings.

Long-term liabilities are those whose maturity dates are more than a year from the balance sheet date. The most common long-term liabilities are mortgages, bonds, and long-term notes.

The owners' equity section of the balance sheet indicates the amount the owners or stockholders have invested in the enterprise. Owners' equity consists of three subcategories: contributed capital, retained earnings, and net income.

Contributed or paid-in capital is the actual money invested in the firm by the owners for use in conducting the business. In a corporation, this is expressed in terms of capital stock.

Retained earnings refer to net income after tax obligations from previous years that have been put back into the business rather than being paid to its owners. Retained earnings reflect internal financing through profits and equal earnings reported over the years minus dividends distributed to owners.

Net income indicates earnings produced during the current period of operation.

An examination of an actual balance sheet of a pure real estate management business can be useful in reaching an understanding of it. By way of illustration, consider the fictitious Arizona Real Estate Management Company's balance sheet, shown in figure 8.1. Assume the company was formed 10 years ago by two property managers. They decided to operate under the corporate form of ownership because it would limit their legal liability and provide them with an opportunity to create savings from preferred corporate tax rates. They elected to have their fiscal year end on September 30 rather than use a calendar year as the period of accounting. The Arizona Real Estate Management Company accounting system is on a cash basis. Consequently, the business reports its financial operations in the differences between cash receipts and cash outlays. This approach has the advantage of simplicity and is the form of accounting used by most real estate management companies. Furthermore, it

Arizona Real Estate Management Company
Balance Sheet (Unaudited)—September 30, 19xx

Assets

Current Assets
Cash in Bank and on Hand	$ 47,727		
Prepaid Expense—Franchise Tax	200		
U.S. Treasury Bills	100,000		
Total Current Assets			$147,927

Fixed Assets	Cost	Accumulated Depreciation	Net Book Value
Rental Property			
Apartments—Marsh Gardens			
Building and Improvements	$367,984	$135,134	$232,850
Administrative Property			
Office Equipment	86,650	45,680	40,970
Automobiles	37,712	7,612	30,100
	$492,346	$188,426	$303,920
Land—Rental Property			
Apartment Site—Marsh Gardens		55,366	359,286
Other Assets			
Deposit—Airline		425	
Loans Receivable—J. Smith		7,897	8,322
Total Assets			$515,535

Figure 8.1. Balance sheet for the fictitious Arizona Real Estate Management Company.

allows some flexibility in tax planning for the two principals of this firm.

The other form of accounting is on an accrual basis. Here, income is recorded when earned, even though it is not necessarily received during the same period, and expenses are recorded when incurred, even though not necessarily paid during the same period. Accrual accounting provides a more accurate determination of the actual financial experience of the business enterprise for a given period of time than cash accounting. However, because real estate management firms in almost all instances receive income—management fees—during the period earned, and since more than 60 percent of expenses are for payroll costs that are paid during the period of accounting, the cash basis is more widely used among management companies.

Arizona Real Estate Management Company's current manage-

Liabilities and Stockholders' Equity			
Current Liabilities			
Mortgages Payable—Estimated Current Portion		$ 12,000	
Accrued Expenses			
Payroll Taxes	$ 96		
Workmen's Compensation and Group Insurance	1,690		
Federal Income Tax Payable	5,395	7,181	
Total Current Liabilities			$ 19,181
Long-Term Liabilities			
Mortgages Payable	307,994		
Less—Estimated Current Portion Above	12,000	295,994	
Tenants' Security Deposits		2,054	
Total Liabilities			298,048
Stockholders' Equity			
Capital Stock—5,000 Shares Issued and Outstanding		15,000	
Retained Earnings—Balance as of October 1, 19xx		141,638	
Net Income		41,668	
Total Stockholders' Equity			198,306
Total Liabilities and Stockholders' Equity			$515,535

Figure 8.1 (continued)

ment portfolio includes approximately 4,000 apartment units, 1,200 condominium units, office buildings totalling 150,000 square feet of net rentable area, and a small neighborhood shopping center. Management fees run approximately $50,000 per month. As is typical of property management companies, its current assets include cash approximately equalling one month's gross fees. Surplus cash has been invested in U.S. Treasury Bills. Several years ago, the company used some of its assets to purchase an apartment house called Marsh Gardens. It owns the property in partnership with three other investors, each investor having equal ownership. The Arizona Real Estate Management Company manages the property for the general partnership. Other funds have been invested in office equipment and automobiles used by the two principals as well as one of the property managers. Other assets include the deposit for an airline travel card and a loan receivable from a former employee.

Under the firm's liability section, current liabilities show the estimated portion of the mortgage for Marsh Gardens that will be due in the coming year. Other current liabilities are accrued expenses for payroll taxes; workmen's compensation insurance; the company's group health insurance; and federal income tax, which is due but not yet paid. Long-term liabilities include the company's share of the mortgage that is payable on Marsh Gardens and its prorata share of tenant security deposits.

The stockholders' equity is divided into the three customary sections: original capital of $15,000, which is listed as capital stock; retained earnings for years prior to the current accounting period; and net income from the most recent year's operations.

This balance sheet reveals a great deal about the company's financial condition. For example, the company has sufficient cash on hand to properly operate its business, as well as a cash reserve, or a current asset reserve, of $100,000. Its current liabilities are small and can be handled easily with its cash balances. Its only long-term liabilities are those related to the ownership of the apartment. During the time since the company was formed 10 years ago, the stockholders' equity has risen from $15,000 to $198,000. The business is in a healthy operating condition. The company has the financial ability to grow and take advantage of new business opportunities.

Profit and Loss Statement

The financial operating results of a property management organization for a given period of time are revealed through a profit and loss (P & L) statement, sometimes called an earnings report, income statement, or operating statement. The value of this statement lies in the fact that it provides vital information about the operating activities of a property management business that can be used in making intelligent management decisions. This report should be seen as the vehicle that indicates if an enterprise has succeeded in fulfilling its purpose of realizing a profit during a given time period. Essentially, it matches the revenue received from selling property management service against the outlays made to operate the company. The result is net income, or net profit if positive and net loss is negative.

The primary source of money received by a management company—management fees—is considered as operating revenue. Subtracted from operating revenue are operating expenses. Among other items, these include depreciation. Most fixed assets have a limited useful life. These assets will be used by the company over a number of years, or accounting periods. Therefore, a fraction of the cost of each fixed asset is properly chargeable as an expense in each of the accounting periods in which the asset is used. The process of this gradual conversion of a fixed asset into an expense is depreciation, that fraction of a fixed asset's cost consumed during a particular accounting period.

The result of subtracting operating expenses from operating revenues is operating profit. To this is added nonoperating, or other, income. This income category could include dividends or interest received by the firm from its investments in securities, fees or royalties earned by the company, etc. The total is taxable income, or the income produced by the management company for a given period of time against which there is an income tax liability to municipal, state, and federal income tax agencies. Subtracting the provision for taxes yields after-tax income.

Total costs and expenses subtracted from total revenues results in net income. This is the sum that is available for dividend payments to owners and for use in the business.

Scrutiny of the profit and loss statement and comparisons of its various elements can be quite informative about a management company's operation. The data indicated on the profit and loss statement may be used to ascertain the operating profit margin, the operating cost ratio, and the net profit ratio. When these ratios are determined on an annual basis, they can be quite revealing in judging the economic soundness of the company.

Company Audit

An independent audit is an inspection of the financial accounting records and procedures by someone specially trained—an auditor—to check their accuracy, completeness, and reliability. The primary function of an auditor is to express an informed, professional, and objective opinion on the financial statements prepared by the property management business. In the case of the balance sheet and the profit and loss statement, the auditor's role is to determine if the former accurately reflects the company's financial status and if the latter truly represents its operations.

The auditor is responsible for his work and, accordingly, the issuance of an opinion based upon his examination of the financial statements and the stewardship of the business enterprise. Before he can give his learned opinion, it is necessary for him to make an exhaustive study of the records and management procedures and controls of the business. The appendix includes a series of documents filled with questions that are likely to be asked in an audit of a real estate management firm and are offered for use in examining if a company is living up to its fiduciary responsibilities to its clients. (Specifically, the documents included in the appendix are: figure A.2, Management Controls Questionnaire; figure A.3, Examination of Management Controls; figure A.4, Questionnaire on Internal Control—Cash; figure A.5, Examination of Cash; figure A.6, Questionnaire on Internal Control—Purchases, Accounts Payable, and Expenses; figure A.7, Examination of Purchases, Accounts Payable, and Expenses; figure A.8, Questionnaire on Internal Control—Payroll; figure A.9, Examination of Payroll.)

Managerial Accounting

Entrepreneurial executives of a real estate management enterprise focus attention on the company's future. To do this, a program of managerial accounting is called for. Whereas financial accounting is concerned with what has happened in the past, managerial accounting's concern is with what will or may happen. It is the aspect of accounting that permits management to make intelligent projections based on past results. Unlike financial accounting, managerial accounting is not auditable. The data presented cannot be certified, as is the case with balance sheets and profit and loss statements. They are forecasts and not actual transactions.

Cost Accounting

One branch of managerial accounting is cost accounting, which provides management with information concerning the cost or profit of a specific portion of a property management company's total operation. Cost accounting has to do with collecting, recording, and controlling the costs of providing property management service and is crucial to the managerial accounting system. The proprietor of a property management company hopes to operate in such a way that he will increase his profits. His accounting records should provide the information that will aid him in accomplishing this goal. Cost control and a good accounting system are synonymous; both are needed in the smallest real estate management office as well as the largest company. Good company management means developing a detailed budget and a parallel system of cost accounting so that the top management can know exactly how the business is responding to its plan and operational programs.

A fundamental difference exists between budgeting and cost accounting. A budget is the financial plan for a management company's programs; cost accounting is the process of measuring expense incurred as a result of actual operations. By understanding the financial facts of operation, the company can budget for operations more effectively in the future. Although they are different processes, budgeting and cost accounting must be compatible. Budgets are for a fixed period of time (not more than one year—otherwise they are long-range plans) and may include monthly, quarterly, and annual reports. Units of cost accounting must be for the same time periods. To further ensure compatibility between the two, fluctuations caused by time must be considered. For example, rent is a fixed, recurring cost at a constant rate and therefore can be analyzed in almost any unit of time. On the other hand, audit expense, payment of annual dues, travel costs, business taxes, and employee bonus programs are costs that do not occur on a regular basis and therefore must be adjusted for seasonal variation.

In order to determine costs of offering property management service, a standard of measurement is needed. The three primary standards of measurement considered practicable in analyzing a real estate management business are the per-unit cost, the per-person cost, and the percentage of gross income.

The property management company whose sole business is the management of apartment units has two choices in establishing its per-unit cost. The obvious choice is a per-apartment unit cost; another is a per-building cost. A principle of mathematics is that the larger the denominator, the more precise will be the measurement. For this reason, it is best to analyze cost based on the number of apartment units rather than the number of buildings. The matter is more complex for the company with a varied portfolio, including apartments, condominiums, office buildings, and retail stores. This calls for establishing equal units of work, using the apartment house and its units as the base unit for comparison. Following is a recommended standard of measurement schedule:

1 Apartment = 1 Unit
1 Condominium = 1 Unit
1 Hotel = 1 Unit
1 Retail Tenant = 1 Unit
1,000 Square Feet (Net Rentable Area) Office Space = 1 Unit
1 Single-Family House = 2 Units
5,000 Square Feet (Net Rentable Area) Industrial Building = 1 Unit
1 Apartment, No Resident Manager = 2 Units

If the company manages unusual properties, such as restaurants, golf courses, parking lots, or garages, and needs a common denominator for establishing its per-unit cost, it is suggested that the definition of a unit be predicated upon the estimated number of bookkeeping entries required to supervise that business. As a basis for comparison, an average of 2.5 bookkeeping transactions is required per month for an apartment unit. Essentially, then, the per-unit definition is predicated upon the management portfolio of the company being considered.

A system of cost accounting based on separately identifying and collecting costs for each unit can be referred to as unit costing. In manufacturing, this would be known as job order cost accounting; service industries, however, demand unique treatment. Unlike the manufacturing industry, there are no costs of materials in a service industry. The major cost is for people, i.e., the employees of the firm.

A property management company's organizational chart may be seen as various cost centers, each engaged in the performance of a single function. A cost center can be defined as any department of a firm for which cost records are allocated. The purpose of isolating cost centers is to provide a means of assigning ultimate responsibility for costs incurred by the person accountable for that center.

The three principal cost centers to be traced in a real estate

Statistical Comparisons

	1976	1977	1978	1979 Budget
Units Managed	5,516	5,906	5,780	6,120
Monthly Fee	$39,715	$46,781	$50,010	$56,000
Fee per Unit	$ 7.20	$ 7.92	$ 8.65	$ 9.15

Payroll

	1976	1977	1978	1979 Budget
Executive				
Payroll				$ 5,600
Number of People				1.4
Average Pay				$ 4,000
Units Managed per Executive				4,371
Percentage of Gross Income				10.0%
Cost per Unit				$ .92
Property Manager				
Payroll				$12,900
Number of People				6.5
Average Pay				$ 1,984
Units Managed per Manager				941
Percentage of Gross Income				23.0%
Cost per Unit				$ 2.11
Secretaries				
Payroll				$ 3,900
Number of People				4
Average Pay				$ 975
Units Managed per Secretary				1,530
Percentage of Gross Income				7.0%
Cost per Unit				$ .64
Bookkeepers				
Payroll	$ 5,850	$ 6,400	$ 7,100	$ 7,800
Number of People	7.5	8	8	9
Average Pay	$ 780	$ 800	$ 887	$ 866
Units Managed per Bookkeeper	735	738	722	680
Percentage of Gross Income	14.1%	13.7%	14.2%	14.0%
Cost per Unit	$ 1.06	$ 1.08	$ 1.23	$ 1.27
Other Payroll Costs				
Total				$ 3,400
Total Employees				21
Average per Person				$ 162
Cost per Unit				$ .26
Percentage of Gross Income				6.0%
Total Payroll				
Number of People				21
Cost per Unit				$ 5.49
Percentage of Gross Income				60.0%

Figure 8.2. Statistical comparisons of per unit, per person, and percentage of gross income payroll costs for the fictitious Arizona Real Estate Management Company, with bookkeeping payroll costs illustrated for three years actual plus the budgeted year.

management operation are labor, other operating expenses, and bookkeeping. The detail of cost accounting warranted for each of these cost centers depends upon the individual company and size of its income and expenses. The following outline suggests a minimum number of categories to be analyzed in a company's cost analysis:

1. Labor (Salaries)
    Executive
    Property Manager
    Bookkeepers
    Secretaries/Receptionist
    Other Payroll Costs
    Total
2. Operating Expenses (all cost categories that are more than two percent of gross income)
    Business Development
    Computer
    Rent
    Telephone
    Travel
    Other
    Total
3. Bookkeeping
    Labor
    Pro Rata Share of Operating Expenses
    Computer
    Total

Figure 8.2 represents the payroll cost centers budgeted for 1979 for the fictional Arizona Real Estate Management Company and includes, by way of illustration, data on the bookkeeper's payroll cost for the previous three years. Performing such a statistical comparison of cost centers on per-unit, per-person, and percentage of gross income bases can provide valuable data for use in making management forecasts and decisions and exercising control.

Chart of Accounts
Because the role of cost accounting is to isolate costs associated with various aspects of the enterprise, a system of assigning these costs is called for. This is accomplished through establishment of a chart of accounts. A chart of accounts is nothing more than a systematic

listing of the accounts needed by the company, usually with an account number assigned to each item on the list. If properly developed to suit the company's particular method of operation, the chart of accounts can be the cornerstone of a successfully functioning accounting system.

In the final analysis, the purpose of a chart of accounts is to serve management as an aid in analyzing business operations and provide units of operating costs that can be scrutinized. Its goal is to clarify, not confuse. To this end, a chart of accounts should include only significant items of expense. Consequently, a large man-

---

Chart of Accounts: Long Form

```
_____  Income Accounts
               _____  Management Fees
_____  Expense Accounts
               _____  Payroll
                              _____  Executive
                              _____  Property Manager
                              _____  Bookkeeping
                              _____  Secretarial
                              _____  Bonuses
                              _____  Payroll Taxes
                              _____  Workmen's Compensation
                                             Insurance
                              _____  Health Insurance
                              _____  Outside Labor
                              _____  Labor Procurement
               _____  Automobile
               _____  Business Development
               _____  Computer
               _____  Dues and Education
               _____  Entertainment
               _____  Furniture and Equipment
               _____  Insurance
               _____  Legal and Audit
               _____  Office Expenses
               _____  Postage
               _____  Printing
               _____  Rent
               _____  Taxes and Licenses
               _____  Telephone
               _____  Travel
               _____  Duplication
```

Figure 8.3.   Chart of accounts, long form, for property management operation with space for inserting account numbers.

agement company usually will require a more detailed chart of accounts than a smaller management firm. As the smaller business grows and becomes more diverse in its business activity, however, its chart of accounts will need to expand as well. A cardinal rule in developing a chart of accounts is that each account always must be meaningful. If the accounts have no meaning, top management will not be provided with the kind of relevant information it needs to manage the business and make rational decisions about its future.

To illustrate and analyze the operations of property management companies, two charts of accounts are included here. The long form (figure 8.3) is an example of what may be used by a larger management company, and the short form (figure 8.4) is illustrative of a chart of accounts used by a smaller firm. Each is for the pure property management operation and contemplates that the only company income is from management fees and the only operating expenses are for property management operations. Since most offices engage in additional real estate activities, it would be necessary for the

---

Chart of Accounts: Short Form

	Income Accounts
	_____ Management Fees
_____	Expense Accounts
	_____ Payroll
	_____ Property Manager
	_____ Bookkeeping
	_____ Secretarial
	_____ Other Payroll Costs
	_____ Business Development (Includes Entertainment)
	_____ Computer
	_____ Dues and Fees (Includes Legal and Audit, Taxes and Education
	_____ Furniture and Equipment
	_____ Insurance
	_____ Postage
	_____ Printing and Supplies (Includes Office Expenses)
	_____ Rent
	_____ Telephone
	_____ Travel (Includes Automobile)
	_____ Duplication

Figure 8.4. Chart of accounts, short form, for a property management operation with space for inserting account numbers.

analyst to make proper allocation of costs when studying other operations. A description of the categories in the long form follows:

Payroll: Executive. This category includes the base salary for the chief executive officer of the firm. If he is not performing this activity full-time, a reasonable pro rata allocation of his time, and consequently of all property managers whose operational responsibilities are to supervise other property managers, must be made. Usual titles for these other executive positions are vice president, branch manager, or general manager. Similarly, if a portion of the chief executive's time or any of the supervisory officers' time is spent managing properties, those portions should be allocated to the property manager payroll at salary rates customarily paid to property managers for supervising similar properties. For example, consider the chief executive officer of a firm whose salary is $5,000 per month and who spends 50 percent of his time in the property management business and the other 50 percent of his time in the firm's real estate sales activities. The management department should be charged only with an executive salary of $2,500. Another illustration involves the vice president of operations who allocates 25 percent of his time to managing properties and the remaining 75 percent supervising others in the management of properties. The company usually pays its property managers $2,500 per month. Therefore, this vice president's compensation would be allocated as $625 per month (25 percent of $2,500) to the property manager payroll and the balance to executive payroll.

Payroll: Property Manager. This category includes property managers, property supervisors, building managers, building secretaries, and all others on the management company's payroll who have primary responsibility for managing buildings.

Payroll: Bookkeeping. The controller and all accountants, bookkeepers, and bookkeeping clerks are included in this category. If an employee's duties are divided between bookkeeping and something else, there should be a pro rata allocation.

Payroll: Secretary/Receptionist. A firm's receptionist, secretaries, and clerks not included in bookkeeping activities are allocated in this category.

Payroll: Bonuses. This category includes all bonuses and retirement benefits paid to property managers, bookkeepers, and secretaries/receptionist. Bonuses and profit-sharing plans paid to executives are included as part of the company's profits.

Payroll: Payroll Taxes. All payroll taxes paid for all classifications of employees are indicated in this account.

Payroll: Workmen's Compensation Insurance. This includes the cost of workmen's compensation insurance for all of the company's employees.

Payroll: Health Insurance. Any health, accident, and life insurance premiums paid by the firm on behalf of its employees come under this account.

Payroll: Outside Labor. Occasionally, firms need to contract for outside labor or part-time help, such as typists or secretarial workers. The applicable costs would be indicated in this account.

Payroll: Labor Procurement. All costs for recruiting new employees, such as employment agency fees, classified advertising, etc., would be noted here.

Automobile. All costs, other than employee parking, that are paid by the company for the operation of automobiles are noted in this category. (Employee parking is included under rent.)

Business Development. This includes all costs for soliciting and procuring new business. Typical costs are for advertising, entertainment, "this property managed by" signs, public relations, etc.

Computer. This account category is to indicate all data processing costs. If the company uses a service bureau, this category includes all costs paid to the service bureau. If the firm has an in-house computer, it includes all lease costs or, if owned, cost of depreciation and interest on investment of equipment and programming maintenance costs.

Dues and Education. This category includes all dues and fees paid to professional organizations, such as realty boards, Institute of Real Estate Management, Building Owners and Managers Association, local and state apartment associations, Community Associations Institute, International Society of Shopping Centers, etc. It also includes costs for sending employees to educational seminars and courses, when those costs are assumed by the company, and subscription costs for any periodicals, newspapers, and books.

Entertainment. The usual costs for entertaining clients, vendors, employees, and business associates should be listed here. Not to be included are unusual entertainment costs of the firm's executives, such as country club and dinner club memberships, etc.

Furniture and Equipment. This category includes costs of depreciation, equipment rental, and equipment repairs.

Insurance. This category includes insurance costs related to the company but not workmen's compensation or health and accident insurance, which is a separate item under payroll.

Legal and Audit. Fees paid to law firms and accounting firms which are necessary in conducting the firm's business are indicated in this category.

Office Expense. This catch-all category includes such things as secretarial supplies, materials used by the bookkeeping department, products needed in the coffee room, etc.

Postage. Postage, special messenger services, and costs of other mail carriers are noted here.

Printing. The cost for all printed matter other than advertising, such as forms, stationery, notices, etc., is classified in this account. (When the management company prints forms that are later to be charged back to the buildings based upon their usage, it may be a good idea to create a separate expense category for these kinds of printed materials.)

Rent. In addition to actual office space, this category also includes employee parking, space maintenance costs, and utilities.

Taxes and Licenses. Many municipalities charge businesses a license or tax for the privilege of operating. That cost would be identified here. This would not include real estate taxes (which should be charged under rent), or city, state, or federal income taxes, which are not considered a business operating cost.

Telephone. Telephone bills and the cost of answering services would be listed in this category.

Travel. This is for all costs of travel, food, and lodging for members of the firm while conducting the firm's business. (The amount employees are to be reimbursed usually is outlined under a travel policy in the policy and procedure manual.)

Duplication. All costs associated with the usage of duplicating and photocopying machines fall under this category.

The short chart of accounts form attempts to present the operating figures in a sequence more appropriate to the smaller management company. This form would be particularly adaptable for the company in which the chief executive officer is also the chief operating officer, manages some property himself, and spends some of his time in other real estate activities. The executive payroll category is eliminated; monies remaining after paying operating expenses are called executive compensation and profit. This does not include the time the chief executive officer spends as an active property manager. If he fills this role in addition to his other duties, a proper allocation of time and related costs should be made and charged to the property manager payroll. If this is not done, the figures will be distorted. Descriptions of the categories are similar to those that applied to the long form.

III

The Acquisition
of Business

9

The Marketing Plan

IN THE FINAL ANALYSIS, a company's ability to grow depends upon its commitment to marketing its services. As Edward S. McKay says in *The Marketing Mystique* (New York: American Management Association, Inc., 1972):

> Marketing is the only business function, with the possible exception of personnel, that continues to be everybody's province. The purpose of marketing is to direct all vision and efforts of the business toward marketing objectives, and to direct all vision and efforts of marketing toward the objectives of the business.

Marketing is a concept that encompasses identification of clients and client needs and coordination of business activities in order to meet those needs. When creating the company plan, the business is defined by determining the clients whose needs the company wants to satisfy. To coordinate its activities in order to meet these needs —to provide management service to those requiring it—a marketing plan must be prepared.

A marketing plan is a short-term business tool designed to generate profits by increasing property management business. The conditions for successful utilization of a marketing plan are (1) commitment from top management, (2) professional marketing leadership, (3) an appropriate trial period, and (4) an environment in which marketing is considered a critical factor in business success.

Without question, the marketing plan is the responsibility of a company's most talented, innovative thinker—the entrepreneurial executive-level manager. Because of the importance of personal con-

151

tact in the marketing of a service, few property management companies have specific marketing departments. Rather, the responsibility for marketing planning is assigned to the professional staff itself. Typically, the chief executive officer of the company assumes personal responsibility for the overall marketing effort. Not only does he have the ability to manage properties effectively but, equally important, he has the innovative skills to devise the marketing approach. However, inasmuch as marketing is an all-pervasive business activity, all professionals within the firm should be involved in planning the market effort. Consequently, the chief executive must work with a team of managers representing the key departments and draw from their expertise to contribute to the planning process.

Since almost all new real estate management business is generated from problem situations, the focus of a marketing effort is on the organization's capabilities to counsel, advise, and provide management expertise toward a sound resolution of a client's real estate investment problems. Since the provider of professional management service is basically a problem solver, the status of a property must be examined in depth to determine its real problems and eliminate those that are imaginary. Thus, a real estate management company markets an intangible—expertise, and its marketing plan must be designed to reflect this.

While marketing plans vary in format and complexity, a plan characteristically contains specific elements, namely the situation analysis, objectives, and strategy. The situation analysis represents the foundation of facts; it is the portion of the marketing plan that defines the company's market, describes its competitive and economic context, and defines its business position and capabilities. The statement of objectives is the quantitative portion of the plan; the objectives establish marketing targets against which the plan's effectiveness will be measured. Marketing strategy is at the creative heart of marketing; it represents a coming together of all the marketing variables and outlines a plan of action for meeting the objectives.

Marketing plays an important role in the business function, and creating a business environment that is marketing oriented rather than production oriented may require a host of employee programs and a great deal of time. Too often, the medium of communication for the marketing plan is an impressive notebook, widely distributed, announced with suitable fanfare, and properly filed in the company's archives. This, of course, does not work. Three steps are required to properly communicate a company's marketing plan.

The first step is to prepare a formal document that includes the previously described elements. The second step is to hold a meeting or series of meetings, with open discussion, to explain, clarify, and sell the concept. The final step is to circulate periodic follow-up publications and bulletins that continue to sell the program, report progress, and make necessary minor adjustments to it. In addition to the introductory program and regularly scheduled marketing management meetings, it may be useful to offer specialized courses or company workshops in marketing or even provide specialized, individual coaching from the more experienced marketing-oriented members of the firm. Hence, the necessity of a well-organized marketing plan may become evident, making the impact on business significant.

The creation of a marketing plan is a sequential process that begins with performing the situation analysis, proceeds to the establishment of objectives, and follows through with the development of applicable strategy. Thus, preparing a marketing plan requires executive management to systematically turn its attention to these considerations in succession.

Situation Analysis

For a property management company, performing a situation analysis calls for an investigation of the company's resources, its competitive advantage, and the opportunities that are available to it.

Appraising Resources

Defining a company's resources means taking a realistic appraisal of its three kinds of assets: people, reputation, and capital.

A broad spectrum of opportunity exists in the field of real estate management. The effective marketing plan correlates these opportunities with the capabilities and experience of the company's management team. Therefore, in evaluating the first asset—people—a practical-minded attitude needs to be adopted. Only an honest and objective appraisal alerts management to the kinds of situations its managers are incapable of handling and those with which its team is equipped to deal. An examination of not only the team's successes but also its failures is called for. A detailed analysis of all management accounts the company has attracted over the past five years, as well as those lost over the same period, is useful in identifying strengths and weaknesses. This requires an in-depth review of how clients were attracted to the office, who supervised those properties, and why any accounts were lost. If this data is compiled annually, market strategists may learn quickly and easily the company's merits and shortcomings.

Crucial to the evaluation of human resources is an examination of property managers in terms of their ability to handle more property. An ideal operating situation exists when property managers are operating at 90 percent of capacity. This permits new business to be added to the management portfolio and assimilated in an orderly fashion, free of immediate pressure to find new people to accommodate new business. If the manpower is not available to handle added business, the marketing strategy is useless. A simple example of a useless marketing strategy is one that calls for increasing a company's management portfolio of high-rise office buildings at a time when the company's capability to manage this kind of real estate rests with one individual whose time is fully committed. A better strategy would be for the company first to seek out new talent in the area of office building management in which it is understaffed and then advance its marketing services to accept professional responsibility in this area.

Similarly, the company's human resources need to be evaluated in terms of the amount of additional executive support required to supervise property managers who are added as the company's management portfolio increases. The company will be positioned for growth if its property manager job description includes the necessary criteria and if only persons who meet these criteria are hired. The property manager should have both an academic understanding of the principles of real estate management and a practical knowledge of its applications to real situations. Furthermore, by selecting and training managers to be entrepreneurs, the company can be assured of having the executive support needed to accommodate growth.

A key factor in marketing professional service is reputation and experience; therefore, the second asset that must be examined in preparation of writing the marketing plan is the company's public credentials. Investors look for management that has a good track record. They want to know the company's reputation for managing specific kinds of real estate and for handling specific kinds of problems. They want to know what its reputation is in terms of the kinds of properties it manages, the clients it attracts, its competitive rating, and its integrity.

A company's reputation can best be measured by input from clients, vendors, and the competition and by reviewing case histories of the performances of properties under its stewardship. If it is repeatedly successful in transforming poorly operated properties into those with high yields, its level of public esteem should be high.

The capital resources available to the company likewise need to be appraised and related to growth potential. Although real estate management is a low cash-intensity industry, the greater the amount of available capital, the greater the number of realistic options for growth. One rule-of-thumb cash requirement for the ongoing operation of a real estate management business is that it needs capital resources equal to approximately 125 percent of one month's gross management fees. Approximately one-half of this is needed for furniture and fixtures and the other half for working capital. If a firm, then, has $25,000 to $50,000 in excess of its working capital and furniture and fixture requirement available to it, it should be in a position to attract new kinds of business situations. For example, it could seek out options on properties it could syndicate and add to its management portfolio or it could purchase another management firm. With excess cash, say $300,000 to $400,000 beyond the requirement, the company could pursue the acquisition of fairly large established businesses. Therefore, the company's cash resources, or its ability to borrow cash, have a direct effect on its planning for growth.

Defining Competitive Advantage

The next stage in preparing a marketing plan is to define the company's competitive advantage. What does it do best, and what is best left to the competition? Again, an objective analysis that relates the company's three kinds of resources to the market place and determines in which markets it has the competitive edge is appropriate. The marketing plan is designed with this competitive advantage in mind. The ability to evaluate, analyze, and execute the marketing plan with foresight and finesse will demonstrate the firm's leadership and credibility in the business world. Or, to paraphrase football notable Vince Lombardi, the company should go to its strengths.

Defining the competitive advantage requires a realistic assessment of the company's composite knowledge and experience as well as familiarity of its competitor's qualifications. Which competitive business areas can be maximized in order that they might appear more attractive to clients? Can management identify vulnerable areas in the competition's management program that spell opportunity for the company?

The competitive advantage in real estate management is the quality of the service at a competitive price. For example, if several companies are being considered for the management and leasing of a 50-year-old, well-located, downtown office building, the competitive advantage will be with the company that is a specialist in remodeling older offices and leasing space in that specific market, has standard procedures for the efficient operation of that kind of investment, has a knowledge of sources for financing and experienced personnel who can be placed on the site, and so on.

Competitive advantage also involves knowing what changes are taking place in a particular market. Rent price, lease terms, rehabilitation allowances, changes in fire and safety code requirements for office layouts, availability of space—all are significant areas of knowledge that affect the ability to successfully compete with other management firms.

Identifying Opportunities

Why do some real estate management businesses prosper while others merely survive and still others fail? With few exceptions, an examination will reveal that the mere survivors and the casualties are lethargic and too readily embrace the status quo. They simply are not competitive. They resist change and lack innovation. They fail to take advantage of new opportunities. At best, they follow rather than lead their competitors and are usually too late to benefit from economic opportunities.

Armed with knowledge of the company's resources and competitive strengths and with relentless attention to economic change, management can construct a marketing plan that encompasses innovative ideas. Wherever the company operates, whatever the types of property it manages, whomever its clients—change is inevitable. Because it is influenced by so many elements within the national economy, the field of investment real estate is particularly susceptible to change. Demographics, interest rates, government influence and regulation, inflation and recession, supply and demand—all affect income properties and make them sensitive to change.

Managers have several alternatives available to them in dealing with change. One, change can be ignored. Those that follow this route, however, will leave, if not be forced out of, the field. Second, change can be studied as it occurs and the necessary adjustments made. Those that take this route probably will do little more than survive. Third, change can be anticipated. Managers who do this are the entrepreneurs who move ahead of the competition and become the industry's leaders. These are the managers who make things happen rather than allowing things to happen to them. A property manager easily can test his ability to recognize change and judge his reaction to it by, first, identifying five important changes that have occurred in the industry within the last five years, and second, honestly answering how these changes were met. Were changes properly anticipated and, if so, what was done about each of them? After all, anticipation without action is of little value.

As previously implied, the nature of property management is such that nearly all new management business is generated from problem situations. When the ownership of a property is experiencing a problem, it turns to the professional property manager and his advice and expertise to provide solutions. Opportunities for new business, then, rest in problem situations, and problems typically occur when there is economic change. Real estate is a cyclical business; consequently, business opportunities often occur in cyclical patterns. An examination of typical problem situations that occur in conjunction with changing economic developments may be valuable:

- New buildings. All new multitenant income properties are management opportunities inasmuch as the problems of merchandising vacant space and building a competent management program are present.
- Overfinanced properties. The well-rounded property manager is an asset manager and conversant with the fluctuations of the mortgage market. From time to time, management opportunities occur because poorly financed properties need professional help. Such situations can be corrected with refinancing and good management.
- Deferred maintenance. Probably the property manager's greatest opportunity to use his professional skills and create value is through rehabilitation of properties that have suffered from deferred maintenance. Such properties not only can be viewed as management opportunities but can be seen as sale or syndication opportunities as well.
- High vacancies or low rents. Inevitably in any real estate market, good or bad, properties suffering from the problem of either a too-high vacancy level or high occupancy but a too-low rent level can be found. A manager's ability not only to merchan-

dise space but also to set accurate, competitive rates creates an economic need for his services.

- Low-yield investment. Whenever an owner is receiving too low a yield on his investment, an opportunity awaits. Solutions here can be found in any of the fundamentals of management, such as raising rents, lowering vacancy, cutting operating costs, or refinancing.
- High operating costs. Rapid inflation has caused a new phenomenon in real estate: Even though a building may be operating at extremely high occupancy, operating costs, in some instances, are increasing faster than the market can afford. When utility costs, real estate taxes, insurance costs, and certain maintenance costs double in a period of three to four years, this causes a unique management problem and, consequently, unusual opportunity and challenge for real estate managers.

In addition to these problem situations, which present obvious opportunities for new business, opportunities may exist as a result of forms of ownership. For example, by their very nature, properties under a form of multiple ownership require management service. These can include large publicly-held limited partnerships, private placements of limited partnerships, real estate investment trusts, and pension funds. Certain public corporations that venture into real estate as a subsidiary activity usually need professional management, as do lender-owned properties, inasmuch as foreclosures by lenders, the U.S. Department of Housing and Urban Development, and receiverships all create management situations. In addition, increasingly popular substitutes for home ownership—specifically, condominium and cooperative ownership—create the opportunity for an agency management situation.

Marketing Objectives

Once the planners have done their homework—appraised the company's resources, defined its competitive advantage, and identified business opportunities—it is time to develop marketing objectives. Astute planning strategists know that continuous success is far more assured if it relies on systematic processing of selective opportunities rather than a scattered, shotgun-like approach. The essential task is to identify, evaluate, and select from all available opportunities those few new business activities that offer the greatest chance of success for the company. This is strategic planning: Screening and evaluating all of the opportunities and zeroing in on those on which the firm should concentrate its resources.

The primary criterion in developing a strategic plan for getting new business is to establish objectives with target performance specifications. In order for any plan to be useful, it must have objectives that include quantitative specifications. Marketing objectives always should include dates by which they are to be accomplished. In addition, objectives should include specifications as to the size and rate of growth that is to be realized. Growth for a property management company can be measured in several different forms, each of which can be quantitatively defined. Several popular methods of setting targets in the property management industry involve monthly gross fees, staff size, establishment of branch offices, and profit margin.

One form of measurement that may be used in setting objectives is the amount of gross fees per month that should be achieved by a certain date. When using gross fees as a quantitative indicator, planners should consider the company's minimum fee for providing monthly management services to a particular property. Another unit of measurement is the monthly fee per unit that is required in order to reach the desired target.

Similarly, staff size may be used as an indicator in setting marketing objectives. This calls for a determination of how many people the existing executive talent can supervise. The executive of a real estate management company is responsible for supervision of property managers and on-site managers associated with properties under his personal direction. A common temptation for entrepreneurial managers in growing companies is to accept additional business without proper planning for the continued executive supervision of the existing properties in the management portfolio. Eager to grow, the entrepreneurial executive becomes too heavily involved in the problems of the newly acquired accounts and lessens his attention to established smoothly operating accounts where the day-to-day management is performed by resident managers. Any new business plan must provide for the leadership needed to properly service the entire portfolio—ongoing as well as new accounts—and take into consideration adequate accounting, secretarial, and property manager support.

Establishment of branch offices may be used as a growth target. With the ease of travel today, it is practical for many property management companies to consider branch units in either outlying areas or other cities. Planners may want to include the establishment of branch units in their expansion plans. In this event, they need to use several measurements—including gross fees and the number of people—to define goals and aspirations.

Net cash flow is a prime measurement of marketing performance. Growth without profit is ridiculous. All too often large full-service real estate companies use property management departments as loss leaders. They are willing to accept management business at fees that do not produce a profit, and sometimes even at a loss, in order to have an opportunity for allied services that often result from managing a client's property. The real estate management industry has become too sophisticated to accommodate these types of operations. In addition, there is considerable risk in assuming the management of someone's real estate investment. A long-range plan that provides for growth without increased profits is a bad plan. A realistic objective is to have a pre-tax profit of 15 percent of gross revenue.

Marketing Strategy

The third step in the sequential marketing planning process is the establishment of marketing strategy. This is the part of the plan in which specific action, designed to meet the marketing objectives, is outlined. Generally, there are three areas of consideration that demand strategic planning: the management service itself, the promotional program, and the pricing system.

Continuous development, upgrading, and changing of the management service being offered by a firm is crucial to company growth. Therefore, it is important that the marketing plan outlines strategy that defines the kind of service the company is selling. For instance, if a marketing objective is to obtain a specified number of condominium management accounts, strategy should outline the method by which the company could provide a premium service and thus capitalize on this specific area of the market.

Promotional strategy revolves around the way the property management firm's service is offered for sale. Incorporated into this strategy would be public relations, advertising programs, and personal selling techniques. (Promotional strategy is discussed in greater detail in chapter 10.)

Pricing strategy relates to the way in which market value is assigned to the property management service that is offered. Price is a major determinant of the market demand for property management service; as such, it has an effect on the firm's competitive position and, subsequently, the company's profit. (The pricing of property management service is elaborated on in chapter 11.)

10

New-Business Development

No SINGLE STRATEGY FOR MARKETING property management service can be applied to the real estate management industry in every city in the United States. Because of variables in customs, practices, ownership records, and methods of communication, effective methods of solicitation vary from community to community. For instance, a direct mail program may be quite successful in Los Angeles, where accurate ownership records are easily obtainable, yet would be difficult to implement in Phoenix, where the necessary information is not available. Radio and television advertising has proven successful in certain Texas cities, yet this kind of advertising would be cost-prohibitive in Chicago.

Despite regional differences, however, at least two fundamental principles should be considered during the development of any business-solicitation program. The first rule is that company executives must encounter, as often as possible, on a one-to-one basis those people who are or could be owners of income properties and consequently may require the services of a property manager. To prove the validity of heeding this principle, a property manager need only examine how he was introduced to existing clients. Chances are he will discover that most introductions occurred through other clients, friends, business associates, members of service clubs and organizations, or other members of the real estate profession or resulted from other previously existing personal relationships. If personal contact was the primary means of meeting clients in the past, it can be assumed that personal relationships will lead to introductions with potential clients in the future.

The second principle is that management must have an effective means of gathering information about the market. By way of illustration, consider the fact that one of the best ways of developing new business is through direct solicitation. Whether solicitation is performed in a methodical fashion or is an uncontrolled expensive use of time depends largely on the data with which a property manager is armed. For instance, it is important for the property manager making a solicitation to speak with a person who is in a decision-making position and represents the ownership of a property needing management service. Management executives cannot afford the time to gather this kind of information regarding property ownership. An intelligence-gathering system is needed to assist it in identifying problem properties and the responsible representatives of ownership.

An effective intelligence system gathers and processes pertinent information about owners, properties, competitors, lenders, architects, accountants, absentee owners, developers, mortgage bankers, presidents of condominium associations, and anyone else in any way related to the real estate profession. The assistance of every member of the firm should be enlisted to gather this information. Some of the more obvious sources of data are articles in the real estate sections of newspapers, ownership lists available for purchase, information received from vendors, neighborhood information reported by resident managers, etc.

The responsibility for overseeing this marketing intelligence system should be assigned to a single person or entity, maybe one of the firm's property managers. Uncoordinated, scattered bits and pieces of information are not sufficient for executing the marketing strategy. Rather, these pieces of information must be coordinated, analyzed, communicated, used or stored as needed, and related to the total organization's marketing efforts.

It takes time to establish a good intelligence system and implement it for an efficient operation. However, its value grows with time as ownership and operating problems of various properties are documented. In the long run, such a system will realize a payoff through effective and efficient use of top management talent in developing new business opportunities.

Public Relations

The term "public relations" here means the various activities undertaken by a company to improve its public image and thereby achieve its marketing objectives. To be effective, a public relations program needs to be a coordinated effort designed to achieve certain well-defined objectives. Here again, the task of planning and organizing falls to the executives of the firm.

Few real estate management firms have effective public relations programs. Top managers lack the time, ability, and image sensitivity to conceive and direct such a program. Since this responsibility cannot be delegated to someone unfamiliar with any of the facets of operation, and since few firms have budgets that permit them to hire competent public relations assistance, few public relations programs get off the ground. Typically what happens is that top management sporadically gives attention to some single aspect of a public relations effort but seldom thinks in terms of an overall program that requires planning, organizing, directing, and controlling. For example, the chief executive officer may give a talk to an interested audience or place a news story about a recent company achievement but provide no means of follow up. When such an effort is fragmented, so are the results.

If the top management of a firm is serious in its desire to establish a public relations program to promote the company and the services it offers, a commitment of time for planning, organizing, and implementing is necessary. Having made the time commitment, management then can direct its attention to establishing an operating public relations policy. This policy should address two elements: the various publics to whom the program should be directed, and the image that is to be portrayed.

Property management deals primarily with five groups of people —clients, industry, community, suppliers, and tenants—and must establish good relations with all of them. (See figure 10.1.) Industry relations involves the interaction of a given property management company with other companies in the real estate industry. This might include participation in professional organizations and related activities. Community relations links the activities of a management firm to the city or neighborhood of which it is a part. A community relations program might include, for example, assisting in chamber of commerce programs, monitoring local planning committees, or providing assistance to educational establishments. Supplier relations is concerned with creating a harmonious, mutually beneficial relationship with those who provide the goods and services required by a management company. Tenant relations is concerned with creating a pleasant, safe place for people to live or work.

But of all of the relationships, the one established between a management company and its clients is the most crucial to the marketing program. More important than getting new business is keeping existing business. Furthermore, satisfied clients often become important sources of new business leads. To these ends, a major part of a company's public relations policy must be its client relations program.

As a rule, the general objectives of a client relations program are these:

1. To communicate effectively with the client.
2. To assure that the company is aware of the client's goals.

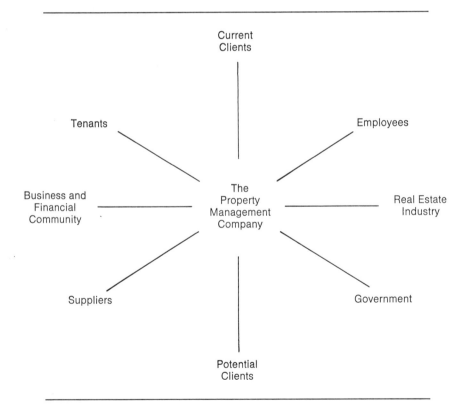

Figure 10.1. Representation of the various publics with which a property management company must establish solid relations.

3. To meet the client's goals and, in the event those goals are not obtainable, recommend alternate courses of action.

The importance of understanding a client's objectives in the ownership of real estate cannot be overemphasized. Owner objectives are key considerations in creating a management plan for a property and subsequently are basic to maintaining good rapport with the client. The company's public relations strategy should include having an officer of the company meet with each client at least once a year to review his goals and objectives and determine if the asset management plan for the property is consistent with them. Having reached an understanding, a management plan for the next year can be prepared for the client's review and approval.

Each client likewise should receive a monthly letter accompanying his financial statement. This letter should report the operating experience of the property and explain any noteworthy items or variances from the management plan. Occasional telephone communication also is needed. This is necessary to keep the client fully and personally informed on what is happening at his property and allow the property manager to be kept current on the client's wishes and objectives.

Apart from this obvious need to keep each client well informed, a client relations program also should include such details as promptly responding to clients' requests for information and offering polite, friendly service at all times. For the company that has adopted a marketing orientation that permeates the entire operation, this kind of attitude will come naturally.

Having identified these relationships, management must determine how it wants to be characterized to the public as a whole and what image it wants to portray. Is it a liberal organization or one characterized by conservatism? How can the company's talent best be described: innovative, strong-willed, cautious, experienced? Sometimes the most important single element of the program comes about through identification of the organization's personality. The creation of personality ranges from the design of the company's logo to the decorations and furnishings of the office to the way property managers, secretaries, and receptionists greet people and respond to tenant and client problems or concerns. Furthermore, creating and maintaining a company personality must be a never-ending operation if it is to continuously reflect the company that changes in response to changes in the economic environment.

Based upon its examination of the various kinds of public relations programs it needs and the image it wants to present, a company is postured to construct a public relations plan. In effect, this is a series of programs for each of its publics, all directed toward the central theme of heightening the public's esteem for the company. Some of the specific communication vehicles that can be used in a real estate management company's public relations program are discussed herein.

Press Releases

A steady flow of news releases to the local press can be one of the most important and effective methods of obtaining a good public image and attracting prospective clients. Most people believe what they read in news columns. If a positive image of the company is portrayed in the news, would-be clients are likely to feel confident that the company is worthy of their management business.

Press releases can take many forms, some of which are these:

- Announcements of new management assignments. The story should identify the client and the property and note its size and gross value.
- Announcements of achievements—awards, promotions, special activities—to members of the firm or the firm itself.
- Special features, including authoritative articles and interviews by management executives on specific topics. These might include management techniques, trends, or problems in the industry. An article on a timely issue, such as rent control or energy conservation, can be especially effective.
- Community service announcements of lectures to be presented, meetings scheduled, or appointments to service positions.
- Tenant features using the borrowed-interest concept to mention the company in relation to one of its major tenants or a tenant activity.
- Features about a specific property. News stories related to the marketing or rehabilitation of a property, for instance, can call attention to a company's accomplishments.
- Announcements of new personnel, the opening of a new office, the offering of new service, etc.

Speaking Engagements

Speaking to the public is another viable means of increasing visibility. There are many opportunities to speak before the public, such as:

- Teaching real estate management courses at local colleges or universities.
- Speaking before trade associations. Real estate boards, mortgage bankers and home builders organizations, appraiser societies, and apartment associations are but a few of the associations that often are in need of speakers.
- Participating in special local seminars at which a professional property manager's input is a major part of the program.

Special Events

Holding special events is another means of improving the various relationships a property management company has. These events should be considered:

- Christmas parties for clients, vendors, and employees. Parties may be held either for the entire management company or for each site.
- Dinner meetings for resident managers of major projects. Such an event would be ideal to enlist their support in developing new business leads.
- Golf tournaments or other outdoor activities for clients, business friends, property managers, etc.
- Special openings and tours of unusual projects under the company's management.

Business Newsletter

One very effective way of keeping a company's name before prospective clients and establishing a reputation as a knowledgeable firm is through the publication of a business newsletter. A two- or four-page letter can describe various operating problems that can afflict income properties, discuss taxation or financing opportunities available to property owners, and provide general information about the real estate industry, all while discussing the company's abilities and activities. The drawback of this form of public relations lies in its preparation. Publishing a good newsletter requires time and talent not normally found among property managers. As a result, few of the companies that start newsletters continue them. However, when published on a regular basis, business newsletters can be effective in communicating with prospective clients.

Advertising

A marketing strategy plan for a real estate management company should include advertising. There is a fundamental difference between public relations and advertising: Public relations, which is not paid for, maintains good relations between the public and the company; advertising, on the other hand, involves paid announcements persuading the public to purchase property management service. The amount of dollars committed to advertising and promoting a company's services typically is one to two percent of gross management fees earned for larger firms and up to five percent of gross fees for smaller firms. Because few property management firms can afford large advertising budgets, it becomes even more important that the paid advertising program be carefully thought out to ensure that the promotional material reaches the largest possible number of prospects. The following list of sources of advertising is arranged in order of importance.

Signage

One of the most visible and effective means of advertising is placement of a tasteful but noticeable sign on every property the company manages, indicating that the building is managed by the named property management company. Such a sign should be placed on the property's street side so that it will be visible to pedestrian and vehicular traffic. It should not be placed near the entrance to the building, where it would be a distraction. Rather, the recommended location is at one of the building's corners, even with the top of the first floor window. Furthermore, a sign should be no more than 18 by 24 inches—a larger sign would be a detraction—and should be harmonious with the building on which it is placed.

Company Brochure

Oftentimes, prospective clients ask for information about the company. A company brochure that lists the services provided, the principals involved, and the company's qualifications as a manager of real estate investments can be an effective response. There is a risk inherent in using brochures, however, and the risk involves timeliness. Because of changes in a management company's personnel and clients, brochures that use pictures of personnel, properties, and client references can become quickly outdated. Furthermore, only a relatively small number of prospective clients will have any interest in

reading a brochure. For both of these reasons, an expensively produced company brochure is not necessarily a prudent use of a company's advertising dollars.

Nonetheless, a company does need some kind of promotional
piece to give to interested prospective clients. In lieu of a costly brochure, a carefully prepared three- to four-page letter may be used.
This letter should be general enough to be applicable to all prospective clients and be reviewed annually to ensure currentness and
presentation of the company in a timely fashion. This letter may be
given graphic appeal and substance by including with it brochures
or photographs of properties currently managed, copies of professional articles written by principals of the company, copies of news
stories pertaining to the company, or any other materials that will
help the reader understand the qualifications of the company as a
property management agent.

Direct Mail Promotion

Direct mail has become recognized as a valuable form of advertising
for professional service companies. This is because direct mail enables management to accurately direct its message to a target audience. If a company maintains an accurate list of names and addresses
of owners of properties compatible with its management portfolio, a
direct mail program can be effective. Developing such a list may be
difficult but can be done if contact with all the sources with whom
the firm has business dealings is maintained and the appropriate
records kept over an extended period of time.

Management should keep in mind that the primary purpose of
a direct mail program is to attract the attention of landlords whose
properties are experiencing operational problems. A good level of
response to a direct mail campaign is one to two percent. A direct
mail piece seldom will obtain new management accounts immediately
upon receipt, but it can put the company's name before prospective
clients. Thus, when they do experience operational problems, they
may contact the company.

A mailing piece need not be expensive. The requirements are
that it be done in good taste and that it carry an appropriate, atten-
tion-getting message. The piece must be sufficiently intriguing to
ensure that it will not be discarded as junk mail and carry a message
that will whet the interest of a potential client. Furthermore, in order
to be effective, direct mailings must be made on a regular basis.
Sending constant reminders that a company can provide professional

management services is critical to making the kind of impact that leads to new business.

Yellow Pages
Every management company should have its name prominently displayed in the real estate management section of the local telephone directory's yellow pages. While it would be unusual for a property owner to use the yellow pages as a primary source for finding a property manager, the directory is a logical place to look when an owner remembers a managing agent's name but forgets the address or telephone number.

Media Advertising
Some firms use institutional advertising in local and national newspapers and magazines to put their names before the public. Often an advertisement of approximately three by four inches is used to state the name of the company and its services or announce the acquisition of a new management account. It must be remembered that one-time advertisements are of very little value. Advertising must have continuity over a reasonable period of time if an image is to be created.

Sales Presentations

Although delivery techniques and personality are highly individual, all successful sales presentations bear common characteristics. This text does not propose to tell a property manager how to make a sales presentation. Rather, the concern here is management's responsibility in organizing, directing, and controlling the sales presentation effort. The following outline can serve as a guide in meeting this responsibility as it relates to locating prospects, pursuing leads, and making sales presentations.

1. Locate a prospect through direct mail program, referral, direct inquiry, neighborhood survey, etc.
2. Identify by name the responsible person who represents ownership and is authorized to make a decision.
3. Decide on the best approach for the initial introduction: phone, letter, or personal visit.
4. Meet with the prospective client to learn his problems and concerns and tell him of the company's capabilities.
5. Visit the property and its neighborhood to gain a better understanding of its operation.

6. Having determined what level of analysis is warranted currently, prepare a written proposal, with an outline of the management plan, and submit it to the potential client.
7. Meet again with the prospective client to discuss the proposal; have a proposed management contract ready for execution.
8. After an appropriate length of time, follow up on the prospective account.
9. If not successful in obtaining the account, find out why.

All steps beyond step two require the personal attention of a property manager functioning as a salesman. While a property management company needs an advertising and public relations program to attract clients, the marketing effort will be ineffective if property managers lack the personal skills of making presentations and salesmanship.

A key step is step four. Its principal objective is to learn why the prospective client is considering agency management and what his investment goals are. In searching for this information, the salesman must ask probing questions while simultaneously explaining the company's capabilities. It is important to focus on the prospect's areas of concern and not use valuable time discussing nonrelated subjects. Only after the salesman has determined the prospect's needs will he be in a position to tell the prospect why he should purchase management service from his company. Furthermore, the salesman should make his presentation on a level that is compatible with the listener's state of knowledge. A presentation that erroneously judges the client's knowledge level and is either above him or below him is very likely to fail.

The salesman of property management services is at a slight disadvantage in making a presentation: He has nothing tangible to show or demonstrate. However, a property manager can be equipped with visual aids. These aids should show the outcome of the company's services as applied to various problem properties. A looseleaf notebook, outlining main topics of conversation with supportive pictures, graphs, or charts, illustrates the sales presentation as well as provides it with a structured format. Naturally, if a presentation notebook is used, it should be professionally prepared. Other supportive aids might include sample copies of management plans, the company's typical operating statement, a list of client and bank references, the company brochure, and reprints of articles from professional journals written by members of the firm.

Throughout the presentation, the property manager must exude an air of confidence in himself and his company. The would-be client must be given a guarantee that the company can provide the services he needs and that professionals will be assigned to operate his property. The feeling of uncertainty that invariably plagues a prospective client must be reduced and replaced with assurance that the problem has been understood and can be solved.

11

Management Pricing and
Contract Negotiation

Establishing the price of property management service is a part of marketing management that demands special attention. Assuming that maintaining a certain level of profit is the chief goal of a business, the price must be accurate if this profit is to be realized. This holds true both if the price of management service is set too high and if it is too low. It is obvious that when the price is too low, the profit margin is narrowed. Likewise, it generally is true that when the price is too high, a reduction in the number of management accounts will be noticed. It becomes important, then, that property management executives understand both theoretically and practically how the company's services should be priced.

Basically, there are two pricing concepts: that of the economist and that of the businessman. The economist's concept of pricing is theoretical in nature. It encompasses the theories of demand, marginal analysis, profit goal, and average cost. The businessman's concept is practical in nature. It encompasses experience, intuition, and cost-plus. The astute entrepreneur's concept of pricing lies somewhere between the two: He is aware of the theories espoused by the economist while remaining sensitive to the experiential knowledge of the businessman. Above all, he has a tested method for determining the price of his service.

Although property managers generally are eager to discuss management fees with their peers, such discussion usually is academic. One reason is the federal government's recent position that discussion about fees among members of real estate associations is in violation of the Sherman Antitrust Act. Another reason is that real estate management fees do not have a common denominator. While fees for other services in the real estate industry (brokerage, leasing, placement of mortgages, sale of land, etc.) are easily learned, real estate management fees are, in the final analysis, fixed by negotiation between agent and owner. The fee depends upon the level of service offered, the term of the contract, and the amount of work that will be required of the agent. While it is common practice to quote management fees in terms of a percentage of gross collections, the entrepreneurial manager performs considerable analysis before he arrives at the proper percentage figure for a given property.

Pricing Strategy

Pricing of property management service cannot be totally determined by statistical analysis of certain factors. An element of strategy—reacting to potential clients and their needs—must be present. However, every pricing plan must include serious consideration of certain elements, discussion of which follows.

Level of Service

In all service professions there are different levels of competence. A law firm may offer the services of recently graduated attorneys at less than half the hourly rate of its experienced specialists. Accounting firms may charge varying rates for varying degrees of expertise. So should it be with property management firms.

The consideration here should lie with the level of service sought by the would-be client and, subsequently, the level of experience needed to provide that kind of service. Not all clients seek the same level of property management service. Some owners want full asset management, while others want little more than assistance in managing their buildings. Having determined this level, the pricing strategist then must ask himself: What level of experience is needed to perform this job? Will it initially require a few hours of a senior partner's time to help establish the management plan and then only periodic review, or is this a difficult situation that will demand a senior partner's full attention for an extended period of time? Likewise, the amount of time a property manager will need to set aside for owner communication and meetings is worth discussing in advance of setting a price. For example, if the property is a condominium, how many association meetings will management be expected to attend? How often will management be expected to report to the association president? As all experienced property managers certainly have learned, it sometimes takes more time to establish owner rapport than it does to manage his property. Thus, when analyzing this factor, the pricing strategist should determine, as accurately as possible:

1. The level and degree of service required by the property owner.
2. The level of property management expertise required to meet the owner's demands.
3. The amount of work (time) required at the property because of its size and management problems.
4. The amount of time required for the owner personally.

Length of Contract

Since the property manager typically charges for his services by the month, he often is exposed to an imbalanced situation relative to his hourly rate. The time commitment to initiate a new property management account, formulate a management plan, and implement the plan is considerably greater than the time commitment necessary to maintain and fine tune an ongoing management situation. Thus, he consistently will be underpaid at the beginning of a new management assignment. For this reason, the manager wants to receive a commitment from the owner of sufficient term that it will enable management to average out its time. Failing to receive a term contract should result in a change in the pricing structure. The manager will need to negotiate for either a higher monthly fee, a start-up fee, or some extra consideration for the heavy time commitment required during the early months of the contract.

Accessibility of the Property

In the final analysis, what a property manager is selling is time. In determining the time demand, he must not fail to give some consideration to the time, as well as direct travel expenses, required to visit the property. If a property is large, the travel time consideration lessens in importance. Managing smaller properties can be quite costly if they are far removed from other properties under the company's management. Conversely, with the flexibility available in airplane schedules, it can be feasible for a company to manage projects that will support monthly fees of $2,000 or more in cities as far as 600 miles from the company's home base.

Management Costs

Knowing the costs of running the management company is fundamental to assigning an accurate price for service. Property managers generally are well informed about costs of operating properties but poorly informed about the cost accounting statistics of operating their own businesses. They can quote unit or per-square-foot costs for utilities, real estate taxes, janitor service, vacancy factors, and even debt service but do not know their per-unit bookkeeping cost, percent-of-gross secretarial costs, or per-employee cost for benefits.

In accounting terminology, cost refers to any expenditure of money, goods, or services for the purpose of acquiring goods or services. Ignorance of actual costs and consequent use of traditional percentage-fee bidding can result in either lost business opportunities because bids are too high or unprofitable business gains because costs are not covered. Either way, the effect can be disastrous. The solution is to implement a cost accounting system that analyzes all of a firm's costs, allocates them to specific functions, and determines just what can be attributed to specific properties. Although the presence of competition in the free enterprise system demands some flexibility in pricing, costs should be regarded as an indication of whether the price a client is willing to pay warrants engaging his account. Accurately and fairly pricing management service requires the same depth of informed judgment as is required for pricing any other service or product in a free market. It cannot be done by guess or industry norms but depends on facts. If the costs are not covered, there will be no profit.

A critical cost consideration when setting the price for providing management service to a particular property is the determination of who—property owner or agent—will be obligated for on-site manager and other on-site personnel costs. For most apartment complexes this clearly is the financial responsibility of the owner. However, custom is less traditional in the management of office buildings, condominiums, shopping centers, excessively large apartment projects, and multi-use complexes. Who is responsible for these payroll costs, as well as for providing the necessary supportive utilities and services, greatly affects the price. (Chapter 8 explains at length the various operating costs of a real estate management business and should be reviewed prior to determining fees for providing management service.)

Fee Structure

Having arrived at a fair and accurate price for providing management service, the property manager must select the most appropriate method of quoting that price to a would-be client. The four accepted methods are based on: (1) a percentage of gross collections, (2) a fixed fee, (3) a minimum fee, and (4) an incentive fee.

Percentage of Gross Collections

The most common method of quoting fees is the system whereby the managing agent will receive a fixed percentage of the monthly gross collections. Inherent in this system is an incentive pay opportunity: The greater the monies collected on behalf of the owner, the larger the manager's fee. Conversely, delinquent rents, vacancies, and other loss of income lower the agent's fee.

Gross collections usually are defined as all monies paid by tenants less refunds to tenants of security deposits and other advance fees. Gross collections normally do not include monies paid by insurance companies for casualty or fire losses, reimbursements by tenants for their share of the cost of improvements to their spaces or specific maintenance, or income that results from real estate rent increases due to tax escalation clauses. It is customary, however, for the agent to receive his normal percentage on rent increases due to operating escalation clauses.

Flat Fee

In many cases, rather than the more common percentage of gross collections, the agent and the owner agree to a fixed monthly fee in exchange for management service. This system is most popular with condominium and cooperative properties. Here, it is important for the manager to have a clear written understanding as to what services are included and a provision that additional work will be met with additional charges. For instance, extra charges in condominium management could arise in the bookkeeping department from changes of ownership of individual units, attending extra association meetings (usually the charge is on a per hour or per meeting rate), handling special mailings or providing photocopying service, or supervising major repairs or rehabilitation projects.

A flat-fee contract should provide for an annual fee adjustment based upon an increase or decrease in the cost of living for the locale.

This avoids the sometimes ticklish problem of renegotiating the fee each year and serves as a hedge against inflation.

Minimum Fee

Regardless of the basis of the rate, every management company should operate under a system whereby no property management account will be handled for less than a predetermined minimum fee. Prudent operators constantly are aware of this minimum so that the firm does not get in a position of providing management services to properties at a loss. The minimum fee is determined on an individual company basis and is dependent on internal bookkeeping procedures and size and location of the accounts; e.g., a company whose management portfolio is mostly widely dispersed apartment complexes will have a higher minimum fee requirement than the firm that customarily manages closely arranged properties.

Incentive Fee

Often an entrepreneurial property owner requests a fee structure that provides the manager with reimbursement of costs plus an incentive for outstanding results. Incentive fee arrangements based upon gross results, such as percentage of occupancy or gross collections, are easy to define and calculate. However, any incentive fee arrangement based upon net results, such as net operating income, cash flow, or increase in property value, must be analyzed carefully.

There are broad guidelines for establishing an incentive fee structure based upon net results. When an incentive fee is based upon net operating income, the property manager must remember that he will be in a position to risk all of his profit. To counterbalance this risk, he should be guaranteed that, if he reaches a realistic, obtainable goal, he will be given the opportunity to earn several times this profit through the incentive fee. An incentive fee determined by cash flow is based on the manager receiving a percentage of all cash flow over a predetermined return to the property owner. Six to eight percent return on invested capital generally is considered quite acceptable. In most cases, a property manager operating under this fee structure receives 25 percent of cash flow after this return requirement is satisfied. Under an appreciation-in-value incentive fee system, a manager receives a certain percentage of all cash realized from the refinancing or sale of a property after the investor has received return of his original capital investment plus a cumulative return of six to eight percent. Generally, an incentive fee is 15 percent of cash realized in excess of this minimum.

Management Agreement

The employment of a management company to assume responsibility for the operation of a real estate investment and the assumption of those responsibilities by the agent are of significant importance to require a management agreement. A written contract is in the best interest of both the owner and the agent, regardless of the size of the property involved or the length of the arrangement. The primary purpose of any written agreement is to avoid misunderstandings. With a contract, it becomes unnecessary for the parties to remember what was agreed to. The understanding is properly established in writing, and a basis for settling any disputes that may arise between the agent and the owner is provided.

Other factors support the theory of having a written agreement. An operative English statute called "frauds" prohibits an agent from signing contracts, including leases, for more than a one-year term without a written agreement from the owner. The written and signed management agreement can bypass this problem. A written agreement also can provide a list of the items that need to be agreed to prior to entering a property management arrangement. If the parties use the agreement as a checklist and review it point by point, there should be a complete understanding of the business relationship and mutual responsibilities when the manager starts managing the property.

Managers' and owners' obligations quite often are complex. The contract, spelling out the agreements of the parties, avoids any misunderstanding as to these obligations. (The management agreement developed by the Institute of Real Estate Management appears as figure A.10 in the appendix of this text.) After the property manager and client have reviewed in detail the requirements of the property and the owner, these understandings should be committed to writing via the management agreement. The agreement should cover certain topics, a discussion of which follows.

Length of Contract

The term of the agreement between the property manager and the owner is dependent upon many factors. The primary consideration in determining the length of term should be the amount of time needed by the property management company to accomplish any agreed upon goals and realize a fair profit for its services.

It is usually in the agent's best interest for the term of the contract to be for as long a period of time as can be negotiated. As mentioned previously, the agent must have sufficient guarantee that the time-consuming activities involved in the takeover of the account will be justified.

Most owners will not object to long-term arrangements. Rather, an owner's concern usually is how he can terminate an agreement should the agent not fulfill his expectations. It is usually in the owner's best interest for the term to be one that can be cancelled for nonperformance on 30 days' notice. The primary problem here lies with the difficulty in agreeing to a definition of nonperformance. Typically, the agent feels that cancellation should be for gross negligence or failure to live up to his obligations as listed in the agreement. The owner, on the other hand, considers this a difficult set of criteria, since, in the final analysis, it may be necessary to seek a court interpretation of the contract in order to decide whether or not the agent has lived up to its responsibilities. Any yardstick other than a quantitative one is difficult to live with. One possible solution is to tie the management agent's performance to a specific net operating income amount. As long as the agent produces net operating income equal to or in excess of this amount, it can be deemed that he is performing satisfactorily. Contracts that are written for several years could provide for escalation of the net operating income amount based on the Consumer Price Index or some other inflation index.

Contracts that are not backed up by the good faith and cooperation of both parties are often difficult to live with. For this reason it is common to have a contract for a base period in which to accomplish certain goals and after which it reverts to a month-to-month agreement. In some cases, a property manager may prefer to be relieved of responsibility rather than continue a difficult working relationship.

Parties to the Agreement

All owners of a property must be named in the agreement, and the agreement must be executed by all owners or their authorized agent. If title to the property is held by a corporation, the agreement should be executed by the authorized corporate officers.

In identifying the property management company, the name of the company, not the name of the chief executive officer or the property manager who will handle the account, should be named.

Commencement Date

The contract must include a date for commencement and termination of services. In certain situations, such as when buildings are being constructed, the commencement date may be identified with the happening of some event. This could be tied with the date upon which a certificate of occupancy is obtained from the local building department, the first tenant moves in, or a certain phase of construction is completed. In any event, it is necessary to have an exact date for the agent's responsibilities to begin.

Property Description

A complete description of the property should be included in the agreement. Identification by specific address is adequate. If the property has a name, as is often the case with larger apartment complexes, office buildings, and shopping centers, this also should be used.

Authority To Sign Commitments

A clause pertaining to the managing agent's authority to negotiate and execute leases and other contracts is needed in the management agreement. Precise and specific instructions in this area are imperative. If the property manager is to execute leases on behalf of the owner, the maximum length of term of those leases must be stated. Customary standards in the industry provide for the property manager to have authority to sign apartment leases for up to three-year terms (although terms beyond one year are uncommon) and office building and commercial property leases for up to five-year terms. In cases of tenants requesting longer terms, the owner would be called upon to approve and sign the leases.

Likewise, the authority of the property manager to execute all types of maintenance and service contracts for the property should be given clearly in the agreement. Usually, however, the agent's authority to commit to these and other kinds of contracts is not authorized beyond a one-year term.

One reason for requiring this written authority harkens back to the statute of frauds. Under this statute, a lease signed by the agent for a term in excess of the limitation may be subject to becoming void. Still, if a property manager is to be held liable for the operation of a property, he must be given the authority to select, within the law, tenants he considers desirable. Likewise, he needs the authority to cancel leases, take legal steps to collect delinquent rent, or perform any action the owner would be able to perform if he were managing the property himself.

Authority To Incur Expenses

Precise instructions regarding the specific amount of money a property manager may spend in connection with certain maintenance repairs and operations of the property is imperative. It must be clearly understood by both parties exactly how far the agent may go before communicating with the owner. Such a limitation should not be perceived as an expression of lack of confidence or a restriction of the agent's ability to perform. Rather, it should be regarded as a viable means for the owner to maintain broad control of his investment and feel that his investment is secure while simultaneously protecting the agent.

This is not to imply that a property manager does not need some kind of additional personal protection in case of an emergency when the owner is not available for consultation or to make an immediate decision in a situation that would require an expense in excess of the limitation. While the property manager has an implied responsibility to take reasonable action in the event of an emergency, especially one that threatens the safety of the property or its occupants, it is best that a provision clearly giving him emergency powers be included in the management agreement.

Advertising

The management agreement should state who is responsible for paying for advertising and promotional efforts related to the property. Most property managers feel that the cost of advertising premises for rent is an operating expense and therefore should be absorbed by the property. If the property manager is given the authority to contract for advertising at the owner's expense, the agreement should state the maximum amount that can be spent during a given period of time without owner approval. This advertising limitation should go far in reassuring the owner that his money will not be spent frivolously.

Indemnification

A hold harmless clause, or indemnification clause, within a management agreement states that the property manager cannot be held responsible for any liability over which he has no control. In this respect, the agreement should require that the property owner who has retained the services of the management agency must maintain an insurance policy covering general liability for bodily injury and property damage. Furthermore, the property manager should be named as an additional insured, although both probably will be named automatically inasmuch as it is better to have the insurance company defending all defendants should the unfortunate need arise.

Insurance

Insurance is needed for the protection of any piece of real estate. A clause that assigns the responsibility for procuring proper insurance coverage and paying the premiums is needed in the contract. If this is to be the owner's responsibility, it should be clearly stated. In such a case, the agent may request that he be allowed to review the coverage to determine its adequacy and make any recommendations he feels are necessary to improve it. If obtaining and maintaining coverage is to be the agent's responsibility, guidelines should be given.

Bank Account

A good management company policy is a requirement that each management agreement the company negotiates contains a clause indicating that there will be no commingling of the funds of the agency and property owner. In fact, most local and state regulatory bodies prohibit commingling of these funds. The clause should state that the funds collected by the agency will be placed in a commercial bank in a trustee account, client account, or some similar account as the owner may direct. These funds are to be the sole property of the owner, not the property manager.

The purpose of having such a clause is as a protection in the event of a failure of the bank in which funds have been placed. This could be disastrous if the amount on deposit exceeds the amount under the protection of federal deposit insurance. Maintaining separate accounts helps guard against the probability of ever having such a large single account. As added protection, the clause also should provide that the agent will not be held liable in the event of failure of a depository.

Employees

A management agreement must have a clause concerning on-site employees. It should provide that any employees needed for the operation of the property will be under the control of the management agent while simultaneously stating that, for compensation purposes, they are employees of the property owner. While management wants authority to hire, fire, train, and supervise on-site employees, the owner must realize that they are compensated from the property's funds. Furthermore, workmen's compensation, social security, etc., are payable whether the employees are those of the property owner or the management firm. (A U.S. Supreme Court decision stated that, from the standpoint of federal wage and hour laws, on-site employees generally are considered to be employees of the management agency. However, this applies only to wage and hour regulations. Under other circumstances these employees generally are considered employees of the property owner.)

Accounting and Reporting

A clause is needed to detail the agent's responsibility for maintaining the books for the property and state the frequency and kinds of operating reports that are to be submitted to the owner. Discussing this during management contract negotiations and reaching an understanding is critical to the owner/agent relationship, since the operating statement becomes the primary means of regular communication.

Two additional points may be included in this clause. One, it can state that the agent's responsibility for making payments for the operation of the property is limited to the amount of money on deposit in the property's account. Two, it can authorize the agent to establish a reserve by withholding from the owner's regular remittance enough money to meet obligations that may come due before the next month's rental income is collected. When this point is included, a specified maximum amount for this reserve should be given.

Cancellation or Termination

A termination clause clearly states under what conditions cancellation of the management agreement can be made. Typically, this calls for written notice of at least 30 days to be given. (Reasons for having a cancellation clause were discussed previously under Term of Contract.)

Management Fee

The agreed-upon management fee for services rendered, the method of paying it, and any supplementary fee structure should be defined clearly in the contract.

Special Services

If an arrangement between an owner and agent calls for special services not usually found in a typical management agreement, a clause providing for these special services should be added. Special services might include maintaining corporate or partnership books, performing special surveys, undertaking or supervising major remodeling, leasing, and brokerage. Naturally, management should guarantee that the contract also discusses compensation for performance of these special services.

12

Assumption of New Accounts

THE BUSINESS OF PROPERTY MANAGEMENT is one in which one business firm (the real estate management company) manages many and separate businesses (properties). Thus, the management organization is involved with planning, organizing, directing, and controlling numerous businesses that have different customers (tenants), markets, financial structures, and ownership. To eliminate all possible confusion, the management company needs to structure its real estate management programs with some uniformity so that the staff can function effectively and efficiently. Certain foundations may be laid to accomplish this objective. Specifically, the duties to be performed upon taking over of a new management account and the preparation of a management plan and budget should be standardized.

New-Account Takeover

Once a property owner and managing agent have negotiated a management contract and the management company has made the commitment to assume the responsibilities for managing the property, an immediate need exists to devote extreme care and attention to the new account.

However, before any action is taken, management must ensure that its liabilities are covered. The managing agent's two greatest liability exposures are (1) personal injury and property damage and (2) its commitment to make cash payments on time. The personal injury and property damage exposure is easily satisfied by having the management company immediately named as an additional insured on the owner's insurance policy. In fact, many insurance policies automatically provide for this coverage; whether this is the case can be determined easily upon examination of the policy.

A more common problem involves management companies that assume the responsibilities of managing a property without making provisions, through the owner, for sufficient cash to meet initial and ongoing financial obligations. Usually this situation can be met either by asking the owner for a fixed operating fund that can be used to finance operations when there is insufficient rental income to meet financial obligations, or by providing for the owner to make the loan payments on the property.

Having dealt with the liability matter, management is ready to turn its attention to the property. It should be remembered that during the first few weeks after takeover of an account, tenants, employees, suppliers, and the owner are testing it for new leadership. The tenants are concerned about the level of service and security they will receive, the employees are concerned about their jobs and their compatibility with the new management company, and the owner is concerned about the productivity and security of his investment. It cannot be overemphasized that the manager must commit a proper amount of time to effectively initiate the new system of management and that he must communicate regularly with all concerned parties to gain their support and quiet their fears.

A change in management inevitably is accompanied by anxiety on the part of tenants, building employees, vendors who provide services and products to the building, and even the owner. The company assuming management is watched very carefully and tested by these people. It is critical at this point that the management company makes a positive first impression on all parties involved. One of the best ways to ensure that the first impression is positive is to adopt a program of affirmative communication that encompasses all persons who are involved with the property.

When a change in management is announced to tenants, they immediately become apprehensive about possible changes in service, security, and the rental rate. A carefully prepared letter to tenants telling them of the company's general plans and explaining its management philosophy will help relieve most of this anxiety.

From the outset it is important that building employees witness strong leadership. The property manager assigned to the new account needs to spend a great deal of time with on-site employees, directing and assisting them in their responsibilities and explaining the way in which the company operates. He needs to instruct them in how to respond to emergencies and tenant grievances. Furthermore, these employees will be concerned about job security and want to know how and when they are to be paid. The managing agent must respond to these anxieties. It is not unusual for the loyalty of these site employees to lie with previous management. The property manager must make every effort to ensure a transfer of loyalty.

The property manager also must meet with vendors and service contractors. This should enable him to determine what products and services they provide and gain an understanding of the value of these products and services. This contact should provide the manager a clearer understanding of the needs of the property.

Starting the management program at a new property is a time-consuming experience for the property manager. A great deal of time must be spent at the property becoming acquainted with it and with the people there to ensure that the management program starts on a positive note. Likewise, many hours must be devoted to gathering statistics and information. The property and its ownership must be properly researched before the manager begins the next important task—creating a management plan.

Maintaining voluminous records and operating data about a property does not necessarily improve its management performance. However, initial thoroughness in gathering all of the important information about the property, its tenants, its employees, and its owners will be worthwhile in the long run. Each management company will want to develop its own checklist of information to be gathered and procedures to be adhered to in the starting of a new management account. Checklists vary from company to company because of the kinds of properties involved, the laws applicable to various states and localities, and the nature of the clientele. However, most checklists share certain steps. The following glossary of items can be used by a management company in developing its own new-account takeover checklist.

Property Description

The typical checklist is headed by the name of the property, its address, and the telephone number of its business office. The description should include what kind of a property it is—apartment house, office building, shopping center, etc.—the land size, and the gross square footage and net rentable area of the improvements. If it's an apartment house, the description might include drawings or verbal pictures of the various floor plans and give the net rentable area for each floor plan. A description of available parking and whether it is covered or not is also important. Amenities, major pieces of equipment, and type of construction likewise are useful and should be listed in the property description when this information is available.

Ownership Data

In addition to the name of the legal entity that owns the property, it also is useful to know how the title is held. For instance, the owner may be an individual, partnership, limited partnership, real estate investment trust, or some other form of ownership entity. If the entity owning the property is a partnership, it is helpful to have a copy of the partnership agreement. Management will want to list on the checklist the names of the people who are to receive the monthly statements and their addresses and telephone numbers and make note of who is to receive the original set of paid invoices. Making note of the names, addresses, and telephone numbers of the accounting and law firms that represent the ownership likewise is advised.

Financial Information

Management must demand complete and accurate information on all loans against the property, the lender, the amount of the monthly payment, the interest rate it bears, and any other unusual clauses relating to the financing. The sophisticated property manager also wants to know the ownership's book value of the property and its current depreciation schedule. A copy of the previous year's tax return is useful if the entity is a partnership.

Another financial consideration is whether or not the owner will fund an operating account. Such an account may be needed to ensure that the property manager will have sufficient funds on hand to meet obligations as they become due.

Insurance

A new-account takeover checklist should call for a complete and current listing of all insurance policies held by the owner. Subsequently, management should review these policies to verify that there is sufficient public liability and property damage coverage, adequate coverage for insuring money from the moment a tenant pays until it is received by the owner, and satisfactory workmen's compensation insurance.

Real Estate Taxes

A reminder to obtain a copy of the most recent real estate tax bill should be in the checklist. The need to identify who will be responsible to make the next real estate tax payment when it's due and note how the funds for that payment are to be arranged for likewise should be considered.

Tenant Data

Not only do tenants need to be notified of the management company's appointment as managing agent, but the accounting department needs a complete and detailed rent roll that shows every tenant, lease expiration dates, size of facilities leased, any security deposits or last month's rent on leases held by the owner, and unusual clauses in leases, such as percentage leases, cost of living index provisions, operating cost escalation clauses, utility charges, etc. The checklist also needs a provision which requires someone to read all of the leases and make notes of special conditions.

Employee Data

The property manager needs to obtain from each employee a W-4 form, a bond application, a signed employment contract, when applicable, and any other payroll information that is required by the bookkeeping department. If the employees are represented by a union, a copy of the union agreement must be obtained and studied.

Management Company Procedures

In addition to gathering necessary information about the property, the property manager usually takes certain procedural steps required by the company's manual of operations. The checklist should ask for the name of the property manager assigned to the account, the date the management agreement begins, the term of the contract, and the management fee. Further procedures may call for erecting special signs on the property, notifying vendors and utility companies in writing that future invoices should be sent in care of the management company, reviewing all contracts currently in force, obtaining and reviewing all guarantees for parts of the building (roof, equipment, air conditioning and heating equipment, appliances, etc.), and obtaining the necessary city permits.

The checklist also should guarantee delivery to the property of all forms used in the property management company's bookkeeping system so that on-site personnel can carry out their responsibilities in such a way as to be compatible with the company's operational method. These forms might include rental agreements, rental applications, occupancy reports, employee manuals, time sheets, deposit slips, endorsement stamps, etc.

The Management Plan

Whenever a property manager takes over the management of a property, he nearly always is starting with a problem situation. In the case of a new building, the problem may be one of renting vacant space. Other common problems are buildings that are over-financed

---

Management Plan Checklist
Page One of Two

I. Income
   A. Scheduled rents
      1. Market analysis
         a. At least five comparable properties
         b. Prepared by resident manager with property manager verifying data
         c. Submit market information on market data comparison grid
   B. Vacancy and bad debts
      1. Turnover
      2. Downtime
      3. Market program
      4. Collection procedures and policies
      5. Non-revenue-producing units—storage, models, cannibalized
      6. Economic trends
      7. Seasonal fluctuations
      8. Rent increases
   C. Other income
      1. Parking
      2. Vending machines
      3. Laundry
      4. Security deposit forfeits
      5. Cleaning dues
      6. Pet deposits and fees
      7. Storage
      8. Furniture
      9. Interest income from reserves
     10. Transfer fees
     11. Late fees
     12. Maid services
   D. Stability of tenancy
      1. Average length of stay
      2. Tenant selection requirements
      3. Type of neighborhood
      4. Occupation of tenants
      5. General physical condition of building
   E. Lease term
   F. Deposit requirements

Figure 12.1.   Management plan checklist.

and having difficulty meeting their obligations, properties plagued by a considerable amount of deferred maintenance and lack of available capital to correct the situation, properties realizing poor cash flow for their owners, and buildings that purely and simply have been poorly managed. Before the operations at these kinds of properties can be turned around and they can begin to produce at a satisfactory level, a great deal of planning and budgeting is required.

Professional real estate managers are retained to solve problems—to improve property values and produce the highest possible

---

Management Plan Checklist
Page Two of Two

II. Operating Expenses
  (Use chart of accounts as a checklist for operating expense items.)
III. Capital Expense Requirements
  A. Major deferred maintenance
  B. Replacement of furniture or equipment (i.e., carpets, draperies, air conditioning units)
  C. City requirements to bring building to code
  D. Major betterments to improve rental value
  E. Major betterments to cure construction defects
  F. Funding program for capital replacement items
IV. Financing Costs
  A. First trust deed
  B. Second, third trust deeds
  C. Land lease
  D. Furniture or equipment payments
  E. Delinquent real estate tax payments
  F. Comparisons of existing constants with constants available in current market
V. Owner Requirements
  A. Ownership structure
  B. Business purpose of ownership
    1. Financial
      a. Rate of return
      b. Cash flow
      c. Tax shelter
      d. Equity buildup
      e. Improved value
    2. Strategic property plan
      a. Hold for investment
      b. Prepare for sale
      c. Trade
      d. Convert
  C. Pride of ownership
  D. Degree of involvement in management
  E. Guarantees to others

Figure 12.1 (continued)

return. No company can achieve these goals and operate effectively unless it adopts a management plan for each and every property under its stewardship.

The easiest way to guarantee that a property operates efficiently is to manage according to a plan. If a manager takes the time to plan, he will achieve better results in less time. He will be able to anticipate problems and foresee opportunities before they occur rather than waiting for them to happen.

The management of a shopping center, office building, or apartment house must be viewed in the same perspective as the management program for a large corporation. The fundamentals are the same; both start with planning. When developing a management plan for a particular property, the property manager has four specific tasks: (1) The mission, objectives, and goals of the property as a business must be detailed. (2) The programs to achieve these goals must be outlined. (3) Approval of the plan and programs must be obtained from the ownership. (4) Like the conducter of a symphony, the property manager must orchestrate a performance using the talents of his organization.

A management plan, generally designed for the short-term operation of a property, typically consists of these elements: regional analysis, neighborhood analysis, analysis of the property's current operation, market analysis, recommended operating plan, analysis of valuation of property before and after changes, and analysis of the financial implementation. A complete management plan deals with staffing requirements, contractual arrangements, methods of correcting deferred maintenance and curable obsolesence, changes in services, marketing programs, and any other suggestions that are needed. (See management plan checklist in figure 12.1.) The overall intent of such a plan is to solve the problem or problems of the property and make it competitive with similar properties in the locale. (A complete management plan with its supplementary budget appears as figure A.11 in the appendix.)

While it is the responsibility of the property manager to write the management plan for the particular property of which he is in charge, this important job should not be tackled alone. It takes a team of competent, cooperative people to create an effective management plan. The property manager should seek the counsel and advice of others. The various experiences of other people should be drawn upon to formulate the marketing, operating, and financial objectives for the investment. Frequently, someone outside of the firm may be contacted for expert assistance. For instance, the specialized services of a construction expert, an interior designer, a mortgage banker, or an accountant may be utilized.

How much time is necessary to complete a plan? If a manager has been managing a project for a long time, it may take only a few hours several times each year to bring the plan up to date. However, it is not unusual, when assuming the management of a new property, to take up to four months gathering the information needed to complete a proper plan. Planning is not an exercise that should be undertaken hastily. Good plans are based upon obtaining accurate data and clearly understanding that data in relation to the problems of the property. It is much more important to be thorough than to be fast. A property manager, therefore, should spend as much time as necessary to prepare a management program in which he has the highest degree of confidence.

No management plan is complete until it has been submitted to the owner of the property and is accepted by him as meeting his objectives. Once the plan is approved, it becomes a program to be implemented for the operation of the property as well as the means for tracking its performance. Furthermore, as a written statement, it becomes the expression of the understanding reached by ownership and management of the goals and objectives they share for the property.

Because nothing is static, management plans must be reviewed on a regular basis and revised as needed. The maximum amount of time a property should go without having its plan reviewed is six months, and this is only for buildings with very stable occupancy levels and relatively little change in performance. A quarterly review is not unreasonable for most properties. Certainly, if a building is operating with many changes or on a tight cash-flow budget, a review every 60 days is not out of order. When a plan needs to be changed, the recommendation should be communicated to the owner for his understanding and approval.

The Budget Process

The financial projection of the management plan and the vehicle for tracking the plan's performance is the budget. Management cannot establish a set of rules that always can be applied when preparing budgets for properties. For example, a property manager may manage two identical buildings—each built by the same developer at exactly the same time—yet if they are held by different owners and are financed differently, budgeted income and operating expenses could be quite different. Every property budget, then, must be prepared individually and independently.

A budget for a property is created by setting realistic and attainable financial goals, establishing a plan for the accomplishment of these goals, and then auditing the results. More succinctly, it states what is to be done and how it is to be done, then evaluates the outcome. In effect, the budget becomes the goal to be attained at the executive level and enforced at the property level. It effectively covers a specified period of time with increments for future income and expenses estimated as realistically as possible. However, there must be some flexibility in the budget to allow for uncontrollable changes. Periodic evaluation becomes necessary to see if execution is necessary or if remedial action is required. This evaluation should

---

Chart of Accounts
Operating Expenses

Payroll
11.00 Resident Manager
12.00 Assistant Manager
13.00 Office/Leasing
14.00 Maintenance
15.00 Security/Doorman
16.00 Janitor/Maids
17.00 Employees' Apartments
18.00 Payroll Taxes
19.00 Employee Insurance
and Benefits

Utilities
20.00 Electricity
21.00 Water and Sewage
22.00 Gas
23.00 Telephone

Maintenance
27.00 Apartment Cleaning
28.00 Carpets
29.00 Draperies
30.00 Pool Service
31.00 Elevator
32.00 Air Conditioning
33.00 Plumbing
34.00 Building
35.00 Furniture

36.00 Painting
37.00 Pest Control
38.00 Rubbish Removal
39.00 Landscaping
40.00 Electrical
41.00 Heating
42.00 Equipment
43.00 Appliances

Advertising
48.00 Paid Advertising
49.00 Tenant Promotion

Other Expenses
50.00 Supplies
51.00 Professional Fees
52.00 Tenant Services
53.00 Security Service
54.00 Insurance
55.00 Unclassified

Taxes and Licenses
58.00 Property Taxes
59.00 Other Taxes
60.00 Licenses

Property Management
61.00 Property Management

Figure 12.2. Master chart of accounts for operating expenses of an apartment management operation.

Market Data Comparison Grid

Comparison Data	Name of Property			
General Information				
Age				
Number of Units				
Manager				
Telephone				
Owner				
Management Company				
Lease (Minimum/Maximum)				
Vacancy (Percentage)				
Type of Tenancy				
Rent and Size				
Single				
Square Feet				
Furnished				
Unfurnished				
One Bedroom/One Bath				
Square Feet				
Furnished				
Unfurnished				
Two Bedroom/One Bath				
Square Feet				
Furnished				
Unfurnished				
Two Bedroom/Two Bath				
Square Feet				
Furnished				
Unfurnished				
Other				
Amenities				
Utilities				
Air Conditioning				
Appliances				
Security				
Pets				
Parking				
Recreation Room				
Pool/Jacuzzi				
Fees				
Security Deposit				
Cleaning				
Comparison to Subject				
Location				
Exterior				
Apartments				
Amenities				

Figure 12.3. Grid for comparing market data upon takeover of a new apartment management account.

be a cooperative effort involving all those concerned with the operation of the property.

In order to prepare an operating budget, certain data must be gathered. Chief among the sources of data is a detailed physical inspection of the property. Every operational detail must be known if an accurate budget is to be drafted. Furthermore, the property manager will need to have at his disposal the company's charts of accounts (see figure 12.2), the company data on comparables (figure 12.3), historical records of the building, a market survey, and tenant and prospect profile sheets (figure 12.4).

Having gathered and evaluated all pertinent information, the actual budgeting process may begin. A management plan budget has five major areas of consideration: income, operating expenses, capital expense requirements, financing costs, and the owner's requirements. These five areas are interrelated.

Income

Rental income and other income are the two basic sources of revenue to a property. When establishing the rental income for a property, a rent schedule must be prepared. This requires paying attention to

---

Tenant and Prospect Profile

This analysis is based upon information from the previous 12 monthly statements and prospect sheets prepared throughout the previous 90 days.

Property _____

Date of Analysis _____Property Manager _____

Tenants
Average Turnover per Month _____
Types of Units Experiencing Unusual Vacancy Problems _____

Profile of Typical Tenant _____

Prospects: Qualified Traffic during Previous 90 Days

Sources	Prospects	Rented
Drive by		
Classified Ad		
Referral		
Other		
Totals		

Figure 12.4.   Form for preparation of tenant and prospect profile of an apartment project upon takeover of a new account.

a variety of details that affect rent, such as view, unit amenities, public amenities, services, design, and age. (See rental income analysis, figure 12.5.) Every unit or space must have a price that is acceptable in the marketplace, and each must contribute to the rental income stream. However, a property manager would do well to remember that it is the user who determines the price of any product, including a rental unit or area.

When establishing a rental schedule, the property manager first should establish the price of the best unit, then compare every other unit to it and subtract for deficiencies. In this way, the highest potential rent schedule is obtained. After establishing this schedule, it must be checked against market comparables (see figure 12.3) to make sure that it is realistic. This comparison may be made either

Rental Income Analysis

Property _____
Data of Analysis _____ Property Manager _____

	Year-to-Date Previous Year (_____ Months)	Year-to-Date Current Year (_____ Months)	Budget Projection (Annual)
Scheduled Rents			
Less Vacancy			
Rental Income			
Security Deposits			
Cleaning Fees			
Other Income			
Gross Income			
Vacancy Percentage			
Cash Basis			
Units-Days Basis			

Unit Rate Analysis

	Previous Year This Month	Current Year This Month	Next Year's Average
Singles, Furnished			
Singles, Unfurnished			
One Bedroom/One Bath Furnished			
One Bedroom/One Bath, Unfurnished			
Two Bedroom/One Bath, Furnished			
Two Bedroom/One Bath, Unfurnished			
Two Bedroom/Two Bath, Furnished			
Two Bedroom/Two Bath, Unfurnished			

Figure 12.5. Rental income and unit rate analyses forms for an apartment management operation.

on a rental-per-unit-per-month basis or a rental-per-square-foot-per-month basis.

The rental income schedule is known as scheduled gross rental income. Subtracted from this are the anticipated amounts for vacancies, loss of rents caused by delay of move-outs and move-ins, and credit losses. Scheduled gross rental income less losses for vacancies and bad debts results in the adjusted (or effective) gross rental income.

Other revenue sources can add significantly to a property's income stream. Potential sources of additional income include these: parking, storage, laundry, vending machines, cleaning charges, forfeited security deposits, pet fees, furniture rental, transfer fees, late fees, maid services, and interest on savings and loans reserve accounts. Gross rental income together with this additional income yields gross income.

Operating Expenses

A property's operating expenses may be divided conveniently into seven categories:

- Payroll. Analyzing this expense requires careful assessment of job descriptions and a consideration of all vacation pay, fringe benefits, salary increases, bonuses, etc. Payroll also may be broken down into subcategories, for instance: manager/assistant manager, leasing agents, janitor/maintenance, security/doorman, employee apartments, payroll taxes, and workmen's compensation.

- Utilities. To make accurate projections in this expense category, a manager must consider all costs of electricity, water, gas, and telephone. An analysis of past utility bills and a complete physical inspection of the property become imperative. Simultaneous to performing the property inspection, the manager can search for ways to reduce energy costs. Furthermore, when breaking the annual budget into monthly budgets, seasonal variations and their effect on utility requirements must be taken into account.

- Maintenance. In determining maintenance costs, the reason for conducting a complete physical inspection of the property becomes obvious. Only by visualizing the property can the property manager accurately anticipate maintenance and repair expenditures. Furthermore, while rental turnover can become very expensive from a maintenance standpoint, this cost can be estimated with extreme accuracy if the manager knows his market and its trends. Whether maintenance is handled by on-site personnel or contracted out or some combination is used, a study should be made commensurate with preparing the budget to determine alternate courses of action and their relative costs.

- Advertising. This expense category covers all types of media advertising, tenant promotions, brochures, floor plans, etc., required by a property's marketing program.
- Sundry. Sundry expenses might include the following subcategories: office supplies, professional fees (legal and accounting), recreation fund, security service contract, insurance, and miscellaneous.
- Taxes and licenses. Included in this expense category are real estate and other taxes and licenses and fees, as required.

Financing Analysis: Existing Loans

Property _____ Year of Purchase _____

Date of Analysis _____ Property Manager _____

	First Trust Deed	Second Trust Deed	Other
Original Amount of Loan	_____	_____	_____
Interest Rate	_____	_____	_____
Annual Payment	_____	_____	_____
Lender	_____	_____	_____

Lock-In Provision
  First Trust Deed   _____
  Second Trust Deed _____
  Other _____
Prepayment Penalty
  First Trust Deed   _____
  Second Trust Deed _____
  Other _____
Assumption Provision
  First Trust Deed   _____
  Second Trust Deed _____
  Other _____

	First Trust Deed	Second Trust Deed	Other
Present Loan Balance	_____	_____	_____
Annual Payment	_____	_____	_____
Present Constant	_____	_____	_____

Total Annual Payments as Percentage of Scheduled Rental Income _____

Owner's Special Requirements and/or Objectives of Property _____

Figure 12.6. Form for performing financial analysis of existing loans upon takeover of a new account.

- Management. The management fee, an operating expense of the property, generally is either a percentage of income collected or a dollar amount per unit. The management agreement should be reviewed to predict this expense category.

Capital Expense Requirements

Capital expense requirements refer to major one-time costs. Major deferred maintenance items, replacement of furniture or equipment, and improvements to increase rental value or cure construction defects are among common capital expense requirements. Because a property manager may consider these capital improvements as critical to the success of the management plan, especially in the case of a problem property, it is important that capital expense requirements be carefully and accurately budgeted.

Financing Costs

Likewise, financing costs must be taken into consideration when the management plan and budget are being prepared. A form for analyzing these costs, such as shown in figure 12.6, can be useful in this part of the budget process. Financing costs include payments for each secured lien against the property as well as lease payments for the land if the property is on a leasehold, chattle mortgage payments for loans on furniture or equipment, and payments on unsecured loans should they exist. Each loan payment should be divided to show how much is attributable to interest cost, the amount paid on the principal, and the balance owed.

Owner's Requirements

Most property owners have several financial requirements. Each will want to realize a positive rate of return on his investment, enjoy a tax shelter, build up his equity, and improve the value of his property. Above all, a property owner will want to realize a positive cash flow from the operation of his property. Upon completion, the budget as prepared by the property manager should indicate anticipated cash flow and appear as follows:

Gross Scheduled Rental Income	$_____
Less: Vacancies and Bad Debts	_____
Gross Rental Income	_____
Plus: Other Income	_____
Gross Income	$_____

Less: Operating Expenses	$_____
Net Operating Income	_____
Less: Capital Expense Requirements	_____
Less: Financing Costs	_____
Cash Flow	$_____

There is a definite relationship between each operating category and the gross scheduled rental income for each type of income property. Thus, from a percentage standpoint, an astute property manager will be alert to expectations based upon these relationships.

Types of Budgets

While the management plan, with its budget as described, is fundamentally a short-term plan for the ensuing year's operation, the plan also can anticipate, and budget for, long-term objectives. Since budgets are financial formulas for operating businesses for future periods of time, the manager will need to understand the differences of the four kinds of budgets commonly used in the forecasting of operating results for income properties. They are the rent-up budget, the annual budget, the stabilized budget, and the cash flow budget.

Rent-Up Budget

Usually a new building experiences unusual marketing and organizational costs during the time required to bring rental income to a well-occupied condition. Rent-up budgets deal with these situations. Rent-up budgets first of all need to estimate the period of time required to attain normal occupancy. Next, the budget forecasts the rate of absorption of vacant space in monthly increments. Absorption rates are not constant; such variables as seasonal influences, available selection, and economic influences all have an effect on absorption rates. Furthermore, operating costs for some categories are inordinately high during this marketing period, while other costs may not as yet need to be budgeted.

Since rent-up budgets are tied to an anticipated marketing result, it may be well to plan such a budget with some flexibility. If the space is absorbed more rapidly or more slowly than expected, this can change the outcome. A manager should budget with possible contingencies in mind so that the rent-up budget reflects expenses for each level of revenue produced. A flexible rent-up budget is more useful than a fixed rent-up projection because it takes into account variable expenses that can be controlled depending on the rate of absorption of the vacant space.

Annual Budget

An annual budget is a 12-month estimate of income and expenses for a mature property. It is the working budget, applied to day-to-day expenditures and including replacements. The annual budget allows for all expenditures to be made during the period covered by it but does not set up reserves for expenditures to be made during a subsequent period of time.

Stabilized Budget

The stabilized budget, on the other hand, includes reserves for those capital items that will need replacement during the period of the budget. In consequence, the stabilized budget is averaged over a longer period of time than the annual budget, usually five or even 10 years. The stabilized budget includes those factors that, while erratic in happening, must be considered over the economic term of the forecast.

Cash Flow Budget

The annual budget predicts the operating results for the year and the resulting annual cash flow. However, the manager and owner also want to know the monthly cash projection. The cash flow budget is designed for this purpose. This forecast lets the parties know how much money is available for major expenses that do not occur on a regular monthly basis, such as real estate taxes, annual insurance premiums, major repairs or replacements that have been anticipated, leasing fees due to brokers for commercial tenants, etc.

A cash flow budget is a useful management tool in that it permits the manager to schedule those costs over which he does have control so that large fixed expenses can be paid on time.

IV
Managing People

13

Personnel Recruitment
and Selection

IN THE FINAL ANALYSIS, a property manager is as much a manager of people as he is a manager of property. While the primary concern is with planning for the operation of a building, maintaining it, and accounting for monies, the job requires constant interaction with people—tenants, clients, vendors, the general public, and, above all, employees. In a typical property management operation, approximately 60 percent of the fee income is applied toward personnel-related costs. Consequently, property management is primarily people management, and it is crucial for the property manager to understand the basic principles of employee management.

Managers have learned not only that they must know how to manage people in order to make work productive, but, subsequent to managing employees, they must know how to recruit good people. Growth of a company, particularly one in the service field, is directly related to the quality of people the firm can attract. Therefore, the recruiting and selection aspects of employee management are keys to building a successful enterprise.

Today's economic market offers extensive employment opportunities to the skilled worker. The economy functions in a highly technological and competitive environment. Members of management recognize that there is an ever-growing demand for skilled workers, and, more than ever before, qualified people have several job choices. Most often they will choose organizations in which they can fulfill their personal work objectives. It is management's job to offer this kind of opportunity.

Hiring a new employee requires a substantial investment. Selecting the wrong person is an expensive error. The cost in terms of payroll and overhead can be measured easily yet in fact probably represents the smallest expense for having selected a new employee who "didn't work out." Management would do well to think instead in terms of the time investment of the person who supervised that unqualified employee, or the loss of income because of poor performance. Still, probably the most expensive management error is not the employee who is selected, trained, and then, after having proved himself inadequate, let go, but rather the marginal employee who is retained. The supervisor continually hopes he can teach the marginal employee how to perform, wasting a great deal of valuable time trying to help the individual who simply does not have the capacity to produce. A startling statistic is that 80 percent of a manager's time is spent working on problems created by marginal producers.

To eliminate this waste, a sound program of employee recruitment and selection must be adopted. A key to a successful career ladder for the property manager and to a successful real estate management organization is quality employees. The property manager must have quality workers in positions subordinate to him, or he will spend a disproportionate amount of his productive time assisting them in meeting their responsibilities. The management company needs a team of quality people to accomplish its goals and successfully contend in a competitive business environment.

Assessing Personnel Needs

A program of employee recruitment and selection demands an assessment of the company's personnel needs. This process begins with an evaluation of existing employees and involves anticipating growth, replacing people who quit, and—an aspect that shouldn't be ignored—replacing marginal employees who are not performing satisfactorily.

An employee procurement program, like all other functions of management, requires planning, and the first element of the personnel plan is a forecast of the company's personnel requirements. Job openings occur for a number of reasons: company growth, promotion or other internal moves, dismissals, death, retirement, transfer to other firms that can better satisfy employment needs, family and health problems. Thus, even in a well-run business environment, employee turnover is a factor to be reckoned with. Responding to turnover through a planned program of employee recruitment and selection is preferable to reacting to crisis situations.

One method of estimating a company's ongoing labor requirement is to calculate its labor turnover rate, a realistic estimate of how many employees are likely to leave the company in a given period based upon past turnover trends. For example, a review of a company's personnel records may reveal that the company's resident managers turn over at a rate of approximately one every three months. Depending upon whether a company expects to maintain its status quo or grow, management, through careful evaluation, can estimate how many vacancies are likely to occur in the future and make the necessary provisions to fill anticipated personnel gaps.

Attracting Job Candidates

Appropriate candidates for specific vacancies must be attracted before actual selection can take place. Essentially, there are two sources of personnel candidates: existing employees within the company and persons outside of the company. Being acquainted with the sources of personnel supply and knowing how these sources may best be used is a prerequisite to having a workable employee procurement plan.

Internal Recruitment

The job of finding someone to fill a vacant job position should begin at the office. Someone already employed in the organization may want, and may qualify for, the vacant position. Promoting people within the firm not only requires little risk, inasmuch as the employee is of known quality, but it also is important to the esprit de corps of the firm. Few things are more damaging to employee morale than hiring an outsider to fill a position that could have been filled with a qualified staff member. Furthermore, although higher level jobs are prime targets for use of existing personnel, lower and entry level jobs should not be ignored. An employee may prefer a lateral move or even a demotion in order to be placed in a more satisfying job. If employees are shown that they have real opportunities to advance or move within the company, they perform accordingly and prepare themselves for possible promotion or job change. The result is that the employees are likely to be of improved calibre.

The property manager of a series of apartment houses should view all employees at the various properties under his direction as one large staff. By offering the opportunity for resident managers and other on-site employees to move to larger buildings and positions requiring greater responsibility, the agency management firm has a distinct advantage in the employee market over the individual property owner who does not offer such opportunity. An employer who views promoting an existing employee as a burden upon management because it requires training for two new jobs rather than one is probably an employer whose organization lacks spirit and strong loyalty.

This is not to imply that all vacant positions should be filled with existing personnel. This source does have its weaknesses. First is the danger of inbreeding: Companies that continually promote from within run the risk of repeating the same mistakes and losing access to people with fresh ideas. The second danger arises out of the limited supply of existing qualified personnel: When numerous vacancies occur, such as during periods of rapid growth, the internal supply will be inadequate.

Promoting from within, therefore, can be effective if the conditions are favorable. The vacancy to be filled must be within the capacity of a present staff member, and the promotion must not weaken the rest of the organization. When handled properly, promotion improves staff morale and encourages employees to improve their performance in an effort to be ready for promotion.

External Recruitment

Even when a company adopts an effective promotion program, it will have to go outside to fill certain vacancies, including those created as a result of promotions. Management, therefore, must be knowledgeable about external sources of job candidates.

The most important source for recruiting new employees is recommendations from people who are well acquainted with the firm. Employees can be important sources for recruits, and clients and vendors can be useful resources as well. The person making a recommendation has a good understanding of the character and reputation of the person whom he is recommending. These personal attributes cannot be tested; they are known only through long-term personal relationships. Thus, when a valued employee, client, or business friend recommends a recruit for employment in the firm, the manager can be assured that he has received a valuable, qualified prospect.

Although a manager may harbor some fear that an employee might recommend a friend who is not suited to the job, this usually is not the case. To the contrary, an employee recommending a friend usually does so with some degree of care and trepidation: He knows that to recommend someone who would be unsatisfactory would damage his own reputation with his employer and, further, that a friend would not appreciate a lead that would not materialize in a good job.

The other most commonly used external recruitment sources are advertisements, employment agencies, schools and associations, and outright recruiting. When performing his search, a manager should know the advantages and disadvantages of using each.

Probably the most popular external search method in the modern labor market is advertising in newspapers, either through classified ads in help-wanted sections or display ads in business sections or sections on career opportunities.

The main drawback of advertising is the range of candidates that may be attracted. This problem can be eliminated in part by writing exact advertising copy that clearly and concisely relays the job description. When using the classified section, the usual medium for hourly and clerical personnel, the ad must be precise and to the point. Classified advertisements are listed according to job title, so it becomes especially important for the title to accurately define the job opening. Furthermore, the job seeker will want to know the pay and the place of employment.

For professional or managerial positions, display ads in business sections are most commonly used. Here it is important to headline the ad with the title of the job, to which considerable care should be given. Furthermore, those elements of the position that would be attractive to potential candidates should be identified and emphasized in the advertisement.

Every advertisement is a sales tool. In this instance, the manager is selling his firm as a source of employment. How the ad is written and how it appears becomes part of the firm's image projection and may affect the attitude of job seekers. Many conclusions may be drawn by prospective job seekers based on an advertisement. The appearance, size, copy, and layout and how the company logo is used combine to form a mental picture of the organization. For example, if a help-wanted ad uses minimal space and delivers its message in the form of cryptic abbreviations, a poor impression of the firm may be formed. A reader might infer that the firm tries to cut corners, is tight-fisted in its spending policies, and does not think enough of the importance of the position it is seeking to fill by offering a decent description of the job. Conversely, ads that are too large or ostentatious may project an image of desperation, high turnover, or lack of stability. The firm's advertising says something about the character and business practices of the company. The image that is created must be a positive one if it is to be helpful in the company's recruitment efforts.

Hiring through private employment agencies has grown considerably in recent years. Some agencies tend to serve primarily in the technical and professional areas, in which case they may be known as executive search firms. Others concentrate in relatively unskilled fields. In essence, the agencies act as brokers, bringing employers and employees together. For this service, a fee, usually computed as a percentage of the salary for a given period, is charged.

A professional employment agency can be useful in recruiting, particularly at the higher levels of compensation, provided both the agency and management make a concerted effort to understand the parameters of the job. The company needs to work with the agency so that it can be presented in a good light. The agency will reflect to potential employees the right image and a positive attitude about the company. In order for this to be accomplished, management needs to tell the agency what kind of people are needed and what a prospective employee will be offered. It is important that the agency does not misrepresent the company by being overzealous in its description. Printed material about the company or the job is helpful to the agency in realistically describing the company.

Oftentimes there is a tendency for agencies to send a client any résumé in which the client might have even the slightest interest. This must be avoided. Unless an agency can deliver several qualified prescreened candidates, its services should not be considered.

Many companies have turned to colleges, universities, and technical schools in their search for desirable personnel. They may send representatives to college campuses to recruit top scholars or offer summer jobs to college undergraduates with a view to permanent employment upon graduation. A well-planned campus recruitment program can become a valuable source of new personnel for the firm that is of sufficient size to support such an effort.

While some candidates may be procured through schools, the primary problem of recruiting people outside of the organization is that most of the people the firm would like to have already are happily employed. A recruiter will have a greater chance of finding the right person for the job if he considers people who are already employed, rather than limiting his market to the unemployed. If a firm enjoys an excellent reputation with the property management profession, it may have an ongoing waiting list of qualified, employed people who want to be interviewed whenever a job opening occurs. For this reason the recruiting effort should never stop; it should be a program that continues even when there are no immediate job vacancies.

Selecting Qualified Personnel

Very high on the list of a qualified manager's skills is his ability to select people for the jobs underlying his responsibility to the firm. His performance as a manager, and the firm's performance as a provider of professional services, is dependent upon selecting people who are intellectually and motivationally compatible with their jobs.

The selection process should not be undertaken in haste. For the employee, a job is more than a paycheck that satisfies financial needs: It is his future, recognition, a status symbol, a source of pleasurable activity, an intellectual challenge, and a sense of accomplishment. It is the company's responsibility to invest in the selection process the time and effort needed to increase the probability of a proper marriage between job and employee. The degree of compatibility between a person and his work is an important facet of the company operation. Unfortunately, too few firms spend the necessary time designing ways to select people. If the wrong person is hired, the company's investment in recruiting, selecting, and training is wasted.

The selection process is an attempt to locate a person to fit a given job based upon available evidence. Typically, it is a matter of trying to predict how a person—often an unknown person—will perform in a given work situation, based upon such things as personal interviews and impressions, employment history, work and personal references, testing, and other informational sources. The decision to hire someone is always a guessing game, but the chance for success is in direct proportion to the amount of intelligent effort that precedes the decision.

Job Specification

The selection process begins with preparing a list of specifications to serve as a guide in decision making. The list should be divided into three sections: the characteristics that are absolutely required of the applicant (the "must" criteria); the highly desirable characteristics; and the characteristics that are desirable but not necessarily mandatory. Candidates who do not possess the "must" criteria should be eliminated automatically from consideration; the others should then be evaluated accordingly. Using a prepared list of criteria forces the manager to plan for interviews with candidates. Also, it provides him with a written document to be reviewed as he considers all of the applicants. This becomes especially beneficial if candidates are interviewed over a long period of time.

Writing specifications for a job requires careful analysis of the position. The process begins with a complete job description of the position to be filled, including the precise job title, purpose of the position, duties, responsibilities, and general qualifications. It then goes a step further than the job description by translating job requirements into statements of human characteristics, such as emotional poise needed for the job, special abilities, and specific educational needs.

A crucial dimension of a job specification is what Paul Renke of Executive Consulting Services, Inc., a management consulting firm in Detroit, Michigan, calls its "behavioral characteristics." According to Renke:

> Each job requires a different set of behavioral qualifications. For example, retail sales jobs take on entirely different types of persons than outside commission sales jobs. An account-type salesman is a different individual than an insurance salesman. The old cliche that a man who can sell, can sell anything is not behaviorally sound. We have seen cases of people who are average in one job, yet outstanding in another job.
>
> If the manager is not aware of the needs of the job in selecting people, his chances of success are limited. The key factor in the selection decision is in the manager's ability to match the behavioral characteristics of a person to a specific job.

This concept is reiterated by Saul W. Gellerman in his book, *Management by Motivation* (New York: American Management Association, Inc., 1968). He says:

> If a man finds his work interesting, reasonably dignifying and capable of providing him with an occasional thrill of accomplishment, the experiences inherent in the job itself will draw his energies and talents to his work. If on the other hand he finds his work a bore, or degrading, or incapable of tossing an occasional bouquet to his ego, no amount of supervisory artistry or anything else can keep him devoted to his work. He may do it in a minimal sense of just doing what has to be done, but he can hardly be expected to lavish any extra care or ingenuity or effort upon it. The crucial difference lies in how well the job is suited to the man.

In addition to having a job description, then, behavioral characteristics connected with the job must be known too. Primary behavioral characteristics and their relationships with job character-istics are these:

- Aggressiveness. Positions requiring problem solving are compatible with an aggressive personality. If the candidate's attitude is negative or passive, chances are he will not be compatible with a job that requires him to provide solutions to troublesome concerns.
- Sociability. Some positions, particularly jobs in service industries, are people oriented and require a high level of sociability.
- Emotional control. People who exhibit a high level of patience tend not to move as quickly as those who are less emotionally controlled. For instance, the telephone receptionist at a property management office may not need to be a fast mover but will need a great deal of patience.
- Need for structure. Accountants tend to prefer a structured business environment. They need to work under rules and regulations. The opposite is true of the entrepreneur, who continually violates structure. He constantly tries new things; if something fails, he does not falter but continues to devise and implement innovative ideas.

Significant to understanding behavioral job characteristics is understanding that people cannot be changed. Psychologists claim that only five percent of the population can alter their basic behavioral patterns. Behavior is how people respond to situations. It is neither good nor bad; it just is. For most, behaviorial patterns are well established by the time the late teens are reached. Therefore, the manager must be aware of a job candidate's individual behavioral patterns because, once hired, it is doubtful he will be able to change them. The executive who spends his time working with a person's behavioral characteristics in an attempt to mold them into those required by a job is fighting a losing battle. The resident manager who lacks aggressiveness will never become a good salesman. Instead, the manager should see his task as attempting to match natural behavior with a compatible job description. The higher the correlation between job and behavioral characteristics, the more productive will be the employee.

Employment Application

In order to obtain much of the basic information about a job candidate that is needed in the selection process, an employment application form often is used. A well prepared application form asks for detailed information in six basic areas: personal data (name, address, age, and social security number), education and special training, family status, financial information, health, and employment history. Additional information may be requested regarding character references, athletic interests, hobbies, avocations, memberships and responsibilities with organizations, etc. The form can be a reliable source for judging an applicant's character and stability. Frequent job changes, lack of credit references, a history of domestic problems, absence of educational experience since high school or college, a void in hobbies and avocations—such instances should be cause for concern and carefully explored during the interview.

Not only does a good application form signal problems; it also reveals candidates with strong potential. The completed application can point out a person with strong character and good potential who has applied himself and has achieved success in his lifetime.

In addition to becoming a means of verifying employment history and references, an employment application may be regarded as a more subtle means of judging an applicant's abilities. For example, it may be seen as a test of a candidate's ability to spell, write legibly, and answer questions with speed and accuracy.

The property manager must be cautioned that it is illegal to request certain information about applicants. Antidiscrimination laws prohibit recruiting and hiring practices that involve race, sex, ethnic origin, and religion. It is advisable to have legal counsel review a proposed application form before use, especially if there is any uncertainty about state and federal laws concerning employment practices.

Furthermore, because a good recruitment and selection program always includes follow through, every person making an application to the firm, whether solicited or not, should be answered. This is especially true of promising candidates. Once a candidate has been identified, management should waste no time with its interview and investigation and analysis of the applicant. Lack of immediate attention may result in a good candidate going elsewhere. A candidate who is ignored leads to creation of a poor image of the firm, and this can discourage others from applying.

Reference and Background Verification

One of the purposes of the employment application is to provide data necessary to verify an applicant's background. Checking into a candidate's background usually is confined to two essential sources of information: employment history and financial status. A third source, personal references, may be useful on occasion, but unless the person offered as a reference holds a responsible position, the reference usually lacks objectivity.

An investigation of the applicant's background is needed to confirm representations made on the application form and establish the candidate's credibility, gain testimony from previous employers, and obtain additional information that may not surface during the interview.

An investigation into the candidate's financial references provides the manager with an important insight of the candidate's fiscal responsibility. The best single source for this information is the local credit bureau. Credit bureaus have detailed information about individual credit ratings; they also serve as sources of evidence of past lawsuits, bankruptcies, or criminal involvements of a serious nature. Other credit sources are previous places of employment to verify wages, bank accounts, and, if a lessee, a landlord to learn rent-paying habits. However, these latter three sources should not be contacted without the applicant's prior permission.

The principal reason for checking on a candidate's previous employment is to learn about his experience and character. This oftentimes may be difficult, particularly if an applicant left under strained circumstances. A pointed interrogation with specific questions addressed to more than one previous employer should reveal the necessary information.

Interview

One of the major purposes of the employment interview is to provide a personal forum for the manager and the job applicant to exchange information. The manager's objective in a job interview is to obtain sufficient information so that he can make the correct personnel decision. Likewise, he has to give the job applicant certain information and assist him in forming a positive attitude about the company and the job. This is best accomplished by creating an atmosphere that is conducive to open, relaxed conversation. A comfortable interview environment is created when the manager shows a sincere interest in the applicant and avoids disagreement with or disapproval of the applicant's opinions and statements. An honest conversation is more likely to take place when the applicant feels at ease and secure with his relationship with the interviewer.

If he feels that he is making a favorable impression, he may be more willing to discuss unfavorable aspects about himself and his background.

In order to establish the right kind of atmosphere, the manager should take some steps in preparing for the meeting. First and most importantly, he should have a thorough understanding of the job specifications, including behavioral characteristics. Secondly, he should review all available information about the candidate. His employment application, job résumés, and letters of reference should all be studied in advance of the interview. Any questions regarding the information provided should be in writing, serving as a reminder.

In asking for specific information, the manager should avoid questions that can be answered with a simple yes or no. Instead, questions requiring longer answers, especially those that will identify the applicant's attitude and knowledge about specific areas of the job, should be asked. Throughout the interview, the manager must listen carefully in order to evaluate what is said and to be alert to what is left unsaid.

One technique used by professionals when interviewing job applicants is to begin the interview with a question that is general and broad in scope. This open-ended type of question does not seek exact information or answers but rather allows the job applicant to respond as to what he believes to be important about that subject. This provides for the burden of the conversation to be carried by the applicant rather than the interviewer. By asking, "How do your plans and goals relate to this job?" the applicant has an opportunity to talk; the interviewer can listen carefully and formulate opinions regarding the applicant's ability to communicate his ideas and organize his thoughts. Once this general or broad question is asked, it is important that the interviewer does not interrupt the applicant's response. Interruption hinders the flow of ideas and obstructs the ability to organize thoughts and communicate effectively.

Another interview technique is to ask questions that require the applicant to make an appraisal of his attitudes, abilities, and experiences. For example, he might be asked this: "You have stated your goal is to become a resident manager. What is there about yourself that makes you think you would make a good resident manager?" Or this: "How would you evaluate yourself as a manager of people? Good? Fair? Poor? What traits do you have that might account for your success?"

The final phase of the interview involves asking the applicant specific questions of fact. Here the interviewer can extract needed information that did not surface during the conversation.

When adequate information has been elicited and the manager has provided the applicant with information about the job and the company, it is well to ask if there are any questions the applicant may have. Having answered those, a brief tour of the facilities and introduction to a few employees in the firm may be considered.

The interviewing process seldom can be accomplished with one meeting. Usually it requires two or three interviews, sometimes with different members of the firm. The amount of time spent in these interviews depends, to some degree, on the importance of the position, but it should not be considered extravagant to devote at least 90 minutes to the initial interview, possibly followed by two 30-minute interviews. The more time people spend talking with each other, the more open the discussion becomes and the greater the chance that a compatible relationship will evolve.

One final rule: The person who does the hiring must do the interviewing. He cannot rely on tests or other people's judgment or recommendations. In the final analysis, the selection of an employee is a judgment call that has its highest degree of success when it is made by the person who does the interviewing.

When a candidate looks promising, a concerted effort should be made to encourage him to join the firm. Everyone involved in the recruitment effort needs to adopt a positive attitude about greeting prospective candidates. Once a decision has been made to extend an offer to an applicant, the firm must act quickly and positively. The employment market for skilled workers is competitive. While it is important to have a very thorough and exhaustive selection procedure, once a decision has been made, time works against the employer. Just as companies need to sell their services to the public, they must have an attitude of selling their company to candidates for employment.

14

Personnel Development

MANAGEMENT'S RESPONSIBILITY extends beyond the selection of appropriate personnel. Having carefully chosen the right person to fill a position within the company, it becomes necessary to provide a proper orientation to the company and, subsequently, an ongoing training program specifically designed for the given job. No employee is without the need for participation in some kind of formal training program. Whether a new employee or an existing one, each requires some degree of supplementary education. An employee training program, when properly planned and implemented, improves the firm's productivity, helps retain people, and more quickly identifies those individuals who do not measure up to the company's predictions.

New-Employee Orientation

The employee training program begins with an orientation to the job, which prepares the new worker for the responsibilities he is to assume. All too often the process of inducting a new employee is given superficial treatment, or, in some unfortunate cases, ignored altogether. This can be quite a mistake. If the company has followed a painstaking selection procedure and has hired someone with whom it is quite pleased, it cannot afford to let that new employee become disenchanted with his new job. Management not only must sell the employee on the company during the selection process but must continue selling the company throughout the term of employment.

A sound orientation program works to the benefit of both employee and employer. It eases the employee's fears by introducing him to his working environment, his fellow workers, and the rules and regulations of the company. Thus, it enables him to make the transition into his new job as efficiently and effectively as possible.

The company should be vitally concerned with the new employee's learning process during the first few weeks on the job. If the company fails here, the employee may become discouraged and leave. In addition to acquainting him with his new job, there are the personal considerations of meeting strangers and perhaps relocating in a new city. Is he being warmly treated by others in the firm? Are his associates and supervisors taking the time to help him establish social relationships as well as become acquainted with his new company? All of this is critically important.

The company must indicate to the employee that it has a sincere interest in acquainting him with the organization and getting him off to a good start. The first step usually is a personal discussion with the employee, or even a group discussion if there are several new employees, concerning the company's general policies and procedures.

This new-employee induction program usually will include most of the following steps:

- An introduction to the company, including information about its history, development, and objectives.
- A statement on the general terms of employment and any disciplinary rules enforced by the company.
- A summary of personnel policies detailing what the new employee can expect from the company and what it will expect of him in return.
- A description of benefits and services.
- A tour of the physical facility and personal introductions to fellow workers.
- An introduction to the department in which the employee will work and a description of his immediate supervisor's duties and the duties of coworkers.
- A detailed description of the job, including its general and specific duties and responsibilities, hours, wage rate, equipment needed, and other pertinent information.

In addition to these obvious areas of discussion, an orientation program also might include information on the following: location of rest rooms; location of eating facilities, both inside the office and nearby restaurants; location and use of the company parking lot, if there is one, or, if not, location of and rates at nearby lots; location of the first-aid facilities; explanation of public transit available to employees.

It is doubtful that the employee will remember all of the details of these programs. For this reason, many companies have personnel handbooks that are distributed to all new employees. This handbook becomes the employee's permanent, personal reference should he have any questions regarding rules, regulations, and policies.

In addition to the structured induction program, subtle indoctrination to the company also might be considered. While an employee is new to a company is an excellent time to encourage him to take a favorable attitude toward his job, his surroundings, and the company. Such an indoctrination would include an explanation of the company's philosophy, the reasons the firm operates the way it does, and how the employee's job is important to fulfilling the overall company plan. A solid indoctrination program is built on the principle of mutual benefit, i.e., what is good for the company is good for the worker. This instills in the employee the sense of team spirit that is so important in the property management profession.

Employee Training Program

No matter how many years of experience a new employee might have filling the same or some similar position at another company, he never will be fully prepared to immediately accept his new job. He will need to adjust to the new working environment and improve the skills he has to meet the responsibilities of his new position. Likewise, no matter how long an employee has been doing the same job for his current employer, it should never be assumed that he has no need of continued education. He should continually hone his skills and increase his knowledge in order to adopt to changing conditions. The training process may be left to chance. However, a wise manager adopts a plan for the personnel development of both new and existing employees.

The purpose of a training program is to make employees aware of the needs of the company and subsequently teach them the skills that are needed to satisfy those needs. This requires a major investment in terms of time, talent, and money. Unfortunately, the basic training program at far too many property management companies is a self-taught program in which the chance of success is dependent on the employee rather than company effort. James Downs Jr., CPM®, in his book, *Principles of Real Estate Management* (Chicago: Institute of Real Estate Management, 1975), put it very well when he said:

> Our observation of the normal procedures in the average office we have visited and studied has revealed an abysmal negligence in the matter of training new employees. Strangely enough, the typical businessman is not as considerate of the performance of a new associate as he is of his new car. When a new automobile is purchased, it is tenderly broken in for the first 200 miles, but when the new employee reports for work, he is usually instructed about like this: "Here is your desk. Start right in. If you have any problems, everyone will be glad to help you." Nobody takes the new employee aside and carefully explains the firm's operating policies, ideals and objectives. The new employee is left to learn his job by himself and pick up whatever knowledge he can get about how and why the organization functions. Usually he is immediately thrown into his work up to his neck. There is no break in, no easing up to the high speeds of ultimate production, and no 500 mile checkup. It is amazing that employees perform as well as they do. Certainly it is not because of adequate or sympathetic training.

This is not to imply that on-the-job training is ineffective. To the contrary, an on-the-job training program very well may be one of the most effective methods of improving employee skills, but only if it is systematically planned and administered. The level of effectiveness of an on-the-job training program hinges largely on whether or not a few simple rules are followed. One of the keys to successful training of property management personnel lies in the selection of instructors. Preferably, an instructor is a subordinate's manager or supervisor. He knows his subject matter and knows how to explain it to his subordinates. Furthermore, by working with them to improve their skills, the supervisor is in a position to gain the loyalty and confidence of his subordinates.

The supervisor must remember that every day, even when formal training is not involved, he is teaching his subordinates how to improve their skills and solve problems: The manager/subordinate relationship becomes one of teacher and student. The nature of the relationship also has a great deal to do with the opportunity for growth that is available to the employee. If, for instance, the manager believes that his subordinates should be tightly controlled, not delegated to, double checked on work assignments, and given only the information absolutely necessary to complete their assignments, there is little opportunity for individual growth and development. Second, the training program has a much better probability of being effective if it is organized. This usually means that one person within the organization is assigned the responsibility for employee training. In the typical property management company, this responsibility goes to a property manager. In addition, each individual lesson must be organized. The supervisor responsible for the training program must be just as prepared as if he were going into a formal classroom. Preparing a written outline of what is to be taught usually is a worthwhile exercise. This helps guarantee that no important information is omitted.

Resident managers are among the personnel that usually need training. For this reason, a special training course may be planned for all of the company's on-site managers. A property manager may consider adapting the following illustrative resident manager training program to his own company's needs:

Resident Manager Training Program

The program currently is designed for resident managers who manage 150-unit buildings. However, it should become a mandatory requirement for all resident managers who manage buildings of 70 units or more and for all new managers joining the company.

Property managers serve as instructors, with guest speakers when needed. Any funds needed for lectures or materials are charged to the buildings of the resident managers in attendance.

The course consists of four sessions of four hours each, given in the afternoon one day per week for four consecutive weeks. Each session consists of lectures, role playing, and question-and-answer periods. Written homework assignments emphasizing real-life situations and problems are given to stimulate the resident managers' thinking prior to each session. A final examination is given; both supervisors and managers are informed of the test results and strongest and weakest areas. Outstanding students are recognized.

The course sessions will be organized in this way:

First Session:	Purpose of course. Ownership, Management, and Managers. Employee Relations. Discussion.
Second Session:	Renting and Marketing. Public Relations. Role Playing. Discussion.
Third Session:	Collections and Records. Legal Aspects. Discussion.
Fourth Session:	Maintenance Procedures. Energy Conservation. Course review. Discussion. Final examination and review.

The course material requires written outlines and notes for the instructors, as well as handouts, examinations, and written homework assignments for the resident managers.

Outline of Resident Manager Training Program

Objective: To develop a course of study to permit the company to attain the highest possible quality of resident managers.

1. Ownership, Management, and Managers
   Reasons for apartment ownership. The management company. The resident manager. Duties of a manager. Budget and expenses. Qualifications of a resident manager.
2. Employee Relations
   Supervisor. Control. Training.
3. Renting and Marketing
   Advertising media. Preparation of space. Tenant selection and qualification. Showing space. Sales techniques. Housekeeping techniques.
4. Public Relations
   Between owner/supervisor and resident manager. Tenant to tenant. Resident manager/supervisor/vendor. Tenant control. Insurance aspects. Tenant comfort and security.
5. Collections and Records
   Rent collections and procedures. Banking. Delinquency policies. Evictions. Rent reporting. Records and receipts.
6. Legal Aspects
   Leases. Lease violations and defaults. Legal notices and proper service.
7. Maintenance Procedures
   Preventive maintenance. Corrective maintenance procedures. Routine maintenance procedures. Emergency procedures. Purchasing procedures. Contract services.
8. Energy Conservation
   Importance of conserving energy utilities. Methods of conserving.

While formal, classroom-type training courses might be most appropriate for resident managers, regularly scheduled symposia should be considered as a training device for more sophisticated personnel, such as property managers and property supervisors. If these meetings are designed to stimulate exchange of experiences and ideas via open discussion, the result may be improved professional growth. Some suggested symposia topics are these:

Corporate Policies and Procedures
Preparing a Management Plan
Time Management
New-Business Development
Developing a Job Description for a Property Manager
Major Problems Faced in . . .
    Employee Relationships
    Client Relationships

Marketing
As a Property Manager
Developing a Personal Long-Range Plan
Resident Manager Performance Evaluations
Basics of Interior Decorating
Asset Management
Developing Purchasing Guidelines and a Vendor List
Employee Recruitment and Selection

Courses and seminars likewise are beneficial and should not be discouraged. Not only should staff be constantly encouraged to participate in programs offered by the company for its employees but also those offered by local colleges and universities, the U.S. Department of Housing and Urban Development, state Departments of Real Estate, and the Institute of Real Estate Management. To further encourage participation, the company may agree to defray all or part of the cost for tuition and books for a course related to the job, assuming the employee successfully completes the course.

Crucial to any effective employee training program is a system of follow-up. The goal of this system is to note the effectiveness of the overall training program by measuring the progress of each employee exposed to it. This not only will serve to get more for each training dollar invested but also make it possible to become aware of deficiencies in the program. Thus, necessary improvements in techniques and practices can be implemented in a timely manner.

15

Personnel Motivation
and Evaluation

THE PURPOSE OF ANY property management company is to provide quality management services. This can be accomplished only through quality employees. To increase personnel productivity, managers need an understanding of how people work, why they work, and how to communicate with them to make them more achieving.

In order to reach this level of understanding, it may be helpful to examine the personnel function in management. The current personnel function is quite different from that which existed 25 years ago. This is owing in part to the fact that the employee of today is better educated and more articulate, enjoys greater economic security, and is more mobile than workers of years past. Furthermore, technological advancements and governmental attitude changes have led management to view workers in a new, more humanitarian light. Concern with the human aspects of employees has expanded to include sociological factors, and there is a growing realization that employees must be dealt with in terms of their own value as meaningful individuals. As a result of this new realization, and with the emergence of management as an important field of study, the personnel department has evolved as an important element of the corporate structure. Industrial psychology, personnel management, and employee relations have gained recognition in all types of enterprises, especially those that are people oriented. Indeed, what subject could be more important for a property manager? In the final analysis, a property manager is as much an administrator over people as he is a manager of property. Certainly as a manager of property,

231

he is concerned with maintenance of buildings, accounting for money, overall planning, and various other functions. However, all of these activities involve people and thus call for expertise in people management.

Motivation

Motivation is the driving force that encourages people to react the way they do. In the past, the management theory of motivation supported the stick and carrot method of encouraging employees to perform. The stick was the constant threat that the employee would lose his job if he failed to produce. The carrot was simply money. The assumption behind this theory was that employees, although basically lazy, were also greedy. It thus was assumed by employers that employees worked solely to satisfy their economic needs. The implication was that work was despised yet was looked upon as a necessary in order to satisfy basic physical needs: the provision of food, shelter, and clothing. The employee's only motivation was considered to be safety and security for himself and his family.

While there certainly may be some element of reality in this theory—some people may work primarily to receive a paycheck or because they fear being fired—it is not a valid comprehensive approach to motivation. The stick and carrot theory has been invalidated by the radical developments that have occurred in this country's social and tax system. The stick is not nearly as threatening: The immediate loss of a job is cushioned by unemployment insurance, greater personal savings, and the probability of getting another job. The carrot must be quite large if it is to be viewed as a real after-tax incentive. Thus, while management justifiably may consider wages and salary as motivators, it must have an understanding of other forms of motivation if it is to be in a position to make workers productive.

Factors of Motivation

An underlying precept of the theory of employee motivation is that one person cannot directly motivate another. The property manager is not a motivator. He cannot motivate his subordinates by specific action or actions. Motivation comes from within. People are motivated by responding to their own goals. A property manager, however, does have a role to play: to create an atmosphere in which motivation can take place. Filling this role requires the manager to

be sensitive to the goals of subordinates. For example, a new resident manager who assumes the responsibility of managing an apartment project must be able to see his own goal achievement in the
organization if he is going to be motivated. A property manager can
establish the necessary environment by working with the resident
manager to define his goals, stressing the idea that meeting those
goals is necessary to the overall success of the organization. Likewise,
it should be conveyed to the resident manager that he will find fulfillment of those goals possible and, subsequently, quite satisfying.

In order to manage people, communication with subordinates
is required. A manager needs to listen carefully and find out what a
subordinate employee wants from management and what he is
looking for in his job. In any business organization, an employer/
employee relationship of mutual dependency exists. Each party expects something from the other. Essentially, the company expects the
employee to competently perform his assigned duties, thus making
a contribution to the company's operation. The employee likewise
has expectations. Obviously, these include a steady paycheck and
proper working conditions. But there are other expectations, possibly
never stated by the employee but certainly considered important to
him. A manager's role is to determine what these expectations are—
these goals that the employee has set for himself—and assure him,
if appropriate, that they are within his reach.

Industrial psychologists generally agree that there are a number
of expectations that an employee may have of his job and of the
company for which he works. These include job security, recognition,
interesting employment, fringe benefits, opportunity for advancement, and physical working conditions. The property manager must
determine which of these factors plays the most critical role to each
of his subordinates. Each employee, after all, has a different set of
values and different abilities. Creating an environment in which
motivation can occur, therefore, must be done on a personal level.
Having determined the relative importance of the various motivating
factors, the manager can increase the value of the pertinent rewards
and make the situation more congenial to the employee's expectations. Consequently, the chances of having a motivated employee
who effectively works toward organizational goals is improved.

It is important to distinguish between true motivators and
satisfiers, sometimes referred to as hygiene factors. Such factors as
recognition, job satisfaction, and promotional advancement are motivators. When the manager creates an environment that is conducive

to satisfying these needs, employees are likely to become achieving workers. Satisfiers, on the other hand, are noticeable only in their absence, and then usually in a negative way. Wages, benefits, and working conditions are primary examples of satisfiers. These are factors that satisfy the most basic needs. Employees automatically expect, and justifiably so, that they will be paid properly, will have a good working environment, and will receive appropriate benefits. If they do not, they feel discriminated against.

A behavioral scientist who contributed much toward the study of this aspect of motivation was Frederick Herzberg. In a book entitled *Work and the Nature of Man,* published in 1966, Herzberg identified six motivators: achievement, recognition, responsibility, advancement, possibility for growth, and work itself. According to Herzberg, the satisfiers, which, when absent, lead to job dissatisfaction, are these factors: supervision, company policy and administration, working conditions, interpersonal on-the-job relations, status, job security, salary, and personal life. Herzberg has been faulted for failing to provide conclusive supportive evidence; however, his theory that people seek pleasing, satisfying work and take pleasure from doing their work well and getting ahead has become widely accepted. A property manager who wishes to apply Herzberg's philosophy first needs a practical understanding of these six motivators.

The achievement-motivated employee is the one who realizes satisfaction by the completion of a specific job or assignment. This employee sees accomplishment of the task as an end in itself, rather than as a means to some tangible reward. Achievement is the motivator for the person who reaps satisfaction from successfully competing with a difficult standard. Simply put, the achievement-motivated worker enjoys difficult jobs.

Recognition by management can be a key motivating factor. There are various ways that a manager can recognize a subordinate. One effective method is for the employer to seek the subordinate's opinion. A property manager, for example, might consult with a resident manager when he is drafting a policy on tenant selection, thus recognizing that the resident manager can bring an element of on-the-job expertise to the task. In fact, the resident manager indeed may know more about the financial limitations of prospective tenants and the parameters that should be established for security deposits, lease, terms, etc., than the property manager. Recognition for this knowledge should be given.

Another form of recognition is letting an employee know what is going on. Few subordinates will be productive if they feel that they are not being fully informed about what is happening in the company, especially as it relates to their own work.

Giving an employee added responsibility, both for his own work and for the work of others, can be an extremely potent motivator. Likewise, improvement in an employee's status can motivate him to higher levels of production. The employee who has learned his job and can perform it well wants to improve his personal growth. As discussed in chapter 1, most people unfortunately view advancement in terms of supervising other people. To the contrary, advancement can be realized in terms of improved professional competence and the application of an expanded knowledge. A manager must create an environment in which this latter form of advancement is recognized.

Similarly, knowing that the opportunity for advancement is present is a critical motivating force. Having mastered his job, an employee must know that a realistic opportunity for moving up within the organization exists. If he does not see opportunity, he will be of the opinion that he will always be doing the same work, which soon will become boring and without challenge: A demotivating influence will begin to take its toll on this worker.

Employees can receive great joy out of work, in and of itself, if that work is meaningful. Management's responsibility is to make work meaningful. The bookkeeping clerk who day after day fills out forms that are forwarded to the computer service center—never understanding the meaning of his work and how it is part of the total bookkeeping system—is not going to be motivated to increased productivity. If that bookkeeping clerk is explained the basics of the bookkeeping system and then asked to participate, even in some small way, in planning a bookkeeping procedure, his interest to learn will be greatly increased.

Likewise, a property manager has a challenge to make work meaningful to the janitorial staff who clean offices, dust, empty trash, clean restrooms, etc. Making their work meaningful and important to them is a measure of his success. For instance, training programs might be established in which maintenance personnel can learn how to lift heavy objects in such a way as to avoid physical injury. They might be taught the importance of their work to tenant satisfaction and therefore the management company's ability to collect rent and subsequently pay them. In both of these examples, the manager strives to create an environment in which all work is meaningful.

Managing by Objectives

Management by objectives (described as a method of organizing work in chapter 2) likewise is a system of motivating employees based on the principle of goal setting. Managing by objectives (MBO) is critical to employee motivation inasmuch as human behavior is typically goal oriented. MBO sets the goals to which employees strive, thus enabling them to feel a sense of achievement. If achievement is to play any part in an employee's motivation, he must know when he has achieved.

In order to be effective, objectives must meet several criteria: They must be realistic, measurable, and specific in nature; they must include timetables for achievement; and they must be established jointly by the manager and his surbordinate. For example, consider the situation in which a resident manager of a large apartment complex, which is experiencing a 20 percent vacancy rate, and his property manager agree to the following objective: "To achieve a 95 percent occupancy within 12 months." If, after the 12-month period, the prescribed occupancy level is reached, the resident manager will have met his objective and thus experience a sense of achievement. If no such goal had been set, no feeling of achievement would be evident. Furthermore, management should commend an employee when an objective is achieved, realizing that recognition is one of the primary employee motivators.

Because employees fill different kinds of roles within a property management business, it is useful for a property manager to think in terms of three types of objectives that may be needed in a complete motivational MBO plan: (1) Routine operating objectives dealing with the normal assignments and responsibilities of a job; (2) innovative objectives dealing with new ways of doing things and new things to do; and (3) developmental objectives dealing with improving performance and/or preparing for promotion.

Many jobs consist largely of duties that must be performed day in and day out. Many first-level supervisory positions, for instance, are characterized by such routine activity. For such persons, routine operating objectives must be established. One example of an employee who needs routine operating objectives is the foreman who supervises the night cleaning crew in an office building. He must see that the offices are cleaned according to a set of exacting standards while keeping close control over man-hours, cleaning materials, and equipment. That is his job, and it will be the same tomorrow, the next day, and the next. Meeting these ongoing standards is, in effect, his MBO.

Other jobs require more innovation—finding new ways to realize goals or even new goals to be realized. Some MBOs can and should be written with the element of innovation in mind. Such an objective might be established for a property manager. For instance, his MBO might be to find a way to compensate resident managers so as to encourage the attainment of a higher gross income than was budgeted in the management plan. The property manager's strategy could include working with resident managers in negotiating for higher rents without increasing the vacancy factor or jeopardizing the building's stable character of tenancy.

The third type of managerial objective focuses attention on improving employee performance. The manager must be a teacher, helping new employees understand their work and encouraging all employees to become full and richer persons. Objectives can and should be written in this area of personnel development as well.

Personnel Evaluation

Determining if employees are performing at the level they should be calls for a formal appraisal of each employee's performance. All employees—and especially new employees who are just joining the workforce—need feedback as to the quality of their work. Having been involved in setting their goals, they must be told whether they are achieving these goals and in what esteem management holds them. When properly administered, a performance appraisal can be a very potent motivating force.

There are several reasons why appraisals must be performed. As Marion S. Kellogg in her book entitled *What To Do About Performance Appraisal* (New York: AMACOM, a division of American Management Associations, 1975) says:

> Every manager faces several situations in which he needs to make an appraisal of an employee. Those most commonly experienced include the "coaching appraisal," in which the manager appraises the employee's performance in an effort to guide his own actions to help the employee improve his performance; the "career guidance appraisal," in which the manager appraises the employee's overall abilities in an effort to counsel the employee regarding career plans; the "salary appraisal," in which the manager appraises the value of the results of the employee's work as a guide to recommending suitable salary action; and the "promotional appraisal," in which the manager appraises the ability of the employee to do the work of a better, open position.
>
> Appraisal is a necessary part of a manager's work. It is his subjective judgment of the value of the individual's ability to do something. It is most likely to be sound if its purpose is well defined and if it is based on

information that is relevant, accurate, and sufficiently complete that no overriding information has been overlooked. It is most likely to be viewed as fair if the employee knows why he is being appraised, what goes into the judgment and how it will be used. It serves primarily as a guide for the manager's own actions with respect to the individual he appraises. A discussion of his appraisal with an employee serves to provide an input for the employee's own appraisal on which he, in turn, will base his actions.

Performance Evaluation
Page One of Two

Employee _____
Department/Supervisor _____
Evaluation Date _____Period Evaluation Covers _____

Purpose of evaluation:
1. To pinpoint strengths and weaknesses of employee performance.
2. To outline and agree upon a practical improvement program.
3. To provide a history of development and progress.

Instructions
1. A copy of this form stating evaluation date is given to employee.
2. Employee and evaluator complete form prior to scheduled evaluation.
3. Evaluator and employee compare completed forms and discuss differences, if any.
4. Employee and evaluator sign completed forms.

Requirements of position:
1. Refer to job description.
2. Specific duties other than those in job description _____

To be filled in upon completion of scheduled evaluation:
Employee only:
How can I improve the quality of work in the position I fill? _____

Evaluator only:
What specific steps can employee take to improve in areas receiving low ratings?

| Evalutor: | Employee: |
| I have discussed the evaluation with the employee and recommend the following: | The above evaluation was discussed with me. I wish to comment as follows: |

Signature _____   Signature _____
Date _____   Date _____

Filing:
1. Copies of both evaluation forms to employee.
2. Originals to employee file.

Figure 15.1.   Form for evaluating employee performance.

Although management's appraisal of an employee inevitably occurs informally on a day-to-day basis as a supervisor unconsciously notes how a subordinate is performing, it is important that a formal appraisal system be established if the appraisal is to be objective. Performing this appraisal calls for two considerations: (1) that specific and measurable goals be set and agreed to by both the sub-

---

Performance Evaluation
Page Two of Two

Rating: E—Exceeds requirements   I—Improvement
          S—Meets requirements   U—Unsatisfactory

Areas of Evaluation	E	S	I	U	Comments
Attitudes and Behavior					
Punctuality and attendance					
Acceptance and completion of assignments					
Adaptability: assistance to others; reactions to stress					
Integrity: acceptance of responsibility for self					
Interpersonal relations: acceptance of counsel; courtesy					
Skills and Knowledge					
Skills for position outlined in job description					
Knowledge of company policies					
Knowledge of company procedures for day-to-day business					
Initiative					
Problem solving and decision making					
Communication skills					
Organizational planning and follow through					
Teaching and evaluating (if applicable)					
Intellectual curiosity and creativity					
Ability to set priorities					
Need for supervision to meet requirements of position					
Personal Impression					
Cleanliness and neatness; poise; personality					

Figure 15.1 (continued).   Checklist for employee evaluation.

ordinate and the employer—a basic principle of the MBO system, and (2) that actual achievements be measured against these objectives. Most companies have a form that is filled out by managers once or twice a year for each employee and serves as a formal judgment of that employee's performance. An example of such an evaluation report is shown as figure 15.1. While completing the form is not the complete appraisal process, it is helpful in documenting the manager's attitude of the employee's work. Ms. Kellogg provides the following "manager's checklist on employee appraisal ethics" which can serve as a guideline to property managers when they are called upon to appraise employee performance:

1. Know the reason for appraisal.
2. Appraise on the basis of representative information.
3. Appraise on the basis of sufficient information.
4. Appraise on the basis of relevant information.
5. Make an honest appraisal.
6. Keep written and oral appraisals consistent.
7. Present appraisal as opinion.
8. Give appraisal information only to those who have a good reason to know it.
9. Don't imply the existence of an appraisal that hasn't been made.
10. Don't accept another's appraisal without knowing the basis for it.
11. Decide on a retention policy for appraisals and adhere to it.
12. Convey appraisal data to a third party only if you've given it to the person.
13. Make written appraisals available to employees.
14. Provide a right of appeal to employees.
15. Open appraisals to employee input.

The performance appraisal, specifically as it relates to property managers, is discussed in more detail in chapter 3.

V
The Management Office

16

The Facility, Staff, and Services

REAL ESTATE MANAGEMENT is a service industry that demands a comparatively small investment in plant and equipment and a large investment in people. Interestingly, a property management firm may be responsible for the operation of assets worth millions of dollars yet require few capital resources of its own. Though by nature a company's capital base is small, it has an extremely high operating cost ratio. If expenses are not carefully managed, the company's operating results are unattractive.

One of the major problems in the property management industry is that too many developers and other real estate institutions and sales organizations have been willing to operate the management department at a break-even point or even a loss. The economic rationalization is that management offers business opportunity for other, more profitable real estate activities. In short, property management acts as a loss leader. However, there is overwhelming evidence that the investment real estate sector is willing to pay a reasonable fee in exchange for competent management service. Consequently, property management can be a viable profit center. The profit level that may be achieved is dependent upon good management of the company as a whole and, specifically, the central management office.

The management office and, above all, the work that takes place there are integral to the total property management operation. The effective office acts as a nerve center, ready to produce records of past and current operations and support the persons directly involved with the properties under management. Consequently, professional property managers must give due attention to the management office, its staff, and the services it provides.

Office Design and Location

When selecting and designing a property management office, several factors should be considered: utilization of space, aesthetic environment, location, and cost.

The first consideration in office layout and planning is the utilization of space for efficiency in work flow, storage requirements, and employee relations. This requires a careful analysis of the space and equipment needs for each person who works in the management office. This analysis is a data-gathering, question-asking step that is necessary if an operative plan for integrated space is to be reached. The integrated office is one that is unified toward a common objective —the establishment of a successful property management enterprise. Each chair, each file cabinet, each table, each typewriter should be where it is because that location helps most in accomplishing the required work. As a general rule, employees involved in similar activities should be together. For example, it usually is most efficient to locate property managers and their respective secretaries and files together in one portion of the office and separate from the bookkeeping department and its equipment, numerous files, and special needs.

This is not to imply that an office must sacrifice aesthetic appeal for utilitarianism. The well-planned office combines a pleasant environment with efficiency, is practical yet impressive. The place in which a person works and how that work is accomplished are difficult to separate. People whose jobs require them to spend their working days in offices consider aesthetics and comfort to be very important factors in making their decisions as to where they are going to work. Lighting, air conditioning, elevator service, security, level of maintenance, neighborhood characteristics, and the prestige of the facility are important considerations in attracting good employees to the company.

Another consideration, and a crucial one for a property management business, is location. Having performed an analysis of its needs, management must locate an office that meets them. For instance, the building must offer an adequate module for efficient use of space, a proper lighting pattern, air conditioning and heating capability, and adequate wiring facilities. But above all, it should be located in an area that serves to meet the company's objectives. In this respect, the value of the location in relation to the ease with which the company is able to attract employees and clients is of great importance. Management should do all it can to locate its central office in an area that is served by adequate transportation facilities, offers sufficient parking, and is convenient to shopping areas, restaurants, and banking facilities. Another consideration for office location is accessibility to properties under management. The travel time of property managers to and from properties can be quite costly if the distance is excessive.

Proper location also can serve as an invaluable public relations tool. There is some advertising value in being located in a prestigious neighborhood and building; often, in fact, the neighborhood is more important than the building. The value of a ground floor location in a prestigious neighborhood is usually too expensive for a property management company; however, the advertising value of a location that allows for good company identification should not be overlooked.

There is one other consideration in selecting an office that is unique to the property management industry: For a property management company, the selection of a location for its central office may mean an opportunity for additional business. It is not unusual for property management companies to have their offices in buildings they manage. The well-established property management firm that moves its headquarters into a large office building and assumes the management of that property offers the ownership a depth of management not available with an independent building manager. In addition, it offers the office building a stable tenant.

The cost of office space, of course, cannot be overlooked. When renting office space, cost is measured in terms of dollars per square foot per year. In a typical real estate company, the expense for office rent may be eight percent of the company's gross income. Certainly there are advantages in renting office space: the possibility of a new management account, as mentioned earlier; the freeing of large amounts of capital; flexibility in changing location; opportunity for the small company. On the other hand, management might give some consideration to the company's owning its own building. This provides for company identification and prestige as well as appreciation in value. Sometimes the company's tenancy and management abilities can be parlayed into forming a limited partnership wherein the company is the general partner that purchases and manages a significant office building. Under this arrangement, there is the potential for a future real estate commission should the partnership decide to sell its investment.

The Office Staff

There is an optimum number of employees for any business venture. For a property management firm, it is the minimum number required to effectively handle its gross volume. Because success depends on the quality of employees, a company must attract people of unusual capabilities through compensation, environment, and opportunity and subsequently use them effectively through efficient systems and policies. Crucial to a successful management operation is a strong supportive staff in the central office. The principal employees who make up the office staff are the controller, accounting personnel, secretaries, and the receptionist.

Controller

One of the key employees in a property management firm is the controller. In addition to performing certain accounting duties (described in detail in chapter 17), the controller usually is the office manager as well. Being responsible for the administration of the central office, he supervises a host of services, facilities, and equipment that support the activities of the business enterprise. These responsibilities encompass the mail function, office equipment and maintenance, supplies procurement, copying and duplicating, telephone communications, and the maintenance of the office premises. To these responsibilities often is added the task of supervising all office personnel—specifically, the receptionist, secretaries, and bookkeepers.

It is absolutely essential that the person selected as office manager be able to get along well with people. Typically, 60 percent of the people employed by a real estate management company are full-time office workers. These employees will look to the office manager for leadership and discipline. The executives of the firm and the property managers are only part-time employees in terms of their presence in the office, inasmuch as the nature of their work requires them to be in the field supervising buildings, not sitting in the office. Thus, the responsibility for morale, training, and motivating of the full-time office staff falls to the office manager.

As the person responsible for more than half the company's

labor force, the office manager must be concerned about determining the optimum number of people in the office and effectiveness of performance of the office staff. Efficiency is sought by developing economical office practices through work centralization, designing effective reports and records systems, and effectively scheduling office work. Similarly, improvement in productivity, sources of trouble spots, relative accomplishments, and the capacity for the organization to grow through more effective use of office staff must be of interest to the office manager.

Accounting Personnel

To provide job descriptions here for employees in the bookkeeping department would be useless. For one thing, there are several different kinds of bookkeeping systems—hand posting, machine, service bureau, computerized—that can be employed to implement one of several different programs of accounting. What is more useful is to point out some operating characteristics of bookkeeping departments.

A direct relationship exists between growth of the enterprise and the bookkeeping department. When a company's business grows to the point at which it needs to add another qualified property manager, it also needs an additional qualified person in the bookkeeping department. Therefore, a guideline for staffing is to have one bookkeeper, exclusive of the controller, for each property manager.

There also apparently is greater productivity when bookkeepers are allowed to handle all aspects of the income and disbursements related to a particular property than when the functions are departmentalized into the accounts receivable and accounts payable functions. This efficiency further increases when a bookkeeper is assigned to a particular property manager. The property manager, his secretary, and the bookkeeper become a team familiar with all of the aspects of managing a particular group of properties. The bookkeeper has the responsibility for producing accurate information on time and becomes familiar with the myriad of operational characteristics that are peculiar to this set of properties or this set of owners. An auditor might argue that this form of team arrangement does not properly measure up to the test for internal audit and control; however, the advantage of increased operational efficiency usually outweighs this concern.

It is critical that the bookkeeping department realizes the importance of the timeliness of monthly reports. If monthly reports to clients are not mailed on time, this becomes a poor reflection upon the management company's capabilities. Missed deadlines should be regarded as a sign that the bookkeeping department is behind schedule in its work. This results in a wave of all kinds of problems: reports to property managers about rental collections become delinquent; vendors are not paid on time and begin calling the office asking for their checks, causing unproductive time for secretaries and property managers and a lag in service to the buildings; payments to mortgage companies, federal payroll agencies, business license agencies, and real estate tax collectors can be missed and lead to penalties for late payment. The whole operation of the company begins to lose efficiency simply because the accounting department is not functioning on a proper time schedule. There is only one solution: Either people work overtime or additional help is brought in until activity is back on schedule.

Interestingly, the highest employee turnover in a property management organization usually occurs in the bookkeeping department. The cost of personnel change is not to be overlooked. It not only costs in terms of productivity at the level of the new employee, but it also costs in terms of executive time to recruit, select, and train new people. Furthermore, company morale can be affected greatly by a constant change of people. For these reasons, special attention should be devoted to administration and development of the bookkeeping staff.

A good philosophy for the operation of the bookkeeping department is that it makes no decisions; rather, it follows instructions. The responsibility for instructing the bookkeeping department lies in the systems and procedures manual, which explains how money is to be received and recorded and disbursements made and who receives various types of reports and statements. The information flows to it from resident managers and property managers. The bookkeeping department, for instance, does not approve bills, establish rates of pay, or authorize the distribution of reports and statements. Rather, it implements the policies established in respect to these concerns. It follows instructions but does not initiate actions. Operating in this fashion, responsibility for performance of a property is where it belongs—in the hands of a property manager.

Secretarial Staff

In a property management office, the main qualification for a secretary is versatility. It is helpful to have good basic secretarial skills, but equally if not more important is managerial ability to handle the myriad of details that face the property manager. A secretary deals with resident managers, tenants, and clients when a property manager is in conference or out of the office. Since the property manager usually is out of the office at least 50 percent of his working hours, he needs a secretary who has a good personality, a lot of common sense, and the ability to handle people. Experience has shown that a highly qualified secretary can handle effectively the needs and responsibilities of two to three full-time property managers.

Receptionist

The receptionist in a real estate management organization plays an important role, as this person often provides the first introduction of the company to the public. It is imperative that a receptionist be an attractive, well-mannered, neatly attired, intelligent person who is well acquainted with the basic operations of the company. Management should not take the attitude that this position is one that can be filled by a young person on the low end of the company's pay scale. The level of responsibility denies the validity of this attitude. The receptionist must have a working knowledge of all departments of the company and all the people therein. Many telephone calls are from people who do not have the vaguest idea of who or what department should be able to solve their problems. A receptionist with a good knowledge of the firm is able to query the caller and direct him to the proper person. The company's public relations image is preserved, and no time is wasted because of misdirected telephone calls.

Since management companies usually have few personal visitors, a receptionist often receives people by telephone. If this reception is unpleasant, the public relations framework that the property managers and company executives have worked so hard to build can be quickly torn down. Smaller offices typically combine reception duties with other tasks, such as typing, opening and distributing mail, preparing certain management information reports from data furnished by on-site managers, or assisting the accounting department. However, none of these tasks should interfere with the primary responsibility as the firm's receptionist.

Record Keeping

The role of the management office is to provide supportive services to property managers who are involved in running income properties. Office services cover a wide range of activities, chief among them that of record keeping.

A common complaint of numerous business organizations revolves around the volume of records needed to operate. In order for businesses to comply with the ever-growing multiplicity of government regulations and information requirements, all companies, even the smallest ones, must keep more records than ever before. One of the purported benefits of an advanced computer system and its technology is that it provides a record-storing system and thus is of great assistance in solving record-storage problems. To the contrary, however, an observation of property management company bookkeeping departments will reveal that computer systems have not solved the problem but indeed have added to the paper volume. Because computers have the capability to produce numerous records and management information reports, the technology actually compounds the paper problem. Unless a business recognizes that record keeping is an operational function that needs direction and supervision, employees can waste tremendous amounts of time simply looking for information.

Some basic rules should be considered by management to solve the paper problem and create a scientific record management system. The term "records" refers to all documents that are filed, including forms, correspondence, reports, reference materials, contracts, leases, memoranda, etc. A program of records management covers four major areas: records creation, records processing, records retention and disposal, and records protection.

Regardless of the size of the organization or the nature of its business purpose, it is important to initiate control over the production of paperwork before it occurs. The first rule, then, is to make sure that each form or report is reviewed in detail and proven to be needed before it is added to the office information system. The goal should be to prove its absolute necessity in terms of legal requirements, how it will be used, who will use it, and where it should be stored. An important technique for proving the validity of a new record is to query the proposer as to why he feels that information is needed in order for him to better do his job and how he's going to use that information. The amount of space required to store records in a real estate management company office can become a problem if this examination is not made. It is estimated that each bookkeeping employee will require 10 cubic feet of storage space and each property manager will require five cubic feet of storage space. Unnecessarily increasing this space requirement can be hazardous.

Each company needs a procedure that streamlines record keeping and the retrieval of information. Management company records and information resources fall into two broad categories: transaction documents and reference documents. Transaction documents are rent bills, invoices, checks, active correspondence with tenants and clients and vendors, the current month's computer runs for bookkeeping operations, etc. These documents are vital to current operations and need to be filed in a manner that will present no special problems for retrieval. The company needs to develop a system of procedures so that as a document travels from one work station to another, it can be located and identified easily. If the system is consistent, all employees in the company can learn the work flow procedures. In consequence, when a transaction document is needed, it can be located without unnecessarily interrupting the entire office staff.

Consider the simple problem of a vendor calling and asking when he's going to get paid for a particular invoice: Typically, the invoice would first go to a property manager for approval, then to the accounting department for processing, then to the computer center for printing of the check, back to the property manager for signing of the check, and then to the mail clerk for mailing. Finally, the paid invoice is deposited in the current month's paid-bills file. This simple process of paying a bill involves a minimum of five procedural steps. This means that a number of people could be interrupted in order to learn the status of the invoice if the company did not have a records processing system that was familiar to all the employees in the office.

The other category of documents—reference documents—refers to reports, research studies, legal documents, and other such records. They are not currently in use but must be available when research is called for. Appropriate files must be created for these reference materials.

Another part of the records processing system is establishment of how files are to be kept and labeled. Is the reference going to be by alphabet, by building number, by client's name, or by some other identification form? The important thing is not what label is attached to the filing system; rather, the rule should be consistency. No one should be permitted to establish a file that does not conform with the company's filing system.

Under the activity of records retention and disposal, the company should establish policies, procedures, and schedules for the disposition of records not required for continuing operations. Such a policy is important not only for economy and efficient use of space but also to protect the company in meeting its legal obligations for the retention of records. In too many businesses, too much material is kept, resulting in row upon row of filing cabinets filled with useless documents. With adaption of a records-retention system, only those records that pass the test of usefulness are kept.

Establishment of a rigid timetable of retention periods for all types of records is part of this system. The statute of limitations is one guideline to be used when establishing policy as to the disposition of records. The legal requirements for keeping records are: public liability laws, seven years; income tax laws, three years; and wage and compensation laws, three years. There is no statute of limitations that bars criminal prosecution; consequently, records that might protect the company against criminal action, while theoretically having a possible use indefinitely, have to be considered in the light of the cost for storage versus the risk of their being needed. All insurance policies that protect the agent and the owner against public liability risks must be kept for seven years. In this regard it is important to keep copies of all letters, statements, and other evidence that may be useful in answering a personal injury claim.

The management company's risk for wage and hour claims by employees—even though those employees may not continue to work at the company—runs for three years. Therefore, all time sheets, pay records, employment contracts, union agreements, and cancelled payroll checks must be kept for this minimum term. Since management companies keep the original cash receipts and cash disbursements ledgers for the operations of a property as well as its general ledger, they should, for the benefit of their clients, keep all bookkeeping records for a period of three years. This is suggested inasmuch as this information may be needed to answer an Internal Revenue Service audit of a client.

Legal requirements, however, are not the sole criterion for establishing policies and procedures on records retention and disposal. The company also must consider its own administrative experience and decide what are practical terms for keeping specific kinds of records. Many records, such as occupancy reports, purchase orders, and interim accounting reports, have no direct relation to the various statutes or regulations. In such instances, it is important to analyze the length of time that they should remain in the operational filing system, when they should be transferred to a dead storage area, and when they should be finally disposed of.

Furthermore, a management company needs to give attention to how it is going to protect certain kinds of records from possible disasters. There are at least three common risks that could destroy a company's records and create enormous problems through their loss: fire, water damage, and mutilation by thieves seeking valuables. In a management company, the primary concern is for accounting data of current month's operations, rental collection records, paid invoices, duplicate copies of checks or cash disbursed ledgers, bank deposits, and employee payroll records—all pieces of information that would be very difficult to reproduce should the office experience a disaster. In response, a company should develop a storage area in which important records can be put at night when the office is left unattended. It should have a minimum two-hour fire rating and be locked securely. The most important documents to protect from a disaster are those sources of information that would be needed to resume the company's operations after a disaster. The company also must consider the value of the data that will be required to re-establish the legal and financial status of the company and provide for its protection. Usually this problem can be solved by keeping duplicate records in separate locations.

The whole problem of records administration continues to grow as property management becomes more sophisticated. Computers add to the ability to create management information reports and accumulate data, and government is forever increasing its requirements for the businessman to keep and store records. If not properly organized, the records administration system becomes a great time waster and has a major adverse impact on the bottom line of the property management company's operating statement. The principal consideration should be to establish procedures and rules that enable all members of the organization to work together and, above all, are simple and easily understood. Usually, the more simple the system, the greater its efficiency.

17

Trust Fund Accounting

A PRIMARY PREREQUISITE a property management company must meet in order to be prepared for growth is the addition of a qualified individual who assumes responsibility for the company's bookkeeping department and especially its trust fund accounting system. The importance of the trust fund accounting function in the management of income property cannot be overemphasized. It represents a major cost center in the operation of a real estate management business, usually requiring 20 to 25 percent of gross fees earned. If this function is not professionally and efficiently administered by a qualified controller, the company's earning ability may be placed in serious jeopardy.

Accounting System Objectives

Establishing an accounting system takes into consideration the authenticating, recording, classifying, processing, summarizing, and analyzing of all financial transactions and events related to properties under management. Trust fund accounting implies the use of a central trust account into which all monies collected for various property owners are put into a single account. The use of a trust account is operationally more efficient than the use of an individual account for each client. The fewer the number of transactions, the more efficient the system. Obviously, it is easier and less time consuming to write one check that covers the water bill for 25 properties than to write 25 separate checks to the water company. Pitfalls do exist in a trust arrangement, however. For instance, management must guard against writing a check to cover an expense incurred by one property that would technically overdraw its account and, by doing so, would require taking money from another property's account. The system should be designed with safeguards to prevent this kind of illegal action to occur.

Furthermore, at no time should there be commingling of the management company's funds with the funds of any of its clients. Clients' funds never should be subject to the liabilities that may be claimed against the company. The practice of placing management company funds and those funds entrusted to the company by clients in the same account is both illegal and dangerous. Commingling of these funds should be avoided for at least two reasons: (1) There is the possibility, either knowingly or by error, of using client funds to pay the liabilities of the company, such as meeting operating expenses or payroll. (2) Should the company's funds be attached for nonpayment of debts, such as payroll taxes or income taxes, the bank account possibly would be tied up for an indefinite period. This would cause a hardship on, and possible penalties to, clients.

A trust fund accounting system should be designed in such a way that it guards against these inherent pitfalls and fulfills certain additional objectives.

Record Income and Expenses

First and foremost, the system must be able to account for all money going into and out of the account of a property. The management company is the agent of each property owner and must assume total fiduciary responsibility for the collection and disbursement of funds relating to each property. Meeting this responsibility requires the establishment of a bookkeeping department to perform the day-to-day activities of collecting and recording rents and other income and paying bills. This must be done according to detailed standard operating procedures and ultimately should result in the collection of data with which accountants can prepare reports to be presented to property owners.

Bookkeeping activities may be performed in one of two ways: on an accrual basis or a cash basis. The accrual method accounts for income as it is earned and expenses as they are incurred. The cash method accounts for money as it actually is received and disbursements as they actually are paid out. Traditionally, property management trust fund accounting systems operate on a cash basis, although property tax and insurance may be handled on an accrual basis. (In accounting for property tax, for example, one-twelfth of the total is accrued each month, even though the actual tax payment is made once or twice a year.)

Collect and Present Data

The second objective of an accounting system is that it properly accumulates data and subsequently presents it in such a way that the data can be objectively analyzed. A good accounting system provides a wide variety of data that can be scrutinized so that management may be more effective. In order to fulfill this objective, cut-off procedures must be implemented. With standard cut-off dates for accumulation of financial data, financial statements are prepared in such a way that they show a property's operating results for equal, or at least relatively equal, periods of time. Normally, financial statement cut-off is on a monthly basis accumulated for the operating year of the property, which may be either a calendar or fiscal year. In a property management environment, the monthly cut-offs usually are at some point other than the end of calendar months. This means, for example, that the cut-off for September would not be the last day of the month, or September 30, but rather, for instance, September 25. Logically, all rents for September are collected by this time, but few, if any, of the October rents have been collected. In ensuing months, the cut-off is maintained as near to the 25th, or five days prior to the end of the calendar month, as possible, taking into account weekends and holidays. Expenses should follow this pattern also; for instance, only one month's services should be paid in a given month. Such services might include trash collection, landscaping, maintenance, utilities, janitor service, and elevator maintenance. Without systematic cut-off dates, accurate comparisons of results are difficult, if not impossible, to make.

Likewise important to performing comparable analysis of operations is information relating anticipated results with actual results. By providing information of past operations, the accounting system enables a property manager to go beyond guesswork and make authenticated projections into and plans for the future. A good operating statement, for instance, includes not only actual operating results but also budgeted figures. Thus, comparisons may be made easily. Management thus can determine if the property is being run according to the management plan; if not, corrections can be implemented. Other operating reports that may be produced by an accounting system for analytical purposes are these: comparisons of current year's operations with previous year's, vacancy factors or occupancy percentages, delinquent and bad debt figures, turnover rates, square foot operating costs, operating costs as percentages of gross scheduled income, cash flow statements and cash flow projections, lease expiration lists, and tenant profiles.

In connection with this, a trust accounting system should be able to produce accurate, timely, and understandable monthly operating statements for property owners. Operating statements should be regarded as client relations tools. In fact, sometimes the only regular contact a management company has with a client is through monthly reports. For this reason, particular attention should be given to the design and appearance of its reports to owners. The format should be simple enough to permit the client to easily understand the financial performance of the property yet complete enough that he can review each major area of concern—income, operating expenses, capital expenditures, and cash flow. The operating statement should be a prestigious, readable document that properly reflects the client's sizeable investment in his property. If it is presented in an attractive cover and accompanied by a letter explaining the month's operations, the image of the management company is sure to be enhanced. An example of a clear and well formated financial operating statement is presented as figure A.12 in the appendix. These elements are necessary to the operating statement:

1. Owner identification and account number.
2. Property information, including property name, number of units, net rental area, and current and year-to-date scheduled gross rent.
3. Current month's operating data.
4. Year-to-date operating data, actual compared with budget. The budget comparison is needed only for major classifications, such as total income, total payroll, etc., although the budget is prepared on a line-by-line basis.
5. Actual numbers as percentages of scheduled gross rents.
6. Cash flow. This is presented on a separate statement to summarize for the client all the cash transactions.
7. "Box score" of occupancy and tenant collections, included in the cash flow statement.

Although numerous formats for financial statements are available, these seven elements cover most of the information needed by clients on a monthly basis. Some additional information may be given to clients in the form of:

- A rent roll, which lists each unit and tenant plus scheduled monthly charges, security deposits, cleaning fees, and collections.
- General ledger detail analysis of expenses.
- Disbursement register of all checks written.
- Cash receipts journal of all cash received by owner.

Classify Income and Expenses

Another objective of an accounting system is that it provides for a means of accurately and consistently classifying sources of income and items of expense. Classification is accomplished through a chart of accounts. If it is to be effective, a chart of accounts must include not only a one- or two-word title and an account number but an in-depth description as well. Without descriptions, the people who are charged with using the chart inevitably use it incorrectly, making improper classifications that evidence themselves in erroneously reported operating results.

A property management company typically has a master chart of accounts that is used in connection with all the properties under its stewardship. (See figure 12.2.) Each property then is assigned from the master chart those accounts it needs. Not every property will need the same accounts as every other. For instance, an office building with a candy vending machine will need an account for vending machine income, while a building with no such machine will have no need of such an account. Only those accounts of which a property has real need should be utilized in connection with it. The purpose of a chart of accounts is to standardize and clarify; unnecessary accounts can only confuse.

Control Accuracy

In addition, a trust accounting system requires a set of internal controls. In a broad sense, internal control is defined as: (1) safeguarding assets or resources from misuse or waste, (2) promoting accuracy and reliability of accounting data, (3) judging the efficiency of property operations, and (4) measuring compliance with established company policies. This discussion is concerned primarily with the second internal control, i.e., the accuracy and reliability of accounting data. In an accounting system, no matter how well designed, errors will occur. The system must have the ability to detect errors within a reasonable period of time after they have occurred. A program should be detailed in written form to spot errors and dishonest acts. One way to establish this internal control is to use flow charting. The object of flow charting is to define the flow of all documents and procedures critical to the accounting function.

Listed below are some practical suggestions for internal control of cash receipts.

1. Endorse all checks immediately upon acceptance from tenant. This stops any attempt of conversion of monies for improper use. To facilitate this procedure, use rubber endorsement stamps, usually provided by banks at time checking accounts are established.

2. Establish, if possible, a no-cash policy. Cash is easily converted to improper use and increases chances of thefts.

3. Prepare in some manner, such as a collection sheet, an original listing of cash receipts that later may be compared with accounting records.

4. Request duplicate deposit slips from bank at time original bank deposits are made.

5. Make bank deposits on a regular basis, daily if possible.

6. Establish a system to test the overall reasonableness of collections. Usually this may be done in apartment management by comparing cash collections to scheduled gross rent (all possible rents if all units were producing rents) and occupancy of the building.

7. Prepare bank reconciliations on a regular basis; monthly is recommended. Care should be given in tracing each collection sheet amount recorded to deposits per bank.

Similarly, certain suggestions can be followed in establishing internal controls of cash disbursements:

1. Establish responsibility for signing of checks with someone other than the person who prepares them or reconciliation.

2. Make payments only from original invoices that have been approved by an authorized person, such as property manager. Avoid paying from duplicated copies (photocopies) or from requests for checks not supported by original documents.

3. Present checks for signing with original documents attached.

Mark in some way that invoice has been paid at time of signing.
4. Again prepare bank reconciliation on a regular basis.

These guidelines should be heeded when internal controls regarding payroll are established:

1. Require as a minimum, before an employee is added to payroll, an authorization in writing from the property manager stating the employee's wages, job description, effective employment date, and any additional compensation, such as an apartment.
2. Require that the employee complete the necessary legal and government documents. These often include a W-2 form, insurance application, employment agreement, fidelity bond, safety program compliance for OSHA, and petty cash agreement.
3. Require that employees be paid on an hourly basis and that approved time cards be submitted to payroll department for all hours worked.
4. Maintain employee personnel file.

These lists represent suggestions of appropriate policies and procedures and should not be interpreted as a complete system of internal control. Establishing internal controls specifically designed for a company's method of operation is a key function of the company controller. If the company has no controller, the use of an outside accounting service to design the controls should be considered. Likewise, outside accountants are used to provide auditing service. The typical feeling is that audits create unnecessary work for bookkeeping departments and connote a feeling of mistrust. However, a property management company should use an audit as a positive tool to improve the system of internal control and assure clients that their funds are being properly handled. Clients usually pay for the audit, and this service can be extremely useful as a client relations tool.

An audit performed by a certified public accounting firm does not guarantee that each accounting transaction is correct or that dishonesty is not present but does certify that the statement fairly presents, in the opinion of the auditors, operations of the entity. Therefore, owners and managers can rely on the information to make business decisions. In addition, an audit usually is accompanied by a management letter detailing improvements that may be made to internal control. This letter should be reviewed with the purpose of consideration of implementing the improvements suggested.

Require Minimum Managerial Time

Another objective of an accounting system is that it not place undue burden upon a property manager's time. A property manager must be involved with the bookkeeping department in the performance of various activities—approving bills, reviewing rent rolls and delinquent rent reports, and approving monthly statements, for instance. Yet the property manager's time is much too valuable for him to be occupied with detailed bookkeeping procedures.

This is in no way a denial of the value of the bookkeeping staff. To the contrary, it is a reaffirmation of the need to have a trained staff and a competent controller who can assume responsibility for managing it. The bookkeeping department must realize that its role within the team is not to make decisions but rather to receive instructions from property managers and respond to them according to prescribed procedures.

Similarly, the property manager must understand clearly and fully his company's accounting system. If he does not, he will make errors, and errors always result in wasted time. Furthermore, he will lack confidence in the reports he submits to his clients. To circumvent this problem, top management should continually examine its property managers as to their knowledge of the accounting system and its accompanying procedures. When evidence of a lack of understanding presents itself, a training session should be conducted to reacquaint the managers with the system and introduce them to any new elements of it.

Necessitate Minimum Expense

Finally, a trust accounting system must achieve all of the previously described objectives at a reasonable cost. Real estate management is in large part an information-gathering industry. A real estate management company's growth is limited to the amount of information it can collect, analyze, and store. Agency management cannot afford unlimited record keeping and analysis. An efficient yet effective trust fund accounting system is one that meets all of the other objectives without exceeding 25 percent of the company's fee income.

Bookkeeping Systems

A good accounting system is one that services the needs of the particular kind of enterprise, in this case property management. An accounting system not designed with the principal activity of the enterprise in mind will be ineffective. The property manager's expertise must be joined with the accountant's expertise in designing a trust accounting system that meets the practical demands of property management and is compatible with generally accepted accounting procedures.

Crucial to developing the overall accounting program is determining what form of bookkeeping system is most suitable to the individual property management firm. This is a decision that rests with the company's top management personnel. There are three types of bookkeeping systems: a hand-posted system, a machine-posted system, and a computerized system. Each has its merits, but each also suffers from shortcomings. The respective advantages and disadvantages must be weighed in relation to the operation of a given property management firm prior to deciding which system is most compatible with that operation. What is important is that whatever bookkeeping system is chosen, it must be able to perform the three primary bookkeeping functions—the cash receipts function, the cash disbursements function, and the payroll function.

Hand-Posted

A hand-posted bookkeeping system, sometimes known as a manual system, is the least costly of the three systems—probably one-half the cost of a computer system—and requires the least amount of technical skill. It is quite effective when used by a property management firm that has a small portfolio, in which case one bookkeeper can handle the three bookkeeping functions. With growth, however, the system becomes cumbersome and restrictive. A management business whose portfolio grows to 800 to 1,000 units or 20 to 30 buildings will find too many limitations in this system. For instance, it requires that the cash disbursements ledger have one column for each account or property managed. If 30 buildings are being managed, 30 columns are needed. This number of columns not only is unwieldy, but, if an error is made, a great deal of time is needed to locate it. The system becomes impossible to control. If there is no control, the system fails to meet a crucial objective.

Machine-Operated

The mechanical system, or NCR or bookkeeping machine, gained wide acceptance during the 1930s and continues to be used successfully by smaller real estate management companies. It customarily is quite effective for a company managing 30 to 100 properties and operating out of one trust fund account with a subsidiary ledger for each managed property. The biggest advantage of this system is that the operator knows at all times the exact balance for each property in the trust account. Knowledge of a property's operations is, after all, one of the keys to sound management. Furthermore, this system guarantees that even the least skilled operator will be unable to overdraw a given property's bank account. Each property has an individual ledger card. Thus, if after writing a check the bank balance is negative, the operator can immediately void checks written for that property. In addition, invoices can be totalled prior to writing checks and tested to the ledger card to ensure that the cash balance is sufficient to cover payments.

Because monthly income and disbursement entries are visible on one ledger card, it is easy to find errors. Thus, inherent in a mechanical bookkeeping system are good controls. Another benefit of the bookkeeping machine is its cost. The ongoing operation of this kind of system costs approximately 75 percent of the cost of a computer system. Likewise, the initial cost for equipment is low; rebuilt NCR machines in good condition may be purchased for about $3,000 to $5,000.

Unfortunately, the machine-operated bookkeeping system does have drawbacks. For one thing, it is very difficult to balance the account of a property containing more than 100 units. The machine-operated system does not produce a rent roll—the rent roll must be hand-posted—so it becomes quite time consuming to identify collections from individual tenants. Also, with larger properties, it is no longer a simple process to locate a posting error. Certainly errors can be detected, but tracking them again requires a major expense of time. Another problem with this system is that it is becoming increasingly difficult to find experienced, stable NCR operators. The older machines were quite noisy, and operators using them were segregated in enclosed rooms for noise control. Although modern NCR machines are much more compact and quieter than the older models, many operators changed employment and now are working for computer service companies. However, of all the disadvantages of the bookkeeping machine, perhaps the greatest is that it does not provide management information via production of reports for property owners. These reports must be prepared manually based on the accounting data gathered in the system.

Computerized

Although the application of electronic data processing (EDP) advancements to the property management industry is still in relative infancy, computer systems are becoming more and more a part of the operations of many offices. In fact, in some instances, computerization is becoming a necessity for efficient modern property management.

The first property management organizations to use computers were those that managed more than 10,000 units and syndicators of significantly large limited partnerships. In 1971, no sophisticated program for property management companies could be found. Computer manufacturers at that time were beginning to recognize real estate management organizations as business opportunities, but no one had developed an operating program. Although a few programs were available through service bureaus, for the most part these had been designed for specific operations and were not applicable to property management functions without considerable reprogramming. Since that time, the market for the use of computers and computer systems in property management has been recognized by both manufacturers and service bureaus. Companies considering computer systems to meet their accounting needs now have a wide range of available choices.

An EDP system is generally accepted as a necessity for any company managing more than 4,000 bookkeeping units, and especially for the company planning for growth. As evidence, on one occasion a specific firm's portfolio grew by 2,600 units within one month. Nevertheless, all reports were mailed on time without interruption in the performance schedule. This could never have been accomplished without a highly effective EDP system. This is not to imply, however, that only large companies will find EDP systems useful. In fact, they can be used by companies managing as few as 1,500 units and have proven to be economically feasible for the agency management firm.

The primary advantage of an EDP system is that it not only maintains accurate, up-to-date books of the business but also provides sophisticated reports for property owners, management company executives, property managers, resident managers, and tenants, specifically those listed in figure 17.1. For the property manager who is cognizant of the value of receiving accurate reports on time, this is an advantage that cannot be ignored.

Property managers have access to two primary types of automated accounting systems: service bureaus and in-house computers. When using a service bureau, the management firm contracts for a company's computer services, including the use of equipment and programs. An in-house system is one installed at a property management office for the firm's exclusive use.

The in-house computer provides for complete control of financial records. Management has access to balances immediately, if necessary, or, as a standard operating procedure, on a daily basis. When errors are made in keypunching or processing, they can be discovered easily and corrected immediately. Furthermore, an in-house system allows great flexibility in tailoring accounting reports to the company's own needs.

Although the in-house system may be more effective than a service bureau, the latter is not without merits. Because in-house computers are smaller than service bureau computers, few in-house systems can produce the quantity of information that a service bureau can. Likewise, service bureaus offer sophisticated programs that will allow for detailed rent rolls and analytical reports beyond the capabilities of most in-house equipment. In addition, a service bureau system shifts the responsibilities for staffing and equipment from the management company to the computer service company. When operating in-house equipment, there is the concern of pro-

Owner Reports	Management Office Reports
Income/Expense Statement	Check Register
Cash Flow Statement	Vendor List
Rent Roll	History File (previous 12 months by
Accounts Payable	month)
	Unit (or Tenant) Status Report
Resident Reports	Accounting General Ledger
Rent Billings	
Past Due Notices	**Property Manager Reports**
Monthly Billings (condominiums)	Property Performance Report (compares month and year-to-date with
Resident Manager Reports	budget)
Rent Payment Slips	Budget (month by month)
Vacating Tenant List	Occupancy Report
Rent Roll	Unit (or Tenant) Status Report

Figure 17.1.   Financial and operating reports that can be prepared by an electronic data processing accounting system.

gramming and program modifications, equipment breakdown that requires specialized manufacturer's maintenance service, and some loss in fiscal control. Lastly, there is the cost consideration. The cost of contracting with a service bureau does not equal the high initial cost of establishing an in-house computer accounting system.

The shortcomings of the service bureau lie in the fact that a real estate management company becomes dependent on the management of another company—the service bureau. Control can be difficult to exercise. If the service bureau has equipment breakdowns, if it experiences rapid growth but has not acquired a large enough staff to handle it, if it gives priority to larger customers, necessary reports are liable to be late and the property management company will suffer. In addition, there is the problem of not knowing exactly what is going on at any given moment, inasmuch as a certain amount of information is undergoing processing at the service bureau at nearly any given time. The typical turnover time from the date information leaves the management company office until it is returned from the service bureau in the form of computer reports is three to five days.

A drawback of both EDP systems is that they are not easy to understand. A great deal of time must be spent teaching employees at all levels—apartment managers, property managers, bookkeepers, secretaries—how to use and understand them. Likewise, both systems require highly skilled and thus highly paid bookkeepers and accountants to supervise the employees in the bookkeeping department. The result is that any EDP system is expensive to operate.

These problems can be minimized to some degree. Prior to converting to any automated system, it is imperative that the company's existing system—either hand-posted or machine-posted—be an effective one. Accurate records must be maintained by the existing system before a successful conversion can take place. A property manager will experience numerous difficulties in imposing a data processing system on a weak data base. *Computer Applications in Property Management Accounting*, published by the Institute of Real Estate Management (Chicago: 1978), indicates that six significant problem areas often are encountered in converting to computer accounting:

1. Employee education and acceptance.
2. Revising and streamlining the old system to be compatible with the computer.

3. Programming actually what is needed.
4. Maintaining the kind of extremely accurate records that must go on the computer.
5. Lack of expertise in programming; familiarizing programmer with the needs of the property management firm.
6. Initial set up of program; debugging; running parallel systems for the first several months.

Although some problems inevitably will occur, many can be eliminated by adopting a systematic approach toward choosing the kind of EDP system to be used. The first step is to conduct a study to determine the company's accounting needs and then determine how these needs may be met. This requires the property manager to thoroughly analyze information produced by the existing program, as well as prepare a realistic list of what information he would like to have; subsequently, he needs to assign estimated costs of producing this information. A study of various computer systems then is ready to be undertaken, after which bids are solicited for the necessary equipment and/or software (the program). While cost is always a consideration, it should not be given undue importance, unless, of course, all of the vendors are offering the same, good service.

Company Controller

Having established the importance of the management company's fiduciary responsibility to its clients and described the enormous amount of detail necessary to meet this responsibility, it is well to scrutinize the individual who is charged with the task of fulfilling this company obligation—the company controller.

The controller, a member of the top management team, typically derives his responsibility from and reports to the president of the company. His responsibilities are numerous; generally he is charged with the following specific responsibilities:

1. Select, train, assign, discipline, promote, and terminate the employment of employees under his direct departmental control.
2. Enforce accounting, data processing, and paper flow routines throughout the company.
3. Inspect, audit, and correct records affecting the flow of money throughout the company.
4. Collect, record, and file all information pertaining to the com-

pany's operations in a manner best suited to the company's needs and in conformance with recognized practices.

5. Maintain the accounting records and the internal audits necessary to assure correctness of entries.
6. Preserve the books of account, company correspondence, etc.
7. Supervise entries posted to journals, ledgers, and subsidiary records.
8. Prepare and audit billings, invoices, and payment notices originating in all company transactions.
9. Record, audit, and authorize payment of accounts payable.
10. Prepare, analyze, and interpret all reports and statistics compiled from accounting records.
11. Prepare all reports to government agencies. This includes income tax reports, for which responsibility is delegated to an accounting firm; the controller retains responsibility for timely filing.
12. Cooperate with the auditing firm employed by the company for verification of correctness of accounting records.
13. Prepare the corporate budgets and forecasts, by department, by branch, and by overall operation.
14. Prepare periodic financial reports and budget analysis for ownership that accurately indicate the performance attained.
15. Report to ownership on departmental and branch costs and suggest corrective action to be taken to end an unfavorable trend.
16. Devise and control all standard procedures, forms, and other written memoranda used throughout the company.
17. Prepare payroll records, listings, and reports.
18. Receive, disburse, and maintain custody of funds.
19. Develop and revise, when necessary, a standard procedure and job description for all accounting and office staff functions.
20. Devise and enforce a procedure for purchasing supplies, equipment, and services and maintenance of offices and equipment throughout the company in a manner to assure ownership against wasteful practices and needless expense.
21. Prepare information and reports for executive officers and managers as needed to assure efficient and smooth operation.
22. Develop and manage a system of cost accounting for the various activities of the company.

The controller likewise is a manager and is given certain managerial duties. For instance, the controller usually is charged with delegating tasks among personnel under his direction in such a manner that the work is distributed evenly and flows smoothly. Similarly, he is responsible for training his support staff to perform in accordance with the company's standard operating procedures and effect limited interchange without disturbing routine. (For the role of the controller as office manager, see chapter 16.) As is true of anyone in a top management-level position, the controller should select and train an understudy capable of filling in for him during his absence.

18

Standardization of Operations

A PROPERTY MANAGEMENT COMPANY cannot permit its employees to operate according to their individual preferences. In order to run professionally, a set of policies and procedures are needed to govern the operation of the company and the operations of all of the properties under its management.

Policies

Policies are established by management to guide the various members of the organization in their decision making. Policies establish the parameters that are needed to ensure that, when a decision is made, it contributes to the fulfillment of the company's objectives. Policies, then, should be designed toward realization of objectives, and establishing them should be integrated with the planning function. Policies usually are formulated by the top property managers of a company—not for themselves but in order to guide their subordinates in making decisions that are compatible with the company plan and its objectives and programs.

A real estate management company needs two kinds of policies: general company policies to guide property managers in making certain decisions relating to the broad operations of the company, the central office, and properties under its management; and specific policies for each of the individual properties' operations. These latter policies should be designed to reflect the unique character and conduct of each property. Each building, for instance, may need a specifically designed policy for tenant selection, levels of maintenance, and lease negotiations. Because these property policies should be compatible with ownership objectives, it is important that they be written with consultation from the property owner.

The reason for having policies is twofold: (1) They provide uniformity in making decisions, and (2) they increase efficiency by eliminating the need to perform the research—often repetitive—that may be required to make a decision. Nevertheless, one of the chief characteristics of a policy is the implied element of discretion. A policy is not a hard and fast rule that dictates one and only one course of action in a given situation. Rather, it is a guide for determining which courses of action are available. The discretion inherent in a policy may be very broad or it may be quite narrow; nevertheless, discretion is present in every policy.

For example, consider a personnel policy on salary review which states: "Salaries are reviewed twice each year, in June and December, with recommendations for increases in salary being based upon either merit increases or increases for the cost of living. However, cost of living adjustments will not occur more often than once every 12 months." This policy fixes the time for salary review to occur only in the months of June and December. Both employees and managers understand from it that the question of salary increases cannot be raised during other times of the year. Also, it establishes that a manager is compelled to consider salary adjustments on behalf of employees at these times. The policy likewise explains the methods by which salaries might be increased. Through this policy, the company creates the framework for quickly and efficiently making decisions regarding salary reviews and ensures that there will be uniformity in the timing and method of them. Simultaneously, room for discretion is provided inasmuch as the actual salary increase is left to the manager.

To better understand the nature of policies, the following guidelines may be helpful. These suggestions should be kept in mind both in establishing policies and in keeping them effective.

1. Policies must be consistent with the plans and objectives of the enterprise. Since the purpose of a policy is to serve as a guide in decision making, each policy needs to reflect the objectives and plans of the business. For example, if a management company embarks upon a major rehabilitation program to correct deferred maintenance at a property and modernize its facilities,

the property's tenant selection policies may be affected: They may become much more narrow and more highly selective during the period prior to the start of the rehabilitation program.

2. Policies must be consistent with each other. If the objective of a property is to upgrade its facilities and tenancy, for example, policies for marketing, selection of employees, and tenant services should be consistent with and reflect the higher rent and higher quality of tenancy that the building is trying to achieve.

3. Policies must be distinct from rules and procedures. The purpose of a policy is to provide guidelines within which a manager can make a decision yet allow him to exercise discretion. Rules allow no discretion.

4. Policies must be flexible. Some policies, such as those governing ethics and professional standards, are unchangeable. Many others, on the other hand, are not. The purpose of a policy is to establish a parameter for acting in accordance with a company's plans and objectives. However, changing economic or other conditions may cause a change in plans and objectives. Policies must be flexible enough for these changes to be reflected in them.

5. Policies must be in writing and accessible to all persons who are affected by them. Communication is greatly improved when the company's policy statements are expressed in writing and circulated to all appropriate parties.

6. Policies need to be explained. Management cannot act under the premise that even the most carefully written of policies will be understood by everyone involved. The various people to whom a policy statement is directed often will interpret it differently. Therefore, management must take every opportunity to explain the meaning of and reason for each of its policies. This can be done through staff meetings, by asking employees to give their written interpolation of policies, or by conducting oral examinations. When a misinterpretation is noted, it should be corrected immediately.

Procedures and Rules

A criterion of a policy is the presence of discretion. Conversely, a criterion of rules and procedures is the absence of discretion. A rule states specifically what can and cannot be done in a given situation. A procedure, often referred to as a standard operating procedure (SOP), is a series of related, chronological steps that are adopted as the accepted way of performing a given activity or function. Neither a well-written rule nor a properly outlined procedure leaves room for alternate courses of action.

Every professional property management company has a set of standard operating procedures for all of its functions. Unless standard procedures are developed for the activities of employees, there can be time-wasting chaos. Standard procedures are designed not only to relieve executives of routine supervisory duties and decision making but also to provide a means for systematic management and control. They encourage people to work in consort toward a common objective while preventing duplication of effort. They establish responsibility as well as give direction as to how a task is to be performed.

The person charged with creating the procedure for a given activity usually discovers that many alternatives are available to him. It is up to him to select the most effective and efficient alternative. The following guidelines may be of some benefit in making this selection and writing the procedure:

1. A procedure must be supportive of the appropriate policy. The intent of a procedure should be fulfillment of a policy; a procedure, therefore, must be designed to lead to this end.
2. Writing a procedure requires scrutiny of the activity involved. A properly designed procedure cannot be written in isolation from the activity with which it is concerned. If a manager is writing a tenant move-in procedure, he needs to participate in the activity, talk to the on-site manager who handles it, and study all appropriate and relevant documents. After this examination, the manager should be in a position to list in sequence the minimum number of steps to be followed to ensure the greatest efficiency and least delay and duplication.
3. A procedure must be clear and succinct. The easiest procedure to adhere to is the one that is characterized by its clarity, conciseness, and simplicity.
4. A procedure must be flexible. When economic conditions change, company policies change; and when policies change, procedures need to be changed. In addition to procedural changes resulting from policy changes, there also may be a need for procedural changes for other reasons. For instance, an employee may discover a quicker way to perform a certain task. If so, his suggestion may be reflected in alteration to the appropriate procedure.

5. On the other hand, a procedure must not be changed without good cause. Changing procedures should not be done haphazardly. For instance, it often is the case that every time a company hires a new head bookkeeper, he immediately wants to install a new system. A general policy to combat this problem would be to forbid an employee to recommend a change until he has been at the company for at least six months. Until new people have a full understanding of the purposes of existing procedures, it is well to supress recommendations for changes. More often than not, a procedural change costs more than the benefits derived from it.

6. A procedure must deal with only one activity. Procedures should not be complicated by unnecessarily entangling different activities or imposing an overall procedure on all functions. Not only is this confusing for employees who must follow the procedure, but it inevitably results in ineffectiveness.

7. A procedure must be in writing and be distributed appropriately.

8. A procedure must be explained. As with policies, procedures should be taught to all employees involved.

Management Forms

The complexity of managing many separate businesses, i.e., properties, with several thousand customers, i.e., tenants, requires a comprehensive system of control and communication. A principal vehicle for establishing this system is the use of forms. A form is a printed piece of paper that provides space for inserting certain information which is to be conveyed to other persons. Even in this age of electronics, a sheet of paper with data posted by the sender is still the most widely used method of communicating information.

Forms offer several advantages to the operation of a property management company: They guarantee uniformity of records. They serve as guidelines in performing assigned work. They eliminate the need to copy oft-repeated information and thus increase efficiency and decrease the possibility of errors. Forms provide information to tenants, on-site managers, property managers, clerks, clients, vendors —literally all the people who are involved with a property management enterprise. Because of this, the image that forms creates becomes part of the company's public relations program, and they must be designed and dispatched with this consideration in mind.

However, while forms can greatly improve a company's operation and enhance its public image, control must be exercised over them if they are to be effective. For this reason, management needs to adopt policies and procedures relative to creating new forms, ensuring that all forms being used are in fact necessary, and changing or abandoning existing forms when called for.

In creating a new form, several factors must be taken into consideration. First, the purpose of the form must be ascertained. A form should be designed in such a way that it incorporates all of the steps required to perform the pertinent task for which it is intended. It should direct employees where to start and where to stop and outline all the steps in between. Second, the information the form is to include must be determined. Third, the order of presenting the data must be determined; the sequence of the items must correspond with the flow of the work. Fourth, the method of presenting the information must be determined. For example, if the form will be completed by hand, adequate space must be given and lines drawn. If, on the other hand, the form is to be typed, the spacing should correspond with typewriter spacing and the lines omitted.

Fifth, the form should be properly identified in accordance with its purpose. For example, "Inspection Report" is incomplete; "Property Manager's Monthly Property Inspection Report" is more descriptive. The form should bear the name, address, phone number, and preferably logo of the management company. One other consideration in identifying a form is numbering for the purpose of exercising control. Such forms as work orders and purchase orders, for example, need identification numbers if they are to be functional. Sixth, the number of copies needed of a form must be determined. Multiple-copy forms provide a quick and easy means of supplying numerous copies; however, the number of copies should be kept to the absolute minimum required so as not to add to the paper problem.

Finally, some consideration must be given to cost. Naturally, the more complex the form and the greater the number of copies, the more expensive it will be to produce. The most effective way to lower the cost of forms, however, lies in reducing the number of forms used by the company. While recognizing that a real estate management business will not be effective without forms, the goal of a form policy should be to have the minimum number of forms needed. They are costly in terms of time to prepare, fill out, and review and in terms of cost for printing, inventorying, and filing. Careful analysis of each existing form should be performed periodically to determine if it should be continued, combined with another form, changed, or eliminated altogether. The goal of this analysis should be a reduction in the number of forms used by the firm.

Unless criteria for adopting forms are established by top management, a number of inefficiencies develop. Typically, individual property managers begin to create their own forms for performing various operations. The weakness that often occurs is duplication of effort between the property manager and the bookkeeping or other department: Each begins to accumulate the same information through different channels.

The central goal of a form is that it serve as a standard vehicle for communicating information. This is particularly crucial for the large company, where the need for extensive communications is obvious, but should be considered equally important by the smaller company.

Among the forms a property management company typically needs are these:

For Tenants

Application To Rent	Store Building Lease
Apartment Lease	House Lease
Office Lease	Lease Extension Agreement
Industrial Property Lease	Assignment of Lease Agreement
Security Deposit	Rent Increase Letter
Pet Deposit	Notice To Vacate
Delinquency Letter or Notice	Rules and Regulations

For Clients
Monthly Operating Statement
Annual Budget and Cash Flow Projection

For Bookkeeping Department

Rent Bill	Collection Journal
Bank Deposit Slip	Tenant Move-In Form
Check Request	Tenant Move-Out Form
Security Deposit Refund	Appropriate Payroll System Forms

For Property Managers

Employment Agreement	Lease Expiration
Management Information System Forms	Employee Performance Evaluation
a. Vacancy Report	Purchase Order
b. Marketing Report	Start-Up Information for New Account
c. Building Inspection	

Manual of Operations

A company's policies, procedures, and forms all come together in one source—an operations manual. This is a written guidebook that contains all of the information, instructions, and suggestions an employee needs to perform his job. A manual eliminates the need for management to constantly repeat explanations and instructions and increases uniformity of activity. A manual commits to writing a company's policies and serves as a convenient reference as to how each task connected with property management is to be done. Furthermore, because forms are by-products of procedures, a manual typically includes all forms used by a management company and instructions on their use.

Often a property management company has separate manuals for various functions. For example, a company may have an accounting manual, a resident manager's manual, and a property manager's manual. What is important is that management make available to each employee the policies, procedures, and forms necessary for him to successfully perform his job.

As previously stated, each company will have to develop its own policies and procedures for the operation of properties under its stewardship. Each company's operations manual, therefore, will be different, depending upon the nature of its business, its clientele, and its management philosophy. Generally, a manual discusses these topics: rent collection and evictions, security deposit refunds, authority for signing leases, buying, decorating, emergencies, tenant selection, tenant complaints, employment records, advertising, and rebates and discounts.

In order to illustrate how an operations manual may be structured, a section from an existing operations manual for property managers of apartments has been included as figure A.13 in the appendix of this text. This section, which deals with the topic of purchasing, begins with a statement of the company's policy about that subject, lists the procedures to be followed, and provides an instructional narrative to assist property managers in carrying out their responsibility as it relates to purchasing goods and services.

In addition to the policies and procedures for operating properties, a company also needs in its manual of operations policies and procedures for the operation of the real estate management company itself. Although not a conclusive list, some of the important ones are described herein.

A policy and procedures for real estate licensees relative to the ownership of real estate and outside interests generally are required. Uniform and consistent interpretation of codes of ethics and laws governing the real estate profession requires practitioners to maintain a high level of ethical and professional standards. A management company has an important fiduciary responsibility to its clients. The relationship is one built upon confidence and trust. The relationship imposes upon the agent the duty of acting in the highest good faith toward his principal. It becomes necessary that the firm have a policy and procedures relative to outside business interests of its licensees.

The fundamental rule is for disclosure of these outside interests before they occur. If the company feels that any outside activity on the part of the employee would endanger its fiduciary responsibility to its client, the company would then have the opportunity to either deny the outside activity or allow the employee the option of leaving the firm.

A policy and procedures for reimbursement of business travel expenses also are needed. Since a property manager needs the use of an automobile in order to fulfill his responsibilities, and because oftentimes management companies operate properties at distances that require airplane travel and overnight lodging, it is incumbent that the company have a policy and procedures for reimbursing the property manager for expenses incurred in connection with his work. The policy should include reimbursement for automobile travel, rented cars and other transportation vehicles, lodging, meals, and any other business-related expenses.

Likewise, a policy and procedures for entertainment expenses may be called for. Opinions differ, but it is often considered unnecessary for property managers to entertain vendors, clients, and prospective clients in order to maintain or encourage business relationships. If such an attitude is adopted, the policy may state that business entertaining is not permitted without prior approval of an officer of the company. There are, however, other entertainment functions that are useful in the conduct of a real estate management business. These might include functions for various groups of employees, i.e., resident managers, property managers, office personnel, etc. When applicable, a company policy on these functions should be included as well.

Another necessary policy and appropriate procedures are needed regarding the purchase of equipment and improvement to the facility. The objective here is to account for the cost, location, and use of all assets purchased by the company. The basic elements of this program are these: (1) The establishment of a capitalization policy for all assets purchased over a certain amount, i.e., the company will capitalize and depreciate all individual purchases over this figure. (2) The requirement that a physical inventory be taken annually and agreed to the facilities and equipment ledger. (3) The requirement that a facilities and equipment ledger be maintained to establish costs and locations of purchases. (4) The requirement that each piece of equipment be assigned an asset number and be identified with adhesive labels applied inconspicuously to the equipment.

19

Insurance and
Property Management

CONSEQUENT TO ITS ROLE AS A MANAGER of property and an employer of people, a property management company is exposed to various risks. By the very nature of the service it provides, a company may be subject to almost every conceivable liability. At a property, a managing agent is exposed to the liability of anyone who suffers a personal injury or whose property is damaged. To his client, the agent is contractually responsible for the level of management services he provides and is accountable for the monies he collects and disburses on behalf of that client. To his employees, the managing agent has a legal obligation to provide workmen's compensation insurance and an administrative concern to provide health insurance protection. If the business owns furniture and fixed assets, as most do, there is the risk that this property may be damaged or destroyed. Furthermore, there is always the risk that a natural disaster may interrupt the operation of the business.

Property management companies exist in a society that places heavy emphasis on legal requirements and rights. Risks must be controlled. Certain steps can be taken to reduce risk. For example, the probability of an employee being hurt on the job will decrease if a conscientious work-safety program is implemented. But all risk cannot be avoided. In some cases, it is preferable to transfer it by contractual means. Managing agents can limit their liability through contracts with others, tenants, employees, and contractors. A well-written management agreement, for example, contains a hold-harmless clause to protect the managing agent. Likewise, a rental lease often stipulates that property maintenance is to be under the care of the tenant who rents the apartment. Although common law prohibits the contracting away of one's legal liability, and all states hold that proven gross negligence and fraud are not defensible, agents can protect their liability exposure through properly drawn contracts.

A number of risks run by a management company can be neither avoided nor contractually transferred. However, they are insurable and can be transferred through appropriate insurance policies.

The cost of providing insurance against risks can be considerable; in some instances, the cost may exceed the estimated probability of risk. Therefore, management needs to make an intelligent and diligent analysis of its probability of loss versus the cost of transferring that risk through an insurance policy. Basic to a program of risk management, then, is analyzing exactly what the company has to lose in the event of an accident. Obviously, a large management corporation with considerable assets runs a much greater risk than does a closely held corporation with a small portfolio.

Having ascertained what it could lose in the event of a loss, management is in a position to outline the kinds of coverages required. What is important is that the company, regardless of size, adopt a program by which risks of accidental loss to which the company is exposed are dealt with in some way so as to protect the assets and earnings of the company.

Public Liability Insurance

When a managing agent executes a management contract with a property owner and agrees to manage the property, he becomes legally liable for personal injuries to others that may occur on the property. As such, he and the property owner as well may be held financially responsible to an injured party as a consequence of negligence. (Negligence exists when there is failure to exercise reasonable care and this failure, though not accompanied by harmful intent, directly results in injury to an innocent party.) Because a management company has an insurable interest in every property under its stewardship and would suffer financially by an occurrence at any one of these properties, it is crucial that the agent is protected against liability risks.

When a liability is alleged, it is up to a jury in a court of law to determine negligence and, if appropriate, award damages. If there is liability and the injury is serious, such as one involving permanent disability, the verdict may be such that, in the absence of adequate insurance, financial ruin could be brought on the management agent. A liability policy offers protection against this. It promises to pay on behalf of the insured party the amount, up to the limit of the policy, that he would become obligated to pay because of the liability imposed upon him by law for damages caused by an insured occurrence.

There are two kinds of liability policies: a bodily injury liability policy and a property damage liability policy. Bodily injury refers to physical injury, mental damage, pain, sickness, disease, loss of services, and death. Personal injuries, such as false arrest, libel and slander, and wrongful entry, are not included under the bodily injury policy but may be added by endorsement. Likewise, medical payments coverage, under which the insurer promises to pay the medical expenses incurred by persons injured through some hazard described in the policy even though the insured is not liable, may be added by endorsement. Property damage refers to physical damage to and loss of use and destruction of real property. Typically, bodily injury and property damage liability and any endorsements that may be called for are combined into a single policy.

While many liability claims are settled out of court or verdicts are reached for far less than the amounts asked for in original court suits, the prevailing attitude of both judges and juries is toward awarding damages. Large claims could destroy a company. Thus, it is not uncommon for a bodily injury liability policy to provide for a minimum amount of coverage of $500,000 per person or per occurrence. However, even this may be insufficient protection. The property manager must determine what he considers to be an acceptable minimum level. A conscientious agent will insist on $3,000,000 in protection. This additional coverage may be purchased through an excess limits policy. Such coverage may be obtained individually by property or through a master policy which covers all properties under the agent's stewardship. In either event, it is customary for the property owner to pay his pro rata cost, inasmuch as he also benefits from the additional protection. In the case of property damage liability, a policy limit is set applicable to any one accident. A typical limit is $5,000.

In addition to obtaining adequate coverage, it is crucial for a managing agent to guarantee that he is named as an additional insured on the owner's liability policy. This is done without cost to either the agent or the owner. In fact, many policies written for income properties have clauses that automatically provide for protection for the agent. However, in order to be sure of proper inclusion, it is best for the management company to adopt a standard operating procedure calling for written notification to be given to each property owner's insurance carrier, verifying that it is named as an additional insured, upon assuming the management of any new property.

A property manager has yet another liability concern: What if he assumes management of a property whose owner allowed coverage to lapse and thus is uninsured? Protection for this kind of occurrence can be obtained. The cost for such a policy would be the agent's, of course, and he alone would be protected by this blanket coverage.

In addition to the liability risks involved with being the managing agent of a property, any management company that maintains an office needs protection as an operator of a business. For example, claims could result from a vendor falling on a slippery office floor or the collapse of a chair in which a tenant was seated. A form of coverage that may be considered is an owners', landlords', and tenants' public liability policy. This covers loss or expense resulting from claims upon the insured for damages on account of bodily injury, death, or property damage alleged to have been accidentally suffered by a nonemployee. The accident must be alleged to have been caused by reason of the ownership, maintenance, ordinary alterations and repair, or use of the premises occupied by the company.

Fidelity Bonds

A property management firm is responsible for each client's monies from the time a tenant pays his rent until the agent submits the monthly operating statement and renders the owner a check for the net proceeds from operations. For this reason it is imperative that the agent have the money insured for all possible losses against criminal acts by employees and others.

Dishonest acts of employees are covered by fidelity bonds. Not only do they guarantee that losses due to employee dishonesty will be made good by the bonding company, fidelity bonds also have the effect of discouraging employees who may be tempted to commit acts of dishonesty because they know an insurance company is prepared to prosecute. Furthermore, the investigation performed by the bonding company prior to providing coverage eliminates the exposure to such losses by bringing to the employer's attention employees with unfavorable records.

A fidelity bond typically is written in one of two forms: on an individual basis or as a blanket bond. The individual bond is written to guarantee against loss growing out of dishonest acts performed by a specifically named individual. Many management companies, however, have discovered that it is preferable to provide protection under a blanket fidelity bond. This form covers all employees of a company without requiring a list of their names or positions. It thus eliminates much paperwork and the possibility of omissions. Furthermore, the blanket bond automatically covers new employees as they join the company. The blanket bond has a distinct advantage in that, if a loss is discovered but it cannot be determined who is responsible for it, protection is provided. Under individual bonding, an act of dishonesty would be covered only if it could be ascertained who the responsible employee is and if he is bonded. Sometimes it is practical for all employees of both property owner and agent to be covered under one blanket bond, with each paying his pro rata share. Key employees of the agent then can be covered with additional insurance through excess limits coverage.

Management needs to ascertain who pays for fidelity bonds. In fact, this should be determined at the time the management agreement is negotiated. Customarily, the owner pays for the bonding of on-site employees, and the agent pays for the cost of bonding his employees. The amount of bonding is discretionary, but a guide is this: up to one month's income for the building employees and up to 10 percent of gross collections for the agency.

Money and Securities Coverage

To complement the fidelity bonding program and in order to have complete protection for dishonest appropriation of money, the owner and agent need an insurance form known as the money and securities policy (broad form). This provides protection for the insured against money and securities losses occasioned by dishonest acts of nonemployees. Coverage is for loss caused by: destruction, which includes any occurrence, such as fire, windstorm, flood, or explosion, resulting in the physical loss of monies or securities; disappearance, which includes loss without any visible evidence of forcible entry into the premises or safe; and wrongful abstraction, the taking of money or securities from a custodian by any illegal means.

The policy can be written with either inside protection, outside protection, or both. Inside protection covers not only the aforementioned losses but also loss of or damage to property caused by burglary or robbery or attempts thereof. Outside coverage affords the same protection to money, securities, and property against robbery or attempted robbery while in the custody of a messenger or an armored vehicle company.

One of the problems with losses that occur at buildings is identifying exactly how the funds disappeared. The building manager will claim an unknown robber broke in after hours and took the cash. But was it a robber, or was it in fact a dishonest employee? By having both this form of coverage and fidelity bond coverage with the same carrier, management avoids becoming the middleman in a dispute between insurance companies.

Apartment houses in particular often experience significant numbers of small—$25 to $500—losses of cash. The cumulative effect may be that it is difficult to obtain insurance coverage. Because of this, it is very important that the agent institutes and strictly enforces a no-cash rent collection policy, insisting that all payments from tenants either be by check or money order. This will remove the attractive nuisance of having cash on hand that can mysteriously disappear. In addition, appropriately worded signs stating that no cash is accepted should discourage holdups.

Professional Liability Insurance

Agency property management is a business that, like many others, is not without risks. When a managing agent contracts with a property owner, he agrees to provide professional service with care, deligence, and earnest effort. If the property is ineptly managed, causing the owner's investment to lose value or him to lose income, the owner very well may make a claim against the agent for that loss.

Original professional liability policies were malpractice policies written to cover physicians, surgeons, and hospitals. Policies now are written to cover many other professionals, including property managers. In contrast to malpractice liability, in which personal injury gives rise to damages, liability for the property manager would be caused by a monetary loss resulting from failure to meet a professional standard or for negligent actions. A professional liability policy, sometimes referred to as an errors and omissions policy, insures the agent against losses he may sustain in such a claim.

Unfortunately, this form of liability insurance is not easily available, nor is it inexpensive. As of this writing, such coverage was obtainable only for firms with less than 49 employees. Furthermore, the recent consumer movement has caused malpractice, errors and omissions, and product liability insurance to skyrocket to premium costs. Consequently, this is one coverage situation in which the professional property management executive may decide it is better to be self-insured.

Nonowned Automobile Insurance

If a property management company expects some of its employees to use their own cars on company business, it should consider protecting itself against this exposure by obtaining automobile nonownership insurance. The premium for nonownership insurance depends on the number of employees and their duties.

Indirect Loss Insurance

Fire is a very real and serious threat, and the direct loss that would occur as a result of a fire is fully understood. The risk of indirect losses of fire and other perils, however, often is not recognized and thus not insured against. For example, if the building in which a property management company's office is located is destroyed by fire, the loss would be a direct one. However, the company would feel a possibly far greater loss—an indirect loss—that would evidence itself in lost profits because of an interruption in operations. Insurance is available to cover such loss.

One form of coverage is business interruption insurance, which provides against the loss of prospective earnings if business is interrupted because of fire or other peril. Essentially, it is designed to keep a business in the position it would have maintained had there been no interruption.

Similar to business interruption insurance, and, in fact, often confused with it, is extra-expense insurance. This form of coverage is very broad and is designed to cover all additional charges incurred by a company in trying to get back into business should full or partial destruction occur at any of its locations. Even if a property management office is destroyed, the company must continue to operate or it will lose its clients. Extra-expense insurance enables it to obtain the extra help, pay overtime wages, obtain temporary office space, or incur other typical costs. It does not, as does business interruption insurance, cover loss of income in any way.

With the advent of the electronic computer, magnetized and

paper tapes containing management data recorded at great expense become important. Likewise, all management agreements, tax and insurance records, and payroll records are quite valuable. For this reason, management should consider obtaining valuable papers insurance. This coverage provides for reimbursement for costs incurred by the insured to reconstruct or replace valuable papers in order to operate normally following damage to or destruction of property. The insurance covers only those papers and records that are maintained in the premises named in the policy; further, they must be maintained in a fireproof safe, except when in actual use.

Property Insurance

In addition to the liability coverage it needs, the company likewise requires property insurance to cover the loss of any real property that may occur. Even if the company does not own the building in which its office is located, it undoubtedly will have office furniture and equipment which, if destroyed, could be a great loss to the company. Property insurance can provide protection against this disaster.

Essentially, the company needs a policy that would protect it against losses caused by fire plus certain additional perils. Possibly an all-risk policy, which protects the company from losses arising from any cause other than some that specifically are excluded, will provide the most comprehensive protection of company property. The amount of insurance needed, of course, depends upon the value of real property owned by the company.

Employee Benefit Insurance

By virtue of workmen's compensation laws in each of the states, an employer is required to provide certain benefits for injuries that occur on the job and some occupational diseases, regardless of fault on the part of the employer or the employee. Workmen's compensation, then, is a form of social insurance, and the cost of bearing it is passed on to the consumer. Workmen's compensation provides for three types of benefits: medical expenses coverage, weekly income payments during incapacity, and rehabilitation. The amount and duration of and eligibility for benefits differs among the states. Rates depend upon the type of job and the employer's claim history.

Although it is not a legal requirement, many employers consider it a duty to provide health insurance. Both medical expense and income reimbursement coverage commonly are available to employees under group health plans. Customarily, an employee is given the insurance as a part of his compensation package as soon as he meets a certain employment time requirement. The coverage typically is available to members of the employee's family as well, generally at a cost borne by the employee.

Dental and life insurance and accident and loss of income coverages are not customary employee benefits but may be considered.

The Insurance Program

A comprehensive program of insurance protection requires careful study of the management firm's liabilities and analysis to determine what risks require protection and warrant the cost of insurance coverage. What follows is an illustrative insurance program for a property management company.

Office Package Policy
Coverages:
1. Deductible: $100 all-risk contents coverage on a blanket basis for an amount at 90 percent coinsurance, including equipment and tenant improvements and betterments at all office locations.
2. Valuable papers: Papers kept in files except during the day at all office locations.
3. Extra expense: Expense incurred by the insured in order to continue normal operations following damage to or destruction of real or personal property. This portion of the policy would repay the company for any monies expended to get back in business should partial or full destruction occur at any of the office locations. The coverage is very broad and literally includes any expense not covered in a separate category that is necessary to re-establish the company in a normal business pattern.
4. Inventory or appraisal: After limit of liability is determined, the insurance would pay up to that amount should the company have to do an inventory or appraisal that is in some way connected with a loss.
5. General liability coverage: Comprehensive general liability covering bodily injury and property damage; personal injury; owners', landlords', and tenants'; and special package.

Workmen's Compensation
Coverage:
Workmen's compensation for all officers and employees of the management company.

Crime Coverage
Coverages:
The coverage provided and the respective limits of liability are as fol-

lows: employee dishonesty, $50,000; money and securities loss inside the premises, $5,000; money and securities loss outside the premises, $5,000; and depositors forgery issued instruments, $100,000.

This policy covers the management company for the dishonest acts of any employee. This also covers any loss of money and securities for the limits specified above. The term "employee" has been extended to include building manager, superintendent, or janitor including spouse and their children over 18 years of age who reside with such employee.

Excess Fidelity Bond Coverage
Coverage:
Commercial blanket bond. This policy provides for excess coverage over and above the limits of liability under the crime coverage policy. For example, if the company decided it wanted to have commercial blanket bond coverage in the amount of $1,000,000, this policy would be for $950,000 with a deductible clause of $50,000 inasmuch the first $50,000 coverage would be provided under the crime coverage policy.

Umbrella Liability Policy
Coverage:
This policy provides liability coverage up to $3,000,000 on those properties managed by the management company and insured through the insurance agency. The policy contains a requirement calling for the underlying primary liability insurance to be maintained at a level of $500,000.

The liability coverage afforded the management company pertains to all properties managed by the company whether or not insured through the primary insurance agency.

20

The Law and

Property Management

THE LEGAL ASPECTS OF OPERATING a real estate management business demand ever-increasing consideration. For anyone engaged in the field of real estate management, whether as a broker, principal of a firm, property manager, or rental agent, a knowledge of the basic rules of real estate law is absolutely essential. For the property manager, there are multiple legal considerations: As a licensee, he must be responsive to the real estate laws of his state; as an employer, he is faced with state and federal employment laws; as an agent providing professional services, he is responsible to the laws of his state; as a businessman, he is responsible to numerous and varied consumer acts and to both federal and state laws regarding discrimination in its many forms.

Although this discussion is by no means an attempt to fully describe all of the legal aspects of operating a property management business, it does focus attention on some of the more important legal responsibilities of property managers and real estate management companies. The intent here is to stress that there may be legal risk in operating a property management business. Furthermore, such laws not only vary from state to state but also may be different from community to community. Its practitioners must understand the basic rules of law that are applicable to the industry and seek competent legal advice, if necessary, to ensure that they operate with practices and procedures that are proper under applicable laws and regulations.

The Law of Agency

Since property managers are agents for owners, it is well for the property manager to understand the basic principles of agency and principal and agent law. An agency is created when one person authorizes another to act in some legal way for him. In law, an agent is a person who is authorized to do some act or acts on behalf of another, who is called the agent's principal. The principal may terminate the agency at any time but may be liable to the agent if the termination is contrary to the terms of the contract creating the agency relationship. The agency generally is terminated on the death of either the principal or the agent. However, it is customary for a management contract to provide that the agreement would be binding upon the heirs, administrators, executors, successors, and assigns of the property owner. Managers operating as sole proprietors realize that their management contracts terminate automatically upon their death unless there is some provision to provide for their continuation.

The law of agency deals with the rights and duties of the principal, the agent, and third persons with whom the agent deals. Agencies are of many kinds, according to the extent of their implied powers. For example, there is the simplest form of agency, such as a travel agent, who is merely authorized to make travel reservations and procure transportation tickets on behalf of the principal. This compares drastically with the attorney-in-fact form of agency, wherein the agent is authorized to perform a business transaction that is legally binding upon the principal. Generally speaking, property management agencies represent a middle ground in activity and responsibility: The agent has the responsibility for the care and protection of the principal's property and to exercise judgment in his stewardship. In addition to the duties of safekeeping and custodianship, the management agent may be expected to render a multitude of services which must be exercised with the same kind of care and judgment that would be required for property held in his own account. On the other hand, the agent should not take actions for which he has no authority. When he does, and third persons are ignorant of such limitations, the agent himself generally is liable for the consequences.

The obligations of the principal to the agent are: to pay the agent's remuneration, to repay all advances made by the agent in the regular course of his agency employment, to honor the obligations lawfully undertaken by the agent on the principal's behalf, and to indemnify the agent against all liabilities incurred by him in the proper execution of his agency contract.

The agent is bound to exercise proper skill, lawful means, and provide appropriate attention for carrying out the functions which he undertakes for the principal. He must devote such care and attention as a man of ordinary prudence does with his own property. He must observe the highest ethics of practice and must not enter into transactions in which his interests are in conflict with the interests of his principal. Thus, when he is employed to buy services or products, he must not be the seller; when he is employed to sell, he must not be the buyer. There may, of course, with full disclosure to and agreement by the principal, be exceptions to this.

While the law of agency in most states provides that contracts between agents and principals may either be verbal or in writing, some states forbid real estate brokers from recovering commissions unless their contracts are written and signed.

State Real Estate License Laws

As in any other profession, the duties and responsibilities of a real estate manager are many. High standards are important. The manager is required to perform his duties and execute his responsibilities with care, skill, and diligence. All states have enacted real estate laws for the purpose of raising standards of the real estate profession and requiring its members to act fairly and equitably with the public. Having once obtained a license, a manager must conduct himself in accordance with requirements of the license law, which means he has the obligation at all times to be honest, truthful, and skillful in the performance of his duties. What follows are some of the principal subjects that are dealt with in most states' real estate license laws.

Fraud

There are two types of fraud: actual fraud and constructive fraud. Actual fraud is defined as the intentional misrepresentation of a material fact in order to induce another person to act on it and consequently to part with property of value or to surrender some legal right. Constructive fraud consists of any breach of duty that, without any fraudulent intent, gains an advantage to the person in fault or one claiming under him, by misleading another, or of any act or omission that the law specifically declares to be fraudulent without regard to actual fraud. Constructive fraud most often is encountered in the breach of duty where the relation of trust and confidence exists, or in the taking of an advantage of incompetent persons, or in otherwise gaining unconscionable advantage.

As attorneys Arthur Mazirow and Arthur G. Bowman point out in their book, *Advanced Legal Aspects of Real Estate for the California Broker* (Los Angeles, 1976):

> Constructive fraud often arises in transactions where there exists confidential or fiduciary relationships that have been abused by the party in whom confidences reposed. In such cases there may be no actual fraud, but fraud is presumed from the fact that the one in whom the confidence is reposed availed himself of that trust to obtain an advantage at the expense of the confiding party, without reference to the question of fraudulent intent. This is particularly true where a relation of dependence, trust and confidence is obtained with gross inadequacy or entire failure or consideration.
>
> Confidential and fiduciary relations are in law synonomous and may be said to exist whenever trust and confidence are reposed by one person in the integrity and fidelity of another. In such a relationship, the party in whom the confidence is reposed, if he voluntarily accepts or assumes to accept the confidence, may take no advantage from his acts relating to the interest of the other party without the latter's knowledge or consent; he must refrain from abusing such confidence by obtaining any advantage to himself at the expense of the confiding party.

The real estate manager's position is one that carries extremely confidential and substantial fiduciary responsibilities. There is no question that unless he performs these responsibilities with the utmost of professional integrity and skill that he be a suspect to a claim for constructive fraud.

Commingling

It is a fundamental of real estate law, as well as part of the Code of Ethics of the Institute of Real Estate Management, that a managing agent will not commingle the funds of a client with one's own personal funds. It is the responsibility of the agent to establish proper trust fund bank accounts for his clients and maintain proper records at all times. These records must disclose, in businesslike fashion, all pertinent information concerning the trust account's transactions. The reason for this, aside from basic consideration of separating trust monies from the agent's monies, is to protect the client's money from the consequences of a legal action which may be brought against the agent.

If the trust account is a true trust account, the client's money may not be attached or "frozen" during a legal battle. If the agent should die or become incapacitated, the client's funds are not exposed to restrictions while the agent's estate is in probate. Another reason is that the client's funds, if they are separately identified in a trust account, are insured up to $40,000 by the Federal Deposit Insurance Corporation. Even though the funds from a number of clients may be handled in one large trust account, each is individually insured up $40,000, if separately identified.

Necessity for Clients To Read Contracts

The fact that an owner signs a contract may not always bind him to its terms. Since a strong personal as well as fiduciary relationship frequently evolves between client and agent, it is not unusual for the client to sign agreements without reading them, based upon the agent's recommendation. If circumstances later develop in which the client wishes to disclaim the instrument, he might state that he was fraudulently influenced not to read the instrument or was lulled into a false sense of security and signed without reading its obligations; the transaction could be excused. Therefore, it is good business practice for the agent to make sure that all property managers review contracts with all the parties concerned in advance of the signing of a contract.

Secret Profit

It is fraudulent for an agent to receive an undisclosed fee, other consideration, or profit. This law not only applies to the agent in the course of managing the property but also applies to his activities as a real estate broker acting on behalf of his clients when authorized to sell, buy, or exchange real estate.

Negligence or Incompetence

Demonstrating negligence or incompetence, while acting as a licensee, is cause for disciplinary action by the license law agency.

Responsibility for Acts of Property Managers

By law, the managing agent is responsible for the acts of his property managers. If he fails to provide reasonable supervision, he can lose his license to do business.

Liability for Out-of-State Acts

In most states, state attorney generals have given broad interpretation to the power of state real estate commissioners. In doing so, they have given them the authority to revoke licenses in cases in which wrongful acts are committed by a managing agent outside of the state.

Antidiscrimination

One of the areas of vital concern to the managing agent relates to antidiscrimination laws. These laws provide for civil action against persons conducting business establishments by aggrieved persons claiming discrimination on account of color, race, religion, ancestry, national origin, or sex. Although the agent frequently may express his desire to do everything possible to abide by the laws, he can encounter difficulty, though unintentional, by not abiding by some recent interpretation or regulation. One of the principal advantages of belonging to a professional real estate organization is that it assists its members in keeping current on these kinds of operational problems.

Antidiscrimination laws are numerous: There are, among others, the Federal Fair Housing Act of 1968, the Federal Civil Rights Act of 1964, state real estate laws, state civil rights acts, and agency regulations at every level of government activity. Since the agent is not only responsible for his own activities but the activities of his employees and independent contractors, it is a good company policy to have a written statement of the company's direction to its employees to abide by the law in all matters of discrimination. In order to prove that each employee has read the policy, should such proof be necessary, each should acknowledge the statement by date and signature.

Employee Safety and Health

In 1970 the U.S. Congress passed the Occupational Safety and Health Act (OSHA), which provides for job safety and health protection for employees. The Act is administered through the U.S. Department of Labor offices throughout the United States. The Act gives considerable authority to government agencies in establishing standards for job safety and health protection. Employers and employees are required to comply with these standards.

Several states have since created their own Occupational Safety and Health Acts. Typical of these is the California Occupational Safety and Health Act of 1973, administered through the State Agriculture and Services Agency and enforced by the Division of Industrial Safety within the Department of Industrial Relations. A brief description of the main points of that legislation follows:

Employers and Employees: The California Act states that every employer shall furnish employment and a place of employment that are safe and healthful for the employees and that every employer and every employee shall comply with occupational safety and health standards and all rules, regulations, and orders pursuant to Division 5 of the California Labor Code which are applicable to his own actions and conduct.

Compliance with Safety and Health Requirements: To ensure compliance with safety and health requirements, the State Division of Industrial Safety conducts periodic job site inspections. The inspections are conducted by trained safety engineers. The law provides that an authorized representative of the employer and a representative of the employees be given an opportunity to accompany the safety engineer for the purpose of aiding the inspection. Every employee has the right to bring unsafe or unhealthful conditions to the attention of the safety engineer making the inspection. In addition, every employee has the right to notify the Division of Industrial Safety if unsafe and unhealthful conditions are believed to exist at the work site.

If the Division of Industrial Safety believes that an employer has violated a safety and health order of the State of California, it issues a citation to the employer. The Division may impose civil penalties.

Citations of violations issued by the Division of Industrial Safety must be prominently displayed at or near the place of violation.

Any employee may protest the time given for abatement of the violation.

An employee may not be discharged or discriminated against in any way for filing complaints concerning unsafe working conditions or work practices in a place of employment, or otherwise exercising rights granted under the Act.

Any employee has the right to observe monitoring or measuring of employee exposure to hazards and the right of access to accurate records of employee exposure to potentially toxic materials or harmful physical agents.

The right to refuse to work under conditions that endanger life or health shall not be denied any employee.

As previously stated, OSHA agencies have broad powers in establishing rules and regulations. Stiff fines may be imposed for violations. Since these laws and regulations are constantly changing, it is important for the property manager to maintain constant awareness of his requirements as an employer. An example of such a change, and the effect that it had, is one that occurred several years after the passage of the OSHA original legislation, wherein the agency made the requirement:

> . . . to every employer to inaugurate and maintain an accident prevention program which must include, but is not limited to, the following:
>
> 1. A training program designed to instruct employees in general safety work practices and specific instructions with respect to hazards unique to the employee's job assignment. General safe work practices will include such things as safe materials handling, proper lifting procedures, good housekeeping and fire prevention. Specific instructions related to unique job assignment would entail such items as safe forklift operating procedures, personnel protective equipment, precautions regarding machinery, hand tool safety, and handling procedures for chemicals or toxic substances.
> 2. Scheduled periodic inspections to identify and correct unsafe conditions and work practices which may be found. Unsafe conditions would include unguarded machinery, broken aisleways or exits. Unsafe practices include such things as improper lifting techniques, grinding or welding without eye protection, and removal of machinery guards or safety devices.

This new requirement added another administrative and record keeping task to the property manager's responsibilities. To be sure that he can prove his effort to comply with these regulations, he needs to keep written records of the training programs and inspections as evidence of his ongoing efforts in maintenance of this accident prevention program. Figure A.14 in the appendix is an example of how a management company can initiate such a program.

Employment or Independent Contractor Contracts

Some state real estate license laws require that an employment or independent contractor contract be entered into between a real estate broker and his licensed salesmen. This regulation also may apply to the relationship between the property management company and certain of its employees, especially property managers.

The property management broker has an unusual fiduciary relationship with his clients. Over a period of time, he acquires and develops clients who confide in him as the manager of their business enterprises. An employee working for the property management broker and assisting in the management of the client's properties has access to much of this confidential information. It can cause the broker great harm when employees leave his employ and attempt to use the confidential information for their own self-interest. For this reason, it is wise for the property management broker to have an employment agreement with his property managers. Figure A.15 in the appendix is such a contract in response to satisfying the state license law requirements and protecting the property management broker for his trade secrets. However, competent legal counsel should be consulted before using any such agreement, inasmuch as legal requirements vary from state to state.

It is also a good business practice to negotiate employment agreements with on-site or resident managers for apartment houses and condominiums. The primary purpose of such an agreement is to establish the hours of employment. Since these positions are unsupervised, in that they are the most senior on-site employees, yet at the same time qualify under the federal wage and hour regulations, a contract is needed in order to regulate the amount of reported working time. In addition to his hours there would be a provision that would explain under what conditions he may be required to work overtime and how he is to be compensated for that work. In addition to satisfying wage-hour requirements, the contract serves other useful purposes. For the employee, there is a clear written understanding of how he is to be compensated and what benefits he is to receive. Figure A.16 in the appendix is an example of an employment contract for resident managers of apartment houses or condominiums.

Conclusion

PREDICTING THE OPPORTUNITIES that will exist for property management in the future is the professional property manager's greatest challenge. Making accurate predictions requires an understanding of the economic, social, and political developments of the past and their relation to and effect on the real estate industry.

The history of real estate since the turn of the century can best be understood by dividing it into five historical segments: the formative years from 1900 to 1920; the period from 1920 to the Great Depression; the years from 1933 through World War II and a wartime economy; the period of continued prosperity from 1949 to 1970; and the 1970s.

1900 to 1920: The Formative Years

The growth of the nation's urban centers and the development of the real estate industry are intertwined, and the years from 1900 to 1920 represent a formative period for both. The century opened with general prosperity, burdgeoning industrialism, and significant social change.

Growing Population and Industrialization

During the last half of the 1800s, the naton had established an extensive transportation network in the form of 193,000 miles of railroads. Prior to their development, urban life in the United States was limited to cities that had good harbors or, later, were located on the canals built to extend water transportation to interior regions. Probably there is no greater example of the impact that railroads had on urban growth than the city of Los Angeles. In 1870, El Pueblo de Nuestra Senora la Reina de Los Angeles was a small village of 6,000 people. In 1882, the Atchison, Topeka, and Santa Fe finished a railroad across the Sierras that was to compete with the Southern Pacific Railroad from San Francisco to Los Angeles. By 1900, the city of Los Angeles had a population of about 30,000 people.

The eastern part of the country was the center of industrialism and population. New York City was the largest metropolitan area with a population of 3,437,202, followed by Chicago with 1,698,575, and Philadelphia with 1,293,697. More than one third of the nation's population lived in urban areas. Manufacturing was replacing farming as a major source of income, and big business was absorbing small business. Despite the passage of the Sherman Antitrust Act in 1890, huge trusts had emerged in such industries as steel and railroads and among banks and financial institutions. The United States Steel Corporation, for example, was formed in 1901 by a merger of 10 companies; capitalized at more than one billion dollars, it became the largest industrial corporation in the world.

While the railroads provided the transportation means for decentralization, it was but one factor among many that was making the United States the industrial leader of the world. The wide use of the corporate form of business organization, which facilitated the pooling of large masses of capital for a single industrial objective, significantly aided economic growth. This form of business organization allowed capitalists and public investors to limit their liability for loss to their actual investment, thus keeping personal fortunes safe in the event of business failure. With the corporate form of business enterprise, risk taking was encouraged. Many investors, both foreign and domestic, could participate.

The development of industrial corporations led to the rapid expansion of activity on the stock market, and this in turn stimulated corporate expansion. Until its collapse in 1929, the stock market was the pulse of industry. A lively market kept business strong as it created an enormous and ready supply of money for new business enterprises or the expansion of established firms.

At the same time, scientific discovery was creating entirely new industries as well as new products. The most important application of new scientific findings was in the field of electricity. Before electricity, wood, coal, and steam dominated American industry as the sources of energy for production. Selection of factory locations depended on convenience to coal mines or waterfalls. Machines used in these factories were constantly overheating, slowing the production rate. But the introduction of electricity into industry changed all of this. By 1900, electric power had come into wide industrial use, and factories were free to locate in urban areas.

These urban areas were an excellent source of labor. Promises of economic opportunity drew hundreds of thousands of craftsmen and laborers to migrate from Europe. These immigrants, on the whole, knew little English and were unable to read or write, even in their own language. Therefore, they tended to associate with their own countrymen in the port cities in which they landed or in the factory towns to which they were directed by company employment agents on their arrival to these shores.

Also having a profound effect on city growth patterns during the 1890s were the electric streetcar and the advent of steel construction, which made the building of skyscrapers possible. The first electric railroad system in the United States was built in Montgomery, Alabama, in 1886. Within 10 years, the electric car was a major source of city transportation in all urban areas. Prior to the application of electricity, urban streetcars were either drawn by horses and mules at about six miles per hour or propelled by steam. Each system severely limited the expansion of cities. As urban steam railroads extended their tracks, trains became longer and required heavier locomotives to pull them. The heavier the locomotive, the more noise and the greater the danger of fire caused by flying sparks. Electric trolley systems were much more flexible than steam railroads. Cars could be powered individually, run singularly or in trains, and switched from track to track with ease. Furthermore, they allowed for single-track lines running down the center of streets. By 1912, 40,000 miles of electric railways and trolley lines, including new urban subway lines, had been laid in the United States.

Advent of the Skyscraper

Meanwhile, the skyscraper was pushing cities up, not out. Prior to the development of the skyscraper, builders using masonry walls had pushed construction to 11 and 12 stories in height. The first steel-frame buildings, usually considered the original skyscrapers, included the nine-story Home Insurance Building in Chicago, which was started in 1884; the eight-story Tower Building in New York, built in 1888; and the 13-story Tacoma Building in Chicago, started in 1888. The popularity of the Tacoma Building, equipped with new electric elevators, established a trend. During the next five years, more than 25 of these buildings were erected in Chicago alone. All were between 12 and 16 stories in height. The typical financial structure of a skyscraper built during this period is of particular interest. Usually, the land was leased from its owners for a 99-year term. The building was built with the equity financed by a stock issue and debt funded through bonds issued, thus being part of the tradition of multi-ownership of income properties in the United States.

In 1914, however, an article on the front page of the *Wall Street Journal* reported that skyscrapers in New York were having difficulties in renting space on upper levels. The article stated that, "With the completion of the Woolworth Building, the maximum height of buildings has been obtained." The article went on to report that there had been a remarkable change in the attitude of tenants within the past few years. Previous to that time, tenants had rushed to get into the newest and loftiest structures; however, this was no longer so. It said that scarcely a building of more than 21 stories in New York was paying a dividend or a decent return on invested capital. One building of more than 30 stories had paid 13 percent the first three years after completion but, at the time of the article's appearance, was not even meeting expenses. Various reasons were assigned for the refusal of tenants to go to upper floors. Some complained of the long elevator journey, others of the comparative isolation, and still others were honest enough to admit a shade of fear or doubt about occupying the upper floors. In the Woolworth Building, with 53 floors of offices available for rent, none above the 41st floor was occupied. The article concluded that the ideal skyscraper seemed to be one of about 15 to 20 stories. Still, monumental office buildings continued to be developed at a rate faster than the market could absorb.

Furthermore, architects and developers had little experience in the erection of new office buildings. For the most part, each new building was a new experience. In a competitive market, many of these buildings failed because of their design faults. Problems such as poor elevator arrangement, light court arrangement, or heating systems made buildings undesirable. Other defects, such as inefficient elevator service, poor window arrangements, impractical office arrangements, and over-adornment, were glaringly apparent in many buildings and materially affected the earning power of the property.

Still another blunder on the part of architects and owners was the desire by both to create monuments and extravagant works of art. They soon learned that these monuments were poor investments and paid low dividends.

The outgrowth of all of this was emergence of a new field of professional real estate activity—that of becoming a specialist in the leasing of office space. Leading real estate offices, particularly in downtown areas, had rent departments. Until about 1915, these departments were unimportant parts of the real estate office, with the work usually assigned to clerks. At that time, the situation changed.

The Automobile and Other Urban Problems

The early 1900s also brought another new force—the automobile. The unique American capability for producing the automobile evolved out of several strengths acquired in the 1800s. From the nation's earliest days, carriage manufacturers had trained skilled craftsmen in the fabrication of wheels, springs, and bodies. During the middle of the century, techniques about building engines were learned through production of machinery, farm equipment, and locomotives. In the latter part of the century, the pneumatic tire was developed by bicycle manufacturers, scientists had learned how to produce a good quality of gasoline through refining of petroleum, and electricity enabled factories to mass produce at feasible prices. These developments and skills were pooled, and in 1908 Henry Ford introduced the Model T, priced at $850. By 1914 he was producing 248,000 cars per year (almost 50 percent of total U.S. production), and the average price was less than $500 per vehicle.

It is interesting to note that in 1911, one of the primary concerns of a national real estate convention was the effect the automobile was having on real estate, both within the immediate central city and in suburban areas. The principal speaker at that convention, John E. Leet of Denver, made these observations: "The next fashion will be a stampede to the suburbs. Exactly as the auto has already ushered in a good road movement, so will it quickly usher a new era of suburban life." He foresaw a new traffic problem, but he also envisioned a new investment opportunity. He prophesied, "The railroads have added 30 billion dollars to the land values of this country. The motor truck will add a hundred billion in one-fourth of the time. Every wagon becomes a branch railroad at reduced rates. Every farmer will run his own train."

In 1911, 92 percent of the roads outside corporate limits were dirt, and the automobile was in its embryonic stages of development. Before the beginning of the next decade, tremendous advances had been made in the road system and in the quality of the equipment. The United States was on its way to becoming a car-born society, with mobility as an inherent strength. As an outgrowth of these forces, it was becoming apparent that comprehensive city planning needed to be a major concern of city government. By 1911, at least 75 cities had engaged experts to make comprehensive studies about city planning. Topics selected for the third national conference of the National City Planning Association held in Philadelphia that year were these: possible standardized street widths, block and lot limits, uniform planning code, housing reform, and the excess use of condemnation. It is notable that the conference concerned itself with the discussion of the automobile's impact on the pattern of cities.

Early leaders in the city planning movement were real estate practitioners, among them J.C. Nichols of Kansas City and Fred G. Smith of Minneapolis, leaders in the National Association of Real Estate Exchanges. Nichols was a particularly important force in the development of city planning codes. In 1912, he developed the 1,000-acre Country Club District of Kansas City and established a notable set of standards for subdivision development. He incorporated plans for park areas and other beautification elements, segregation of residential from business and apartment areas, and building restrictions that would safeguard the permanent attractiveness of the home. Parks and boulevards were deeded to the city. Transportation lines were constructed, then turned over for regular street car service. A fund was established to keep vacant lots in order. Nichols's thesis was that "it pays in the long run to follow such standards. Now our last lot is always the highest priced lot sold. It really does pay, in order to make your grades right and to ruin a few lots if necessary. It really does pay to have regard for city plans as a whole."

The first comprehensive zoning law in the United States was adopted by New York City in 1916. It was to influence cities over the country. The New York measure was comprehensive in that it regulated city-wide the manner in which land might be used, the maximum heights of buildings, and the minimum size of lots, yards, and courts. During the next 10 years, most of the major cities of the nation enacted some form of zoning ordinance.

Another major problem for real estate during these formative years was taxation. The major source of government income had been taxes levied against real estate. By 1900, government was beginning to become a costly operation, and real estate continued to foot the bill. The California Realty Federation pointed out that real estate was paying more than 80 percent of all taxes in the state of California and that banking institutions and other businesses were paying very little. During the next 20 years, there was a concentrated effort toward tax reform that would require real estate to pay only its fair share of the tax burden, at the same time establishing a fair method for setting the value of separate parcels of real estate.

During these formative years, real estate considered one of its major problems to be that of bad housing. Housing reform came into the national consciousness and vocabulary as a result of the profound movement of the early 1900s for social advance. In describing the substandard housing problems of 1911, Lawrence Veiller, secretary of the National Housing Association, said this:

> The housing problem as we know it in America is largely a sanitary problem. It is chiefly the problem of good municipal housekeeping, removal of garbage and rubbish, cleanliness of streets and alleys, provision of proper sanitary conveniences. In New York there are over 100,000 dark, unventilated rooms without even a window or an adjoining room, and over one million people have no bathing facilities in their homes.

More than 60 years later, the national housing problem remains one of the great challenges for property managers.

Acceptance of Apartment Living

Despite the problem of poor housing, important changes in residential real estate were occurring. These changes revolved around the advent of apartment living. Architects design apartment houses to reflect the lifestyle of the times, and so it was in the early 1900s. City life was exploding. Many new jobs were being created within the urban areas. Not only was there a movement from farm to the city but also from the single-family home to the apartment. The first apartment house to be developed in Chicago was in 1870, and in Detroit in 1892. These were patterned after apartment buildings that had been built in New York City and Boston. When the first buildings were built in Chicago, public opinion was low. Nevertheless, the market was very strong. All apartments built during the first few years were rented in short order, and a vacancy presented no operating problems.

A phenomenal period of residential construction began in 1909 and lasted until World War I. Prior to this time, apartment house development had been confined to very small buildings. The duplex and four-flat were popular, and the four-story walk-ups served the housing needs of middle- to low-income people. The growth of the cities brought on two important new apartment markets. Luxury apartments became a popular form of living for the well-to-do who were seeking greater independence and a way of lessening the management of household affairs, since it was increasingly difficult to secure help. Luxury buildings offered such services and conveniences as domestic cleaning and central laundry facilities. Some buildings even had chutes via which the housewife sent the laundry to an electric laundry in the basement. There people waited to care for her laundry needs. The design of apartments was utilitarian as well. Built-in furniture, such as sideboards, linen closets, china closets, and a central vacuum-cleaning aparatus, iceless refrigerators, steam heat, and new electric ranges all contributed to making the ideal apartment "a never living abode to the family desiring carefree existence from the turmoil and labors of housekeeping."

The other new market for apartment houses was single employed persons or married couples on limited budgets. For this market was developed the first single or studio apartment, as it is known today. An article in the *Kansas City Star,* describing a new apartment house in that city, said that this "new mode of living" was a "scientific assault on the high cost of housekeeping." The article claimed that the architects had "simplified housekeeping to the extent that six rooms, without sacrificing utility, had been compressed or consolidated into a space of 18 x 20 feet." The key to this achievement was a combination room, convertible in a moment into a lodging room, a dining room, or a bedroom. In the architects' "scientific analysis" of the needs for living space, they had calculated that dining rooms were, in effect, rather useless, because they were used so few hours during the day, and that bedrooms, while used from eight to nine hours a day, were used mostly for hours of "unconsciousness." Therefore, by combining the uses of a dining room and a bedroom with that of a living room, there was greater use of space and certainly was less costly in rent to the tenant. This first "single apartment" solved the dining room and bedroom problem by providing a small alcove off of the living room, similar to a pullman car's drawing room. It served as an eating area in the daytime and converted into a sleeping area in the evening. All of these space-saving features were designed to attract the tenant who was moving from a home and turning toward a new, popular mode of living—the apartment.

The apartment buildings themselves, however, were not small. Articles pointed out that a building of from eight to 12 stories seemed to be the most practical size. Elevator service was becoming important, and this size was large enough to afford the space and construction costs of an elevator. Furthermore, it was of sufficient size to afford competent on-site management. As a rule, buildings were measured to be successful if they showed a return of eight percent on the owner's investment.

Probably the greatest risk the apartment developer and owner assumed was one of a changing neighborhood. Cities were growing so rapidly that the property owner could experience a change in use of his neighborhood from residential to business or even industrial. With no zoning laws, indiscriminate change in the use of land in a neighborhood could seriously affect the value of surrounding real estate.

Establishment of Retail Districts

This risk of shifting population centers and changing neighborhoods also had an impact on retail properties. Initially, retail store operators chose to have short-term lease commitments. By the turn of the century, however, downtown areas were becoming more clearly defined, and values for choice property appreciated accordingly. Department stores required longer leases, and neighboring merchants began to commit to 10-year leases. Department stores established the best retail districts because of their heavy advertising and the resulting foot traffic. An example of the value of choice downtown property was in Philadelphia, where the city's best location sold in 1910 for $15,000 per front foot.

By 1917, the shopping habits of the new American city dwellers were sufficiently established to make downtown retail properties prime real estate investments. Chain store operations had begun to flourish, department store locations stabilized, and commercial leases lengthened. Retail stores of moderate size in these locations offered the investor land values that were increasing faster than the building

310 The Practice of Real Estate Management

depreciated. With new store fronts every 10 to 15 years, a property could be kept in style without great expense. If the location was good, there was no need to worry about vacancies. Rent values were regulated to a large extent by the number and character of the people passing by, not by management, advertising, style, or accident. Increased taxes and operating costs were assumed by the tenant.

Birth of Professionalism in Real Estate

This dynamic growth of major urban areas and the development of the railroads, which opened up millions of acres of land to investors, offered unprecedented opportunities for the fraudulent operator in real estate. Unfortunately, it was not uncommon for fraudulent operators to sell land to which they did not possess title or create false values by offering parcels of real estate with a low down payment, carrying back a piece of paper as a mortgage, and then selling the mortgage to unsuspecting persons. Another fraudulent practice was to sell land owned on a contract for sale, the contract being on terms the vendor never intended to fulfill. Still another problem of the day was ignorant and incompetent real estate operators selling real estate to unknowledgeable buyers. R. Bruce Douglas, then president of the Milwaukee Board of Realtors, had a glimpse of the answer when he said:

> In the State of Wisconsin it is easier to become a real estate man and handle thousands of dollars worth of property and money than to become a barber, charging 10¢ for a shave. The barber must go to the investigating board. If he is not a good barber, they won't give him a license. A real estate man has no preliminary examination to meet. He is not questioned as to his mental training, education, honor, or anything of that kind.

While local real estate boards were the watchdogs of fraudulent practices, their efforts were only successful in prohibiting fraud from continuing rather than punishing offenders. Through public pronouncements, they could warn the public against certain land speculation and could ostracize these practitioners from their organization, but they lacked legal authority. The resulting solution to the problem was enactment of statewide license laws to control the practices of agents and subdividers.

As a matter of interest, one of the primary reasons for the founding of the National Association of Real Estate Boards (NAREB), now the NATIONAL ASSOCIATION OF REALTORS®, was self-discipline. When the idea to organize the industry was proposed in 1907 by Edward Judd, he suggested that this national body might well give its attention to real estate license laws. Modern regulatory real estate license laws are, in fact, an implementation of real estate's national code of business ethics. The first state license law to be enacted and made operative was the California Act of 1917; however, after a few months it was held unconstitutional. The first regulatory license systems to be permanently established were set up in 1919 by two states, California and Michigan.

It was during these formative years of real estate that efforts were first made toward recognition of real estate as a profession. In order for any occupational activity to earn the status of a profession, it must meet four basic tests: (1), The practitioners must subscribe to a code of ethics; (2) the individuals must pass an examination and be licensed by the state; (3) the claimants must meet certain educational requirements, usually including the earning of a college degree; and (4) the public must accept the work activity as a profession. Real estate was on its way toward professional status in that it had a code of ethics, it was beginning to have state licensing laws, and it had recognized the need to educate its practitioners, as evidenced by real estate courses being offered all over the country.

In fact, formal educational courses in the methods of real estate are older than the NATIONAL ASSOCIATION OF REALTORS® itself. They go back to 1904, when first courses in real estate were taught at the West Side Y.M.C.A. of New York and sponsored by the Real Estate Board of Brokers in New York City. Teaching of the first university-level real estate courses began in 1905. Courses were offered that year at the University of Pennsylvania's Wharton School of Finance and Commerce and its evening school. In 1908, the University of Pittsburgh's evening school of economics opened a course that was still being offered six years later. By 1915, the National Association of Real Estate Boards began to focus on the need for real estate education. The minutes of NAREB's national meetings show that, from 1915 to 1920, a good deal of effort was spent in the planning for sponsorship of a "uniform course of real estate instruction" and for development of a real estate encyclopedia, "a big undertaking, but no five or ten books written by separate individuals can cover all of the subjects." United States entry into World War I in 1917 caused the Association to put aside this work for an analytical real estate educational course and other activity not directly related to its tangible war service. It was not until 1923 that a systematic development of technical real estate education was to be achieved.

1920 to the Great Depression:
From Shortage to Surplus

"Roaring Twenties" was a slogan that not only described an American lifestyle but also expressed the activity of urban real estate. Houses, factories, office buildings, apartment buildings, and retail properties were becoming important assets on the national balance sheet. Keyed to a wave of technological advance and tremendous industrial expansion, the 1920s marked an unparallelled period of urban prosperity and the greatest wave of building construction the country had ever known.

This major turning point of America's economic history was reached with the decade ending in 1920. As World War I was ending, the population was turning from one that was predominantly rural to one predominantly urban. At the beginning of the century, 39 percent of the population were city dwellers; by the 1920 census, more than 51 percent of the population lived in urban areas. The 1920 census also noted that the percentage of the population that owned homes had been declining since the year 1912. With apartment living now popular as a ready way to enjoy modern heating, lighting, and plumbing, an increasing number of Americans were becoming tenants rather than home owners.

War-time Housing Shortage

While the advance of technology had a great deal to do with the enormous amount of industrial and commercial construction that occurred during the twenties, increased residential building was brought on by a major housing shortage that began in the 1920s. About a year before U.S. entry into the war, American industry began the transition from peace-time to war-time production. In 1916, Congress created the Council of National Defense, the chief concern of which was the living conditions of war workers. With war production at a fever pitch came two inevitable needs: conservation of war materials and production of emergency housing for war workers. The shortage of housing for the thousands of newly employed defense workers began to be felt in 1917 in such places as the government shipyards of Hog Island. Furthermore, the placing of huge contracts for explosives in relatively remote places created its own specialized housing problems. By mid-1918, practically no vacant houses could be found in war-industry centers.

Despite this need for housing, Secretary of the Treasury William McAdoo discouraged any building, arguing that materials were needed for the production of the implements of war rather than for the housing of the businesses and people who manufactured these weapons. It was not until mid-1918 that Congress reacted to the shortage by forming the United States Housing Corporation. Because of its late start, the Housing Corporation had not one new single-family dwelling built and occupied before the war was over. (In later years, however, it did build and manage 25 projects containing about 5,000 single-family units plus some apartments. The agency was to continue its existence until it was liquidated in 1952.) By January 1918, building materials were costing at least 50 percent more than their pre-war rates. Of course, the problem was somewhat academic in that the government was discouraging and even prohibiting the development of additional housing.

As an emergency measure, the first federal rent control law was enacted in 1917. It applied only to the District of Columbia. Subsequently, emergency rent controls of various types were enacted in 13 states. The housing shortage did not end immediately upon the end of the war. Some state rent control laws had been declared unconstitutional, but New York extended its rent control, and other states, notably Pennsylvania, were considering peace-time control. Federal rent control in the District of Columbia had been extended to the post-war period and was not finally terminated until 1925.

Immediately following the war, the government, through the U.S. Department of Labor, sought industry's cooperation to get authentic information on which to base post-war resumption of construction. The Department of Labor also initiated a huge advertising program urging Americans to renew construction of houses. The advertising program included a series of widely distributed posters carrying such slogans as "Own a Home for your Children's Sake," "Thrift Put Savings into a Home," "Construct Now for a Greater and Still Happier America," or "Keep Good Times by Building NOW." The nation was in its first country-wide housing shortage. In 1920, the Senate established a select committee on reconstruction and production which reported that about 60 percent of the population were tenants. In Boston, for example, only two new housing units, built to house six families, were constructed in the entire year of 1918. In 1920, Philadelphia needed 20,000 units, St. Louis was short 10,000 homes, Cleveland needed 15,000 units, and over 10 percent of the Detroit population were unable to find permanent homes.

"A national emergency exists in housing conditions in all centers of population, largely aggravated by the drain of mortgage money for construction," declared the National Association of Real Estate Boards at its 1920 convention. So it was. There was a tremendous demand for new construction, the government was actively encouraging builders and buyers to get construction going, but there was a dearth of mortgage money.

Changes in Financing Practices
The major source of real estate mortgage money was private lenders, and the usual term for a real estate loan was five years. However, two recent developments had made real estate loans less attractive to the individual investor. The first was the advent of income taxes, which became effective in the year 1913. The new federal income tax law classified interest income as taxable income yet provided that a federal tax exemption be given to investors who put their money in municipal, state, or federal securities. Wealthy private investors, wanting to place their money largely in tax-exempt securities, were recalling their real estate loans for this purpose. It was estimated that $14 billion that had been invested in real estate mortgages were transferred to tax-exempt bonds. The second development was that national banks in federal reserve cities were not allowed to make real estate loans, and those in other cities could lend only one-third of the bank's time deposits. After state banks had invested all of their funds allowable for real estate loans, they could lend no more except from sale of those mortgages. Building and loan associations were experiencing a diminishing influx of money, and insurance companies up to that time had avoided the small construction loans.

A host of legislation, aimed at relieving the money shortage for real estate, was offered in Congress. Bills were introduced to establish a Federal Urban Mortgage Bank and create a Federal Home Loan Bank System. These were followed by proposals to repeal the excess profits tax on real estate sales, require federal reserve discounting of mortgages, provide federal income tax exemption for building and loan stock, and create a post office savings bank system directed toward becoming a credit supply for home mortgages. Although none of these issues passed, it is interesting to note that government participation in mortgage financing was first proposed during this time.

Ultimately, the law of supply and demand, not government action, was what eased the housing and mortgage and money shortage that followed World War I. The only important legislation to deal with real estate mortgages was a bill, initiated in 1923 and not passed until 1927, that allowed national banks to lend greater percentages of their net worth in time deposits on real estate. Under the new regulations, banks were permitted to lend 25 percent of their capital and surplus and 50 percent of their time deposits on improved real estate, providing the loan had a maximum term of five years.

The result of government ineffectiveness was that practically all of the real estate construction of the 1920s was financed by private sources. Insurance companies had learned that real estate loans were a good investment. The bond market had fluctuations in price depending on the market yield of bonds at a particular time, but real estate loans were always worth par. Metropolitan Life Insurance Company, then the largest life insurance company in the world, led the parade of life insurance companies back into the mortgage lending field. In 1920, it announced that it was placing $50 million in home mortgage money for new houses and apartments and that this money was going to be placed on terms that would provide for a 15-year loan payment plan with prepayment privileges. Prudential Insurance Company shortly followed suit.

The mortgage investments of 104 life insurance companies in the United States in 1928 yielded an average return of 5½ percent. Typically, their investment in real estate mortgages had almost doubled since 1921. During the 1920s, life insurance companies emerged as one of the principal sources for real estate financing. Interest rates were generally placed at one point higher a yield than the current corporate bond market, and the loans were amortized over a 15-year term. Most companies would not lend more than two thirds of the appraised value of the project, and many preferred 60 percent loans.

The early twenties also saw the emergence of building and loan associations as vehicles for real estate financing. By 1922, they claimed to be the fourth largest source of real estate loans, preceded by private investments, insurance companies, and commercial banks and savings banks, in that order. By today's standards, savings and loan associations (then called building and loan associations) were very small, the largest being the Railroad Men's Building and Loan Association in Indianapolis, with $24 million in assets. Collectively, however, they loaned a half billion dollars on real estate.

Real estate bonds first came into vogue in 1916 when corporations, rather than individuals, became the principal developers of large properties. Prior to that date, most real estate was owned by individuals, and real estate loans were negotiated primarily with insurance companies and savings banks. By creating real estate securities, the public found it possible to participate in the financing of large properties, which in the past had been confined to the very wealthy.

Real estate bonds were advanced during the 1920s to finance most of the large new apartment and office building developments. This was a program whereby mortgages were created in local communities for individual projects and marketed to large companies that oftentimes formed pools. They in turn would put the bonds in trusts by appointing trustees, issue bonds or collateral trust certificates against the pool of mortgages, and then supply the bonds to distributing companies, through which they would be passed on to individual investors.

The duties of the trustee under the trust indenture or mortgage to secure a bond issue was an important function of the whole operation. If it had been feasible to finance a mortgage transaction running into thousands or even millions of dollars by finding one lender for the entire amount, the trustee would have been a superfluous position. Ordinarily, however, this could not be done. Financing large properties in the 1920s required numerous investors, each lender committing a given sum of the total and then receiving evidence of the indebtedness through a bond. The impracticability of making the mortgage in favor of all such investors was obvious. Since all of the bonds were to be secured by the same property, the logical procedure was to execute a single mortgage, secured by as many bonds as that particular situation demanded, in favor of a trustee. The trustee was duly authorized to hold the lien created by the mortgage for the benefit of all the bondholders, certify the bonds, receive and disburse principal and interest payments, enforce the lien or the mortgage in case of default, and, upon payment in full by the mortgagor, execute a full release in satisfaction of the obligation. The trustee became the impartial third party who saw that the rights and obligations of both the mortgagor and mortgagee of the bondholders were protected and enforced. The need for trustees to fulfill this important duty caused the development of trust companies, who had the fiduciary powers to act in such a capacity.

The real estate bond business grew from modest beginnings to a gigantic size, disposing of approximately $1 billion worth of securities a year, until 1926. At this time it was threatened with disaster after the failure of G.L. Miller & Company in the summer of that year. Publicity of the most harmful nature was broadcast through newspapers and magazines. In a wave of hysteria, in part actively inspired by hostile forces, public confidence in the industry was badly shaken. Drastic measures of every kind were proposed by public authorities; the National Association of Security Commissioners, after a dramatic meeting, appointed a committee of commissioners to investigate and report on the industry.

The first mortgage bond industry, well aware that its industry needed regulation by the security commissioners of the many states, formed a committee to meet with the security commissioners. These two committees remained in almost continuous session for two months. Working together, they came out with a paper that became commonly known as the Chicago Agreement. The agreement had been approved by a large number of dealers in first mortgage bonds and was adopted in substance through departmental regulations by the security commissioners of many states. Essentially, the agreement charged the house of issue with keeping its own house in order, checking and supervising the acts and omissions of the borrower, and protecting the investor with respect to payments and defaults. A series of guidelines was drafted to ensure that this was done.

Shortly after the signing of the Chicago Agreement, the National Association of Real Estate Bond Houses was organized, with adherence to the Chicago Agreement in letter and spirit as a prerequisite for membership. Its first activity was in working with the commissioners on the matter of appraisals of projects and properties for which the bond houses would be selling bond securities to the public. Although the firms that composed the real estate bond houses were to fail during the early years of the Depression, which was only a few years away, their relationship between industry and the officers charged with the administration of securities law demonstrated how industry and government could work together to give the public the greatest possible measure of safety against fraud and sharp practices. The Chicago Agreement became the forerunner of governmental regulations of public offerings of real estate securities of today.

Numerous examples can be cited of the abuses afforded this form of financing when it flourished with no supervision by either federal or state government. One involved an investigation by the New York Assistant Attorney General, which in 1929 disclosed that 15 corporations in that state had 1,105 outstanding issues of real estate bonds that involved a face liability of over $1 billion. All of these issues depended on the earnings of the buildings that secured them. Of these, more than 98 percent were sold and the proceeds collected and held by the bond houses before the ground was broken for the buildings. In none of these issues was there any recourse by the bondholder to any property except the projected building. The funds collected by the bond house from the public through the sale of these securities were all dumped into one fund in each of these companies; the proceeds of the bonds then were used indiscriminately to make over and operate buildings that had defaulted or failed. Of the 1,105 issues, over 40 percent defaulted on interest and amortization payments and were not self supporting. In every such instance, the bondholders were not notified of these defaults or failures, but the coupons were paid out of the general fund. In other words, the bad bonds were floating at the expense of the good bonds.

Another popular form of financing during the 1920s was the second mortgage. Oftentimes it was made without amortization, was of short term, and could not be renewed. With the comparatively short term first mortgages that were the primary method of financing, the borrower was greatly dependent upon a rising real estate market in order to refinance when a second mortgage became due.

One of the great services performed by the National Association of Real Estate Boards during the twenties was to conduct a study to establish three criteria for second mortgages: the method of financing homes, including what safeguards should be used in such financing; the actual degree of risk involved in the ownership of first mortgages and second mortgages on homes based upon members' experience; and the cost of second mortgages to the homebuyer. Significant among other matters studied were insurance companies' loans, amortized loans and debentures against them, bond issue loans, safety and mortgage securities, participating certificates, contract sales, subdivision finance, ethics of mortgage lending including the ethics of collecting commissions on loans, appraisal for city loans, and appraisal for farm loans.

This study became a milestone for real estate history. It established a key fact then surprising to most people—the relatively low degree of risk involved in small home financing—laying the foundation for the mortgage revolution of the 1931–34 era. It also brought out the high cost and painful prevalence of second mortgage home financing. These revelations paved the way for the home loan and bank system and the Federal Housing Administration.

The Business Boom
Coupled with the housing and capital shortage during the early 1920s was the great advance in industrial and manufacturing efficiency caused by the increased use of power machinery, mass production methods, standardization of parts and processes, and electrification of 70 percent of the country's industry. By 1923, more than half of the industrial wage earners were concentrated in four percent of those factories employing 250 or more workers.

When President Coolidge declared in 1925 that "The business of America is business," he was putting it mildly. Three full years had passed since the end of post-war recession, and business had become a national obsession. The economy was spiraling upwards at a record clip, and everyone was spending avidly.

Production was up. The torrential output of consumer goods included such desirable new products as radios and electric refrigerators along with countless improved models of standard items—faster cars, shinier bathroom fixtures, even plusher caskets. Competition for sales was stiff and growing stiffer all the time.

Corporate profits were up. Thanks to new techniques of mass production, many manufacturers netted huge sums that they plowed back into plant expansion. In 1923, U.S. Steel was operating so efficiently that it was able to reduce its workday from 12 hours to eight hours and at the same time hire 17,000 additional workers, raise wages, and, amazingly, show an increase in profits.

Income was up in most lines of endeavor. Even industrial workers, whose strikes for higher pay had availed them little in the previous decade, benefited from company profits and enjoyed a higher standard of living. To round out this happy picture, prices were stable, savings and life insurance policies doubled, and business was given added impetus by the growth of chain stores and installment buying. With all these factors reinforcing the upward spiral, prosperity seemed to have no ceiling.

This atmosphere of swollen profits and abundant credit was the climate in which this country went on the wildest get-rich-quick speculative binge in its financial history. By 1928, the prices of stocks had soared beyond the point of safe return as thousands of small investors braved the hectic market, seeking a share of overnight windfalls. At no time in the twenties were there more than 1.5 million Americans involved in the market, but their much publicized success fueled the reckless optimism of the country at large. Business, most people came to believe, would provide everyone with a steadily increasing share of the ever-expanding prosperity. It seemed almost unpatriotic to exercise restraint in buying. For people everywhere, easy credit opened up broad new vistas. Time purchases in 1929 accounted for 90 percent of all piano and sewing and washing machine sales; over 80 percent of vacuum cleaner, radio, and refrigerator sales; 70 percent of furniture sales; and 60 percent of auto sales. Between 1920 and 1929, installment purchases quintupled, reaching $6 billion annually.

To the business community of the twenties, salesmanship was the greatest of performing arts. The soft sell of the early twenties hardened as competition increased the pace with the volume and variety of manufactured goods. The modern advertising agency emerged as a sophisticated team of highly paid specialists who often named, packaged, priced, and promoted the distribution of new products. Great ad men could and did bestow instant success on fledgling products and sick businesses. The decade's dominant and identifying trend in advertising was the increasing use of psychology, the deepening appeal to the secret emotions that motivated people to buy.

The Construction Boom

Meanwhile, the wave of residential construction was reaching a crest. The peak building for single-family dwellings came in 1925, for apartments in 1926 and 1927, for total construction dollar value in 1926, and for the number of persons employed in construction in 1926. The early starts for new private permanent nonfarm dwelling units in 1925 totalled 927,000 units, a rate not again to be reached until 1949. One movement that began to flourish was the cooperative apartment movement. Reportedly, the first cooperative apartment house was built in New York City in 1876. This project was undertaken through the desire on the part of several wealthy people to minimize the cares incidental to the administration of a private home yet retain the chief advantages of individual home ownership while living in the central part of the city. To quote an author of that period:

> They wanted freedom from the furnace man, snow shoveler, watchman, plumber, tinsmith, and other nightmares of housekeeping. They wanted to be free to go away and return to their individual apartments ready for occupancy. Add to this the ability to decorate and treat interiors as one wishes, no longer to fear moving troubles, and to experience a diminishing output for household expenses.

While there were a few such buildings in New York City built prior to 1920, it was not until that time that the cooperative apartment movement really began to flourish in the United States. This had become a logical solution of the problems of urban living, inasmuch as land values and taxes were high and the expense and trouble of maintaining an individual home were considerable. Cooperative apartments had become such an important part of the real estate business that by 1928 NAREB had a Cooperative Apartment Division with membership composed of people from most of the large cities in the United States.

Likewise in the early 1920s, office buildings were becoming a popular form of investment, particularly in the larger cities. The early twenties was a time of skyscraper construction. The influences of electric power and the internal combustion engine continued to push urban growth upward. Although skyscraper construction stayed active throughout the decade, orderly recession of general construction was the story in 1927, 1928, and 1929.

Curiously, with all of this activity, unemployment by contemporary standards was very high. It was estimated that in 1921, 25 percent of the total labor supply was unemployed, and, in 1929, when it reached its lowest point, 10 percent was still unemployed. (Today, a seven percent unemployment rate is thought of as a recession economy.) For the employed, there were changes in work patterns. People had greater leisure time, the basic eight-hour day and 44-hour week, with Saturday a half-holiday, having been established as standard in most industries during the war period.

It was a different story for the farm economy, however. War-expanded farms did not share in this prosperity. With the war's end, farmers suddenly lost their $2.00 or $3.00 per bushel wheat market and went into a depression. By 1924, cultivation had been abandoned on 13 million acres that had been tilled during the war years. After a wave of foreclosures, the farm crisis and its causes were studied by Senate committees and a committee appointed by President Warren G. Harding. As a result of their studies, the government entered the rural real estate business in 1923 by providing for immediate term government farm loans through intermediate credit banks under the auspices of Federal Land Banks, which were made permanent institutions. Farmers used the new federal banking aids chiefly to refinance existing mortgages. Although the farm-to-city population shift became more noticeable, as evidenced by a citywide movement of over 1,000,000 people in 1922 alone, the farm depression gradually wore off.

While the six years from 1922 to 1927 were the best years that real estate practitioners had ever seen, by 1928 market conditions had slowed considerably. It was no longer a seller's market, but instead a buyer's market. Values had stabilized; the nation was in an over-built condition. There were too many hotels, large apartment houses, theaters, and office buildings. The increased efficiency of industrial labor and new types of machinery resulted in less floor space necessary to produce the same amount of goods. A survey taken by the Brokers Division of NAREB indicated that the vacancy rate in office buildings was 12 percent.

The Retail Explosion

In spite of this condition, however, an increased demand was reported for the better retail business locations in both large and small cities. These properties were bringing higher rentals and were being keenly sought by a new dimension to the merchandising revolution: the coast-to-coast network of chain stores. For the housewife and the chain alike, economy was the ruling passion. Chains cut costs through volume purchasing and heightened efficiency and passed on a part of the savings to the customer. The gigantic A&P chain, which bought a half billion dozen eggs per year, could afford to set its prices per dozen several cents lower than that of the small-scale independent grocer, or the so-called ma-and-pa operation. Comparable cost price benefits stemmed from a different source at the F.W. Woolworth Company. Its five-and-ten stores were stocked with rewarding economy by expect buyers. Savings were even more important to a trailbrazing company in the fiercely competitive grocery business. One particular firm, Piggly Wiggly, featured a method of operation new to the field at the start of the decade. Under the proud slogan of "scientific merchandising," Piggly Wiggly created a self-service system with its markets laid out according to a patented traffic pattern. These first supermarkets were known popularly as grocerterias until the handier term was coined.

By 1928, the Great Atlantic and Pacific Tea Company had 16,000 stores under its control, Kroger Grocery had 5,500 stores, and Woolworth had 1,500 five-and-ten-cents stores. Chain store organizations were expanding in every direction. Hardly a week would pass without the announcement of the birth of some new syndicate group that intended to form a chain store operation for some part of the retail business.

Two new terms were added to the real estate vocabulary—the "100-percent location" and "percentage leases." The 100-percent location was defined as "the location that checks the highest with due regard to the traffic desired," a definition that emphasized the kind of traffic being sought. Although rare, larger cities could have more than one 100-percent location. In smaller communities, ordinarily only one 100-percent location existed. In 1928, for example, the 100-percent locations for major chain store operators were as follows: In New York City, the north side of 24th Street, between Fifth and Sixth Avenues; the north side of 42nd Street, between Fifth and Sixth Avenues, and Fifth Avenue on both sides of the street from 34th Street to 40th Street. In Baltimore, the south side of Lexington Street, between Park and Howard Streets. In Chicago, the west side of State Street, between Washington and Monroe. In Detroit, the west side of Woodward Avenue, between State Street and Grand River. In Los Angeles, the west side of Broadway, between Fifth and Seventh Streets. In Atlanta, the corner of Peachtree Street and Ellis Street.

Sites with a 100-percent rating were determined by three basic considerations:

1. The type of location. Almost all locations were divided into two classes—men's clothing, hats, shoes, sporting goods, and other lines patronized by the alleged head of the house. A women's location was the buying center in which five-and-ten-cents stores, variety stores, and department stores were located and in which all lines of female apparel were sold. Public markets and food stores quite often located in secondary women's locations. A good men's location usually was found to be on the side of the street opposite the women's center or on the adjoining block. Most often, it was in the location of the larger office buildings or banks, i.e., the focal points of the male traffic. Women's locations usually were the most high priced, made so by the fact that women did most of the family shopping and spending.
2. Location percentage. This was determined by the use of a stopwatch. Checks were made at various points in the retail district, all of uniform periods of time. Locations that checked the highest, with due regard to the traffic desired, were termed 100 percent. Other locations of the same type were graded therefrom.
3. Purchasing power. This was determined by the relation to the quality of traffic passing at a given point. What sometimes happened to be the highest traffic point did not necessarily represent the highest purchasing power. Traffic and transit condi-

324 The Practice of Real Estate Management

tions usually governed. For instance, the heaviest traffic point in New York City was the west side of Sixth Avenue and Broadway, between 33rd and 34th Streets. However, the north side of 34th Street, between Fifth and Sixth Avenues, was the best popular-priced center in the metropolitan area.

Ownership of the 100-percent location in any community was one of the best investments a person could have. Consequently, determining how much rent the merchant could pay was a new science that began to develop. No merchant could pay rent in excess of the volume of business transacted on his premises and still show a profit. Therefore, a schedule of percentages evolved that was based on total business realized by a merchant in a given line of business. Studies were made throughout the country to learn what average rents different lines of businesses were paying or could pay. Two of the principal studies were conducted by the Bureau of Business Research at Northwestern University and by Harvard University's Business Research Department. From these studies lists began to be published, primarily through the National Association of Real Estate Boards, providing guidelines on the percentage of a business's gross income it could afford to pay for rent.

1933 through World War II: From Depression to War Economy

The genesis of the modern real estate management business was the Great Depression, during which the individual owner was liquidated and the bulk of income real estate in the United States fell into the hands of lenders.

Shortly after the New York Stock Exchange opened on the morning of October 24, 1929, stock prices started to drop dramatically. The volume of trading broke all previous records. By 11:30 a.m., panic selling prevailed. In the offices of J.P. Morgan and Company, a group of top investment bankers met and, in an effort to reverse the tide, sent Richard Witney, vice president of the Exchange, to the floor to purchase millions of dollars worth of key stocks. This action was successful and prices began to steady. But four days later, prices again tumbled. This time the bankers did not try to halt the decline. On October 29, panic selling increased. The ticker tape fell two and a half hours behind, and, by day's end, a record 16,410,030 shares had been sold. The stock market lost $14 billion in a single trading session. Thousands of investors saw their fortunes wiped out.

Buying on margin was the straw that broke the market's back and signaled the end of Coolidge-Hoover prosperity. Before the market crashed, stocks not only were priced far above their real values but were being bought for marginal down payments of as little as 10 percent, the bulk of the purchase price being financed by brokers' loans. As stock prices slumped, overextended investors were required to put up additional margin. Many could produce the capital only by selling off shares at distressed prices. This drove the market into a steeper, broader descent—and redoubled the brokers' demands for margins. Between late October and mid-November, stocks lost more than 40 percent their total valuation, a drop of $30 billion in paper value.

Those few weeks were a nightmare. Market-wise reporters struggled in vain to describe adequately the phenomenon on the stock exchange floor. Broker Fred Schwed later wrote ironically, "Like all life's rich emotional experiences, the full flavor of losing important money cannot be conveyed by literature." Only slowly, as personal antecdotes fleshed out the appalling statistics, did the scope of the crash become amply evident. The economy was unsound. Banks and corporations were structurally weak and in many cases undermined by skullduggery and fraud. America's trade policies were self-defeating. The market for consumer goods was both glutted and untapped: 90 percent of the nation's wealth was concentrated in the hands of only 13 percent of the people. Meanwhile, large segments of society, among them farmers, textile workers, and coal miners, lacked sufficient income to buy much more than minimal needs. The stock market crash was far more than a private retribution for greedy speculators. It was a clear warning for all. The Great Depression had begun. In the rigors of this disaster, the strength of America would be sorely tried.

The Depression Economy

Even after the crash, economists, bankers, and politicians believed that the economy was still sound and that the market would soon recover. Yet examination of statistics revealed an increasing unemployment rate during the year prior to the crash and a great decrease in construction activity. In 1930, the prosperity propaganda continued, a strong stock market recovery was noted during the first four months of the year, and the Dow Jones average rose from a low of 198 to 294 during the period. But unemployment, which stood at 1.5 million in October 1929, rose to four million by the spring. The stock market again declined sharply in May. A terrible drought during the summer months in the Ohio-Mississippi Valley caused much suffering and worsened the already bad farm situation. Increasing bank failures during the latter half of the year culminated in December with the failure of the Bank of the United States. By October, President Herbert Hoover recognized publicly that 4.5 million were unemployed. By 1931, the number was at nine million, and that year saw 2,294 bank failures. The movement of people from the farm to the city was reversed for the first time as, in some industrial cities, one out of three workers was unemployed. Nonetheless, the farmer was taking a financial beating as well. Commodity prices were about 60 percent lower than two years before. By the presidential inauguration day in 1933, one third of the labor force was out of work, and many who had jobs were working for as little as 10 cents an hour. The year proved to be the bottom of the Depression.

During the turbulent thirties, a new economic philosophy, credited to Lord Keynes of England and adopted by the Roosevelt Administration, evolved. The philosophy was that when an economy suffers a reversal, such as the Depression of 1929–1933, government can reverse adverse trends by pumping the economy via wholesale spending. When commercial and industrial activity has reached sufficient velocity, then the government can recapture its original investment through increased taxes.

Even though the country today is several hundred billion dollars more in debt than when this economic philosophy evolved, both political parties tend to embrace it as national policy. This has an important effect upon the business of real estate management, inasmuch as real estate values follow dollar values. There are bound to be fluctuations in the economy ranging from serious recession to serious inflation; however, as long as government follows this economic philosophy, the dollar will continue to grow less valuable in purchasing power, and real estate will grow higher in price. Therefore, while at times real estate may face overproduction with high vacancy, lower percentage lease income, and lower net operating income, eventually, in stable neighborhoods, the situation will improve. A student of real estate must have a sufficient knowledge of these fluctuations of the economy and the timing of them to adjust to an intelligent businesslike manner as they occur.

The Depression took a toll on the real estate industry. Specifically, it was a period of high vacancy rates, for which there were four causes:

1. Undoubtedly, too many living quarters were built in the United States during the boom years of the mid-1920s. Probably 10 to 15 percent of the vacancies were due to this oversupply.
2. Although impossible to measure, there was a tremendous doubling up of families due to unemployment.
3. There was a back-to-farm movement. Because of unemployment, many people had been forced to leave large cities and return to rural communities.
4. As the unemployment rate increased, the declining marriage rate, which had been dropping since 1924, greatly accelerated during the period beginning in 1930.

Probably the best survey of the vacancy problem was made by Real Estate Analysts, Inc., of St. Louis, which reported that one out of five apartments was vacant, two out of seven apartment hotel units were vacant, stores were experiencing one vacancy out of every seven, and two out of nine offices were vacant. Industrial properties also were experiencing vacancies, these at a rate of about 10 percent.

By 1934, economic conditions began to improve. About 2.5 million of the unemployed found jobs, and wages began to rise. Still, 11 million needed work, and the relief rolls were maintained at between 16 and 18 million. Farm prices increased markedly, partly because of the subsidy and crop limitation efforts of the government. The stock market turned upward, and industrial production increased slowly.

In 1935, the real estate market began to turn around; occupancy improved. That year saw an actual increase in rents as well as occupancy, rates increasing on the average about eight percent. The next year showed continued recovery in all sectors of the real estate economy. It is interesting to note, in a recovery period, those areas that are affected first and last. The recovery first was apparent in the reduced vacancy level and next in apartment rentals. Retail stores followed, then industrial properties, and, lastly, office buildings.

In 1937 and 1938, the economy experienced a short recession. Congress again financed relief measures and public works projects, and the economy began to strengthen. Although residential rents continued to climb, building costs showed a slight drop, and, of course, residential construction was dropping. By 1939, the country was again on its road to recovery; the recession had been short-lived. Real estate activity was increasing. Foreclosure rates were down. Construction had reached a new peak in December 1938, its highest point since 1928. An index of the bid price of 16 prominent office building bonds had reached its low point—about 35 percent of par value in 1933. By 1939, they had recovered only to 41 percent of par value. Office buildings in 1939 were still experiencing an 18 percent vacancy factor, indicative of the type of real estate that had not recovered well from the depths of the Depression.

Mortgages for Middle America

The most significant change in real estate to come out of the Depression was recognition of the need to provide homes for middle America. When applying the traditional formula that a family can afford to pay 25 percent of its income for housing, the National Bureau of Economic Research found that 84 percent of the families in the United States could not qualify to buy a home with civilized conveniences and modern facilities. Leonard P. Reaume, president of NAREB, in 1930 proposed a program with four fundamental changes in method and public policy needed to reach the goal of providing affordable decent homes: (1) a reduction in the cost of homesites by more efficient, less wasteful land use; (2) new techniques to reduce the cost of building; (3) reduction in the local tax load then penalizing home ownership; and (4) a reduction in the homebuyer's financing cost. His first three points received immediate attention from developers, legislators, and manufacturers and were somewhat effective in reducing the production cost of a new home. However, it was his fourth point, reduction in the homebuyer's financing cost, that would start the wheels of construction in the homebuilding industry and provide for a wider ownership of real estate in the United States.

The typical means of financing a house before this time was a first mortgage of short duration, many times only five years, which customarily was renewed upon expiration. In addition, many houses had second mortgages, also customarily renewed. As the Depression hit and these mortgages became due, the second mortgage money market practically disappeared. Owners caught with a need to renew their five-year mortgage loans were finding it impossible to obtain money comparable to that which prevailed when they undertook the original payment. The result was that their equities disappeared.

As early as 1931, NAREB was investigating the feasibility of a central mortgage banking system to stabilize and aid the financing of real estate. The association, through its spokesmen, president, Harry Kissell, and secretary, Herbert U. Nelson, campaigned for the proposition of a "need of a reserve system that would stabilize all long-term mortgage credit." An article by these gentlemen in the magazine *Wall Street* caught the attention of President Herbert Hoover. The officials of the association were asked to confer at the White House on the proposal. The plan contained revolutionary concepts in the field of home finance. It proposed a central residential mortgage bank and regional banks initiated by the federal government with banks, building and loan associations, and mortgage companies as members subscribing to the needed capital. A regional bank would purchase first mortgages only from its members and issue bonds secured by such mortgages as well as loan capital and surplus and possibly by further guarantees or commitments by members from whom these mortgages were purchased.

Mortgages eligible for regional banking purchases would be limited to amortized long-term first mortgages on urban residential properties of no more than 55 or 60 percent of the property value. Long-term financing of say 20 years with installment payments on principal not exceeding four percent per annum and with certain rights of prepayment would enable the family to accumulate a reserve for times of stress. Congress finally enacted the Home Loan Bank Act in July 1932, but the plan was of meager effectiveness because it was restricted to use only by savings and loan associations and a relatively few savings banks. It gave so small an appropriation that for five years the banks could be used only for bailing out member institutions, not for lending to new construction. Further, the mortgages handled could be of no more than 50 percent of value. Though whittled down and "tragically delayed," as Hoover put it, the Home Loan Bank Law was the start of a mortgage revolution that strengthened and widened home ownership.

By June 1933, foreclosures on home mortgages were taking place at the rate of about 1,000 a day. Cordell Hull, chairman of the Senate Banking Committee, was shocked by a decision of a leading life insurance company to pull out of residential lending in his home state of Tennessee. He reacted by creating legislation, passed by Congress in June 1933, authorizing a home rescue agency, the Home-owners Loan Corporation (HOLC).

The corporation initially was authorized to issue $2 billion of

18-year, four-percent, tax-free, government-guaranteed bonds. These were to be exchanged for home mortgages not exceeding $20,000 in value. The HOLC was authorized to accept mortgages up to $14,000, or 80 percent of the current appraised value, whichever was smaller. It then took a new amortized mortgage from the owner of the property for 15 years at five percent interest. Thus, every mortgage guaranteed by HOLC became a modern amortized mortgage at the currently most liberal interest rate of five percent and with a 15-year term. This program was later amended by Congress in 1939 to provide for 4½ percent interest and a term of up to 25 years. Of course, this was to be tremendously influential on the course of home ownership in the United States. This financing provided one fifth of the then existing mortgaged urban homes. The program also financed the mortgages foreclosed upon by banks that had been closed or institutional lenders who themselves were in liquidation. Thirteen percent of the total monies funded by the HOLC was used for "rescue mortgages" for these institutions in bankruptcy. The total amount of the loans taken over by the HOLC was over $3 billion.

This program was later to demonstrate the tremendous stability in the value of a house used as a home. The HOLC program was to terminate 21 years later. It had started by taking the poorest risks in the national home mortgage portfolio, at the depth of the nation's worst depression, and, through cumulative earnings, had returned the entire funding capital of $3 billion plus a $14 billion profit to the government. This profit was after paying off the bonds, salaries, interest, office rentals, service fees, and other expenses and without cost to the government of any kind. A key factor in the success of HOLC was its use of fee appraisers, real estate brokers, and property managers from the private sector. In all, it employed 2,700 qualified fee appraisers, nearly 3,000 contract management brokers, and 3,000 contract sales brokers.

The HOLC was a program of direct federal refinancing of home mortgages during a national crisis. Still the administration, through its National Emergency Council, was seeking a long-range plan to stabilize the house mortgage market. In June 1934, it devised a plan that was to carry the mortgage revolution to its height. The plan was for the federal government to create an agency to provide home mortgage insurance. The government became a supervising agency that guaranteed repayment of loans made by private lenders to private borrowers. For this service, the government charged an insurance premium based on the amount of money borrowed for the home loan. The premiums collected went into a central fund used to reimburse lenders for loans that went into default. For many years, people misunderstood the government's function and thought it to be a lender of money. It was not. It was an insurer of loans. The plan was adopted by Congress and became the Federal Housing Administration (FHA), a borrower's mutual insurance agency.

With the FHA set up, the mortgage revolution was over the hump, and home ownership was possible on a truly wide scale. The important features of the plan were: high loan-to-value ratios, making low down payments possible without involving second mortgages; long-term amortization, making low monthly payments possible; monthly payments that included reduction of principal, interest, local real estate taxes, hazard insurance, and mortgage insurance premium all in one package payment; and the limitation on the rate of interest to be charged on the insured loans. Originally the limit was set at five percent exclusive of the insurance premium, but under special conditions it could go up to six percent. The ratio of loan-to-value was limited to 80 percent; the term limit was 20 years.

Within eight years, the FHA was serving 25 percent of the nation's home mortgages. By 1940, the FHA was paying all of its operating expenses out of income; in March 1954, it repaid all of the money that had been advanced by the government in setting up its program, plus interest calculated at a rate of 2¼ percent. The FHA program proved so successful that the terms for homebuyers were later liberalized by increasing the maximum loan-to-value ratio to 90 percent and extending the term to 30 years. The program continued to be a sound fiscal plan until the 1960s, when Congress committed the program to be used as a vehicle in attempting to solve the social housing needs of the nation.

The War Effort

The overproduction of income real estate during the 1920s was beginning to disappear by 1940. Higher employment and new jobs, fundamental to the housing demand, had reduced the vacancy factor in apartments to normal standards, and rental rates were actually experiencing escalation. New jobs and additional purchasing power had reduced the oversupply of commercial retail space; new construction was even underway in this segment of the real estate economy. As the nation shifted again from peacetime to wartime economy, industrial space became a specialized focal point because of the need for defense production. Office building space throughout the country had been slow to recover; the defense period of 1940 and 1941 found vacancy rates in most large cities still quite high.

Upon the outbreak of World War II, the nation made a commitment to victory that was unparalled in history. The entire nation shifted to wartime economy and accepted controls on prices, the right to strike, the right to buy, and wages. A new generation of government alphabet agencies appeared, the purpose of which was to develop defense production and distribute war materials and manipulate the economy through wage and price controls.

The first segment of the real estate economy to be of importance to the war economy was the industrial property sector. On the day following the Japanese bombing of Pearl Harbor, the Society of Industrial REALTORS® (SIR) formed a committee and met with officials of the Office of Production Management. Together, they formulated a plan to inventory the vacant industrial properties of the country. Within a few weeks, the government had a report listing some 10,000 available buildings that could be used effectively in the war effort. SIR also developed standard formulas for measuring factory and warehouse properties, which were adopted and used by various branches of the government. The highly specialized knowledge of practitioners in industrial real estate enabled both government and industry to obtain, in advance of purchase, skilled analysis of plants or locations covering raw material supply, labor, transportation, fuel, and power, as well as equipment and construction.

During World War I, housing for defense workers had been managed poorly, resulting in stifling shortages. A recognized principle in World War II was that good housing is closely tied to good morale among war workers. While the government realized the serious need to conserve materials needed for defense, it was also well aware that, with the creation of millions of new jobs and the redistribution of those jobs, it had to create healthy and safe housing for its defense industry workers. Several pieces of legislation provided this housing. The Lanham Act provided for 1,320,000 dwelling units: Private production was allocated 200,000 new units; remodeling was expected to produce an additional 260,000 units; a war guest plan was expected to use 650,000 dwellings. The balance was in public war housing. Also enacted was FHA Title VI, a plan whereby private builders were able to produce total war housing, privately constructed and financed, of about one million units. Construction standards were limited: The maximum size permitted for a three-bedroom house was 960 square feet of floor space; no more than 4,420 board feet of lumber could be used; floor space for a one-story, one-bedroom house could not exceed 560 square feet.

Rent Control

Despite these commitments to housing for war workers, a housing pinch existed. As early as March 1941, a rent control bill for the District of Columbia was before Congress. As it became apparent that rent control in residential properties was a wartime necessity, the National Association of Real Estate Boards supported the imposition of rent control as a part of the national plan to avoid inflation. Rent control became a fact on April 29, 1942. Residential rent control fell under the direction of the Office of Price Administration (OPA) and its Rent Division. What followed was a classic example of a government agency's overreaction to new-found authority. Unfortunately, rather than assuming a position of fair regulation to both landlord and tenant, it became a pro-tenant, anti-landlord agency that produced regulations that were both unfair and counterproductive to the housing needs of the nation. For example, it did not deal with questions about a reasonable length of time for eviction notices nor did it encourage homeowners to open their homes to war immigrants by removing the fear that a roomer proving recalcitrant could not be evicted. Among the regulations the agency made were these: (1) It required a 50 percent down payment on all residential purchases, which had the effect of taking properties off the rental market; (2) it denied private housing the right to increase rentals even though these rents had been frozen at the below-market levels; and (3) it set aside and overrode state and local eviction laws and acted entirely beyond its scope of authority, invading the constitutional rights of citizens. Because of its lack of fair dealing with owners of properties, an antagonistic relationship developed between property owners and the OPA. It was to last until its final days of regulation, long after the end of the war. In 1943, a congressional investigation of rent control was made by the House Select Committee To Investigate Acts of Executive Agencies Beyond the Scope of Their Authority. The Committee found that the OPA's administrative methods had failed to carry out the mandate of Congress. Many of its administrative inadequacies were corrected through amending legislation passed by the 79th Congress.

The war ended in August 1945. However, wartime controls on construction remained in force on building materials, the size and price of dwellings to be created, and rents. These controls were not budged until the Housing and Rent Act of 1947. It is important to remember that a backlog of housing demands had accumulated during the war years and carried forward into the post-war period. As some 10 million men and women were released from the Armed Services, the country was racked by the most difficult housing shortage in its history. Further, the accelerated rate of family formation and an accelerated birth rate pointed to an even greater housing demand in the immediate future. Rent control could not cure the housing shortage; in fact, it worsened the shortage. It had brought a continuous decrease in the rental housing supply and made new rental construction practically impossible. Taxes, maintenance, and operating expenses had increased since 1942. Income from rents had not. By 1946, some two million units had been withdrawn from the rental market. Meanwhile, demonstrating the elasticity that exists between rental and sales housing, home ownership had shot up. A 1946 Bureau of Census Report showed that owner-occupied homes in the United States had increased by nearly one-third since 1940. Although four of those six years were war years, home owners had increased in number from 15,200,000 to more than 20,000,000. Tenant-occupied buildings had declined by 2.1 million.

Federal rent control, as first enacted in 1942, was an exercise of the war powers of Congress as a viable means of stabilizing and conditioning the nation's economy to the impact of total war. The new basis for continuing rent control well into the years of peace was contested in *Wood* v. *Miller,* which went to the U.S. Supreme Court. In 1947, the Court held:

> We deal here with the consequences of a housing deficit greatly intensified during the period of hostilities by the war effort. The legislative history of the present Act makes it abundantly clear that there has not yet (1947) been eliminated the deficit in housing which in considerable measure was caused by the heavy demobilization of veterans and by the cessation or reduction in residential construction during the period of hostilities, due to the allocation of building materials to military projects.

The Court, therefore, held that federal rent control during peacetime was constitutional.

The National Housing and Rent Act of 1947 was truly the most important piece of legislation enacted for solving the nation's housing shortage. The act provided that all new construction was freed from wartime controls. All construction—commercial, industrial, and residential—was released from the shackles of rationing of materials. Rent control was removed not only from all new buildings but also from properties that were rented for the first time. The act provided for large-scale construction of rental housing with two greatly broadened sections of the FHA Act, Sections 68 and 603. These sections literally provided developers with 100-percent financing for new apartments. Furthermore, recognizing the rising costs to property owners, the act granted a rent increase of 15 percent, if landlords would provide a tenant with a year's lease.

Following in the steps of this act, Congress granted the states a local option provision that would enable them to free themselves from rent control, if approved by the state legislatures. Wisconsin was the first state to do so, and others followed. In 1950, a law was enacted that made the decontrol of rents mandatory on December 31, 1951, except where the city council should take specific action to the contrary. By January 1951, the results of rent decontrol could be measured: There was an increase in the housing supply and widespread renovation of rental units. Rental rates had increased, but only moderately—about 15 percent, according to one report. A study provided by Roy Wenzlick, a noted real estate economist, showed that the range of increases in large cities varied from a 9.4 percent increase in Los Angeles to a 30.3 percent increase in Birmingham, Alabama.

The Korean crisis caused postponement of the decontrol of rents in some 1,100 communities, including many large cities. Nearly half of these communities had accepted the choice of going free, but the federal government declared that they still had a substantial housing shortage and requested an extension until April 1952. This was later amended, and federal rent decontrol finally was achieved on July 31, 1953.

The effects of rent control during a peacetime economy were very aptly described in 1952 by Henry G. Waltenade, president of NAREB. He said of the effects of decontrol of rents:

> Rents did not skyrocket. Riots did not rock the cities. Some rents did go up, yes, but the vast majority of these only to a degree commensurate with the rising costs which owners had incurred. Many rents remained unchanged. Some rents moved downwards, as owners were forced to compete in an open market with newer buildings.
>
> Increased housing immediately became available as many owners offered for rent units which they had refused to subject to the whims of the local rent board. Builders were encouraged to step up construction of rental units. Owners of existing buildings, who could not

afford to maintain their units adequately under subeconomic incomes allowed by controls, launched a gigantic renovation and repair movement which made thousands of tenants happy.

The experience proved that the solution to a housing shortage is not the control of rents but rather the production of additional housing units in a free market.

1949 to 1970: Continued Prosperity as the National Economic Policy

The real estate industry during the quarter century following World War II was characterized by three significant factors: America's affection for the automobile; the federal government's adoption of a program of a managed economy with prosperity as the national political commitment; and, "war babies," who were to cause a dramatic change of values in work and life.

Growth of Suburbia

It was the automobile, which provided a popular expanded transportation system to outlying areas where new housing could be developed on inexpensive land, that permitted the growth of suburbia following World War II. During the war, no automobiles were produced for the public market, as the total production capability was committed to the manufacturing of vehicles needed for the war effort. With the surrender by Japan and cessation of hostilities, the automobile industry geared up for a public market with enormous demand. By 1949, the industry was producing more than five million new cars a year. By 1954, the U.S. registration of automobiles totalled 58,622,524 vehicles, two thirds of the world's supply. Seventy-one percent of all U.S. families owned at least one car, typically the largest asset owned by a young family. This was true even among home owners, inasmuch as a house could be bought under a G.I. Bill of Rights or with a very low or even no down payment. The importance of the automobile industry to the national economy can be pointed out in the statistic that by 1960 it was estimated that one out of every eight employed Americans worked at a job that was related to producing or operating an automobile.

The single most important factor influencing the demand for all types of real estate was to become the automobile. With few exceptions in major northeastern cities, there was, and is, no mass transportation in America. The entire population has become dependent on the auto. It has become a necessity, not a luxury, for most Americans, who take for granted the mobility that the car has given them. The auto intensified the flight from central cities to the suburbs. As gasoline historically was inexpensive in the United States, it became economical to live long distances from places of employment. Since suburban land also was inexpensive, the American dream became a suburban house with trees in the back yard, a two-car garage, and a safe place for the children to play.

The growth of suburbia and new techniques in merchandising caused the development of supermarkets and outlying shopping centers. The shopping facilities developed after World War II moved away from rows of proprietor-owned shops along main streets to concentrated shopping centers, developed and owned as single entities. This basic change in the shopping patterns of Americans over the next 25 years was to grow in popularity until it accounted for nearly 50 percent of all retail sales. The strategy of these centers was to provide the customer with convenience, excitement, and a large variety of goods and services by concentrating a cross-section of stores in close proximity to residential areas with vast amounts of free parking.

As the population moved to the suburbs, so did the jobs. Industrial development followed residential and commercial development. The techniques of manufacturing had been greatly advanced. Methods of production had changed, and buildings occupied by industry were well-maintained facilities. Suburbs offered cheap land that could be assembled in large parcels. Buildings could be built to accommodate new methods of construction. Employees could be provided with adequate parking. Probably most important of all, the travel time for both executives and employees from home to work was reduced drastically. It was easier to attract good employees and good executives because of the plant's proximity to their suburban homes.

Keynesian Economics
While the growth of suburbia was changing the nation physically, it was being affected economically by the government's commitment to a managed economy. It all started with the Keynesian economic philosophy. Both political parties embraced the philosophy of prosperity as the national policy. It made little difference which political party was in power, because each supported a managed economy. During times of recession, extra money was pumped into the economy

to encourage prosperity; when the economy began to heat up with too much inflation, an attempt was made to curtail it through conservative monetary policies. What was learned during the 25 years following World War II was that political economic managers could not do a perfect job. The science of economics had greatly advanced during this phase, and statistics such as population, inventories, supply of money, amount of credit, and indeed the gross national product, could be measured much more accurately. Still, they could not react quickly enough to major swings in the economy. Although these 25 years experienced neither depression or runaway inflation, there were short periods of economic difficulties. For example, in 1954, the inflation spiral accelerated too fast when the easing of credit was allowed too long; in 1957 and 1958, the government had restricted the economy too long and caused undue unemployment.

Well-located, income-producing real estate was one of the chief beneficiaries of this economic policy. There was a tremendous financial advantage in being able to borrow money for long periods of time at fixed interest rates while the income from the property rose with other prices during the inflationary process. Highly leveraged real estate experienced greater overall profitability than the much more conservatively leveraged U.S. industrial corporations.

Another experience also was learned from this period of a managed economy: Not only could the country experience short swings in inflation and recession but also serious capital deflation. In real estate, capital deflations occur even during inflationary times if there is overproduction of a particular kind of real estate. The supply and demand forces of economics become applicable. (This occurred in 1963, for instance, when there was an overproduction of new apartment houses in the San Fernando Valley section of Southern California. Savings and loan institutions had found themselves with a significant increase in deposits, a new-home market that had produced to the point at which inventory was increasing rather than being absorbed, and an apparent need for more new apartment houses to be built. Anxious to get their money working, they made commitments to apartment developers for very highly leveraged loans. With this supply of money available to them, the homebuilder-turned-apartment-developer overproduced. The result was a significant increase in the vacancy factor. In 1960, the apartment vacancy factor was five percent. By 1963, it had accelerated to nine percent. Competition set in for the tenant. Property owners began cutting rents, with the result that the rent price went down, the vacancy increased, and, because of the natural effects of inflation, operating costs increased. With this decrease in net operating income, the value of the properties went down. The owners experienced capital deflation. Perhaps an even better example of capital deflation was what happened to the stock market in 1966. On February 9, 1966, the Dow Jones average was 785. This amounted to an 18 percent deflation in capital wealth in one year, an example of the loss in public confidence in a particular form of investment. Likewise, major changes in interest rates are deflationary to capital. In 1966, when interest rates went up, value of bonds fell. During the first eight months there was a 25 percent loss of capital value in the bond market.)

The Housing Market

A 10-year review of rental housing made in 1956 showed that the FHA had insured about two thirds of the one million apartment units built since World War II. However, by 1955, the FHA participation in the production of rental housing was down to less than 10,000 units per year. In 1957, a substantial increase in the construction of new multifamily units was noted for the first time in four years. The private sectors of the mortgage banking industry, particularly savings and loan associations, were seeking new sources for mortgage funds now that the shortage in single-family housing had stabilized. Apartment developers, for the most part homebuilders who were looking for new markets, were offered attractive terms for the construction for new apartment projects.

In part, the rental market for new apartment projects was a result of the decentralization process that started following the war. Homebuilders, anxious to supply the great demand for veterans and FHA housing, had gone to the suburbs to build large housing tracts. The shopping center and assorted retail strip stores followed the homebuilders. As this growth pattern continued, there eventually developed the need for small rental housing to accommodate those who worked in the suburban service and retail businesses. During this decentralization movement a pattern developed: It usually took about five years between the time the first development of the new single-family house in the neighborhood until the time that there was a market need for rental housing. By 1957, with the lessening demand for loans for single-family houses, lenders became interested, for the first time in almost 30 years, in providing funds in significant amounts for the construction of privately owned and financed rental housing. Furthermore, the 1950 census found that about one fifth of the national population moved during a single year. Families were changing their dwelling place frequently. This mobility made a significant contribution to the demand for more rental housing. And yet another significant factor that aided the desirability of owning income properties was the change in the income tax laws. The Federal Tax Act of 1954 encouraged investment in income properties by providing for a greater depreciation deduction in the structure's earlier years of life, under a declining balance method rather than by a straight line method.

As the fifties turned into the sixties, the population continued to be mobile. Owners of houses and condominiums moved on the average of every 12 years, and renters every 2½ years. The decade started with a period of relatively high stability and a firm and constant supply of financing for housing. In about 1962, rental housing was experiencing very high occupancy and rents were rising. This soon changed. Market conditions, coupled with a money market that provided easy financing, encouraged builders to develop an extraordinary number of new apartment buildings. The result was a period of oversupply. For the first time since 1938, rent prices actually fell, and foreclosures increased to their greatest rate in 30 years. With the oversurplus of 1966, the spigot for financing new projects was turned off. The money market conditions changed, and construction of new apartments was at a slowed-down pace. By 1969, the industry, again, was approaching a point of shortage in some areas. As a result, during the decade of the sixties, the apartment market experienced a complete cycle, moving from stability to surplus to shortage.

The decade also saw a change in the marketing of apartments to particular demographic groups. Historically, the apartment market had been divided into three segments of the population: the single employed, the married employed without children, and the retired. During the 1960s, developers began to build for very specific markets. The elderly received particular attention. FHA financing was created specifically for senior citizen housing. It resulted in such developments as Leisure World, 8,000 units built in Southern California expressly for senior citizens. Nonprofit corporations were able to build high-rise apartments totally tenanted by senior citizens. The full-life care homes for the aged became popular, particularly in the warmer climate areas.

As the war baby reached the legal age of 18, his highest priority was to strike out on his own. The father's first priority after returning from service in World War II had been to buy an automobile. The son or daughter's first priority was to move into an apartment. What followed were projects designed specifically for this market. Typically, these were small, 400-square-foot, furnished apartments that could be rented for $90 to $120 a month, including all utilities. Later, as the divorce rate dramatically increased and public mores changed, the market developed for "adult swingers." Companies like R&B Development Company of California developed and owned 18,000 apartment units in several major metropolitan areas catering to this market. Buildings were quasiluxury with full recreational facilities, such as tennis courts, swimming pools, billiard rooms, saunas, gymnasiums, restaurants, and whirlpools, and social programs.

Still another market—empty nesters—developed. These were the people whose children had left and who no longer needed large homes with their associated maintenance and care problems. High-rise luxury apartments began to spring up and do well, as mom and dad sought carefree and secure shelter. Likewise, some developments were specifically for the market of families with children. These buildings had playgrounds, babysitting services, and small swimming pools.

Also during the sixties, the government entered the housing market with massive programs for low-income families. Government-subsidized housing was to become a major form of property needing real estate management services.

The Office Building Boom

The 1960s witnessed an enormous amount of construction in the office building industry. There were several causes for this demand, the most important of which was the change in the nature of jobs in the United States. At the turn of the century, most people earned their income from agriculture. Later, most were employed in industries in which they developed natural resources or made things. By the late 1960s, 70 percent of the working population of the United States was employed in government, retailing, and services. A good portion of these people were housed in office buildings. Another factor contributing to the construction boom was that as businesses grew and became more prosperous during this 25 years of inflation, they simply outgrew their existing quarters and needed to relocate. While the rent per square foot was considerably higher in new office buildings, it offered a number of advantages: The prestige of a more important address, improved employee comfort and consequent increased productivity, and efficient use of space. For these reasons, most businesses using office space have relocated into buildings constructed after World War II.

The need for more office space was accelerated with the growth in complexity of operations of the companies that used such space. Firms needed facilities that were not available in the older buildings: special rooms for computers, executive dining rooms, libraries, meeting rooms, and employee cafeterias. The amount of office space required per employee grew by almost 70 percent.

With this demand for new office space, the nation's most courageous entrepreneur, the real estate developer, answered the call of opportunity. Although the market was sometimes overbuilt, resulting in a vacancy rate that was higher than had been anticipated, that overdevelopment was absorbed in due course without catastrophic economic results. During this period, too, many large companies developed office buildings for their own use and for the advertising value they offered. Most often such buildings were considerably larger than the housing needs of the business, the extra space available for growth and, in the meantime, being rented to other tenants.

The suburban office building or office park was popularized in the 1960s. Office buildings followed the houses, retail shopping centers, industrial buildings, and apartments in suburban areas. After all, to a large extent, the businesses and services an office houses is dependent upon those other facilities being in place. An exception to this rule was when companies decided to move major parts of their work force to suburban locations. Probably the first type of enterprise to do this were research and development companies that moved their "think tanks" to the suburbs where there was considered to be a more creative atmosphere.

The competitive market that developed for tenants of office buildings proved the value of location. Buildings in prime central areas experienced an average of less than five percent vacancy for the decade. Conversely, secondary location buildings experienced much higher vacancy. Thus, while there was a market for competitive office space, tenants remained highly selective, there being a substantial inventory of available office space in secondary locations. Enumerable examples could be cited of new office buildings in poor locations that simply could not attract tenants. There were also instances of previously well-located, well-maintained, well-tenanted office buildings that experienced a change in the security and desirability of the neighborhood and found that they could not attract, nor indeed keep, tenants. Older office buildings, even in well-located areas, modernized in order to maintain tenants. Such upgrading was often very expensive, since it usually required the installation of a central air conditioning system and automatic elevators. Office interiors also had to be remodeled with lowered acoustical ceilings, new and attractive interior wall and door design, upgraded electrical systems, and carpets and draperies. Public restrooms, hallways, and elevator lobbies needed to be rehabilitated as well. Owners of well-located older properties who could not make these improvements found that their equities gradually eroded away.

Increase of Shopping Center Construction

Meanwhile, shopping centers continued to make inroads in the total retail trade market. The term shopping center covers everything from a neighborhood center with an average size of 52,000 square feet to the super regional mall of 2,000,000 square feet. Most centers are located near middle and upper income areas and are accessible to major roads.

Shopping centers are classified as being of five different types. Neighborhood centers are generally 50 to 150,000 square feet of gross leasable area in size. The principal tenants with AAA credit rating typically are supermarkets, drugstores, and variety stores; the remainder are local merchants offering convenience goods and services. In highly developed metropolitan areas, such centers are generally found about two miles apart and serve a population of 10,000 to 25,000 persons. The second type, community centers, are 150,000 to 300,000 square feet in size and have the same AAA tenants as the neighborhood center, plus one or more AAA junior department stores, clothing stores, and shoe stores, together with local merchants. These centers generally are located three to five miles apart and serve 25,000 to 100,000 people. Regional shopping centers are 300,-000 to 2,000,000 square feet and consist of two to five major full-line department stores, plus up to 150 smaller stores. These centers are generally five to 10 miles apart and serve populations of 100,000 or more. Specialty centers range in size from 50,000 to 150,000 square feet and cater to upper income discretionary spending with an occasional emphasis on the young. The tenant mix offers fashion goods, atmospheric restaurants, gift and novelty items, and other specialty merchandise. Typical store sizes are 1,000 to 2,000 square feet, with major tenants being less than 20,000 square feet each. Some are laid out in a bazaar style with little or no wall separation. The fifth type are free-standing discount stores. These are large warehouse-type stores, often specializing in a particular type of merchandise, such as durable goods.

By the end of the 1960s, 60 percent of all new chain stores were located in shopping centers. In fact, they almost completely dominated expansion plans for variety, general merchandise, department, and shoe chain operations, as more than 90 percent of their new units went into shopping centers.

Although central business districts did suffer somewhat because of the surgence of demand for office space in the central business districts, the demand for downtown retail space was relatively strong at the end of the 1960s. In some cities, urban renewal programs led to central city development of apartments, particularly in the luxury class, adding to the retail sales in downtown areas.

The real victim of this change in the merchandising habits of the American public were the so-called strip stores and secondary retail areas peripheral to or outlying central business districts. Because these were both inconvenient and lacked adequate parking, they lost their value as retail buildings and found lower uses, such as becoming warehouses, distribution centers, or parking lots.

The decade closed with the economy at an all-time high. Real estate was in its strongest position since 1955, and unemployment nationally was at a low 3.3 percent. However, underlying forces were going to cause the most dramatic change in real estate at any time since the Great Depression.

The 1970s: Period of Dramatic Change

Real estate and real estate management are service businesses, providing the physical structures that shelter people in all their daily activities—buildings for commercial use, buildings in which to buy and sell goods and services, facilities that provide places for employment and production of materials, and places to live. How the demand for these various types of real estate will be met, where new construction will occur, and what shape these structures will take is a result of a combination of factors, the two most important ones being population and demographic trends and the overall health of the national economy.

Economic and Demographic Trends

During the forepart of the 1970s, it was the national economy that had everyone's attention. A new phenomenon, double-digit inflation coupled with extremely high unemployment, was being experienced. Inflation was caused primarily by huge government spending programs, the result of social legislation passed by Congress in the previous four years, and the financing of the Vietnam War. In effect, the nation's money managers blundered. First, they fed too much money into the system; then they pushed interest rates up to dangerously high levels in an attempt to check the inflation of 1973 and 1974. The 1974 recession hit hard and was one of the contributing factors to a high unemployment rate. Another cause was the dynamic way in which the labor force was growing. The labor force rose from 72 million workers in 1960 to nearly 83 million in 1970. In 1975, the labor force had grown another 12 percent, or by almost 10 million people, to 92.6 million and was projected to rise to 102 million by 1980. This growth occurred as the post-World War II babies reached working age and as more women sought employment outside of the home.

By the mid-1970s, the managers of the economy were doing a more skilled job, providing money for growth but not for inflationary expansion. However, the unemployment problem continued, the economy being unable to create additional jobs. Because new jobs add to the demand for both housing units and industrial, office, and commercial space, employment is the single most important statistic in real estate. With low employment, the real estate industry suffered.

As the United States celebrated its bicentennial year, it was estimated that it had a population of 215.3 million, making it the fourth most populous country in the world (behind China, 823 million; India, 613 million; and the U.S.S.R., 255 million). During the 1950s, the total population grew by 28.4 million, or an increase of 18.6 percent. During the 1960s, the growth rate decreased to 13.3 percent, 24.2 million more Americans being added to the population. The most widely accepted estimate for future growth is based on a fertility rate of 2.1 children per woman of child-bearing age. This assumption brings the country to zero population growth by the twenty-first century but leads to substantial increases in population to 1990, averaging about a one percent growth rate per year.

At the same time the overall population has grown, significant changes have occurred in age composition. The most important age groups are the retired or elderly, who comprise over 10 percent of the total population, and the war babies, whose numbers and new values toward work and life are causing dramatic change in the economic and social structures. As the baby-boom babies reach the most productive age group, they should increase demand for new housing and shopping and employment facilities.

The effects of the age composition change already are being seen in increases in family and household formations and a declining median age from 30.2 in 1950 to 28.1 in 1972. At the same time, the rapidly expanding economy has permitted these increases in population to grow wealthier, although at a slightly slower rate in recent years.

A second major impact of demographic changes has been the increased mobility of Americans and their migration from one section of the country to another. The United States developed historically from east to west. The early European settlers in the country founded large merchant and trading centers in major eastern harbors, such as Boston, New York, Philadelphia, Baltimore, and Washington. As the nation grew and the Industrial Revolution developed, the population pushed westward, primarily along the northern border, and established major manufacturing centers in such cities as Pittsburgh, Cleveland, Detroit, Chicago, and Milwaukee. As these centers have grown, land has become dearer, and businesses as well as individuals have sought new opportunities in the southern and western parts of the country. During the 25 years following World War II, the far-west region, dominated by California, had the greatest percentage growth in population of any section. Here, individuals and businesses found land less expensive and more plentiful, the cost of living lower, and, in some sense, a higher quality of living. During the 1950s, 25 percent of the total population increase was absorbed in California. A trend also developed for people to move to the warmer climates of Florida and Arizona as they reached retirement age.

Acceptance of Multiple Real Estate Ownership

Historically, the ownership of income real estate has been an entrepreneurial business in which one or a few individuals pool their resources to develop and/or own income properties. It changed during the thirties, when lenders acquired the ownership through foreclosure of great numbers of properties. Their plan, however, was to dispose of these properties as soon as they were healthy again. By the 1940s and 1950s, most of the real estate again was owned by individuals. Beginning in the early 1960s, financial entrepreneurs began the movement to let small public investors into the action. Three new equity investors began to look at the real estate market. These three new sources of capital, which became inter-related by the early 1970s and became significant forces in what happened to the real estate market, were these: (1) mortgage and/or equity real estate investment trusts; (2) public corporations which entered the business of developing multifamily housing; and (3) public syndication of real estate investments. To encourage small-investor participation in real estate and energize a slack property sector, Congress in 1960 adopted a new section of the Internal Revenue Code establishing real estate investment trusts (REITs). This allowed pass-through tax treatment for the REIT and hence no corporation taxation on income subject to certain conditions; i.e. at least 90 percent of taxable earnings had to be distributed. REITs originally were conceived as mutual funds to allow small investors to obtain the advantages of real estate ownership while maintaining a degree of liquidity with their money.

Trusts invested either in equities or mortgages, including construction finance. Some funds acquired both mortgages and equities. Usually the trusts were operated by banks and insurance companies; these were little noticed during the first half of the decade. During the latter part of the 1960s, however, Wall Street realized that REITs offered opportunities at a time when other equities were slack. Because of their attractive tax structure, ability to make wide-ranging real estate investments, and the likely onset of a housing shortage, Wall Street analysts felt the trusts should be extremely successful. By the end of 1970, over $2.5 billion had been subscribed. This was at a time of rapid economic expansion, and the maxim, "growth is good," was followed blindly. Banks and insurance companies became heavily involved in the creation and management of REITs, which borrowed heavily from the same institutions that created them in order to lend on real estate projects. Banks were anxious to loan this money, as these loans were written at floating rates above prime and provided a large boost to bank earnings.

By the end of 1973, the REITs' total assets stood at $21 billion, over half of which was in construction and development loans. Unfortunately, the REITs had achieved much of the expansion by incurring debts at floating rates and lending on generally unsatisfactory projects at fixed rates. This was primarily the result of inadequate and unseasoned management. Secondly, due to the high rate of interest charged, the REITs were forced into more speculative loans. The institutions had established relationships with the best developers over the years and, therefore, had the pick of the best projects. In addition, slack managements had resulted in poor controls over payouts and project management during construction.

When prime interest rates were low, the policy survived. When the prime rate rose to 10 percent, the construction loans went to over 15 percent; developers could not support these costs and defaulted. REITs soon found their income insufficient to cover their own debt service. The house of cards came down. The requirement to pay out earnings severely restricted the REITs from making satisfactory reserves; indeed it diluted their equity base. Some, like the Chase Manhattan Bank, which even has loss provisions three times greater than its reserves, were brought close to bankruptcy.

During the decade of the 1960s, many non-real estate corporations entered the development field. Sometimes, these companies had significant land holdings as a part of their regular business (i.e., railroads). Sometimes, other corporations, such as department stores and airlines, entered the field of shopping center malls and hotels, respectively. Similarly, other corporations, such as suppliers of construction materials and firms in the aluminum, cement, steel, wood products, and construction components industries, felt that real estate was a natural adjunct to their operations and could be used as a related business activity to demonstrate how their products were used in new construction. Several financial institutions that had long associations with real estate lending also entered the development field, as did many public corporations that had no previous real estate experience in any form and decided that real estate development would become a profitable diversification and a new profit center. For these companies, the local apartment house developer became a very hot commodity. Public corporations with cash and good lines of credit wanted to get into the real estate bonanza. Some who did this were American Standard, Equity Funding, Shareholders Capital Corporation, ITT (International Telephone and Telegraph), and Pennsylvania Railroad through its subsidiary Great Southwest Corporation. They began producing apartment units by the thousands.

The public corporation developer was not an investor in real estate but rather a manufacturer of real estate requiring a customer to whom he could sell his product. The historic owner of real estate, the large single investor or the general partnership with each investor making a significant capital contribution, was not sufficiently available to absorb this product. So they adopted a form of ownership that had been devised and approved in the 1950s—the widely held limited partnership. The marketing of these public syndications was still another problem. The developer sought out marketing experts, with the result that major security firms (usually on a best-efforts basis) became the underwriters of large issues covering many properties. The largest banks created tax shelter divisions and marketed these to their customers, usually on a property-by-property basis. New marketing firms entered the field and offered their services as general partners for these newly formed partnerships. Soon after 1970, the industry was creating a tremendous oversupply, although not apparent until 1972. There were other problems. Projects were costing more than they should have because of high interest rates. Construction interest rates added to the cost of the project. Permanent loans were requiring 9.9 percent interest; although the payback had been advanced from 25 to 30 years, this constant was still higher than the property's ability to produce net operating income and had a devaluing effect on the value of the investment. Marketing costs for real estate were high. By the time the developer had paid the cost of registering the new partnership with the SEC, paid the underwriter for marketing the limited partnership interests, and tagged on his own direct marketing cost, he was paying from 15 to 18 percent of the amount of money raised for marketing. The public corporation that had become a developer of real estate projects was faced with still another problem: inability to attract competent management. Although local real estate developers were intelligent, successful entrepreneurs with established records of success, they were not equipped for corporate atmospheres that required increased production of real estate projects. Unable to acquire experienced, competent people, what resulted were poorly designed, improperly located, high-cost projects.

The final problem from all of this activity was tremendous oversupply. For example, apartments developed in 1971 that were supposed to rent for $175 per month and have five-percent vacancy factors ended up renting for $145 a month with 10-percent vacancy factors. Oftentimes a developer, in order to sell a project to the publicly held limited partnership, would guarantee a minimum return of five or six percent for a period of three or five years or even would guarantee any deficit cash flow for an extended period of time. By 1972, a great number of these public corporations had become disenchanted and applied their energies toward getting out of the real estate business and minimizing their losses.

Foreign and Institutional Investment

While there has been fairly continuous interest in real estate by individuals, foreign investment by companies became a significant factor in the early 1970s. There was some activity by overseas property companies in the early 1960s when predominantly British companies started development or investment operations in the United States. Few achieved lasting financial success as oftentimes an overseas company became a joint venture partner with a U.S. developer in overly ambitious projects. An example here was the British company, Dollar Land, which joined with William Zeckendorf in the development of the Pan Am Building in New York City. While the project was to become successful, it was not profitable to the original investors because, as owners, they had to assume existing lease commitments of incoming tenants and many of these commitments could not be relet.

Prior to the 1970s, a number of countries had regulations that prohibited the transferring of funds for investment to the United States. These exchange regulations continually barred the creation of any significant foreign-based investment program in the United States. The 1970s saw large increases in oil prices and a resultant accumulation of wealth in the Middle East. With this accumulation of wealth, the Arabs began to show considerable interest in U.S. real estate. Coincidental with the interest from the Middle East, a growth in demand for real estate in the United States came from countries in Western Europe, particularly from the U.K., West Germany, and Holland. Individuals, corporations, as well as pension funds, especially the U.K. state-owned ones (the post office, steel corporation, and electrical supply pension funds) actively sought investment in the United States. Investors from Japan, Hong Kong, and Korea became aggressive buyers of U.S. real estate, particularly in Hawaii and on the West Coast. Canadian investment accelerated. At least 12 of the major Canadian investor/developers embarked on U.S. investment programs. These included companies like Trisec Corporation, Cadillac-Fairview, Oxford Leasehold, Abbey Glen Properties, and M.E.P.C. Less expensive U.S. borrowing costs and increased hostility by the Canadian government toward foreign-owned real estate encouraged this movement. The Province of Ontario initiated a 20 percent transfer tax on all foreign-acquired property. Much of the Canadian interest was centered on apartment buildings in the western part of the United States. However, significant purchases of office buildings and shopping centers also were made.

Why did these foreign investors buy properties in America? Investment, if it is to be secure and of long-term benefit, demands certain conditions which the U.S. property market can meet. Among the more important are political stability, private property rights, and a minimum of government intervention. The political stability of the United States is one of its strengths. The U.S. Constitution protects the owners of property from expropriation and unjust restriction. Even though all U.S. practitioners in the field of real estate investment continually complain as to the degree of governmental interference with which they are saddled, it is miniscule compared to the regulations and restrictions imposed upon real estate owners in foreign nations. Also, there is relative economic stability. The inflation rate is lower and more controlled in the United States than it is in most other industrialized countries. The natural resources provide a substantial competitive edge for the future. Land is less costly, and the combination of this and relatively low building costs results in prime commercial properties in New York, Chicago, or Los Angeles for substantially less than the cost of similar properties in London, Paris, Tokyo, or Hong Kong.

Another significant factor in attracting foreign capital to U.S. property investment is the way in which real estate investment deals are put together. Despite the fact that yields in many cases are higher in the United States than they are in most European and Asiatic countries, it is possible to further increase yields by high debt-to-equity leverage. Long-term, self-liquidating, relatively low-interest mortgages are not available in most foreign countries. The advantages of leveraging then is another unique investment characteristic of the U.S. property market.

The motivations of foreign investors are diverse and include fear of creeping socialism and the possible future confrontation with the East, yet the main driving force is economic. The West Germans clearly fear that their economy has peaked, while the U.K. pension funds need to invest to beat inflation.

By the late 1970s, it became quite apparent that the supply of quality properties was not adequate to meet the demands of foreign investors, particularly when coupled with the increasing appetite for equities by such U.S. sources as pension funds and managed funds. The interest of individual investors also increased following the closing of other tax shelter schemes in the Tax Reform Act of 1976, which left real estate as the most significant tax-shelter opportunity. A marked yield differential began to emerge between foreign and domestic buyers. U.S. buyers were unwilling to drop much below their historic yield requirement of plus or minus nine percent. Foreign buyers, on the other hand, were willing to be much more competitive for prime properties. Yields as low as six percent were quoted, and it became clear that competition between foreign funds was a major force in pushing the rate down. While the foreign investor was willing to accept a lower yield and therefore was more competitive in acquiring prime real estate through its willingness to pay a higher price, it had a distinct disadvantage over the U.S. investor. The foreign investor needed management capability of high quality, and oftentimes this restricted interest in investments to situations for which management could be found. A common solution was for the foreign investor to form a partnership with a U.S. firm that would provide the management, often with the foreign investor receiving a preferred return over his U.S. managing partner.

Real estate is a unique hedge against inflation, and it was the concern about long-term inflation, along with the devaluation of equities in the stock market, that renewed interest of pension funds in prime income property. As investors in real estate, pension funds saw five advantages in real estate equities: (1) return on investment higher than the yield to be received from most other forms of equity investment; (2) a protection against inflation; (3) the potential for capital appreciation; (4) security; (5) a variety of tax advantages unavailable in most other forms of investment. With these benefits for investing in prime income properties, domestic pension funds, under pressure to diversify, began looking in greater and greater numbers toward real estate investment. Some major insurance companies and banks accommodated them with the introduction of the commingled real estate fund, a vehicle that overcomes the barrier of unfamiliarity with real estate which most pension fund managers face.

Rehabilitation and Recycling

During the 1970s, a new word was added to the real estate jargon—recycling. The double-digit inflation spread of the early 1970s accelerated building costs so much that there was an unusual spread between existing rent levels for established properties and the rental rates needed for new construction to be feasible. This significant difference in rental rates for existing versus new created an economic opportunity for the rehabilitation or recycling of existing structures. The term "rehabilitation" refers to restoring value for a present use. Apartment houses, office buildings, shopping centers, etc., are rehabilitated to correct maintenance and, indeed, modernized in order to achieve higher rents while maintaining the same use of the real estate. The concept of recycling refers to a change of use of an existing structure by converting it to a new use. Physically sound buildings that have become obsolete due to changes in neighborhoods, local economic conditions, or design are stripped to their shells and then rebuilt to accommodate a new use. For example: Multistory manufacturing buildings may be made into office buildings, furniture marts, or shopping malls; office buildings can be converted into apartments; a motel may be changed into a specialty shopping center; strip stores may be converted to offices, and schools to apartments. A property has a potential for recycling if the value of the obsolete property plus the improvement cost is less than the replacement value of a new facility.

In addition to the rising cost of construction, other social and economic changes occurred in the 1970s that accelerated the rehabilitation and recycling of properties. It became increasingly fashionable for families to buy older homes in inner-city neighborhoods and refurbish or restore them as places to live. Oftentimes through this process, whole neighborhoods are resurrected, with the result that income properties in those neighborhoods can be rehabilitated or recycled. By the late 1970s, this already had occurred in Boston, San Antonio, Philadelphia, Washington, D.C., and Portland, Oregon.

The federal government, through HUD, has made a long-term commitment to offer various forms of financing for the rehabilitation of inner-city neighborhoods. The government has recognized that if it is going to effectively improve the standards of housing in the United States, much of its financial support will need to go toward restoring or rehabilitating existing properties rather than trying to solve the problem by simply creating new housing. Furthermore, the emergence of the no-growth movement as a political fact of life for developers places a greater opportunity for the recycling and rehabilitation of existing structures. In the late 1960s and early 1970s, many local governments began to initiate ordinances designed to stop or at least slow down new development. Coupled with this was environmental impact legislation which further restricted development. In 1969, Congress passed the National Environmental Policy Act (NEPA). It required federal agencies to file an environment impact statement to focus on the impact of all federally funded projects. This was followed in many states with similar state laws requiring environmental impact statements for state and local projects as well as major private development projects. With this continued restriction of use of vacant land in the suburbs and the scarcity of vacant land in the city, opportunities for increasing values of existing inner-city properties evolved.

The property manager has some unique talents important in the recycling or rehabilitation of an existing structure. Because of his long experience in the maintenance and marketing of existing income properties, he is better informed than any other professional as to potential feasibility of this recycling or remodeling process. Neither the architect, builder, nor developer is experienced in improving older properties, since the work of each has always focused on new building on vacant land. On the other hand, the property manager, through his years of experience in managing properties, is familiar with improving properties with new air conditioning systems, elevator equipment, electrical systems; the degree of improvement that is required in order to satisfy a particular market; and the time required in order to make these kinds of improvements and how they can be interfaced with existing tenancy.

Increasing Government Involvement

The decade of the 1970s was marked by the increasing involvement by government, at both federal and state levels, in housing, welfare, consumer protection, and the environment. Other than providing buildings for its own use, government at all levels had previously played a relatively minor role in the development, ownership, and control of real estate. Except for initiatives in housing, new community development, and urban renewal, government policies had been designed to keep real estate within the domain of the local entrepreneur and the individual investor while providing controlling legislation to promote an orderly and environmentally sound process. Government supported the development process under the assumption that growth was good for the community. New real estate creates employment opportunities, increases property values, and produces a new basis for property taxation. However, this sentiment changed in the 1970s, and no-growth movements began in many communities. Environmental impact legislation passed in both the federal level and many states in 1969 and the early 1970s had a great impact on the cost of new developments in the future.

Since World War II, the federal government played several important roles in real estate development, primarily related to housing activities. In 1949, Congress set as a goal "a decent home and a suitable living environment for every American family." To achieve this goal, the Department of Housing and Urban Development (HUD) was established, headed by a secretary appointed by the president. Projects are originated and managed from a central bureaucracy in Washington, D.C., with the aid of regional offices around the country. To achieve the housing goal, HUD became actively involved in constructing housing units of all types for low-income families in major cities throughout the country. In the early 1970s, new legislation was passed and funds were appropriated to build new communities in rural areas surrounding large metropolitan cities. In most cases elaborate projects including golf courses, swimming pools, and retail units were prematurely installed before the development generated enough cash flow to support the cost of these services. In 1976, the 13 communities that had been started were either bankrupt or had questionable financial structures. In 1978, the program was abandoned.

In general, the story of the federal government's participation in the direct development of housing has been at best disappointing; at worst, many buildings have had to be torn down. By 1976, HUD was placing weekly advertisements in almost every city to sell thousands of properties, at well below cost, that were bankrupt, vacant, or otherwise noneconomic. The government had learned an expensive lesson: That development of property is a highly localized process and a national bureaucracy cannot effectively or efficiently produce housing. As a result, HUD activities in the latter part of the decade focused on tax-incentive programs for private developers and direct subsidies to low income rent payers to enable them to obtain units in privately developed market rate units.

To provide liquidity and an assured source of funds for real estate markets (primarily housing), the government established several government and quasigovernmental agencies. Through the Federal Housing Administration (FHA) and the Veterans Administration (VA), the government insures mortgage loans of qualified applicants, permitting these individuals to purchase homes with low down payments. For a fee, the payments on these loans are insured with the full faith and credit of the American government and, as such, can become marketable securities. To facilitate the transfer of these insured mortgages, several agencies have been established to allow mortgage capital to flow into regions that cannot generate a sufficient supply locally. The principal agencies are these:

- Federal National Mortgage Association (FNMA or Fannie Mae). Originally chartered in 1938, it became a private corporation in 1970 with its stock publicly traded on the New York Stock Exchange. Its purpose is to maintain an active secondary market for FHA/VA loans by buying and occasionally selling mortgages. Although it is empowered to deal in conventional loans, its primary activity has been with mortgage brokers and government backed loans.
- Federal Home Loan Mortgage Corporation (FHLMC or Freddie Mac). Created under the Emergency Home Finance Act of 1970, this government agency serves the secondary market needs of the savings and loan industry by making future commitments to buy mortgages at a fixed rate. This has provided some stability in the market, as a lender can be assured a selling price for the mortgage pool and fix a price to the buyer which will hold regardless of interest rate changes in the marketplace.
- Government National Mortgage Association. (GNMA or Ginnie Mae). This is a wholly-owned government corporation operating within HUD. Although it also has some responsibilities for giving assistance to low-cost housing, its primary function is to guarantee the timely payment of interest and principal on securities backed by mortgages. It is by these guarantees that mortgaged-backed securities have become attractive to new types of institutional investors—even private individuals.

In addition to the agencies that provide liquidity for mortgages, the Federal Home Loan Bank (FHLB), a regulatory agency for savings and loans, redirects funds to thrift institutions in times of tight money. The FHLB borrows funds on the open market, issuing bonds with the full faith and credit of the federal government, and then reloans the funds to mortgage institutions that cannot generate a sufficient supply in the local marketplace.

Probably the most important role the federal government plays in real estate development is the generation of equity capital by providing tax incentives to private individuals who invest in real estate. In certain low-income housing projects, investors are allowed to write off the full cost of the investment in five years. This and other accelerated depreciation provisions allow property owners to deduct substantial noncash charges against current property income, usually resulting in no tax payments on the property income. In addition, losses due to depreciation deductions exceeding property income can be taken against ordinary income from other sources to reduce personal tax liabilities. In recent years, legislation has been contemplated that would reduce the individual's ability to shelter non-real estate income with property losses.

The federal government also has played a relatively small role in shaping the location and usage of U.S. land. This function has largely been assumed by the local governments using zoning restrictions. However, the National Environmental Protection Act has had a significant impact on real estate development. This law requires that before any new development of significant scale can proceed, an analysis of the building's impact on the total environment must be made. This includes an assessment of the impact on air and water quality. These studies can be quite costly and time consuming and developments cannot proceed until the studies have been approved.

Recent years have seen an increased interest in the preservation and reuse of existing buildings of all types. As a result, the government created the quasipublic group called the National Trust for Historic Preservation to promote the preservation of historic structures on a national basis. In addition, a National Register of Historic Places was established to record buildings of important architectural and historical significance. Federal money cannot be used to demolish buildings listed on this register, and the most recent tax legislation disallows a deduction for the demolition costs if a developer destroys a building on the National Register and provides accelerated depreciation benefits if a Register building is restored to a new use.

State governments have relatively little direct involvement with real estate development, other than requiring additional analysis to be included in environmental impact statements. Some states, however, e.g., California, have passed stringent fire-safety regulations that require building owners to install extensive equipment to protect the safety and well being of inhabitants in case of fire. These requirements can have substantial impact on future building costs. In addition, California has introduced a coastal protection law severely limiting all development within 1,000 yards of the shoreline.

In general, local city or town governments have the greatest control and impact on real estate development. The jurisdiction of local planning agencies normally is restricted to the legal boundaries of a community; however, in some limited instances, such as in Minneapolis-St. Paul, Minnesota, metropolitan planning commissions have been established to develop guidelines and zoning controls for several municipalities. Local governments have become involved with real estate in two major ways: via zoning controls and local development activities.

The most important tool for controlling land use at a local level has been zoning laws. With one notable exception—Houston, Texas—nearly every city has zoning regulations that determine the uses, heights, densities, etc., that are allowed in any given area. These laws are enforced by either a planning commission or the local building department. These powers, combined with the ability to provide or deny public facilities, such as water and sewer lines, have been utilized by local governments to control the amount and shape of development in their communities.

Local communities likewise have become involved in development directly through locally created redevelopment authorities, often called urban renewal agencies. Primarily funded through federal grants, these authorities can condemn land through the powers of eminent domain and clear existing structures from the site, then sell the land at below cost to developers who construct new commercial facilities. During the 1960s, considerable support was given to these activities as agencies purchased and cleared large numbers of city blocks. Although this program has now come to a virtual halt as federal funding has all but dried up, many imaginative and innovative projects were constructed. In Atlanta, Georgia, Peachtree Center, an office, retail, and hotel complex, was built on redevelopment property, as was the Embarcadero Center in San Francisco. In Boston, the refurbishment of the Faneuil Market complex was completed by the Boston Redevelopment Authority, which has since leased the buildings to a shopping center developer. However, in many cities, these agencies overestimated market demand for new facilities; many blocks were cleared prematurely. Overall, there was much greater destruction than construction. As a result, many urban centers are today a sea of parking lots.

The Future of Property Management

What does the future hold for the practice of real estate management? Will management's range of responsibility be more encompassing and more involved? In light of an awareness of the history of the real estate sector from 1900 through the present, it should be abundantly clear that the practice of real estate management is subject to dramatic change. Granted, not everything changes. The professional property manager continually must meet certain fundamental requirements; specifically, he should have a full working knowledge of the management process, including ability in planning, strategy setting, decision making, communicating, organizing, controlling, and directing. Furthermore, a clear concept of opportunity-focused company goals and a plan for achieving them must be crystalized. Property managers who establish goals and set their courses solely upon past experiences and historical practices will be unable to maintain their status quo—much less make noticeable advancements—in a fast-moving, ever-changing economic community.

Cyclical Considerations

Any prediction for the practice of real estate management must be tempered by an awareness of the cyclical nature of the business economy, which presents short-term periods of economic difficulty. Ironically, opportunity in the real estate management industry is usually counter-cyclical to the national economy. The greatest need for management services generally occurs when properties are experiencing operational adversity and particularly when there is a surplus of rental real estate. For example, the demand for property management weakened following World War II, when a housing shortage made attracting and accomodating tenants a simple task.

The periods of surplus and shortage within the nation's economic structure reoccur in almost predictable cycles, each new cycle apparently accompanied by a unique set of circumstances. The first real estate boom, which occurred at the turn of the century, was caused by a massive movement from an agrarian to an industrial society. This was followed by a major property shortage felt during World War I, when use of construction materials was centered on the war effort. Then came an unprecedented construction boom, made possible by new methods of financing through public underwriting of mortgage debt. With the outbreak of World War II came another shortage. Subsequent to the war, the government via FHA financing provided the vehicle for the constructon boom that resumed. By the mid-1960s, oversurplus again evidenced itself; financing became tighter and development slowed. This lasted until the late 1960s and early 1970s, when tremendous development of investment properties was made possible by public investment organizations, i.e., REITs, limited partnerships, and public corporations, entering the real estate investment business.

Currently real estate management is in the down-swing of one of its cycles. New economic and political forces are discouraging development of investment real estate. Excessive inflation, rapidly increasing constructions costs, and high interest rates have created too large a spread between rental rates for existing properties and rental rates that must be charged for new developments in order to realize a profit. Some of this interference is political and involves restrictive zoning and building ordinances, environmental constraints, and rent control legislation. However, there are some statistics that, government interference and inflation aside, cannot be ignored. Between the years 1980 and 2000, the U.S. population is expected to grow from 223 million to 263 million. This growth, coupled with the element of real estate obsolescence, will create a need for urban America to expand by at least 25 percent of its current size. More and more housing units will be needed, inasmuch as households are being formed even faster than the population rate as families become smaller and fewer people live in each dwelling unit. Further, as the population grows, so does the available work force. New office buildings, shopping centers, and industrial parks must be provided for this increasing labor pool.

The property manager's business opportunity during this period will be different from the past, particularly for managers in housing management. Inflationary and political forces have caused single-family ownership to be affordable to a smaller and smaller percentage of the population. The resulting effect sponsors the popularity of condominium ownership as an alternative method of owning real estate. This creates an opportunity for the property manager to provide specialized accounting, common area maintenance, and consulting services to the condominiums' associations. This new form of property management service will be recognized as an economic opportunity for those innovative management firms that can profitably create management programs which meet the needs of the associations at fees lower than those charged for management of similar sized apartment projects. New investor-owned, luxury rental housing quite probably is becoming a relic of the past. Unless there are significant changes in the federal income tax laws, the economics for building or renting luxury multifamily housing is in favor of condominium ownership rather than investor ownership.

Social Considerations

At the same time, it is quite probable that much of the new construction of medium- and low-income family units will need to be government subsidized in some form. Socially cognizant property managers realize that this means tenant participation in management programs. Property managers who foresee participatory management as the wave of the future believe that future federal legislation will insist upon tenant approval of any significant change in a property's management program and may even include changes of ownership.

In addition to a social awareness of tenants, property managers of the future will need to develop a social awareness of its employees and their needs. Management increasingly will be called upon to exhibit an understanding of human behavior in order to provide the type of leadership under which investment goals of clients and personal goals of employees will be achieved. Organizing and directing a management team means more than the ability to supervise and delegate. The manager's success will hinge largely upon ability to motivate employees to greater levels of production. The more aware a manager is that success is dependent on skill in accomplishing work through others, the more significant will be his understanding of the motivational forces that affect people.

Tomorrow's real estate manager, like his counterparts in other industries, also will be forced to accept a greater responsibility to the community. The free enterprise system represents a special privilege available to American businessmen, but it requires support from its participants. Tremendously complex patterns of inter-relationships and interdependencies demand the support and skills of professional managers in order to maintain the system. As the society grows increasingly complex, it becomes more evident that a glaring weakness of management capability exists in government and community organizations. The property manager can find outlets for his professional skills in civic programs that permit him to utilize his unique expertise—rather than participating in some aspect of community life that is unknown to him and, as a result, is time consuming—to sustain the free enterprise system.

Asset Management

Still, the most important opportunity for tomorrow's property manager is as a complete asset manager. Property management may very well play one of the most critical roles in affecting investment decisions regarding income-producing property, casting new light on the importance of professional management in ever-increasing competitive markets. As an equity investment, real estate can provide an investor a current yield with certain tax benefits. Investors seeking protection from inflation through capital appreciation will continue to seek real estate projects in the future at a far greater rate. Each real estate investment demands an analysis as an independent operating business within its particular environment. This analysis must deal with a myriad of issues of varying importance, some of which are of a subjective nature. Through skilled analysis, the property manager can suggest and implement changes in the operation and maintenance of a project in order to alter the levels of income and expenses to a greater extent than any other participant in the income property's operation. Each property operating as a separate business requires this kind of thorough, knowledgeable, ongoing attention that can be provided only by an entrepreneurial asset manager.

The professional property manager will be postured to accept added responsibilities that accompany new opportunity only if he is well versed in the management discipline. Only if the property manager accepts the challenge to become a dynamic, decision-making, active force will the real estate management enterprise be prepared to meet the challenges that the next business cycle, and all subsequent cycles, will bring.

Appendix

INSTITUTE OF REAL ESTATE MANAGEMENT
CODE OF PROFESSSIONAL ETHICS
OF THE
CERTIFIED PROPERTY MANAGER®

Introduction

To establish and maintain public confidence in the honesty, integrity, professionalism and ability of the professional property manager is fundamental to the future success of the Institute of Real Estate Management and its members. This Code and performance pursuant to its provisions will be beneficial to the general public and contribute to the continued development of a mutually beneficial relationship among CERTIFIED PROPERTY MANAGERS®, REALTORS®, clients, employers and the public.

The Institute of Real Estate Management as the professional society of property managers seeks to work closely with all other segments of the real estate industry to protect and enhance the interests of the public. To this end, members of the Institute have adopted and, as a condition of membership, subscribe to this Code of Professional Ethics. By doing so, they give notice that they clearly recognize the vital need to preserve and encourage fair and equitable practices and competition among all who are engaged in the profession of property management.

Those who are members of the Institute are dedicated individuals who are sincerely concerned with the protection and interests of those who come in contact with the industry. To this end, members of the Institute have subscribed to this Professional Pledge:

I pledge myself to the advancement of professional property management through the mutual efforts of members of the Institute of Real Estate Management and by any other proper means available to me.

I pledge myself to seek and maintain an equitable, honorable and cooperative association with fellow members of the Institute and with all others who may become a part of my business and professional life.

I pledge myself to place honesty, integrity and industriousness above all else; to pursue my gainful efforts with diligent study and dedication to the end that service to my clients shall always be maintained at the highest possible level.

I pledge myself to comply with the principles and declarations of the Institute of Real Estate Management as set forth in its Bylaws, Regulations and this Code of Professional Ethics.

1. Fiduciary Obligation to Clients

A CERTIFIED PROPERTY MANAGER® shall at all times exercise the utmost business loyalty to the interests of his or her clients and shall be diligent in the maintenance and protection of the clients' properties. In order to achieve this goal, a CERTIFIED PROPERTY MANAGER® shall not engage in any activity which could be reasonably construed as contrary to the best interests of the client or the client's property. The CERTIFIED PROPERTY MANAGER® shall not represent personal interests divergent or conflicting with those of the client, unless the client has been previously notified in writing of the actual or potential conflict of interest, and has also in writing assented to such representation. A CERTIFIED PROPERTY MANAGER®, as a fiduciary for the client, shall not receive, directly or indirectly, any rebate, fee, commission, discount or other benefit, whether monetary or otherwise, which has not been fully disclosed to and approved by the client.

2. Disclosure

A CERTIFIED PROPERTY MANAGER® shall not disclose to a third party confidential information which would be injurious or damaging concerning the business or personal affairs of a client without prior written consent of the client, except as may otherwise be required or compelled by applicable law or regulation.

3. Accounting and Reporting

A CERTIFIED PROPERTY MANAGER® shall at all times keep and maintain accurate accounting records concerning the properties managed for the client, and such records shall be available for inspection at all reasonable times by each client. A CERTIFIED PROPERTY MANAGER® shall cause to be furnished to the client at intervals to be agreed upon with the client, a regular report in respect to that client's properties.

4. Protection of Funds and Property

A CERTIFIED PROPERTY MANAGER® shall at all times exert due diligence for the protection of client's funds and property in the possession or control of the CERTIFIED PROPERTY MANAGER® against all reasonably foreseeable contingencies or losses.

Figure A.1. Code of Ethics of the Institute of Real Estate Management.

5. Relations with Other Members of the Profession

A CERTIFIED PROPERTY MANAGER® shall not make, authorize or otherwise encourage any unfounded derogatory or disparaging comments concerning the practices of another CERTIFIED PROPERTY MANAGER®. CERTIFIED PROPERTY MANAGERS® subscribing to this Code shall not exaggerate or misrepresent the services offered by him or her as compared with competing CERTIFIED PROPERTY MANAGERS®. Nothing in this Code, however, shall restrict legal and reasonable business competition by and among CERTIFIED PROPERTY MANAGERS®.

6. Contract

The contract, if any, between a CERTIFIED PROPERTY MANAGER® and his or her client shall provide for the specific terms agreed upon between the parties and shall be in clear and understandable terms, including a general description of the services to be provided by and responsibilities of the CERTIFIED PROPERTY MANAGER®.

7. Duty to Firm or Employer

A CERTIFIED PROPERTY MANAGER® shall at all times exercise the utmost loyalty to his or her employer or firm and shall be diligent in the maintenance and protection of the interests and property of the employer or firm. The CERTIFIED PROPERTY MANAGER® shall not engage in any activity or undertake any obligation which could reasonably be seen as contrary to the obligation of loyalty and diligence owed to his or her employer firm, and shall not receive, directly or indirectly, any rebate, fee, commission, discount or other benefit, whether monetary or otherwise, which could reasonably be seen as producing a conflict with the interests of his or her employer or firm. A CERTIFIED PROPERTY MANAGER® shall at all times exercise due diligence for the protection of the funds of his or her employer or firm against all reasonably foreseeable contingencies or losses and shall as agent of his or her employer or firm exercise the highest degree of responsibility for the safekeeping and preservation of these funds.

8. Preserving and Protecting Property of the Client

It shall be the duty of the CERTIFIED PROPERTY MANAGER®, as a skilled and highly trained professional, to competently manage the property of the client with due regard for the rights, responsibilities and benefits of the tenant. A CERTIFIED PROPERTY MANAGER® shall manage the property of his or her clients in a manner which takes due regard for his or her obligations to conserve natural resources and to maximize the preservation of the environment.

9. Compliance with Laws and Regulations

A CERTIFIED PROPERTY MANAGER® shall at all times conduct his or her business and personal activities with knowledge of and in compliance with applicable federal, state and local laws and regulations, and shall maintain the highest moral and ethical standards consistent with membership in and the purposes of the Institute of Real Estate Management.

10. Continuing Professional Education

A CERTIFIED PROPERTY MANAGER®, in order to assure the continued retention and further growth and development of his or her skills as a professional, shall utilize to the highest extent possible the facilities offered to him or her for continuing professional education and refinement of his or her management skills.

11. Incorporation of NATIONAL ASSOCIATION OF REALTORS® Code of Ethics

The Code of Ethics of the NATIONAL ASSOCIATION OF REALTORS®, as in effect, from time to time is incorporated by reference into this Code and in relevant parts shall be binding on CERTIFIED PROPERTY MANAGERS® as other articles of this Code.

12. Enforcement

Any violation by a CERTIFIED PROPERTY MANAGER® of the obligations of this Code shall be determined in accordance with and pursuant to the terms of the Bylaws and Rules and Regulations of the Institute of Real Estate Management. Disciplinary action for violation of any portion of this Code shall be instituted by the Institute of Real Estate Management in accordance with the Bylaws and Rules and Regulations established by the Governing Council of the Institute. The result of such disciplinary action shall be final and binding upon the affected CERTIFIED PROPERTY MANAGER®, and without recourse to the Institute, its officers, councillors, members, employees or agents.

Figure A.1 (continued)

Management Controls Questionnaire
Page One of Two

Reports	Yes	No
1. Are accounting reports issued promptly enough to be useful? (How soon after end of period? _____)	____	____
2. Do the periodic reports compare actual experience with		
a. Budgets?	____	____
b. Cost per unit or per square foot?	____	____
c. Are prior periods shown in above reports?	____	____
3. Are budgets reviewed and is actual performance compared by individuals other than those directly responsible for the operation?		
4. Are reports effectively used as a basis for corrective action?	____	____
5. Are reports accompanied by interpretations written by a responsible individual?	____	____
6. Are annual budgets prepared?	____	____
a. Are they reviewed and updated quarterly?	____	____
b. Are they reviewed and updated semiannually?	____	____

Accounting	Yes	No
1. Is a chart of accounts in use?	____	____
a. Is it supplemented by definitions of items to be recorded in the various accounts?	____	____
2. Are the account ledgers arranged in a logical manner so as to facilitate the monthly balancing of statements without analysis or reclassification?	____	____
3. Are accounting records adequate for the reporting needs of the business?	____	____
4. Is there in use an up-to-date accounting manual with adequate written instructions on accounting policies and procedures?	____	____
5. Are journal entries approved by a responsible employee?	____	____
6. Are journal entries properly supported by identifiable data?	____	____
7. Are journal entries uniquely numbered?	____	____
8. Are clerical measurement devices used?	____	____
9. Does the company have a methods and procedures department?	____	____
10. If so, does it operate effectively?	____	____

Figure A.2.   Questionnaire to test management controls.

Management Controls Questionnaire
Page Two of Two

	Organization	Yes	No
1.	Is there an organization chart?	_____	_____
2.	If the answer to (1) is yes, does it adequately portray individual responsibilities and reporting relationships?	_____	_____
3.	If the answer to (2) is yes, is the company functioning in accordance with the chart?	_____	_____
4.	If the answer to (2) is no, does the company appear to function with a proper segregation of duties, i.e., is record keeping divorced from custody and control of assets?	_____	_____
5.	Are all employees responsible for record keeping and custody of assets required to take an annual vacation (or are the jobs rotated)?	_____	_____
6.	Is their work performed by someone else during the vacation period?	_____	_____
7.	Is there an organization manual?	_____	_____

	Miscellaneous		
1.	Is there an internal audit staff?	_____	_____
2.	Does the company have an established written policy prohibiting officers and employees from affiliating with other business organizations with which the company has significant dealings?	_____	_____
3.	Is this policy disseminated to all employees?	_____	_____
4.	Are officers or employees in key positions unrelated to one another?	_____	_____
5.	Are employees in accounting or other sensitive positions bonded?	_____	_____
6.	Is the purchasing function effectively tested by the company annually? (Date of last test _____).	_____	_____
7.	Are other areas besides purchasing sensitive in the company's type of business tested by the company annually? (Indicate areas and dates of last tests on reverse.)	_____	_____

Figure A.2 (continued)

Examination of Management Controls
Page One of Two

Audit Operation	Performed by	Remarks

1. Compare the company's performance with:
  a. Similar industry data obtained from the company or industry publications.
  b. Prior year's performance.		

2. Inquire of controller of accounting procedures and principles.		

3. Obtain copies of:
  a. Chart of accounts.
  b. Accounting manual.		

4. Review procedures used in balancing monthly statements.		
5. Review procedures for preparation and control of journal entries.		
6. Discuss extent of use of clerical measurement devices with appropriate officials.		
7. Review reports and plans of methods and procedures department.		

8. Obtain for the permanent file:
  a. Copy of certificate of incorporation.
  b. Copy of bylaws.
  c. Copy of organization chart.
  d. Copy of chart of corporate relations showing principal companies, subsidiaries, affiliates and associated companies, with nature of business for each company.
  e. List of officers, directors, and employees authorized to sign and approve.
  f. List of all directors and their company affiliations.		

Figure A.3.   Examination of management controls.

Examination of Management Controls
Page Two of Two

Audit Operation	Performed by	Remarks
9. Review organization chart for lines of authority and proper segregation of functions and determine that company is operating in this manner. If no chart is available, sketch one and obtain assurance from management of its accuracy.		
10. Review list of directors and officers for possible outside activities having a bearing on the scope of the examination and the company's own internal procedures.		
11. Review vacation or rotation policy and discuss compliance with appropriate officials.		
12. Review with appropriate official procedures followed by the company to determine if conflict of interest situation exists and evaluate effectiveness.		
13. Examine or test examine evidential matter in connection with review of conflict of interest procedures.		
14. Examine fidelity bonds covering employees to see that coverage is in line with individuals' responsibilities and confirm with insurance company that the policy is still in force.		

Figure A.3 (continued)

Questionnaire on Internal Controls—Cash
Page One of Three

	Receipts	Yes	No

1. Are check receipts deposited intact daily? _____ _____
2. Are the duties or functions of all persons receiving or directly supervising the receiving of cash completely segregated from the following duties or functions:
   a. Following up delinquent rents? _____ _____
   b. Mailing or delivering receipts to tenants? _____ _____
   c. Preparing or approving lists of NSF checks to be written off? _____ _____
   d. Reconciling bank accounts? _____ _____
   e. Opening incoming mail? _____ _____
   f. Preparing or approving invoices for payment? _____ _____
   g. Preparing or signing checks? _____ _____
   h. Posting the ledger? _____ _____
3. Is mail opened and distributed by person or department other than one having access to cash? _____ _____
4. Is a list of receipts prepared by mail opener? _____ _____
5. If so, is such list effectively used as a check against deposits? _____ _____
6. Are receipts given directly by mail opener to cashier? _____ _____
7. Are remittance advices, letters, or envelopes that accompany receipts separated and given directly to the accounting department? _____ _____
8. Are duplicate detailed deposit slips:
   a. Prepared? _____ _____
   b. Stamped by the bank? _____ _____
   c. Checked against the record of receipts? _____ _____
   d. Checked by someone other than the person receiving the money? _____ _____
9. Are bank charge-backs checked by someone other than the person handling the receipts? _____ _____

Figure A.4. Questionnaire to test internal cash controls.

Questionnaire on Internal Controls—Cash
Page Two of Three

	Disbursements	Yes	No
1.	Are the duties and functions of all persons preparing or supervising the preparation of checks completely segregated from the following duties or functions:		
	a. Reconciling bank accounts?	___	___
	b. Preparing or approving invoices for payment?	___	___
	c. Posting the ledger?	___	___
	d. Signing checks?	___	___
2.	Are the following approvals by properly responsible persons required before invoices are submitted for payment:		
	a. Approval of prices?	___	___
	b. Approval of receipt of goods?	___	___
	c. Approval of footing, extensions, discounts, etc?	___	___
	d. Approval of account distribution?	___	___
	e. Final approval for payment?	___	___
3.	Does the procedure require that at least one check signature and final approval for payment be made by different individuals?	___	___
4.	Are invoices and supporting data examined by at least one person signing the payment check?	___	___
5.	Are invoices and supporting data effectively cancelled upon payment?	___	___
6.	Is the signing of checks in advance prohibited?	___	___
7.	Are blank checks adequately safeguarded?	___	___
8.	Are all checks prenumbered?	___	___
9.	Are all voided checks retained?	___	___
10.	Are check protectors used?	___	___
11.	Are mechanical check signers used? If so:	___	___
	a. Are facsimile signature plates properly safeguarded?	___	___
	b. Are mechanical counting devices on the check signers?	___	___
	c. Does the person whose signature is mechanically signed approve invoices for payment?	___	___
	d. Are totals of the mechanical signers regularly checked against the number of checks written?	___	___
	e. Are persons operating the check signers denied access to blank checks?	___	___
12.	Are all checks countersigned?	___	___
13.	Are there limitations on the amounts of checks that require only one signature?	___	___

Figure A.4 (continued)

Questionnaire on Internal Controls—Cash
Page Three of Three

Petty Cash	Yes	No
1. Are petty cash funds on an imprest basis?	____	____
2. Is there one custodian for each fund?	____	____
3. Are the funds limited to reasonable amounts for the needs of the building?	____	____
4. Are individual petty cash disbursements limited to a maximum amount?	____	____
5. Are petty cash vouchers:		
a. Prepared for each disbursement?	____	____
b. Supported?	____	____
c. Written in ink or typed?	____	____
d. Dated?	____	____
e. Fully descriptive of the item paid for?	____	____
f. Clearly marked to show the amount paid?	____	____
g. Receipted by the person receiving the cash?	____	____
6. Are petty cash reimbursements made payable to the custodian?	____	____
7. Are petty cash vouchers effectively voided at the time of reimbursement so as to preclude their re-use?	____	____
8. Is the use of petty cash funds prohibited as to:		
a. Cashing of checks?	____	____
b. Making change?	____	____
c. Making advances?	____	____

Bank Reconciliations		
1. Are all bank accounts and signers authorized by the board of directors?	____	____
2. Are banks notified immediately when an authorized signer leaves the employ of the company?	____	____
3. Are bank accounts reconciled by persons who do not sign checks or handle or record cash?	____	____
4. Are bank accounts reconciled regularly?	____	____
5. Are bank statements and paid checks delivered unopened to the persons reconciling the accounts?	____	____
6. Do reconciliation procedures include:		
a. Inspection of checks for signatures?	____	____
b. Inspection of checks for endorsements?	____	____
c. Comparison of checks to check register for numbers, payee, date, and amount?	____	____
d. Accounting for all check numbers?	____	____

Figure A.4 (continued)

Examination of Cash
Page One of Two

Audit Operation	Performed by	Remarks
1. Obtain the bank reconciliation as of the beginning of the period.		
2. Obtain direct from the bank, if possible, the statement as of the end of the period. If not possible, obtain the statement before it has been reconciled.		
3. Using the reconciliation at the beginning of period, foot check the balances to the ledger and bank statement, and investigate all reconciling items.		
4. Check deposits for the period to bank statements from the cash receipts record, observing that dates correspond as an indication that receipts are being deposited promptly. Account for any receipts not shown as deposits on the bank statement and for any credits on bank statement not reflected as receipts on books.		
5. Trace deposits in transit to the bank statement of the subsequent month.		
6. If bank statements are not obtained direct from the bank, ascertain, so far as it is practicable to do so, that the paid checks and bank debit and credit memoranda are all accounted for.		
7. Examine all bank debit and credit memoranda and determine that they have been posted to the appropriate accounts.		
8. Review the cash receipts and disbursements records for a period up to the period under examination, noting and investigating any unusual items.		
9. List from cash receipts and disbursements records the dates and amounts of interbank transfers for the week or more immediately before and after the reconciliation date. Ascertain that each disbursement and the related deposit are both entered in the same period.		

Figure A.5. Examination of cash.

Examination of Cash
Page Two of Two

Audit Operation	Performed by	Remarks
10. Compare paid checks with cash disbursements record as to date, amount, and payee and compare prior dated checks with the opening reconciliation.		
11. If checks are not obtained direct from the bank, examine perforations to determine that checks were passed through the bank during the period under review.		
12. Review check endorsements, paying particular attention to any check having second endorsements.		
13. List and investigate checks drawn to cash or employees.		
14. Prepare a list of check signers and compare to list of authorized signers.		
15. Investigate all reconciling items other than outstanding checks.		
16. Trace checks dated on or prior to the reconciliation date to the disbursements records and the outstanding check list.		
17. Trace checks for material amounts dated subsequent to the reconciliation date to the disbursements records.		
18. Examine dates of bank endorsements on checks selected in previous step to ascertain that they had not been issued prior to the reconciliation date.		
19. Investigate and vouch outstanding checks of a material amount not returned by the bank.		
20. Investigate all items deposited prior to the reconciliation date but returned by the bank at a subsequent date.		
21. Review petty cash transactions for a period of time and inquire into any unusual items. Review vouchers passed through the petty cash fund to see that they have not been raised nor do they represent duplicate payments.		

Figure A.5 (continued)

Questionnaire on Internal Controls—Purchases, Accounts Payable, and Expenses
Page One of Two

	Yes	No
1. Is there a separate and distinct purchasing department?	_____	_____
2. Is the purchasing function completely separated from:		
a. Accounting?	_____	_____
b. Cashier or persons signing checks?	_____	_____
3. Are purchase requisitions used?	_____	_____
a. If so, are they approved by building managers or property supervisors?	_____	_____
b. If not, are purchases approved by someone other than the purchasing department?	_____	_____
4. Are purchase orders:		
a. Used?	_____	_____
b. Used for all purchases?	_____	_____
c. Prenumbered?	_____	_____
d. Copy sent to accounting department?	_____	_____
5. Are purchase order numbers routinely accounted for?	_____	_____
6. Are receiving documents used?	_____	_____
a. If so, are copies sent to the accounting department?	_____	_____
7. Is a record kept of return purchases?	_____	_____
8. Is the account distribution indicated on the purchase order?	_____	_____
9. Does the accounting department:		
a. Compare invoice prices, terms, and quantities with purchase orders?	_____	_____
b. Check extensions on invoices?	_____	_____
c. Review the account distribution?	_____	_____
d. Match invoices with purchase orders and receiving documents?	_____	_____

Figure A.6. Questionnaire to test internal controls of purchases, accounts payable, and expenses.

	Yes	No
10. Are invoices approved by managers or supervisors prior to payment?		
11. Are invoices reviewed for reasonableness and necessity and approved by a responsible employee outside of the originating department?		
12. Are invoices periodically audited by examination of advertisements, obtaining quotations, or other means? (If by other means, explain on reverse.)		
13. Is an employee designated to maintain a record of payments of recurring charges (utilities, etc.) and approve such charges to prevent duplicate payments, skipped payments, etc.?		
14. Is the distribution of charges reviewed in the accounting department by a person competent to pass on the propriety of distribution?		
15. Are trial balances of accounts payable prepared at least monthly?		
16. Does an employee other than the accounts payable clerk check the trial balance and control totals?		
17. Are invoices reviewed for completeness of supporting data, checked by an officer or employee not responsible for the preparation thereof, and approved by him?		
18. Are invoices and supporting data furnished to the check signer and reviewed by him prior to signing the check?		
19. If an invoice is received from a vendor not previously dealt with, does an officer or employee take steps to ascertain that the vendor is not fictitious and is actually engaged in business?		
20. At time of payment, are invoices and supporting documents satisfactorily cancelled?		

Figure A.6 (continued)

Examination of Purchases, Accounts Payable, and Expenses

Audit Operation	Performed by	Remarks
1. Compare invoices selected with purchase orders as to vendor, price, and quantity.		
2. Examine bids, quotations, etc., in support of prices.		
3. With respect to any vendors on the invoices selected for test that are not readily recognizable as authentic, check by reference against Dun and Bradstreet Reference Book, telephone directory, or other source.		
4. Compare approvals with lists of those authorized to approve expenses of the particular type.		
5. Review company's working papers relating to the audit of invoices and determine that satisfactory tests were made of the propriety of the charges.		
6. Review the invoices for conformity with the chart of accounts and established policies regarding differentiation between capital items, expense, etc.		
7. Trace the invoices to the disbursement records noting that the distribution is the same.		
8. Total selected accounts payable registers for the period and trace to management report and general ledger.		
9. Obtain list of unpaid invoices at end of period, prove footings, and compare total with property status report.		
10. Examine invoices selected for approval for payment by proper official and for effective cancellation.		

Figure A.7.   Examination of purchases, accounts payable, and expenses.

Questionnaire on Internal Controls—Payroll
Page One of Two

	Records	Yes	No
1.	Is an individual personnel file maintained for each employee?	____	____
2.	Are personnel records inaccessible to persons who:		
	a. Prepare payrolls?	____	____
	b. Approve payrolls?	____	____
	c. Distribute payrolls?	____	____
3.	Does the personnel file contain:		
	a. A signed employment application?	____	____
	b. A signed W-4 form?	____	____
	c. Properly approved on-payroll authorization?	____	____
	d. Properly approved change notices?	____	____
4.	Do procedures provide that all authorizations be transmitted promptly to the payroll department?	____	____
5.	Are time cards or sheets used?	____	____
	a. If so, are they approved by someone other than the person who prepares payroll?	____	____
6.	Are overtime hours and other special benefits approved by someone who supervises these activities but who does not:		
	a. Prepare payrolls?	____	____
	b. Distribute payrolls?	____	____

	Preparation and Approval		
1.	Is the person who prepares the payroll independent of hiring and firing functions?	____	____
2.	Is he excluded from the distribution of the payroll?	____	____
3.	Is the payroll checked by an employee who takes no part in its:		
	a. Authorization?	____	____
	b. Preparation?	____	____
	c. Distribution?	____	____
4.	Is the payroll approved by an officer or responsible employee?	____	____
5.	When practicable, are the totals of current payrolls reconciled to the previous payrolls by showing specific changes?	____	____
6.	Is the accounting distribution of the payroll charge checked by someone not involved in its preparation?	____	____

Figure A.8.   Questionnaire to test internal controls of payroll.

Questionnaire on Internal Controls—Payroll
Page Two of Two

Payment	Yes	No
1. Are all employees paid by check?	_____	_____
2. Is the payroll bank account reconciled on a regular basis by someone who has no connection with the:		
a. Preparation of the payroll?	_____	_____
b. Distribution of the paychecks?	_____	_____
3. Are endorsements compared, at least on a test basis, with signatures on file?	_____	_____
4. Are unclaimed wages returned to other than the payroll department?	_____	_____
5. Are payments of unclaimed wages at a later date made only upon:		
a. The basis of appropriate evidence of employment?	_____	_____
b. Approval by an officer or employee who is not responsible for the payroll preparation or the reporting of time?	_____	_____
6. Are W-2 forms accounted for and mailed by persons who took no part in:		
a. Approving payrolls?	_____	_____
b. Preparing payrolls?	_____	_____
c. Distributing payrolls?	_____	_____
7. Are returned W-2 forms forwarded for investigation directly to someone who took no part in:		
a. Approving payrolls?	_____	_____
b. Preparing payrolls?	_____	_____
c. Distributing payrolls?	_____	_____

Figure A.8 (continued)

Examination of Payroll

Audit Operation	Performed by	Remarks
1. For a limited number of employees appearing on the selected payrolls, check files for: a. Employment applications. b. On-payroll authorizations. c. Current wage rates. d. Increase authorizations for those whose current rate differs from their starting rate.		
2. For those selected employees, obtain time cards or sheets and: a. Check to payroll sheets. b. Check for approvals of overtime hours or other deviations from normal working requirements.		
3. For the selected employees: a. Check the calculation of earnings. b. Check the calculation of deductions. c. Crosscast the amount of net pay.		
4. Foot all columns of the selected payrolls. (If voluminous, a test check of certain columns is satisfactory.)		
5. Trace totals of all payroll columns to the accounting distribution, monthly management reports, and the general ledger.		
6. Compare checks for the selected payroll as to name, date, and net pay.		
7. Compare endorsements on the checks of the selected employees to signatures on file.		
8. If practicable, perform pay-off of selected employees.		

Figure A. 9.   Examination of payroll.

Between

OWNER_____

and

AGENT_____

for Property located at_____

Beginning_____19_____

Ending_____19_____

MANAGEMENT
AGREEMENT

In consideration of the covenants herein contained,_____

_____(hereinafter called

"OWNER"), and_____(hereinafter called "AGENT"),
agree as follows:

1. The OWNER hereby employs the AGENT exclusively to rent and
manage the property (hereinafter called the "Premises") known as_____

_____

_____

upon the terms hereinafter set forth, for a period of_____years beginning

on the_____day of_____, 19_____, and ending on

the_____day of_____,19_____, and there-
after for yearly periods from time to time, unless on or before _____ days
prior to the date last above mentioned or on or before _____days prior
to the expiration of any such renewal period, either party hereto shall notify
the other in writing that it elects to terminate this Agreement, in which case
this Agreement shall be thereby terminated on said last mentioned date.
(See also Paragraph 6(c) below.)

Figure A.10. Institute of Real Estate Management standard
management agreement.

2. THE AGENT AGREES:

(a) To accept the management of the Premises, to the extent, for the period, and upon the terms herein provided and agrees to furnish the services of its organization for the rental operation and management of the Premises.

(b) To render a monthly statement of receipts, disbursements and charges to the following person at the address shown:

Name   Address

_____   _____

_____   _____

and to remit each month the net proceeds (provided Agent is not required to make any mortgage, escrow or tax payment on the first day of the following month). Agent will remit the net proceeds or the balance thereof after making allowance for such payments to the following persons, in the percentages specified and at the addresses shown:

Name   Percentage   Address

_____   _____   _____

_____   _____   _____

_____   _____   _____

In case the disbursements and charges shall be in excess of the receipts, the OWNER agrees to pay such excess promptly, but nothing herein contained shall obligate the AGENT to advance its own funds on behalf of the OWNER.

(c) To cause all employees of the AGENT who handle or are responsible for the safekeeping of any monies of the OWNER to be covered by a fidelity bond in an amount and with a company determined by the AGENT at no cost to the OWNER.

3. THE OWNER AGREES:

To give the AGENT the following authority and powers (all or any of which may be exercised in the name of the OWNER) and agrees to assume all expenses in connection therewith:

(a) To advertise the Premises or any part thereof, to display signs thereon and to rent the same; to cause references of prospective tenants to be investigated; to sign leases for terms not in excess of _____years and to renew and or cancel the existing leases and prepare and execute the new lease without additional charge to the OWNER; provided, however, that the AGENT may collect from tenants all or any of the following: a late rent administrative charge, a non-negotiable check charge, credit report fee, a subleasing administrative charge and/or broker's commission and need not account for such charges and/or commission to the OWNER; to terminate tenancies and to sign and serve such notices as are deemed needful by the AGENT; to institute and prosecute actions to oust tenants and to recover possession of the Premises; to sue for and recover rent: and, when expedient, to settle, compromise and release such actions or suits, or reinstate' such tenancies.

Figure A.10 (continued)

(b) To hire, discharge and pay all engineers, janitors and other employees; to make or cause to be made all ordinary repairs and replacements necessary to preserve the Premises in its present condition and for the operating efficiency thereof and all alterations required to comply with lease requirements, and to do decorating on the Premises; to negotiate contracts for non-recurring items not exceeding $_____and to enter into agreements for all necessary repairs, maintenance, minor alterations and utility services; and to purchase supplies and pay all bills.

(c) To collect rents and/or assessments and other items due or to become due and give receipts therefor and to deposit all funds collected hereunder in the Agent's custodial account.

(d) To refund tenants' security deposits at the expiration of leases and, only if required to do so by law, to pay interest upon such security deposits.

(e) To execute and file all returns and other instruments and do and perform all acts required of the OWNER as an employer with respect to the Premises under the Federal Insurance Contributions Acts, the Federal Unemployment Tax Act and Subtitle C of the Internal Revenue Code of 1954 with respect to wages paid by the AGENT on behalf of the OWNER and under any similar Federal or State law now or hereafter in force (and in connection therewith the OWNER agrees upon request to promptly execute and deliver to the AGENT all necessary powers of attorney, notices of appointment and the like).

4. THE OWNER FURTHER AGREES:

(a) To indemnify, defend and save the AGENT harmless from all suits in connection with the Premises and from liability for damage to property and injuries to or death of any employee or other person whomsoever, and to carry at his (its) own expense public liability, elevator liability (if elevators are part of the equipment of the Premises), and workmen's compensation insurance naming the OWNER and the AGENT and adequate to protect their interests and in form, substance and amounts reasonably satisfactory to the AGENT, and to furnish to the AGENT certificates evidencing the existence of such insurance. Unless the OWNER shall provide such insurance and furnish such certificate within _____ days from the date of this Agreement, the AGENT may, but shall not be obligated to, place said insurance and charge the cost thereof to the account of the OWNER.

(b) To pay all expenses incurred by the AGENT, including, without limitation, attorney's fees for counsel employed to represent the AGENT or the OWNER in any proceeding or suit involving an alleged violation by the AGENT or the OWNER, or both, of any constitutional provision, statute, ordinance, law or regulation of any governmental body pertaining to fair employment, Federal Fair Credit Reporting Act, environmental protection, or fair housing, including, without limitation, those prohibiting or making illegal discrimination on the basis of race, creed, color, religion or national origin in the sale, rental or other disposition of housing or any services rendered in connection therewith (unless the AGENT is finally adjudicated to have personally and not in a representative capacity violated such constitutional provision, statute, ordinance, law or regulation), but nothing herein contained shall require the AGENT to employ counsel to represent the OWNER in any such proceeding or suit.

(c) To indemnify, defend and save the AGENT harmless from all claims, investigations and suits with respect to any alleged or actual violation of state or federal labor laws, it being expressly agreed and understood that as between the OWNER and the AGENT, all persons employed in connection

Figure A.10 (continued)

with the Premises are employees of the OWNER not the AGENT. The OWNER's obligation under this paragraph 4(c) shall include the payment of all settlements, judgments, damages, liquidated damages, penalties, forfeitures, back pay awards, court costs, litigation expense and attorneys' fees.

(d) To give adequate advance written notice to the AGENT if payment of mortgage indebtedness, general taxes or special assessments or the placing of fire, steam boiler or any other insurance is desired.

5. TO PAY THE AGENT EACH MONTH:

(a) FOR MANAGEMENT:_____per month or_____

percent (_____%) of the monthly gross receipts from the operation of the Premises during the period this Agreement remains in full force and effect, whichever is the greater amount.

(b) APARTMENT LEASING_____

_____

_____

(c) FOR MODERNIZATION (REHABILITATION/CONSTRUCTION)

_____

_____

(d) FIRE RESTORATION_____

_____

_____

_____

(e) OTHER ITEMS OF MUTUAL AGREEMENT_____

_____

_____

_____

_____

6. IT IS MUTUALLY AGREED THAT:

(a) The OWNER expressly withholds from the AGENT any power or authority to make any structural changes in any building or to make any other major alterations or additions in or to any such building or equipment therein, or to incur any expense chargeable to the OWNER other than expenses related to exercising the express powers above vested in the AGENT without the prior written direction of the following person:

Name   Address

Figure A.10 (continued)

except such emergency repairs as may be required because of danger to life or property or which are immediately necessary for the preservation and safety of the Premises or the safety of the tenants and occupants thereof or are required to avoid the suspension of any necessary service to the Premises.

(b) The AGENT does not assume and is given no responsibility for compliance of any building on the Premises or any equipment therein with the requirements of any statute, ordinance, law or regulation of any governmental body or of any public authority or official thereof having jurisdiction, except to notify the OWNER promptly or forward to the OWNER promptly any complaints, warnings, notices or summonses received by it relating to such matters. The OWNER represents that to the best of his (its) knowledge the Premises and such equipment comply with all such requirements and authorizes the AGENT to disclose the ownership of the Premises to any such officials and agrees to indemnify and hold harmless the AGENT, its representatives, servants and employees, of and from all loss, cost, expense and liability whatsoever which may be imposed on them or any of them by reason of any present or future violation or alleged violation of such laws, ordinances, statutes or regulations.

(c) In the event it is alleged or charged that any building on the Premises or any equipment therein or any act or failure to act by the OWNER with respect to the Premises or the sale, rental or other disposition thereof fails to comply with, or is in violation of, any of the requirements of any consititutional provision, statute, ordinance, law or regulation of any governmental body or any order or ruling of any public authority or official thereof having or claiming to have jurisdiction thereover, and the AGENT, in its sole and absolute discretion, considers that the action or position of the OWNER or registered managing agent with respect thereto may result in damage or liability to the AGENT, the AGENT shall have the right to cancel this Agreement at any time by written notice to the OWNER of its election so to do, which cancellation shall be effective upon the service of such notice. Such notice may be served personally or by registered mail, on or to the person named to receive the AGENT's monthly statement at the address designated for such person as provided in Paragraph 2(b) above, and if served by mail shall be deemed to have been served when deposited in the mails. Such cancellation shall not release the indemnities of the OWNER set forth in Paragraphs 4 and 6(b) above and shall not terminate any liability or obligation of the OWNER to the AGENT for any payment, reimbursement or other sum of money then due and payable to the AGENT hereunder.

7. This Agreement may be cancelled by OWNER before the termination date specified in paragraph 1 on not less than __ days prior written notice to the AGENT, provided that such notice is accompanied by payment to the AGENT of a cancellation fee in an amount equal to __ % of the management fee that would accrue over the remainder of the stated term of the Agreement. For this purpose the monthly management fee for the remainder of the stated term shall be presumed to be the same as that of the last month prior to service of the notice of cancellation.

This Agreement shall be binding upon the successors and assigns of the AGENT and their heirs, administrators, executors, successors and assigns of the OWNER.

Figure A.10 (continued)

IN WITNESS WHEREOF, the parties hereto have affixed or caused to be affixed
their respective signatures this _____ _____ day of _____ _____ _____ , 19 _____

WITNESSES: OWNER:

_____   _____

_____   _____

_____   _____

                                              _____

                                              AGENT:

                                              Firm _____

_____   By _____
Submitted by

Figure A.10 (continued)

19xx Management Plan
Pinehurst Apartments
Page One of Two

The Property:

This 86-unit, three-story, garden-style apartment building is located in the northwest section of the San Fernando Valley. The building was constructed in the middle 1960s and provides housing primarily for blue-collar, middle-income, adult tenants.

The style of the building conforms to the standards prevalent in 1965 and includes amenities such as central air conditioning, built-in appliances, swimming pool, saunas, and covered parking. The apartments are relatively large (750-square-foot one-bedroom units, 950-square-foot two-bedroom units) and have wall-to-wall carpeting, standard draperies, and balconies/patios. There are 55 one-bedroom apartments and 31 two-bedroom apartments; of the latter, five are being rented as furnished units.

The building has struggled, always, with higher than normal maintenance costs, due primarily to the sophisticated year-round air conditioning system. Recently, the cost of utilities, paid by the tenants, has become a major obstacle, with monthly electric bills running as high as $60.00.

The building has sustained high occupancy for the last three years because of the increasingly attractive rental value that it offers and the generally stronger market the area has experienced.

The Budget:

This year's operating budget, which will be submitted to the owners in December 19xx, shows an expected cash flow of $50,000 for 19xx. (The proposed budget is attached to this report.)

The budget anticipates the continued employment of the current managers, who are paid additional salaries for cleaning and painting of vacancies and for performing certain duties outside of the scope of a resident manager's normal responsibilities.

The service functions for the property are to be handled in conventional fashion by outside contractors and have been determined to be currently priced at the best available levels.

The Property Improvement Program:

In accordance with the intentions and objectives of the owners, portions of the actual, and expected, cash flow will be utilized to accomplish continuing improvement to, and/or maintenance of, the capital investment represented by the property.

In 19xx, the building was reroofed and a snow coat reflective covering was added. This has resulted in a significant increase in the livability of the top-floor apartments. These improvements were funded out of cash flow.

In 19xx, all existing hallway and exterior incandescent lighting fixtures were changed to the more efficient flourescent lighting. This proposal provided that an investment of $4,000 would result in a continuing savings of approximately $300 per month at current electric rates. These savings significantly improved the cash flow position of the property and increased the capitalized value of the investment. The cost of the change-out was funded from cash flow.

Figure A.11. Management plan for the hypothetical Pinehurst Apartments (without supporting documents).

19xx Management Plan
Pinehurst Apartments
Page Two of Two

A less cost-effective improvement, accomplished in 19xx, was the redecoration of the hallways and lobby areas of the building. The cost for this program was $7,500.

In 19xx, management intends to install a system that will make the building a full-security apartment structure. Because of the property's close proximity to Canoga Park High School, there is a continuing nuisance and petty vandalism problem caused by some of the students. The full-security system will provide that no one can gain entrance to the building unless he has a key or has identified himself through a speaker system to an occupant of the building who in turn has pressed a button in his apartment that releases the door lock. The cost for this system is $9,000 and will be funded from cash flow.

The Plan:

The items listed below outline management's concept of the short-term program for the operation of the property:

• Rents will be raised, one-third of the building at a time, during January, February, and March in order to increase the scheduled gross income by 8.1 percent for 1978. It has been determined that the proposed 98 percent collected occupancy is realistic, based on a market study of the area's competing buildings. That study also indicates that the proposed rent increase of 8.1 percent is the correct amount to result in maximum collections.

• Maintenance costs are projected to increase by 17 percent. In addition to cost increases caused by inflation, a higher allowance is provided for repairs of air conditioning units and appliances. Since the property is 12 years old, these items are beginning to require replacement more frequently.

• Property taxes could be greatly influenced by voter approval of Proposition 13. Management will keep abreast of this situation.

• Management will continue to maintain and improve the property through utilization of portions of the proposed net operating income.

Figure A.11 (continued)

19xx Management Plan Budget
Pinehurst Apartments

	19x1 12 Month Actual	19x2 12 Month Actual	19xx Annual Budget	19xx Monthly Budget
Scheduled Gross Income	$192,382	$218,705	$242,004	$ 20,167
Less Vacancy	4,344	3,268	4,800	400
Rental Income	188,038	215,437	237,204	19,767
Other Income	3,391	3,964	3,600	300
Gross Collections	191,429	219,401	240,804	20.067
Expenses				
Payroll	10,851	11,690	13,200	1,100
Utilities	12,083	11,973	13,920	1,160
Maintenance	21,750	23,612	27,600	2,300
Adv./Sundry	4,750	3,614	4,440	370
Insurance	3,077	3,598	3,900	324
Property Taxes	36,379	43,632	45,000	3,750
Management	7,661	8,776	9,336	778
Total Expenses	96,551	106,895	117,396	9,783
Net Operating Income	94,878	112,506	123,408	10,284
Capital Improvements	4,116	7,525	9,000	750
Debt Service				
Interest	40,478	38,979	37,728	3,144
Principal	23,650	25,149	26,400	2,200
Cash Flow	$ 26,634	$ 40,853	$ 50,280	$ 4,190

Figure A.11 (continued). Supporting budget for the Pinehurst Apartments management plan.

PREPARED BY		ACCOUNT NO.	STMT. DATE	PAGE
WILLIAM WALTERS COMPANY		2 02	5/31/78	1

509 S. GRAND AVE.
LOS ANGELES, CALIFORNIA 90017

PROPERTY INFORMATION
PROPERTY NAME

OWNER:

CHATEAU DE VILLE

WILLIAM WALTERS CO
509 SOUTH GRAND AVE
LOS ANGELES CA 90017

TOTAL NO. OF UNITS	TOT. NET RENT AREA(NRA)
254	209,738

SCHEDULED GROSS-RENT (SGR)

CURRENT MONTH	YEAR-TO-DATE
58,930.00	288,755.00

INCOME AND EXPENSE STATEMENT

DESCRIPTION	CURRENT MONTH		YEAR - TO - DATE				PER NRA
	MAY	% OF SGR	ACTUALS	% OF SGR	BUDGET	% OF SGR	(OR PER UNIT)
INCOME							
RENTAL	55,478.06		279,407.78				
FURNITURE	1,874.03		10,521.57				
SEC DEP COLLECTED,NET	886.49		4,385.75				
SEC DEP REFUNDED	493.49-		2,529.75-				
SEC DEP FORFEIT	100.00		1,683.01				
CLEANING FEES	720.00		5,280.00				
VENDING	828.22		4,378.29				
MISCELLANEOUS	106.50		401.50				
DAMAGES	71.00		345.27				
TOTAL INCOME OPER.	59,570.81	101.1	303,873.42	105.2	294,000.00	101.8	.29
EXPENSES							
MANAGER	981.74		6,309.80				
ASSISTANT MGR	310.36		1,763.50				
MAINTENANCE	350.76		1,962.18				
EMPLOYEE APTS	420.00		2,100.00				
PAYROLL TAXES	234.55		1,405.41				
COMP/EMP INS	331.02		1,754.57				
TOTAL PAYROLL	2,628.43	4.5	15,295.46	5.3	15,455.00	5.4	.01
ELECTRICITY	796.97		3,959.15				
WATER	1,126.65		2,288.64				
GAS	271.86		1,290.27				
TELEPHONE	113.62		558.18				
TOTAL UTILITIES	2,309.10	3.9	8,096.24	2.8	6,500.00	2.3	.01
APT CLEANING	615.25		4,754.80				
CARPETS	2,848.43		5,760.80				
DRAPERIES			4,720.25				
POOL SERVICE	320.00		4,813.00				
PLUMBING	55.99		1,711.51				
BUILDING	998.61		7,002.86				
FURNITURE	2,181.57		3,855.40				
PAINTING	1,341.53		7,462.98				
PEST CONTROL	95.00		275.00				
RUBBISH REMOVAL	275.94		1,835.94				

Figure A.12. An illustrative income and expense statement of a property's operation prepared by a computerized bookkeeping system and submitted as part of the monthly statement to the owner.

PREPARED BY			ACCOUNT NO.	STMT. DATE	PAGE
WILLIAM WALTERS COMPANY			202	5/31/78	2
609 S. GRAND AVE.					
LOS ANGELES, CALIFORNIA 90017			PROPERTY INFORMATION		

OWNER:

	PROPERTY NAME
	CHATEAU DE VILLE

WILLIAM WALTERS CO
609 SOUTH GRAND AVE
LOS ANGELES CA 90017

TOTAL NO. OF UNITS	TOT. NET RENTAREA(NRA)
254	209,738

SCHEDULED GROSS-RENT (SGR)	
CURRENT MONTH	YEAR-TO-DATE
58,930.00	288,755.00

INCOME AND EXPENSE STATEMENT

DESCRIPTION	CURRENT MONTH		YEAR - TO - DATE				
	MAY	% OF SGR	ACTUALS	% OF SGR	BUDGET	% OF SGR	PER NRA (OR PER UNIT)
LANDSCAPING	1,335.75		7,049.59				
EQUIPMENT	66.80		118.66				
APPLIANCES	126.24		1,128.09				
TOTAL MAINTENANCE	10,261.11	17.4	50,488.88	17.5	64,650.00	22.4	.05
PAID ADVERTISING			772.25				
TENANT PROMOTION	300.00		1,100.00				
TOTAL ADVERTISING	300.00	.5	1,872.25	.6	2,250.00	.8	
SUPPLIES	327.29		829.38				
PROFESSIONAL FEES	206.50		4,643.28				
SECURITY SERVICE	190.50		952.50				
UNCLASSIFIED			16.00				
TOTAL OTHER EXPENSES	724.29	1.2	6,441.16	2.2	4,875.00	1.7	.01
PROPERTY TAX	7,200.00		35,400.00				
LICENSES			185.00				
TOTAL TAXES/LICENSES	7,200.00	12.2	35,585.00	12.3	35,185.00	12.2	.03
PROPERTY MANAGEMENT	2,084.80		10,635.37				
TOTAL PROP. MANAGEMENT	2,084.80	3.5	10,635.37	3.7	10,285.00	3.6	.01
TOTAL OPERATING EXP.	25,507.73	43.3	128,414.36	44.5	139,200.00	48.2	.12
NET OPERATING INCOME	34,063.08	57.8	175,459.06	60.8	154,800.00	53.6	.17

Figure A.12 (continued)

PREPARED BY			ACCOUNT NO.	STMT. DATE	PAGE
WILLIAM WALTERS COMPANY			202	5/31/78	1
609 S. GRAND AVE.					
LOS ANGELES, CALIFORNIA 90017					

PROPERTY INFORMATION

PROPERTY NAME

CHATEAU DE VILLE

OWNER:

WILLIAM WALTERS CO
609 SOUTH GRAND AVE
LOS ANGELES CA 90017

TOTAL NO. OF UNITS	TOT. NET RENTAREA(NRA)
254	209,738

SCHEDULED GROSS RENT (SGR)

CURRENT MONTH	YEAR-TO-DATE
58,930.00	288,755.00

CASH FLOW STATEMENT

DESCRIPTION	CURRENT MONTH		YEAR-TO-DATE				
	MAY	% OF SGR	ACTUALS	% OF SGR	BUDGET	% OF SGR	PER NRA (OR PER UNIT)
BEGINNING BALANCE	8,203.66						
RECEIPTS							
TOTAL OPER. INCOME	59,570.81	101.1	303,873.42	105.2			
FROM BANK			57,210.31	19.8			
INTEREST EARNED			3,666.01	1.3			
TOTAL RECEIPTS	59,570.81	101.1	364,749.74	126.3			
DISBURSEMENTS							
TOTAL OPERATING EXP.	25,507.73	43.3	128,414.36	44.5			
PROPERTY TAX PAYMENTS			41,792.00	14.5			
DEBT SERVICE							
PRINCIPAL	1,668.24	2.8	8,211.26	2.8			
INTEREST	25,243.76	42.8	126,348.74	43.8			
OWNER DISTRIBUTION	15,000.00	25.5	76,954.99	26.7			
TOTAL DISBURSEMENTS	67,419.73	114.4	381,721.35	132.2			
ENDING BALANCE	354.74						
****************************							
* TOT. POSSIBLE RENTS	58,930.00		288,755.00				*
* RENTS COLLECTED	55,478.06		279,407.78				*
* % OF POSSIBLE RENTS		94.1			96.8		*
*							*
* TOTAL UNIT DAYS	7,874		38,354				*
* UNIT DAYS FILLED	7,718		37,255				*
* OCCUPANCY FACTOR		98.0			97.1		*
*							*
* NO. OF UNITS	254		1,270				*
* NO. TENANTS LEAVING	12		79				*
* TURNOVER RATE		4.7			6.2		*
****************************							

Figure A.12 (continued). An illustrative cash flow statement prepared by a computerized bookkeeping system and submitted as part of the monthly statement to the owner.

Purchasing Policies and Procedures
Page One of Seven

Policy

A. It is the company's policy to obtain the best possible purchases for the owners the company represents.

B. It is the responsibility of each property manager to obtain good buys for each property supervised. Good buying policies include: right kind, right quality, right place, and right price. The dependability of the vendor is the most important aspect of supply and can save the property manager a tremendous amount of time.

C. To help enable the property manager to make good purchases, each office will have a current detailed vendor list, with one property manager at each office responsible for keeping the list current. Each property manager is responsible for reporting good and bad vendor information to update the list.

Procedures

A. Each property manager should take the following items into consideration when selecting vendors and contractors:

   1. Legal
      a. Federal and state minimum wage laws
      b. Warranties
      c. Law of agency and contracts
      d. Lien laws

   2. Protection of client funds: Procedures should be properly established and supervised to protect clients' money and the company's reputation.

   3. Integrity of vendors and contractors: Shortages, incorrect quality, overcharges, duplicate invoices, and late billing can be very costly to clients as well as the company. Therefore, honest and dependable vendors must be chosen and proper internal procedures must be followed.

   4. Cash Discounts: Procedures should take advantage of all cash discounts and avoid all penalties or sizeable losses may accrue; i.e., if the company fails to get a two percent discount for cash, then this is equivalent to 36 percent per year if cash is available, or 24 percent if money is borrowed at six percent.

   5. Central Control: Centralization of authority results in more specialized and capable leadership over purchasing and thus savings to clients and company.

B. Speculative Purchasing

   One cannot be exposed to purchasing very long without coming face to face with the realization that, since most market prices change frequently and widely, there are numerous opportunities for gain and loss. Thus, when purchases are made at a low price and prices move up, the company may realize a profit not only on manufacturing, but also on the increase in inventory values.

   There may be a temptation, therefore, to purchase at one time more than is required for immediate production requirements when the purchaser holds the opinion that prices are going to move up. If such a purchase is made and if prices increase sufficiently to affect the cost of carrying the inventories beyond the usual period, a large profit may be earned with seemingly little effort.

   But there is a dark side to this bright picture. Prices may not rise as expected. They may fall precipitously. In such a case, the losses may be great. In one rubber

Figure A.13. Policy and standard operating procedures for ensuring that best possible purchases are obtained.

Purchasing Policies and Procedures
Page Two of Seven

company, the president had brought rubber for 20 years but guessed wrong on the market in one particular year. When he guessed wrong, profits fell from $8 to $1½ million in one year even though volume of business had not changed materially from one year to the next.

Whether or not speculative purchases should be attempted is a matter of company and owner's policy. Speculative purchasing is the policy of buying excessive quantities in the hope of gaining inventory profits yet recognizing the risks of large losses. Such purchasing is normally frowned upon. Nevertheless, it is practiced in cases where conditions seem propitious.

C. Who Can Purchase and How Much

Property managers have complete authority to purchase supplies and services under the guide of the management contract, building budget, and owner's direction using usual company vendors, policies and practices.

Resident managers should have authority and responsibility to purchase and order above services and supplies from vendors authorized by their supervisor, under guidelines of the building budget, and up to a maximum of $100 for any one item.

Petty cash in an amount of from $25 to $100 should be in the hands of each resident manager. This, not rent money, should be used. Managers should be limited to a maximum one-item petty cash expenditure of $25 and one-month total equivalent to the total of the petty cash fund. Anything in excess of this requires property manager approval.

Exceptions to any of the above should be in writing and signed by the property manager and resident manager.

All purchasing by maintenance men must have prior resident manager approval.

D. Company Purchasing Guides

1. (See attached vendor billing instructions.) Exceptions to the following guides must be approved by the supervisor.

    Use existing company vendors except where substantial savings or better service can be obtained.

    Advance payments to vendors are to be used only under rare circumstances.

    Pay from invoices only—not statements.

    All vendor checks are to be mailed directly to the vendors by the accounting department.

    Vendors must give discounts if bill is paid within 30 days of receipt of invoice.

    Invoices are to be mailed by the vendor to the central company office, not left with the resident manager.

    Vendors must allow the company 30 days to pay without calling for payment. It is the company's responsibility to be sure bills are approved promptly and payments made on a timely basis.

    Vendors should bill at least monthly.

    Mortgages, taxes, insurance, utilities, and telephone must be in the name of the building or owner.

    All purchase contracts are to be in name of owner; the company can sign as agent only on items approved in the management contract.

    Anything not specified in the management contract should be signed for by owner, or the company should have written authorization in its files to sign as owner's agent.

Figure A.13 (continued)

Purchasing Policies and Procedures
Page Three of Seven

2. Group Purchase Discounts: Where substantial discounts are available by group purchasing on one account, then the company will set up accounts in its name. These must be established through a company officer. Property managers may not establish accounts in the name of the company.

3. Legal Liability: It must be remembered that when things are purchased in the name of the company, it assumes the responsibility to pay if the owner does not. If the building has insufficient funds, the company is liable. It can sue the owner to recover, but in the meantime, the company is legally liable to pay the vendor. In addition to legal liability, the company has a business reputation to protect. This reputation is extremely important.

   If the owner will sign the attached vendor billing instructions, then the company can be relieved of this liability except if it misleads the vendor, i.e., if the company knows a building is in financial trouble and does not disclose this to the vendor.

   Where the rental agreements, charge accounts, and contracts are in the name of the building, a "Fictitious Name Notice" must be filed using a strict legal procedure if the building name is not a legal entity.

4. Advertising: On the Times and the Register accounts, the company is responsible for all charges. Therefore, any building whose financial condition will not permit paying bills in the same month's business as received must be set up as a separate account in the owner's name. In the Times, this means that the building must run its own daily rate holder or pay higher rates. On the Register, a separate account can mean an increase of 10¢ or more per line per day.

E. Independent Contractor or Employee

There is no clear-cut answer to the question of whether the company can be found liable for an injury sustained by an independent contractor. The rules regulating who is an employee versus an independent contractor are continually changing due to findings made by the local appeals board.

Employees are covered under the state worker's compensation insurance laws for "disability for injuries and for the reasonable cost of medical, surgical and hospital treatment, including nursing, medicines, medical and surgical supplies, crutches, apparatus, and artificial members."

Not only is injury and liability involved, but more important, if an individual is found to be an employee, then all wage and hour laws, both federal and state, apply. This would mean that the company would have to pay for work done, even if unsatisfactory. The company could terminate but would have to pay for hours to date.

If found to be an employee, the company would be protected since it has proper insurance. However, the company could experience substantial loss under wage laws.

This is particularly important in cases in which a contractor is doing all or a substantial amount of the work himself. If a contractor works only for the company and works full time as a worker, he may be an employee even if all other tests show him as a contractor.

Definitions and Guidelines: According to Labor Code Section 3353, an independent contractor means "any person who renders service for a specified recompense for a specified result, under the control of his principal as to the result of his work only and not as to the means by which such result is accomplished." An employee can be defined as one who performs services for another

Figure A.13 (continued)

Purchasing Policies and Procedures

Page Four of Seven

and who is subject to the direction and control of his employer in the manner in which the work is done.

Several factors tend to establish an employer/employee relationship. The one receiving the service:

1. Controls the details or manner of doing work. He tells the person doing the work what to do and how to do it.
2. Has the right to terminate the relationship before the completion of the work. There is no contract for a specific job.
3. Pays salary or wages and makes deductions for unemployment disability insurance, social security, etc.
4. Furnishes materials or tools.
5. Requires performance during specific days or hours.

An independent contractor relationship can be established by the following factors. The one receiving the service:

1. Has no control over the details of the work performed.
2. Has no right to terminate the relationship before the completion of the work. There is usually a written or unwritten contractual relationship.

To protect the company, the following alternatives should be considered:

1. Request a copy of the contractor's business license.
2. Request a certificate of insurance from the contractor showing his worker's compensation coverage.
3. Keep in mind that if less than 50 percent of the contractor's business is with the company, the company will have a better chance if the case should be brought before an appeal board.
4. Have a written contract for the work to be performed indicating that the party is an independent contractor, is bonded, and has liability insurance coverage.
5. Have on file a copy of a contractor's business card, letterhead, and invoice form.
6. Have a list of other people contractor has, is, or will work for as a contractor.
7. Be sure he is not doing same type work as an employee for someone else— in other words, he should be a contractor for all work.
8. Be sure that other people working for the contractor are doing so as his employees with taxes withheld, etc.

F. Major Contracts and Bidding

1. Taking bids
   a. Make a specification sheet for job and give to each bidder; should include time limits.
   b. Get at least three comparable bids.
   c. Analyze bids: Determine if they are using same quantities and same quality of products. Check out their references.
2. Preparing the contract
   a. Include names of contractor and subcontractor and their license numbers.
   b. Include scope of work and specifications of materials and quantities to be used.
   c. Include special conditions; i.e., when work is to be done and completed and any late penalties.
   d. Any drawings or plans become part of the contract.
   e. Make sure contract language includes that subcontractor will not violate any codes or laws.
   f. Include warranties or guarantees.
   g. Bonding may be required, in case of default.

Figure A.13 (continued)

Purchasing Policies and Procedures
Page Five of Seven

       h. Contractor should submit certificate of insurance for: liability, worker's compensation, and vehicles.
       i. Lien releases should be submitted before final payment is made.

G. The following forms can be used as guidelines for working with vendors and outside contractors.

To:

Gentlemen:

We have enclosed two copies of our information sheet regarding the procedure we would appreciate your following in billing us for services you perform for property managed by our company.

After you have read this information sheet carefully, please sign one of the copies where indicated on the second page and return to our office for our files.

Thank you for your cooperation.

Cordially,

_____

Enclosures

P.S. Our resident managers are authorized to purchase supplies and/or service as managing agents for apartment buildings but not to sign contracts for continuing services.

Figure A.13 (continued)

Purchasing Policies and Procedures
Page Six of Seven

Information for Vendors Regarding Billing for Materials and Services

Because the company manages more than 150 pieces of property for almost as many different owners, it is necessary that we receive a separate invoice for each call at or each purchase for each different building that we manage. In some apartment complexes, the buildings are owned by more than one owner and, therefore, a separate invoice may be required for each building in the complex Our employees should indicate this to you or, if the job is ordered through our office, we will indicate this to you.

All invoices should be billed to either the owner of the building or to the building by name and sent c/o the company. It is important that the following items be indicated on every invoice received:

Note: Our accounting is set up to pay from only invoices, not statements.

1.   Each invoice should show the address to which the material was delivered or the work performed or where materials are to be used if these are picked up.

2.   Each invoice must have a description of the work done, including any hours and materials used in detail. The hours should show each employee, the beginning and ending times, the total time, and the rate of pay. If the invoice is for a monthly service, then the beginning and ending date of the period covered should be shown on the invoice. If more convenient, these details may be on an attachment to the invoice.

3.   Each invoice should show the apartment number, office number, or area in or about the building where the work was performed or material used.

4.   Each invoice should be signed by an authorized employee of the management company. Usually this would be a resident manager or other resident employee on the premises. In a case where there are no resident employees and the work is being done in a resident's space, then you should ask the resident to sign the invoice. Residents are not permitted to originate purchases or service calls. If the work is performed on an exterior of a building with no resident employee, then a signature is not required.

5.   All invoices should indicate all discounts that apply so that there is no misunderstanding as to the discounts applicable.

6.   Invoices are not to be left at the buildings but are to be mailed directly to the company. Any items left at the buildings with the manager will not be processed for payment.

7.   If your company also mails a monthly statement showing the items incurred during the month and the payments or outstanding balance, we suggest that much confusion can be saved if you will hold all of your invoices and send them to us along with your monthly statement. That way, we are sure that we have received everything and that all items have been processed properly to get you prompt payment.

8.   If you have not received payment of a specific invoice within 60 days, please contact us. Do not send duplicate invoices unless we specifically request these and you plainly mark them as duplicate invoices per our request.

Figure A.13 (continued)

Purchasing Policies and Procedures

Page Seven of Seven

Also, as a condition of our billing procedure, you agree to the following statement:

It is hereby acknowledged and agreed that it has been disclosed that the _____ company is acting as an agent only in this matter and that no liability of any nature whatsoever shall attach to the _____ company, its employees, or any of its agents arising out of this agreement. That the undersigned shall look to the _____ company's principal only for any breaches of this agreement, and that this agreement does not bind the _____ company, its agents, or any of its employees. The _____ company acknowledges that it is acting as agent for several property owners in this manner.

By _____

Company _____

Address _____

Business License Number _____ City _____

State Contractors License   Yes _____ No _____

Number _____

Emergency Phone Number _____

Figure A.13 (continued)

Work Safety Program
Page One of Five

Date: _____

Bulletin to: All _____ Company Employees

From: _____, Vice President

Subject: Safe Working Conditions

The attached safety rules have been established to help you avoid work-related illness that may cause pain or loss of pay to you and loss of productivity to the company.

We have spent a considerable amount of effort to make working conditions safe and to determine safe work methods to protect you from injury.

Accidents can be prevented with your cooperation. It is essential that you learn and follow the safety rules and always keep safe working habits foremost in your mind.

If you have any doubt about the proper way to do a job, be sure to contact your property manager before you start, and always remember that you must remain alert to avoid serious injuries to yourself or your fellow workers.

Within 48 hours after you receive this bulletin you will be expected to do the following:

1. Read the entire bulletin.

2. Be sure you thoroughly understand all of the rules and guidelines. If you are in doubt about any part of the bulletin contact your property manager for clarification.

3. Complete the attached acknowledgment form by signing, dating and returning it to the _____ Company.

Safety Policy Statement

The _____ Company acknowledges and accepts its responsibility to provide a safe and healthful working environment for its employees. We endorse the concept that this responsibility cannot be discharged passively but requires the active effort and support of every level of management through constant training and supervision of its employees and continual review of its facilities and processes.

Specifically, it is the policy of the _____ Company to:

1. Comply with the requirements of federal, state, and local codes as they pertain to safe and healthful working conditions.

2. Develop, adopt, and enforce adequate safety standards and criteria for all operations.

3. Supply exposed employees with necessary and approved protective equipment and insist on its use when hazards cannot be engineered out of a process.

4. Develop and teach employees safe working habits and techniques.

5. Maintain in our employees a continuing awareness of safety habits and techniques through constant supervision.

6. Encourage each employee to take an active interest in his own safety by developing good working habits and by bringing unsafe working conditions to the attention of his property manager.

General

1. Report all injuries at once. Failure to do this may lead to several unforeseen complications, such as infection, increased medical expenses, or possibly the denial of a claim.

Figure A.14.   Work safety program for compliance with OSHA regulations.

Work Safety Program
Page Two of Five

2. If you are not sure how to do a job safely, ask your property manager.

3. Horseplay and practical jokes are strictly prohibited.

4. Put equipment away after use. Do not leave tools, chairs, brooms, boxes, etc., in passageways.

5. Broken chairs and ladders, loose and worn carpets, missing lights, and other equipment needing maintenance may cause accidents. Report these at once to your property manager in writing. Make certain that no one can use broken equipment until it has been repaired.

6. All first-aid kits should be kept current and must be maintained in the manager's apartment or office. If you do not have a first-aid kit, see your property manager about purchasing one.

7. All fire extinguishers should be properly mounted and unobstructed.

8. Report any unsafe condition to your property manager at once.

Safe Lifting Procedures

1. Follow the rules listed below for safe lifting practices:

   a. Size up the load. If it seems more than you can easily handle yourself, get help. Do not move furniture or appliances without both proper lifting equipment (dollies and hand truck) and other people.

   b. Face the load squarely.

   c. Secure a firm footing with your feet properly spread.

   d. Bend your knees.

   e. Get a good grip on the load.

   f. Keep a straight back and lift by straightening your legs.

   g. Lift gradually, not suddenly.

   h. Keep the load close to your body.

   i. Do not twist your body.

Housekeeper and Custodian

1. Mops, buckets, and other equipment should be placed where no one can fall over them.

2. Put trucks, dollies, etc., out of the way when you are finished with them.

3. Tools with defective electrical cords or plugs are not to be used.

4. Wear rubber gloves when using strong solutions and when cleaning toilets, urinals, ovens, and baths.

5. Safety glasses must be worn when cleaning ovens.

6. When moving tall items or tall pieces of furniture, pull them, do not push them.

7. Tools or equipment that is not working properly should be reported to the property manager immediately and not used until repaired.

8. When your hands are wet or you are standing on a damp floor, do not touch light switches or handle electrical equipment.

9. Use a proper ladder to reach high places; do not climb on furniture or bath fixtures. Never stand on the top two steps of a ladder.

10. Walk; do not run. When going up or down stairs, grasp the handrail securely.

Figure A.14 (continued)

Work Safety Program
Page Three of Five

11. Be alert to things that may cause accidents. Remove them when possible or report them to the property manager.

12. Observe the rules for safe lifting. Use a dolly when moving furniture.

13. Do not try to repair machines or equipment with which you are not familiar.

14. Do not run hands along surfaces that you have not first checked for razor blades, broken glass, etc.

15. Hold wastebaskets by the sides and empty over a newspaper or open refuse bag.

16. Do not attempt to physically compact trash in dumpsters.

17. Do not attempt to light gas heaters or hot water heaters without proper instruction.

18. Wear a leather-type shoe with a hard sole that completely encloses the foot and toes.

Office

1. Keep the floor clear of electrical cords, waste paper, paper clips, and all other material that may cause a fall.

2. Chairs have four legs. Be sure you use all four, not just the back two.

3. Close file or desk drawers when you are finished with them. Never go away and leave a drawer standing open.

4. Office machines can be quite heavy. Obtain help when moving equipment and follow the safe-lifting rules.

5. Report defective electrical cords on office equipment to your property manager immediately. Ground electrical equipment. Eliminate multiplug outlets.

6. Never repair or clean office machines without shutting off power by unplugging the machine.

7. Always walk; do not run in the office areas.

Painters

1. Safety goggles must be worn when doing preparatory work, mixing paints, or using an airless or compressor spray unit.

2. Flammable paints and spirits must be stored in approved and properly marked containers.

3. Never store paint products in rooms that contain a water heater or other type of heater.

4. Be sure that sufficient ventilation is available whenever you are working.

5. Know the location of fire extinguishers.

6. Use a respirator when spraying or mixing paint.

7. Do not smoke in paint shop or while using flammable paints.

8. Clean up work area immediately after job is completed.

9. Wear a leather-type shoe with a hard sole that completely encloses the foot and toes.

Maintenance Personnel

1. Gloves or loosely fitting clothes are not to be worn around the bench grinder, etc.

2. Do not work with faulty tools or machinery.

Figure A.14 (continued)

Work Safety Program
Page Four of Five

3. To avoid a serious electrical shock, do not handle electrical tools, machines, switches, or connections with wet hands or when standing on damp floors.

4. Turn off electricity before making repairs to machinery; unplug whenever possible. If you are working out of sight of the switch, leave a tag at the switch stating that the machine is under repair.

5. Never overfuse or overload a circuit or bypass a safety switch.

6. See that ladders are in perfect repair at all times.

7. Always use ladders to reach high areas.

8. Always wear goggles when grinding or cutting wood and steel, iron, and other metals.

9. Do not try to make repairs to equipment with which you are not familiar.

10. Make sure lighting is adequate to perform a job safely.

11. Do not handle flammable liquids in enclosed areas.

12. Do not smoke when working with flammable liquids.

13. Clean up anything dropped or spilled.

14. Have a place for every tool and machine and keep it there.

15. Do not try to operate machinery you do not understand.

16. Think safety first at all times, and take safety precautions to protect yourself, your fellow employees, and residents.

17. Keep heavy objects and sharp tools on low shelves.

18. Wear a leather-type shoe with a hard sole that completely encloses the foot and toes.

Gardeners

1. Wear protective goggles when power edging.

2. Never check or adjust moving parts of power machinery with motor on.

3. Check that all power equipment is equipped with a spark arrestor or ignition cut-off.

4. Wear protective goggles when using the power sprayer.

5. Wear rubber gloves when mixing or transferring bulk chemicals.

6. Always wash hands thoroughly after mixing or spraying insecticides or herbicides.

7. Always wear a respirator when mixing, dusting, or fogging with chemicals.

8. Avoid skin contact with plastic solvent when performing pipe repairs.

9. Use tool holster for carrying sharp objects, such as pruners, shears, etc.

10. Do not remove factory-installed features on equipment.

11. Observe safety-lifting rules.

12. Return all tools to designated storage areas. Never leave equipment in walk areas.

13. Do not use faulty electrical equipment. Report frayed electrical cords immediately.

14. Wear hard hats when pruning trees.

15. Store gasoline in approved and properly marked containers; never store in the same area as a water heater or room heater.

16. Wear a leather-type shoe with a hard sole that completely encloses the foot and toes.

Figure A.14 (continued)

Work Safety Program
Page Five of Five

    I hereby acknowledge receipt of a copy of the above bulletin and attest that I have read the bulletin in its entirety. I further attest that I thoroughly understand the rules and guidelines it contains. I agree to keep a copy of the bulletin handy for easy reference should I have any questions regarding safe working procedures.

———————————————
Name of Property

———————————————
Printed Name of Employee

———————————————
Employee's Signature

———————————————
Date

Figure A.14 (continued)

Property Manager Employment Agreement
Page One of Four

This agreement, by and between _____, a _____
Corporation, hereinafter referred to as "Employer," and the undersigned person, hereinafter referred to as "Employee," is made as of _____ with reference to
the following facts which the parties agree are true:

A. Employer is in the general real estate business and provides services to owners, buyers, sellers, and occupants, which services include but are not necessarily limited to management, leasing, financing, brokerage, and consultation.

B. Employer has been engaged in the above described business and has provided
the above described services for many years.

C. Employer has developed, maintained, and will develop in the future a list of
clients for whom Employer has, does, and will perform said services.

D. Employer has acquired and will acquire its clients through great efforts.

E. The clients of Employer are not readily discoverable.

F. Employer has acquired and will acquire information concerning its clients in
relation to:

1. What property owners will use professional property managers, brokers,
and consultants.

2. Their goals and objectives in owning, selling, buying, leasing, and financing real property.

3. Their financial resources.

4. Their future desires relative to buying, selling, and financing existing
properties and additional properties.

5. Information concerning the financial details of their properties, such as
rent schedules, financing information, repair frequencies, operating costs,
and other matters relating to the operation and ownership of the properties.

G. The list of Employer's clients and the above information concerning them is
confidential, is a trade secret, and every firm in a business similar to that of
Employer and/or providing services similar to that of Employer carefully protects said information.

H. That the above information could or will be disclosed to Employee, by virtue
of this Agreement, who will be in a confidential relationship, and were it not
for Employee and Employer executing this Agreement, the information would
not be disclosed to Employee.

Now, therefore, in consideration of the mutual covenants herein contained, Employer
does hereby employ Employee and Employee does hereby accept employment on the
following terms and conditions:

I. Term

A. The term of this agreement shall be for a period of one year.

B. This agreement shall automatically be renewed on an annual basis thereafter.

C. This agreement may be cancelled by either Employer or Employee without
cause at any time by the giving of two weeks written notice by the cancelling
party.

II. Compensation

A. Employer shall pay Employee a monthly salary of $_____, payable semi-
monthly on the 15th and last day of each calendar month during the term
hereof.

B. Employer shall pay Employee $_____ per month as an automobile allow-
ance.

C. Employer shall (not) pay for Employee's parking.

D. Employer shall provide and pay for Employee's individual group health plan
and $_____ of life insurance.

Figure A.15. Employment agreement for the property manager.

Property Manager Employment Agreement
Page Two of Four

E. Employer shall reimburse Employee for travel costs as provided for in the Company Policies and Procedures Manual.

F. Employer shall pay Employee's dues, if any, for the following Associations: NATIONAL ASSOCIATION OF REALTORS®, California Association of REALTORS®, Local Board of REALTORS®, National Institute of Real Estate Management, Local Chapter Institute of Real Estate Management, and Community Associations Institute.

G. Employer shall pay for all educational course tuitions and travel costs (i.e. airfare) that Employee incurs, which has been approved by Employer.

III. Services by Employer

Employer will provide to Employee all reasonable services required which would be necessary for Employee to fulfill the employment services as provided by this agreement. These would include, but not be limited to, office space, secretarial services, bookkeeping services, supplies, equipment, telephone, etc.

IV. Services by Employee

A. Employee shall use his best efforts to acquire, service, and maintain property management accounts for Employer.

B. Employee shall use his best efforts to solicit and acquire other related business accounts for Employer consistent with the services which Employer has the capabilities to provide, i.e., leasing, brokerage, financing, consulting, etc., all as directed by Employer.

C. Employee shall use his best efforts to accomplish the following goals:

1. Assist owners in achieving their investment objectives through quality professional property management services.
2. Provide these services through methods and procedures established by company policy and programs.
3. Make recommendations to improve the profit and productivity of Employer.
4. Identify and develop new business opportunities for Employer.
5. Develop his own professional abilities.

D. Employee shall at all times follow all policies and procedures as promulgated by Employer in the Company Policy and Procedures Manual.

V. Standards of Conduct

A. Employee shall at all times maintain as a minimum a State Real Estate Salesman's license in the state of his employment and assign said license to Employer.

B. Employee shall pursue the attainment of the CERTIFIED PROPERTY MANAGER® (CPM®) designation and subsequently shall maintain said designation.

C. Employee shall at all times abide by all rules and regulations as published by the Real Estate Commissioner of the State.

D. Employee shall at all times abide by the Code of Ethics of the NATIONAL ASSOCIATION OF REALTORS®.

E. Employee shall at all times abide by the Code of Ethics of the Institute of Real Estate Management.

F. Employee shall report all personal real estate activities to Employer in writing.

G. Employee shall notify the President in writing of all personal ownership of real estate or partnership interests in organizations owning real estate or stock purchases in corporations owning investment real estate.

H. Employee shall not engage in a real estate business activity with a Company client without prior knowledge and written approval of Employer.

I. Employee may not purchase a property which is in any way related to Employer's operations without the prior knowledge and written approval of Employer.

J. Employee shall not purchase goods and/or services from any firm and/or

Figure A.15 (continued)

Property Manager Employment Agreement
Page Three of Four

vendor in which Employee has an interest without the prior knowledge and written approval of Employer.

K. Employee shall not engage in nepotism without the prior knowledge and written approval of Employer.

L. Employee shall not accept any gifts from business clients, vendors, firms, etc., with a value of over $25.00, without the prior knowledge and written approval of Employer.

M. Employee shall at all times abide by the State Real Estate Laws and Civil Codes.

N. Employee may invest in any partnership where Employer or affiliates of Employer is the managing or General Partner.

VI. Buying, Selling and Leasing and Consulting Commission Schedule

It is the usual and normal practice of Employer to have Employees involved in the various phases of Employer's business activities. These activities are a part of Employee's services for which Employee receives compensation as described in Section II as outlined above. However, from time to time Employer may call upon Employee to perform services outside the normal realm of his services and work schedule. The following sections outline the agreement of compensation for the rendering of additional services when requested by Employer:

A. All clients for whom Employer manages properties are considered Employer clients. Employee has a proprietary interest in the following clients _____
_____.

B. When Employee is given an assignment relative to Employer's client's account, the fee, if any, that Employee is to receive for the assignment will be agreed to in writing between Employer and Employee prior to commencement of the assignment.

C. During the term of this agreement, when Employee has a proprietary interest in a client, Employee will be entitled to the following:

   1. A listing commission of 50 percent of the total commission received by Employer for the listing side of the transaction if and when the client's property is listed and/or sold.

   2. Employee shall have the right of first refusal for any commissionable assignment related to that client.

D. If Employee produces a new buyer or seller, the Employee will be treated as a salesman; i.e., Employee will receive 50 percent of the commission received, if any, by Employer for the listing side of the transaction, and/or Employee will receive 50 percent of the commission received, if any, by Employer for the selling side of the transaction.

E. If Employee produces leasing commissions, Employee will be treated as a leasing agent; i.e., 50 percent of commission received by Employer will be paid to Employee.

F. From time to time certain circumstances may exist which would require an adjustment to the above fee schedules. In such cases, Employer and Employee shall agree in writing as to said adjustment prior to the commencement of the work.

VII. Termination

Employee agrees that from the date of this Agreement and for a period of One Year, immediately following the termination of this Agreement, Employee, either directly or indirectly:

A. Will not make known or divulge the names or addresses of any of the clients of Employer or the location of any parcels of real property owned by clients of Employer or divulge or make known rent schedules, repair frequency, costs of operating, or any other financial data of properties belonging to clients of Employer, to any person, partnership, firm, or corporation engaged in the general real estate business.

Figure A.15 (continued)

Property Manager Employment Agreement
Page Four of Four

    B. Will not, neither for himself nor for any other person, partnership, firm, or Corporation, call upon or solicit or attempt to call upon or solicit from clients of Employer the property management business of such clients.

    C. Will not, neither for himself nor for any other person, partnership, firm, or Corporation, sell or attempt to sell, exchange or attempt to exchange any real property belonging to clients of Employer.

    D. Will not, neither for himself nor for any other person, firm, partnership, or Corporation, sell or offer to sell real property to any clients of Employer.

    E. Will not, neither for himself nor for any other person, partnership, firm, or Corporation, induce, attempt to induce, or cause to be induced any other employee of Employer to terminate his employment with Employer.

    F. Will not, neither for himself nor for any other person, partnership, firm, or Corporation, solicit or attempt to solicit any other real estate services to or for any clients of Employer.

VIII. General Provisions

    A. Violations of any section or any part of this Agreement while Employee is in the employ of Employer may be grounds for dismissal.

    B. Any violation of this Agreement shall be a basis for Employer to obtain an injunction to restrain such activities that are in violation of this Agreement.

    C. In the event of litigation between the parties hereto concerning this Agreement, the prevailing party shall be entitled to reasonable attorney's fees.

    D. This Agreement may be modified, changed, and/or amended upon the written agreement of the parties hereto.

    E. This Agreement contains the entire understanding between the parties and supersedes any prior understanding and agreements between them respecting the within subject matter. There are no representations, agreements, arrangements, or understandings, oral or written, between and among the parties hereto relating to the subject matter of this Agreement which are not fully expressed herein. This Agreement shall be governed and construed in accordance with the Laws of the State of _____.

In Witness Whereof, the parties hereto have signed this agreement this _____ day of _____, 19_____.

_____Company

_____
Date

_____
Employer

_____
Date

_____
Employee

Figure A.15 (continued)

Employment Agreement

Page One of Two

Employment Agreement entered into this _____ day of _____, 19_____, between the _____ company, a Corporation, hereinafter called the Employer, and _____, hereinafter called the Employee.

Whereas, the Employer employs the Employee as a Manager for the _____ _____, City of _____, State of _____.

Now, therefore, it is mutually agreed as follows: The compensation for such employment shall be an apartment and utilities, all of which have a market rental value of $_____ per month. However, for the purposes of computing wages, this facility shall be valued at $_____. In addition to the apartment, the employee shall receive cash wages. The total compensation shall be computed at $_____ per hour.

It is further agreed that the employee and an agent of the employer have reviewed the tasks to be performed, and that both parties agree that these tasks can normally be performed during _____ hours each working day. The employee shall post office hours at the building, which will advise tenants and visitors to the building of the hours that the Manager will be available to conduct the business of the property, and that these posted hours shall not exceed the time specified above. The employee agrees to take the following day off each week: _____. It is recognized that the Manager may be disturbed for emergencies at hours other than those posted, and it is mutually agreed that this "inconvenience time" shall be computed at _____ hours per working day.

The employee further agrees that, if there should be work that cannot be done in the hours specified above, the employee will notify the employer *in writing*, and such work shall not be done until permission is obtained in writing from the employer.

The employee acknowledges receipt of a copy of the Payroll Procedures of the employer, and agrees to abide by those Procedures in order that he may be properly paid.

Employment may be terminated at any time upon written notice by either party to the other without liability for compensation, except such as may have been earned at the date of such termination, and said apartment will be vacated and surrendered immediately upon the termination of said employment.

In the event the employer shall bring an action against the employee to recover possession of the premises under the terms of this agreement, and the employer wholly or partly prevails in any such action, then in that event, the employee shall pay the employer, in addition to the costs of such action, reasonable attorneys' costs and fees to be fixed by the court hearing such action.

It is further agreed that there are no other or further agreements between the parties not contained in this instrument.

By _____

_____

Employee   Employer

Figure A.16.   Employment agreement for the resident manager.

Employment Agreement
Page Two of Two

This form is intended to help in filling out and explaining this Individual Employment Agreement.

The Fair Market Rental Value of Apartment No. _____ that you will occupy is $_____ per month. In addition, the utilities have a value of $_____ per month. Therefore, the total Fair Market Value of this apartment is $_____. The law requires that when lodging is furnished by the employer as part of the minimum wage, it may not be valued in excess of the following: "two-thirds ($\frac{2}{3}$) of the ordinary rental value and in no event more than $140 per month if only an individual is hired. When a couple are both employed by the employer, in no event more than $210 per month." (If a couple is hired, the apartment allowance can be divided between them.)

Apartment Allowance:

$_____ x $\frac{2}{3}$ = $_____
Fair Market Value   Value To Be Used in Establishing
(Including Utilities)   Hourly Wage

Monthly Wages:

In calculating the total hourly payroll rate:

Total monthly salary $_____(subject to appropriate taxes)
Add apartment allowance value _____
Total monthly wages $_____

$_____ x ___12___ ÷ ___52___ = $_____
Total Monthly Wages Months Per Year Weeks Per Year Weekly Salary

As additional information, your payroll checks will show the following apartment allowance deduction:

$_____ x ___12___ ÷ ___26___ = $_____
Apartment Allowance Months Per Year Pay Periods Payroll Deduction
                                                    Per Check

Weekly Hours and Inconvenience Time:

Hours to be worked per week:

Inconvenience time should be allocated for at least ½ hour per working day per person; and, if the inconvenience time is in excess of 40 hours per week, the employee should be paid these hours at a time and one-half rate.

_____ x 1½ = 4½ + _____ = _____
Inconvenience Hours   Weekly Hours   Total Weekly Hours

Hourly Rate:

$_____ ÷ _____ = $_____
Total Weekly Salary Total Weekly Hours Hourly Rate

(Hourly rate must be equal to or greater than $2.90 per hour as of January 1, 1979.)

Figure A.16 (continued). Computation form for explaining resident manager employment agreement.

Glossary

Abatement A reduction of rent, interest, or other amount due.

Absorption rate The rate at which a market can absorb space designed for a specific use, i.e., office space.

Account A detailed statement of receipts and payments of money.

Accountant A person trained in accounting, either employed by a firm or working independently.

Accounting The theory and system of establishing the books of a business organization and classifying, recording, and summarizing financial transactions and interpreting the results.

Accounts payable Monies due to others for services rendered or goods ordered and received.

Accounts receivable Monies due from others for services rendered or goods ordered and delivered.

ACCREDITED MANAGEMENT ORGANIZATION® (AMO®) A designation conferred by the Institute of Real Estate Management to real estate management firms that are under the direction of a CERTIFIED PROPERTY MANAGER® and comply with stipulated requirements as to accounting procedures, performance, and protection of funds entrusted to them.

Accrual basis accounting Method of recording expenses incurred and income due in the periods to which they relate rather than recording actual flow of cash.

Achievement Successful accomplishment, especially of a challenging assignment and by means of skill and perseverance.

Actual fraud Intentional misrepresentation of a material fact in order to induce another person to act on it and consequently to part with property or value or surrender some legal right.

Adjusted gross rental income Scheduled gross rental income minus vacancy factor and bad debts; also *effective gross rental income.*

Administration Executive management and direction.

Administrative assistant Someone who assists a property manager or property supervisor by assuming responsibility for certain specified operational details.

Advertisement An individual notice designed to attract public attention; also *ad.*

Advertising. The placing of paid public presentations or announcements about a product, service, or activity, with the objective of persuading the public to buy that good or service or accept a certain point of view or concept.

Agency management Management by an agency, authorized to do so, of property owned by another.

Agent The person who is authorized by another to act for him within the limits of that authority.

Agreement A document that expresses assent between two or more parties.

All-risk insurance Policy under which a loss resulting from any cause other than those causes specifically excluded by name is considered to be covered.

Amenities Features of a property that render it more useful and/or attractive, such as a swimming pool, scenic beauty, etc.

Amortization Of assets, a method of gradually reducing the book value of a fixed asset by spreading its depreciation over a period of time; of debt, a method of gradually retiring an obligation by making regular payments of both principal and interest over a period of time.

Annual budget A 12-month estimate of income and expenses for a mature property.

Annual report A formal financial statement, issued once a year by a corporation to shareholders, listing assets, liabilities, and earnings and indicating the company's standing and profits at the end of the business year.

Annual statement A fully detailed and annotated statement of all income and expense items covering a 12-month period of operation of an individual property.

Antidiscrimination laws Statutes that provide for civil action against persons conducting business establishments by aggrieved persons claiming discrimination on account of color, race, religion, ancestry, national origin, or sex.

Apartment   Residential unit.

Apartment building   A building designed for the separate housing of two or more families; also *apartment house, complex,* or *project.*

Appreciation   An increase in the value of property.

Articles of incorporation   Certificate by which a corporation formally comes into existence; also *corporate charter.*

Asset   Any physical property or right that is owned and has a monetary value, generally appearing as one of the major categories on the financial balance sheet.

Asset management   A sophisticated form of property management under which the managing agent organizes, operates, and assumes the risk of the total real estate business venture and whose concern extends beyond net operating income.

Attachment   The legal seizure of property or rights as a safeguard for possible satisfaction of a legal judgment.

Attorneyship-in-fact agency   An agency in which the agent is authorized to perform a business transaction that is legally binding upon the principal.

Audit   An inspection of accounting records and procedures conducted by a trained person to check their accuracy, completeness, and reliability.

Auditor   A person trained to conduct an audit.

Authority   Power or right conferred on a person.

Balance sheet   Statement of the financial position of a business firm at a particular time, indicating its assets, liabilities, and owner equity.

Bank debits   The total of checks and other instruments charged to the accounts of a bank's depositors.

Bank failure   The inability of a bank to honor the withdrawals of its depositors.

Bankruptcy   The legal proceeding whereby the affairs of a person or business unable to meet its obligations are turned over to a receiver or trustee in accordance, in the U.S., with the bankruptcy act.

Base period   In constructing an index number, a selected period of time, frequently one year, against which changes in other years are calculated.

Basis point   A unit of measure for the change in interest rates for bonds and notes.

Batch processing   A form of data processing in which information is accumulated over a period of time before being loaded into a computer.

Beneficiary   The person who benefits from a trust fund, contract, will, or life insurance policy.

Betterment   Substantial improvement upon real property.

Blanket fidelity bond   Insurance to cover loss of money or real or personal property when such a loss is due to dishonesty of any employee of the company.

Blanket mortgage   A mortgage that encompasses more than one parcel of real estate.

Blanket policy   An insurance policy covering several kinds of property at one location or one kind of property at several locations.

Board of directors   The persons elected by the shareholders of a corporation to set company policy.

Bodily injury liability insurance   Protection against loss arising out of insured's legal responsibility and as a result of injury, illness or disease, mental damage, loss of service, or death of another person.

Bond   A promissory note from a corporation that is evidence of a debt, usually of relatively long term, on which the issuer (borrower) usually promises to pay a specified amount of interest for a specific period of time and to repay the principal on the date of expiration or maturity date.

Bonus   Any compensation to an employee over and above his regular wage or salary.

Bookkeeping   Maintaining the financial records of a business by recording all transactions in which it engages.

Bookkeeping unit   A cost accounting standard of measurement tied to a specified number of bookkeeping entries.

Book value   The amount an asset or group of assets is said to be worth in the books of account, which may differ from market or intrinsic value.

Break-even analysis   An investigation, useful in pricing strategy, of how changes in volume of production affect costs and profit.

Brochure   A pamphlet designed to provide, via illustrations and narrative, complete information on a specific subject.

Broker   A person who, for compensation, acts for another in a real estate or related transaction.

Budget   An itemized estimate of income and expenses for a given period of time in the future.

Building code A set of rules and specifications established by local government authorities for the construction of buildings or other permanent structures.

Business cycle A pattern of periodic fluctuation in economic activity, characterized by alternate expansion and contraction.

Business interruption insurance Form of property insurance that provides against loss of prospective earnings if business is interrupted because of fire or other peril.

Cancellation Termination before the time of expiration.

Capital The total assets of a firm; any form of wealth capable of being used to create more wealth.

Capital asset An asset needed to create a product or service, normally acquired with the intention of being kept rather than being resold.

Capital budget A long-range financial plan for acquiring and financing capital assets.

Capital expense A major one-time cost representing the purchase price of a capital asset.

Capital gain A profit from the sale of a capital asset.

Capitalization The treatment of future income as though it were part of the firm's capital; the process employed in estimating the value of a property by the use of a property investment rate of return and the annual net income expected to be produced by the property, the formula being expressed as: Income ÷ Rate = Value.

Capitalization rate The percentage used to determine the value of income property through capitalization.

Capitalized value The value of assets in terms of their expected future earnings.

Cash An accounting category made up of currency, negotiable money orders, checks, and demand deposits.

Cash-basis accounting A system of recording income and expenses when cash is actually received or paid out and without regard to when it was earned or incurred.

Cash flow The amount of cash available after all payments have been made for operating expenses and mortgage principal and interest.

Cash flow budget Monthly or other projection of a company's cash position.

Cash flow statement Financial statement of all income and expenses and consequent actual cash flow for a given period of time.

Central business district Downtown area of a major city.

CERTIFIED PROPERTY MANAGER (CPM®) The professional designation conferred by the Institute of Real Estate Management on individuals who distinguish themselves in the areas of education, experience and ethics.

Certified public accountant (CPA) An accountant with a state license indicating that he meets certain requirements for the public practice of accounting.

Chain store One of a group similar centrally-owned retail stores that have centralized control over their operations.

Chart of accounts A systematic classification or arrangement of account items.

Chattel mortgage A mortgage on moveable personal property.

Chicago Agreement A document prepared in 1926 that provided regulations for the mortgage bond industry.

Classified advertisement A form of advertising usually relegated to special sections of newspapers and magazines consisting of a brief announcement.

Client One who hires another person as his representative or agent and agrees to pay his fee.

Code Collection of laws, rules, or regulations.

Coinsurance A requirement that the insured, in order to purchase insurance at a preferred rate, carries at least a specified proportion of insurance to the value of the property at the time of loss; if there is failure to do so, the insured will not collect in full for partial losses and becomes a coinsurer in proportion to the amount carried in relation to the amount required.

Collateral Security, which has monetary value and usually is readily convertible into cash, that is deposited with a creditor as a pledge for repayment of a loan.

Collateral trust certificate A bond secured by collateral deposited with a trustee.

Collection A sum of money collected, such as rentals.

Commercial paper Short-term promissory notes of highly reputable business firms.

Commercial property Real property used for the conduct of retail or service business that invites public patronage by display of signs, merchandising, advertising, and other stimulants for public participation.

Commingling The illegal act of a real estate agent in mixing the money of other people, i.e., clients, with his own.

Commission A fee paid to an agent or broker for negotiating a sale; a wage incentive that rewards for the amount of responsibility assumed and the level of productivity achieved.

Community shopping center Type of shopping center that covers approximately 150,000 to 300,000 square feet, serves a population of 25,000 to 100,000, and houses department stores and local merchants.

Company An association of individuals for the purpose of carrying on some joint business or enterprise, whether incorporated or not.

Compensating balance The balance a borrower must keep on deposit in a bank, representing a given percentage of the loan.

Competition A state of rivalry among sellers, each of whom is trying to gain a larger share of the market and greater profits.

Compound interest Interest charge computed by applying the percentage rate of interest not only to the principal but also to successive increments of simple interest, i.e., interest upon interest.

Computer An automatic, high-speed calculating machine that accurately performs a variety of mathematical computations by reducing them to arithmetical operations by means of electronic devices, has the ability to be programmed to perform limitless sequences of operations, and is capable of storing and retrieving enormous amounts of data.

Condemnation Taking private property for public use; officially terminating the use of real property for nonconformance with governmental regulations or because of the existance of hazards to public health and safety.

Condominium The absolute ownership of an apartment or unit, generally in a multi-unit building, by a legal description of the air space the unit actually occupies, plus an undivided interest in the common elements that are owned jointly with the other condominium unit owners.

Condominium association Private, automatic, usually nonprofit organization responsible for the operation of the condominium community; also *homeowners' association (HOA)*.

Constant A percentage derived by dividing the annual principal and interest payment by the original amount of the loan; also *loan constant*.

Constructive fraud Any breach of duty, trust, or confidence that, without fraudulent intent, gains an advantage to the person in fault or one claiming under him by misleading another, or any act or omission that the law specifically declares to be fraudulent without regard to actual fraud.

Consumer good   A product used directly to satisfy human needs or desires.

Consumer price index   A figure constructed monthly by the U.S. Bureau of Labor Statistics that weighs products by their importance and compares prices to those of a selected base year, expressing current prices as a percentage of prices in the base year; formerly *cost-of-living index.*

Contract   An agreement entered into by two or more legally competent parties under which one or more of the parties, for a consideration, undertakes to do or refrain from doing some act.

Contributed capital   Actual money invested in a firm by the owners for use in conducting business.

Control   Exercise that regulates and guides operations of business, guaranteeing that all is proceeding as intended.

Controller   Chief accountant of an organization who is responsible for instituting and operating a system of accounts and external financial reports, preparing and filing tax returns, countersigning checks and preparing and implementing the budget, and often supervising office administration; also *comptroller.*

Conventional mortgage   A mortgage loan that is not insured or guaranteed by a governmental agency.

Cooperative   A residential multidwelling building with title in a corporation that is owned by and operated for the benefit of persons living within, each possessing a proprietory lease and each a stockholder owner.

Corporate income tax   Tax levied by the federal government and most states on the annual net earnings of a corporation.

Corporation   A form of business organization created by statute law and consisting of owners who are regarded legally as a single entity.

Cost   Any expenditure of money, goods, or services for the purpose of acquiring goods or services.

Cost accounting   A branch of accounting concerned with the collection, determination, and control of the costs of producing a particular product or service.

Cost-benefit analysis   A systematic technique for judging alternative ways of trying to achieve the same objective by comparing costs and benefits of each alternative.

Cost center   Any department, process, or other element of a firm for which cost records are maintained and to which fixed costs, along with direct labor and material costs, may be allocated.

Cost of living The money cost of maintaining a particular standard of living in terms of purchased goods and services.

Cost-plus pricing A common method of setting prices by determining the cost of providing the good or service to which is added a percentage to cover expenses and profits.

Credit bureau A firm specializing in investigating consumers' credit ratings.

Credit rating Evaluation of the financial trustworthiness of a company or individual, particularly with regard to meeting obligations.

Curable obsolescence A loss in value caused by a property becoming outmoded that can be remedied.

Current asset An asset that can be readily converted into cash, sold, or consumed in the near future through normal business operations.

Current liability A liability expected to be satisfied within a relatively short period of time.

Cyclical fluctations Regular changes in the business cycle characterized by fluctations in employment, money income, and output, especially of capital goods.

Cyclical industry An industry whose sales and profits are greatly affected by and reflect the ups and downs of business cycles.

Damages Legal compensation for loss or injury.

Data Known available information, including facts and figures; information that is to be processed in a computer program.

Data processing The gathering, interpreting, and transmitting of data for reference and as the basis for decision making; also *electronic data processing (EDP)*.

Debt Money, goods, or services owed by one person or organization to another.

Debt service Principal and interest payments on a mortgage.

Decentralization Reorganization of a company into numerous autonomous companies that remain under central control; principle of establishing a business where it is most appropriate.

Deductible coverage An insurance clause providing that the insured will assume any losses below a specified amount.

Deduction Any expense or cost set off against revenue.

Default Nonperformance of a duty or failure to meet an obligation when it is due.

Deferred compensation	Income postponed until a later time, usually upon retirement.

Deferred maintenance	Ordinary maintenance of a property that has not been performed and which noticeably affects the use, occupancy, welfare, and value of the property.

Deflation	Abnormal decline in the general price level owing to a decrease in total spending relative to the supply of goods on the market.

Delegation	Assignment of a task and related responsibility.

Delinquency	An overdue debt, such as rent not paid when due.

Demographics	Characteristics and vital statistics of human populations.

Demotion	A lowering in job rank.

Deposit	A credit to an individual's or firm's bank account.

Depreciation	Any decline in the value of a physical asset, usually resulting from physical deterioration (ordinary wear and tear), functional depreciation, and economic obsolescence; the process of gradually converting a fixed asset into an expense.

Depreciation reserve	A series of credits on the asset side of the balance sheet that show the reduced value of a fixed asset.

Depression	A prolonged period in which business activity is at a very low point.

Developmental objective	Goal designed to improve employee performance and prepare an employee for promotion.

Developer	A person who organizes and supervises the construction of improvements on land, often on a speculative basis.

Direct mail	A form of advertising through letters, cards, brochures, etc., sent by mail to potential customers and which relies heavily on specialized mailing lists.

Disbursement	An actual payment in cash or by check.

Discount	Reduction in price, usually as a reward for paying a charge prior to the date of delinquency, buying in quantity, or taking some advantage.

Display advertisement	A large paid notice designed to attract the public's attention and which usually has a border and includes artwork.

Distressed property	Income property that yields an insufficient return or is in difficulty for other reasons.

Diversification	Expansion of the scope of business activity, usually into related areas of business.

Dividend	The part of a corporation's profits that is distributed among the stockholders in proportion to their shares of ownership.

Double entry   A system of bookkeeping in which every transaction is recorded twice, representing a debt in one account and an equivalent credit in another and the net balance of accounts always equaling zero.

Downtime   A period when machinery equipment or employees are idle because of breakdowns, adjustments, etc.

Duly authorized   Properly authorized to act for another in accordance with legal requirements and in conformance with a written series of conditions and covenants.

Earnings   The operating profits of a business.

Economic   Pertaining to the economy; economically advantageous.

Economic alternatives   The determination of highest economic and most productive use after a study of alternative uses.

Economic life   The number of years during which a building will continue to produce a high net percentage yield.

Economic obsolescence   Impairment of desirability or useful life or loss in the use and value of property arising from economic forces, such as changes in optimum land use, legislative enactments that restrict or impair property rights, or changes in supply-demand relationships.

Economics   The science that deals with the production, distribution, exchange, and consumption of goods and services.

Economy   The management of resources.

Efficiency   Ratio of work done to energy expended.

Eminent domain   The right of a government body to acquire private property for public use through court action.

Employment agency   A firm in the business of finding jobs for persons seeking employment and employees to fill vacant positions.

Employment contract   A formal agreement between an employee and employer outlining conditions and terms of employment.

Empty nester   Someone whose children have left home permanently.

Endorsement   Signature placed on the back of a check transferring the amount of that instrument to someone else; a form attached to an insurance policy that includes alternatives to the original terms of the policy.

Energy conservation   Program of reducing energy waste.

Enhance   To improve value or benefit.

Entity   Something that has a real existence.

Entrepreneur One who undertakes and develops a new enterprise at some risk of failure or loss.

Environmental impact legislation Any of a series of laws aimed at regulating construction as it relates to its effects on the environment.

Equity The excess of a firm's assets over its liabilities; the interest or value an owner has in real estate over and above any mortgage on it.

Escalation clause Clause in a lease, contract, etc., providing for increases in wages, rent, interest, etc., based upon fluctuations in certain economic indexes, costs, or taxes.

Estimate Form an appropriate opinion; the opinion itself.

Ethics The rules of conduct or code of principles recognized in respect to a particular class of human actions.

Eviction Legal process to oust a person from possession of real estate.

Excess limits liability insurance Policy which pays, up to a maximum, liability claims against an insured but only to the extent that each claim exceeds some specified limit of primary insurance.

Executive search firm Employment agency specializing in professional and technical areas.

Expense Any kind of business cost.

Experience Observing, encountering, and performing things that occur in the normal process and course of time.

Expert A person who has special skill or knowledge in some particular field.

External recruitment Program of processing candidates for employment from sources outside of the existing staff.

Extra-expense insurance Insurance to provide for reimbursement expenses incurred in resuming business should full or partial destruction of the property in which business is located occur.

Federal Deposit Insurance Corporation (FDIC) An agency established to insure up to $40,000 on the individual deposits in all Federal Reserve member banks and in any state bank that qualifies for such insurance.

Federal Home Loan Bank System of 12 regional banks established in 1932 to provide a credit reserve for savings and home-financing institutions.

Federal Home Loan Mortgage Corporation (Freddie Mac) Agency created in 1970 to serve the savings and loan industry by making future commitments to buy mortgages at fixed rates.

Federal Housing Administration (FHA) Federal government agency created in 1934 whose chief function is to insure loans and mortgages issued by private lending institutions for the purchase of single-family dwellings, private residences, rental housing, cooperatives, condominiums, and mobile homes.

Federal land banks System of banks that grant long-term mortgage loans to farmers and ranchers for buying land, refinancing debts, or other general agricultural purposes.

Federal National Mortgage Association (Fannie Mae) A government-sponsored private corporation that buys mortgages from banks and other lending institutions and sells them to investors to create a fund for mortgage lending.

Federal Tax Act of 1954 Law that, among other things, encouraged investment in income properties by providing for greater depreciation deduction in early years, or adoption of the declining-balance method rather than the straight-line method.

Fee A payment for a service.

Fidelity bond Kind of insurance against an employer's loss of money or other property through dishonesty of an employee.

Fiduciary Relationship based on faith or confidence in which one person is entrusted to hold and manage money or property for another.

Financial accounting Technical aspects of collecting, recording, summarizing, and reporting financial data.

Financial analysis Projection of income and expenses, financing considerations, tax implementations, and value charged.

Financing Availability, quantity, and terms under which money may be borrowed to assist in the purchase of real property using the property itself as the sole security for such borrowings.

Fire and extended coverage insurance Property protection that covers loss by fire as well as perils of windstorm, hail, explosion, riot attending a strike, civil commotion, aircraft, vehicles, and smoke.

Fire insurance Insurance on property against all direct loss or damage caused by fire.

First mortgage A mortgage that has priority as lien over all other mortgages.

Fiscal year Any 12-month accounting period ending with a date other than December 31.

Fixed assets Assets of a relatively permanent nature, not intended for resale within the regular operation of the enterprise.

Fixed expense Cost that remains relatively stable.

Fixture Article that has been installed in or attached to a building or land in a more or less permanent way so that legally it is considered part of the real estate.

Flat fee A uniform rate charged for service.

Flow chart Graph that illustrates the movement of money, credit, goods, documents, or some other element or function through various critical stages.

Foreclosure A court action initiated by the mortgagee for the purpose of having the court order the debtor's real estate sold to pay the mortgage.

Form Printed piece of paper that provides space for inserting certain information that is to be conveyed to other persons.

Fraud Intentional deception practiced in order to secure unlawful gain.

Free enterprise An economic and political doctrine holding that a capitalist economy can regulate itself in a freely competitive market through the relationship of supply and demand and with a minimum of government intervention.

Fringe benefits Extra compensation to an employee with payments by an employer on behalf of an employee that accrue to his benefit but are not direct cash remuneration; i.e., pension plans, hospitalization provisions, vacations, etc.

Funding Providing money to finance a particular project.

General partner A co-owner of a partnership who is able to enter into contracts on behalf of the partnership and is fully liable for debts of the partnership; in a limited partnership, the individual or firm who manages the limited partnership and is its fiduciary.

General partnership The business activity of two or more persons who agree to pool capital, talents, and other assets according to some agreed-to formula and similarly to divide profits and losses and to commit the partnership to certain obligations.

Goal The purpose toward which an endeavor is directed.

Goodwill An intangible business asset arising from a firm's high reputation, good relations with customers and suppliers, favorable location, etc.; an intangible asset for which a specific sum is paid.

Government National Mortgage Association (Ginnie Mae) A federal government-owned corporation formed in 1968 in order to invest in mortgages not suitable for the private Federal National Mortgage Association, such as those for government-subsidized housing.

Graduated rent Rental payments that begin at a low fixed rate and increase at set intervals as the lease term matures.

Great Depression The slump in the business cycle that began in 1929 and continued until 1933, during which private capital investment came to a virtual standstill and consumer expenditures declined by nearly one-half.

Gross collections All monies paid by tenants less refunds to tenants of security deposits or other advance fees.

Gross income The total monthly or annual revenue from all sources before any deductions, allowances, or charges.

Gross possible income The total monthly or annual possible income before uncollected income is deducted.

Group insurance An insurance plan subscribed to by an employer or professional organization for various kinds of insurance, usually life and health insurance.

Guarantee A warranty or formal assurance.

Habit An action that becomes permanent by persistent repetition.

Hand-posted bookkeeping system A manual method of maintaining financial records.

Hardware The electrical, electronic, and mechanical devices that make up a computer.

Hazard In insurance, a cause of probable loss; also *peril.*

Health insurance An insurance program covering medical expenses and/or income lost owing to illness or accidental injury.

Highest and best use The most productive use to which real property may be put for the most desirable period of time considering all economic quantities.

High-rise A building with 10 or more stories.

Hold harmless Declaring that one is not liable for things beyond one's control.

Home Loan Bank Act An act passed in 1932 that was authorized to create eight to 12 Home Loan Banks to extend emergency credit to homeowners.

Homeowners Loan Corporation (HOLC) Established in 1933 as a home rescue agency to provide for direct refinancing of home mortgages during a national crisis.

Housing act Any one of several laws passed by the U.S. Congress creating programs and procedures for federal assistance in the creation and improvement of residential facilities for U.S. residents.

Housing and Reconstruction Act A federal enactment passed in 1947 that freed construction from wartime controls, including rent controls.

Housing reform A movement to improve housing conditions.

Hundred-percent location The site in a downtown business district that commands the highest land value and rental rate and reflects highest desired traffic count.

Hygiene factors Motivators that are expected and noticed only in their absence.

Improvement Something done or added to real property in order to increase its value.

Incentive A payment that is tied directly to standards of productivity and represents a financial inducement to perform.

Incentive fee Type of management fee tied to level of productivity.

Income The returns that come in periodically from all sources.

Income accumulation Maintaining corporate earnings rather than distributing them as dividends.

Income approach The process of estimating the value of an income-producing property by capitalization of the annual net income expected to be produced by the property during its remaining useful life.

Income property Property that produces an income, i.e., that is leased or rented.

Income tax Tax levied on the annual incomes of households and unincorporated businesses after certain deductions and exemptions have been taken into account.

Incorporation The legal forming of a corporation via charter from a state.

Indemnification The act of promising to make good or secure against a foreseeable loss or damage.

Independent contractor A person, not an employee, who contracts to do a piece of work for another by using his own methods and without being under the control of the other person regarding how the work should be done.

Indirect loss An insurable loss not resulting immediately from property damage or destruction but consequent to such damage or destruction.

Industrialization The development of industry, considered by most economists essential for economic growth and prosperity.

Industrial park A controlled parklike development designed to accommodate specific types of industry and providing public utilities, streets, etc.

Industrial psychology Application of science of human behavior to personnel-related matters.

Industrial relations A broad term for all relations between management and individual employee groups concerning conditions and terms of employment.

Industry A specific branch of business activity in which a number of firms produce the same kind of commodity or service or are engaged in the same kind of operation.

Inflation Undue increase in the currency of the country with resultant decrease in the worth of the unit of that currency and generally associated with rising wages and costs, large money supply and decrease in purchasing power.

Innovation The practical application of a new product, service, or method following its original invention and representing an improvement important to economic growth.

Innovative objectives Goals that deal with new things to do and new ways of doing things.

Installment purchase Buying consumer goods, usually relatively expensive ones, and paying for them plus carrying charges over a period of time in periodic partial payments; also *buying on time.*

Institute of Real Estate Management (IREM) A professional association affiliated with the NATIONAL ASSOCIATION OF REALTORS® for persons who meet professional standards of experience, education, and ethics with the objective of continually improving their respective managerial skills by mutual education and exchange of ideas and experiences.

Insurance An agreement whereby one party promises to pay a sum of money to another if the latter suffers a particular loss in exchange for a premium paid by the insured.

Insured The person who receives the promise; also *policyholder.*

Insurer The person or firm who undertakes the risk; also *underwriter.*

Integrity Moral soundness in business dealings that tests steadfastness to truth, purpose, responsibility, and trust.

Interest The charge, usually quoted as an annual percentage, for borrowing money.

Interest rate The price of borrowing money.

Internal audit Internal system by which assets and resources are safeguarded from misuse or waste, accuracy and reliability of accounting data is judged, efficiency of property operations is verified, and compliance with established procedures is tested.

Internal recruitment Program of procuring job candidates from among existing personnel.

Internal Revenue Service (IRS) The federal agency that administers and enforces most U.S. tax laws.

Inventory Materials owned and held by a business firm; a detailed list of such items showing the value of each.

Investment Purchase of some form of property that will be held for a relatively long period of time, during which it is expected to increase in value.

Investment trust A company or trust formed for the purpose of pooling the members' resources to invest in other companies with participants sharing in the profits or income in proportion to their trust shares or cash invested.

Invoice An itemized bill for goods delivered to a buyer.

Job description A listing of regular and ongoing tasks to be performed by the person occupying a given position and assignment of parameters of responsibility and authority.

Job-order costing System of cost accounting in which costs are collected separately for each job or order accepted.

Job specification List of required and desirable criteria for a given position.

Journal An accounting book in which original entries concerning transactions are recorded and from which they are later transferred to the appropriate ledger accounts.

Keynesian economics A theory, based upon the concept that propensity to consume is related to income, which theorizes that the economy can be controlled through appropriate government programs.

Keypunch A computer operation whereby holes representing characters, digits, etc., are punched into data processing cards as information that is fed into computers for classification and storage.

Labor   The human effort expended to produce income.

Labor cost   The total salaries and wages paid to workers.

Labor relations   Relations and transactions between employers and groups of employees concerning job terms and conditions.

Labor turnover   An estimate of the number of employees who are likely to leave a company based upon evaluation of past trends.

Landlord   One who owns property and leases it to a tenant.

Lease   A contract granting possession and use of property in return for rent or some other compensation.

Lease conditions   The provisions setting forth the agreed privileges, obligations, and restrictions under which a lease is made; also *lease terms*.

Leasehold   Land held under a lease.

Ledger   The final accounting book of entry for recording a business's financial transactions.

Legal description   The description of real property used to identify it in legal instruments setting its dimensions, metes and bounds, or other definite identification in accordance with the description recorded in official governmental records.

Leverage   Use of borrowed funds to purchase investment property with expectation that investor will realize a profit not only on the investment but also on the borrowed funds.

Liability   An accounting debt owed by a business or individual; legally, a required obligation or responsibility from which a claim against an individual or business may arise.

Liability insurance   Insurance arising out of insured's legal responsibility and resulting from injuries to other persons or damage to their property.

Libel   Defamation that maliciously or damagingly misrepresents by written or printed words.

License   A form of permission granted by a government or other authority to engage in some activity that is regulated by law.

Lien   A claim or attachment enforceable by law to have a debt or other charge satisfied out of the debtor's property, usually by selling it.

Life insurance   A kind of financial protection that involves death benefits for a deceased person's survivors or enforced savings to build a reserve of funds, especially for old age.

Limited liability   Responsibility for the debts of a business that is restricted to the size of one's investment in it.

Limited partner   A partner in a business who by agreement shares in the profits of that business but is not liable for any portion of any net losses or other obligations of the business beyond his original investment.

Limited partnership A business arrangement that limits certain of the partners' liability to the amount invested and also limits the profit they can make.

Liquid asset An asset that is readily convertible into cash or consists of cash.

Liquidity The ease with which a person, firm, or organization can meet its obligations without selling fixed assets.

Loan A sum of money borrowed at interest for a specific period of time with the promise of repayment.

Loan payment The payment of an installment on the principal balance plus accrued interest on the entire unpaid balance.

Loan payment cost The cost paid by the borrower for securing a loan.

Logo A trademark or company name or other identifying device.

Long-range plan Formal written statement that details beforehand the means of accomplishment of an objective; also *strategic plan.*

Long-term liabilities Liabilities whose maturity dates are more than a year from the date on the balance sheet.

Loss In accounting, any excess of costs over income; in insurance, the basis of a valid claim for damages or indemnity under the terms of a given policy.

Loss leader An item sold very cheaply to attract customers to a store in the hope that they will buy more profitable items as well.

Low-rise A building containing five stories or less.

Machine-operated bookkeeping system Method of maintaining records of financial transactions via use of a mechanical system or machine.

Maintenance Care and work needed to keep a property in good physical and operating condition and appearance.

Malpractice Failure of a professional to provide proper services as a result of ignorance, negligence, or criminal intent.

Management The job of planning, organizing, and controlling a business enterprise; the persons in an organization who are engaged in management.

Management agreement A contract between the owner of a property and the designated managing agent that describes the duties and establishes powers, rights, responsibilities, and obligations of the parties thereto.

Management by crisis   A system of management in which there is little or no planning and attention is directed to sudden, unstable situations on an individual basis.

Management by exception   A system of management control in which attention is warranted when any exception to that which is expected is noted.

Management by objectives (MBO)   A system of organizing work and setting objectives in an attempt to motivate workers to a higher level of performance.

Management fee   Monetary consideration paid monthly or otherwise for the performance of management duties.

Management firm   A real estate organization that specializes in the professional management of real properties for others as a gainful occupation.

Management information system   A program whereby top management obtains the information, both physical and financial, it needs to make decisions.

Management plan   The fundamental document for the short-term operation of a property that represents a statement of facts, objectives, and policies and details how the property is to be operated during the coming year; usually includes the annual budget.

Management records   Historical and accounting documents designed for the interpretation and understanding of the physical and financial welfare of a managed property.

Management survey   A detailed expert analysis of the physical condition, income, expenses, operating procedures, trends, and other factors that affect the highest and most productive use of a property.

Managerial accounting   The use of accounting information and analysis for managerial decision making.

Managing agent   An agent duly appointed to direct and control all matters pertaining to a property that is owned or controlled by another.

Man-hour   A unit of measure to estimate labor cost, productivity, etc.

Market analysis   A determination of the characteristics, purchasing power, and habits of a given segment of the population.

Marketing   All business activity involved in moving goods and services from producers to consumers.

Marketing plan   Short-term business tool to generate profits by increasing business.

Marketing strategy Plan of action for meeting marketing objectives.

Market rate of interest The interest rate determined by the supply of money available for lending and the demand by those wishing to borrow it for capital investment.

Market survey A detailed and comprehensive inspection for a given market which provides market research data.

Medical payments insurance Form of insurance whereby the insurer promises to pay medical expenses incurred by persons injured through some hazard described in the policy even though the insured may not be liable.

Merchandising An aspect of marketing that involves advertising, promoting, and organizing the sale of a particular product or service.

Minimum fee The lowest fee for which service can be provided while maintaining a profit margin.

Minimum wage The lowest hourly wage rate permitted either by state or federal law or a labor contract.

Mission The statement of purpose, as expressed in a plan.

Money and securities insurance Form of insurance coverage whereby the insurer provides protection against losses of money and securities occasioned by dishonest acts of nonemployees.

Mortgage A legal agreement that pledges real property as security for the payment of a debt.

Mortgagee The lender in a mortgage loan transaction.

Mortgage lien The claim on real estate given to the mortgagee when the mortgagor executes a mortgage or trust deed to secure his note.

Mortgage loan insurance A program for insuring mortgages and loans made by private lending institutions for the purchase, construction, rehabilitation, repair, and improvements of single-family and multifamily housing.

Mortgage market The demand for and supply of mortgages; those seeking to borrow mortgage funds and lenders willing to invest in mortgages.

Mortgagor The borrower; the owner of the real estate who conveys his property as a security for the loan.

Motion study A detailed analysis of any industrial operation in terms of every hand and body movement used in its performance.

Motivation A stimulation or incentive to action.

Motivator That which serves as an incentive to action.

NATIONAL ASSOCIATION OF REALTORS® National nonprofit corporation whose membership is composed principally of local members in subscribing local real estate boards throughout the United States and which is dedicated to the highest principles and performance by real estate license members; founded in 1909 as the National Association of Real Estate Exchanges, later known as the National Association of Real Estate Boards.

National Environmental Policy Act (NEPA) A law passed in 1969 that requires federal agencies to file environmental impact statements on all federally funded projects.

National Environmental Protection Act Law that requires an analysis of a building's impact on the total environment before development can proceed.

National Register of Historic Places Federal agency established to record and preserve buildings of architectural and historic significance.

Neighborhood A district or locality, often defined in reference to its character or inhabitants; a limited area as to size and used for residential, commercial, or other purposes or a combination of such uses integrated into an accepted pattern.

Neighborhood shopping center Retail area of from 50 to 150,000 square feet of gross leasable area serving an immediate neighborhood population of approximately 10,000 to 25,000 and usually containing a supermarket and several local merchants offering convenience goods and services.

Negligence Failure to exercise reasonable care which, though not accompanied by harmful intent, directly results in an injury to an innocent party.

Negotiation Dealings between two parties—buyer and seller—in order to reach an agreement on price, quantity, quality, payment, or other conditions of the sale or agreement.

Net income The difference between total sales and total expenses over a given period, usually one year; the earnings produced during a current period of operation.

Net operating income Cash available from collected rental income after all operating expenses have been deducted and before capital expenses and debt service have been deducted; also *net prior to debt service (NPDS)*.

Net profit Remainder after deduction of business operation expenses from sales income for a given period.

Net rental area   Actual square footage of a building that can be rented.

Net taxable profit   Corporate income subject to federal corporate income tax.

Net worth   The excess of assets over liabilities, which represents the equity of the owners.

Nonowned automobile insurance   Insurance that would cover exposure of employees who use their own cars on company business.

Notes payable   The amount owed by a business to lenders in the form of short-term loans.

Notes receivable   The amount owed to a business on promissory notes from customers and other debtors.

NSF check   A check drawn on a bank account that does not contain enough cash to cover the check; also *insufficient funds*.

Objective   A quantitatively defined goal toward which an effort is directed.

Obligation   In accounting, any form of indebtedness.

Obsolescence   A loss in value brought about by a change in design, technology, taste, or demand.

Occupancy report   Statement on the number of units in a building occupied and, consequently, the vacancy factor.

Occupational hazard   Any danger of accident or disease directly associated with performing a particular kind of work.

Occupational Safety and Health Act (OSHA)   Law, passed in 1970, that set up an independent U.S. government agency to reduce occupational hazards by requiring employers to comply with certain job safety and health standards.

Office building   A single- or multistory building designed for the conduct of business, generally divided into individual offices and offering space for rent or lease.

Office of Price Administration (OPA)   Executive agency created in 1941 that was given statutory power to control prices and rents and establish penalties for violations.

Office park   A controlled parklike development composed of office buildings and providing public transportation, streets, etc.

On-the-job training   Learning how to perform a given kind of work while actually employed to do it.

Operating budget   Estimate of income and expenses required to maintain a property or business and keep it productive of its services for a given period, usually one year.

Operating expense   Periodic and necessary expenses essential to the operation and maintenance of a property or enterprise.

Operating profit   Earnings from regular business operations exclusive of revenues from other supplementary sources.

Operating ratio   A way of measuring success by performing calculations of various income statement items in some way.

Operations manual   A guidebook that contains all necessary information, instructions, policies, procedures, and forms for performing a job; also *standard operating procedures manual.*

Opportunity   Favorable or advantageous combination of circumstances.

Organization   The apportionment of authority and responsibility among the employees of a business.

Organizational authority   The right of one person to require another to fulfill specific duties because of rank and position within the company organization.

Organization chart   Graphic depiction of levels of employee responsibility.

Overdraft   The amount by which a check exceeds the funds on deposit.

Overhead   A general item for all business costs that are neither direct labor or material; indirect costs.

Owners equity   Owners' share of an enterprise; also *stockholders equity.*

Ownership   Legal right of possession.

Owners', landlords' and tenants' public liability insurance   Form of insurance whereby the insurer promises to pay claims against a property owner, landlord, or tenant arising from personal injury to a person at a subject property and including any improvements and any other contiguous areas for which the insured is legally responsible.

Paid-in surplus   Capital that is contributed by stockholders over and above the par value of the stock; also *capital surplus.*

Partnership   Form of business organization formed by agreement in which two or more enter into business as co-owners to share in profits and losses.

Payroll   Total amount owed by business to employees for work performed during a given period.

Penalty   Loss or forfeiture imposed for failure to fulfill obligation to another.

Pension fund   Fund into which allowance or other regular payment is made by an employer and/or employee to provide means of payments to employee upon retirement.

Percentage fee   Regular compensation based on a given percentage of monthly gross collections.

Percentage lease   A contract, usually negotiated in connection with retail property, whereby all or part of the rent is based on a percentage of the tenant's yield from the property.

Per diem   Allowance, payment, charge, or rental established on a daily basis.

Performance appraisal   Formal evaluation of an employee's fulfillment of duty.

Performance contract   A statement of written objectives agreed to by a superior and subordinate and designed to improve the subordinate's level of performance.

Personal injury   False arrest, libel and slander, wrongful entry.

Personal injury liability insurance   Insurance against loss arising out of personal insults, such as slander, libel, or false arrest, allegedly delivered by the insured.

Personal property   Any property other than real property that is moveable and not permanently affixed to real property.

Personnel management   Managing an organization's employees, including recruiting, selecting, training, supervising, motivating, and discharging in an orderly fashion.

Policy   A statement of general intent that tells what is permitted or expected; in insurance, an insurance contract.

Population   Total of all individuals in a fixed or stipulated geographical area.

Population movement   Shifting of a large number of people from one place to another over a period of time.

Premium   The sum of money the policyholder agrees to pay the insurer for an insurance policy.

Prepaid expense   An expense incurred for future benefit, or paid before it is currently due.

Press release   An announcement of news or a publicity item issued to the press.

Preventive maintenance   Keeping property and equipment in good repair so as to minimize the need for costly major repair work or replacement.

Price   The exchange value of a good or service at a particular time as expressed in terms of money.

Price-earnings ratio The current market price of a share of stock divided by the issuing company's earnings per share for a 12-month period.

Pricing The system of setting a price.

Prime rate The interest rate charge by commercial banks for short-term loans to corporations whose credit standing is so high that little lender risk is involved.

Principal In finance, the original amount of capital invested; in law, the individual being represented in a business transaction by an agent authorized to do so.

Procedure Specific series of related, chronological steps that are adopted as the accepted way of performing a given activity or function.

Product liability insurance Insurance protection against claims that result from alleged injury from products improperly made, labeled, or packaged.

Profession An occupation that requires considerable education and specialized training.

Professional liability insurance Insurance against a monetary loss caused by failure to meet a professional standard or for negligent actions.

Profit Any excess of revenues over the costs incurred to obtain those revenues; the surplus earned above the normal return on investment of capital in a business, created when the price received for a good or service exceeds the cost of producing it.

Profit and loss statement A summary of the revenues and expenses of a business firm or other organization for a particular period of time, generally one year; also *operating statement.*

Profit margin Gross profit expressed as a percentage of net sales.

Profit sharing The practice of distributing some of a firm's profits to some or all of its employees as a kind of bonus and in addition to regular wages and salaries.

Pro forma An unofficial financial statement that treats hypothetical events as though they actually had occurred.

Program A sequence of instruction for achieving a specific outcome; in computer technology, the process of producing a sequence of instructions which, when carried on a computer, results in specific data-processing results.

Promotion The overall activity of furthering or advancing a business, particularly through increasing the sales of its services and products; appointment to a position of higher rank.

Property analysis   In-depth investigation of the various characteristics, i.e., financial, physical, etc., of a property.

Property damage liability insurance   Insurance against liability for damage to property of others that may result from occurrences in or about a specified property or for which the insured is legally liable.

Property insurance   Any insurance that protects against loss of or damage to real or personal property.

Property management   A professional activity in which someone other than the owner oversees the operation of a parcel of real estate and assists the owner in achieving his investment objectives.

Property manager   Knowledgeable professional who has the experience and skills to operate real estate and understands the fundamentals of business management; chief administrator of a particular property or group of properties.

Property supervisor   Service- and detail-oriented individual who oversees operations of a property or group of properties and is responsible for the performance of personnel and maintenance of properties under his supervision in accordance with company policies and procedures.

Property tax   A tax levied on various kinds of real and personal property by state and local governments.

Prospect   A potential customer.

Prospect profile   A study and listing of characteristics of prospects.

Psychology   The science of mental processes and behavior.

Public area   A space at a property for general public use and not restricted for use by any lease or other agreement.

Public corporation   A corporation formed for purposes of government and the administration of public affairs.

Public housing   Low-rent housing provided in the U.S. for low-income families by local housing authorities with federal assistance.

Public relations   Activities undertaken to improve the public image between the general public and a firm in order to meet marketing objectives.

Purchase order   Written authorization to an outside supplier to provide certain goods or services in a given amount, at a given price, and at a certain time and place.

Purchasing   The acquisition of goods required to carry on the enterprise; also *buying*.

Purchasing power   The ability to buy, particularly as distinguished from the possession of money.

Quantitative indicator   A measurable index or standard of performance.

Real estate   Land and objects permanently attached to it.

Real estate investment trust (REIT)   A real estate lending organization set up to sell shares to investors and use the funds to invest in real estate holdings.

REALTOR®   An active member of a local real estate board affiliated with the NATIONAL ASSOCIATION OF REALTORS®.

Rebate   The return of part of a payment representing a deduction from the full amount previously charged and paid.

Recession   An extended, substantial, and widespread decline in economic activity.

Recognition   Acknowledgment or favorable notice.

Reconciliation   Bringing into agreement two or more accounts or statements that show a discrepancy.

Record   Any document that is filed.

Records administration   Management of creation, storage, and termination of documents.

Recycle   Convert a property to a new and different use.

Reference document   Record not currently in use but one that must be available for research when necessary.

Refinance   Obtain a new loan to pay off an existing loan.

Regional analysis   Detailed study of a region to determine the force of various factors affecting the economic welfare.

Regional shopping center   Retail centers of from 300,000 to 2,000,-000 square feet serving a population of 100,000 or more and containing several full-line department stores and up to 150 smaller stores.

Rehabilitation   Restoration to former or improved condition.

Remodel   Convert a building to another or better use by effecting structural changes or additions.

Rent   Periodic payment made for the use of a property over a period of time.

Rentable area   Total interior area in a building, usually expressed in square feet, that may be leased to tenants.

Rental schedule   Listing of rental rates for units or space in a given building.

Rent control   Government regulation imposed on rents in order to keep rents from rising inordinately.

Rent loss Deficiency increment resulting from vacancies, bad debts, etc., between total project rental and actual rents collected or collectible.

Rent roll A record of rents and other income payable and paid by tenants.

Rent-up budget Projection of income and expenses for a newly developed property.

Reputation Esteem in which a person or organization is held by the public.

Reserves Funds set aside for foreseeable expenses or charges.

Resident manager On-site employee charged with overseeing and administering day-to-day building affairs in accordance with directions from manager or owner.

Responsibility Quality of being accountable for the performance of delegated duties.

Retained earnings Income left to a company after taxes and dividends have been paid; source of funds for expansion without increasing obligations.

Return Rate of profit earned in relation to value of capital investment required.

Risk The probability of losing money or making a profit on one's investment; in insurance, a general term for any possibility of loss.

Risk management A method of controlling risks, generally through insurance, and managing losses.

Role playing Dramatization of probable events in an attempt to predict or learn.

Routine operating objective A quantitative goal set for performance of a normal assignment or responsibility.

Rule Statement of specifically what can and cannot be done in a given situation.

Salary The earnings of a professional paid on a weekly, monthly, or other basis.

Satisfier Type of motivator that is noticeable only in its absence.

Savings and loan association An institution that provides both a safe form of investment and funds for financing, primarily of home mortgages; also *building and loan association.*

Scheduled gross rental income Total revenues possible from an income property.

Scientific management An objective method of solving problems via the application of scientific principles and techniques to business management.

Scientific merchandising The application of scientific techniques to merchandising of consumer products.

Seasonal variation A regularly recurring pattern of change that occurs in nearly all business and economic activities owing to periodic climate changes, holidays, etc.

Second mortgage A mortgage loan secured by real estate that previously has been made security for a prior mortgage loan.

Secured lien Lien backed by a mortgage or pledge of collateral.

Securities and Exchange Commission (SEC) An independent federal regulatory agency that administers statutes designed to provide the fullest possible disclosure to the investing public.

Security deposit An established amount of money advanced by a tenant and held by an owner or manager for a specific period of time to cover possible damages and ensure the faithful performance of the lease by the tenant.

Service bureau Company that provides computer service, including equipment and programs, in exchange for a fee.

Shareholder Owner of a corporation; also *stockholder*.

Sherman Antitrust Act An act passed in 1890 that declared trusts and monopolies illegal and provided for fines and imprisonment of violators.

Shopping center A group of retail stores planned, developed, and owned as a unit and usually providing off-street parking.

Short-term plan A detailed program worked out in advance in order to meet immediate objectives; also *operational plan*.

Simple interest An interest charge computed by applying the percentage rate of interest to the principal of the loan only and not to previous interest charges.

Situation analysis Factual foundation of a marketing plan that defines the market, competitive and economic context, and business position and capabilities.

Social responsibility Responsibility to exercise positive control over impacts on people.

Society of Industrial REALTORS® (SIR) An international organization of specialists in meeting the real estate needs of industry, marketing industrial properties, and coordinating all phases of industrial real estate activity.

Software A computer program.

Sole proprietorship A form of business organization in which an individual owns and manages the entire enterprise.

Span of control The number of subordinates a person supervises.

Specialization Narrowing the scope of output or job responsibility.

Specialty shopping center Retail area that offers fashion goods, atmospheric restaurants, gift items, and other specialty merchandise and caters to upper-income discretionary spending.

Stabilized budget Long-range estimate of income and expenses which includes reserves for capital items that will need replacement during the period of the budget.

Start-up fee Level of compensation sometimes required by management upon takeover of a property.

Statute of frauds That part of a state law which requires that, in order to be enforceable, certain instruments must be in writing.

Statute of limitations Any of numerous laws that limit the period of time during which certain rights are legally enforceable.

Stock option Right to buy a specific number of shares of company stock at a stated price within a definite period of time.

Strategy Specification of programs for attaining desired objectives.

Strip store An adjacent horizontal group of small stores along a roadway serving an outlying neighborhood or passing traffic.

Studio apartment Small, efficiency apartment.

Subchapter S corporation Form of business corporation that permits corporate income to pass through to shareholders as personal income; also *small business corporation*.

Subsidized housing Federal program of housing based on government grants that reduce cost of housing and as a result lower the rental charged to the occupant.

Supplier relations Relationships with vendors who provide goods and services to the enterprise.

Surtax An extra tax levied in addition to a normal tax, usually applied to incomes at the top of the scale to make an income tax more progressive.

Symposium A meeting for the discussion of some specified topic.

Syndication A combination of persons or firms to accomplish a joint venture that is of mutual, usually financial, interest.

Target performance specifications Quantitative goals toward which employee or other production is aimed.

Tax A governmental levy usually made on a regular basis and based in principle upon the relative value of the object being levied.

Taxable income Income for a given period of time against which there is an income tax liability to municipal, state, or federal income tax agency.

Tax deduction An expenditure that legally may be deducted from taxable income.

Tax-exempt Certain kinds of income not subject to income tax, such as income from state or municipal bonds.

Tax shelter A device whereby a taxpayer may reinvest earnings on capital without paying income tax on them.

Tenancy Occupying or holding land or other real estate on a rental basis, with or without a written lease.

Tenant One who pays rent to occupy or gain possession of real estate.

Tenant mix The combination of occupant types within a building.

Tenant profile A study and listing of the similar and dissimilar characteristics of the present tenants of a property.

Termination The process of leaving a job, either voluntarily or involuntarily; the ending of a contract, usually when the conditons have been carried out.

Time deposit A deposit in a bank account that must remain for a given period of time.

Time log A record that facilitates recording time usage.

Time sharing A system of computer utilization whereby a number of customers at scattered locations use the same computer, each paying for their proportionate share of computer time.

Time study Detailed analysis of any operation in terms of the precise performance time for the entire job and each of its parts.

Trade association An organization formed by companies in a particular industry or field for the purpose of promoting their mutual interests.

Transaction documents Records vital to current operations.

Trust An arrangement whereby title to a property is transferred from the grantor to a third party to be held and managed by it for the benefit of another.

Trust company Financial organization whose chief function is to act as trustee, fiduciary, or agent for individuals or firms in a variety of capacities.

Trustee The person to whom property is transferred in order to hold for the benefit or use of a third person.

Trust fund accounting Use of a central trust account into which all monies collected for various properties are maintained.

Turnover Number of units vacated during a specific period of time, usually expressed as a ratio between the number of units vacated and the total number of units at the property.

Umbrella liability insurance Protection against losses in excess of amounts covered by other liability insurance policies.

Unemployment compensation System of insurance whereby those who lose their jobs receive periodic payments from an unemployment compensation fund for a period of time presumably long enough to permit them to find new jobs.

Union An organization of workers formed for the purpose of collective bargaining with employers concerning terms and conditions of employment.

Unit A single, distinct part of the whole; a single apartment.

Unit mix The combination of apartment unit types within a property.

U.S. Department of Housing and Urban Development (HUD) A federal department created in 1968 to supervise the Federal Housing Authority and a number of other government agencies charged with administering various housing programs.

Unsecured loan A loan secured only by the borrower's good name and not a pledge.

Urban renewal Any of the various programs undertaken by government and private business to redevelop and improve portions of cities.

Valuable papers insurance Insurance that provides for reimbursement costs incurred by the insured to reconstruct or replace important documents in order to operate normally following damage or destruction to property.

Valuation The result of the process of appraising property for tax purposes.

Value The worth or usefulness of a good or service expressed in terms of a specific sum of money.

Vendor Any seller or supplier.

Veterans Administration (VA) An independent federal agency established in 1930 to administer laws covering a wide range of benefits for former members of the U.S. armed forces and their dependents and beneficiaries, among them ensuring that qualified applicants may obtain mortgage loans.

Wage   Any regular payment to an employee for labor by the hour, week, or some other period.

Wage-hour laws   State and federal statutes that govern the number of hours that may be worked and consequent compensation.

Workmen's compensation   Payment to workers or their families for work-related injuries or disease, regardless of fault, as required by state laws.

Yield   Rate of return on any investment.

Zoning   Establishment of districts in which specific enterprises may be located, designed to regulate and control the character and use of property.

Index

Economy, management of, 13, 326, 336, 337–38
  effect on real estate, 344–46
Electronic data processing (EDP). *See* Accounting, computerized method of
Embarcadero Center, 358
Employee(s). *See also* Performance appraisal; Personnel management
  development of, 44–5, 54, 223, 225–29
  management account takeover and, 190–91, 193
  motivation of, 232–35, 361
  orientation of, 223–25
  promotional advancement of, 211–12
  recruitment of, 146, 209–10, 218, 221
  safety and health of, 296–98
  selection of, 209–10, 215, 217, 218, 223
Employee benefits, 63, 66–7, 288–89
Employee relations, 128, 190–91, 231
Employee turnover, 210–11, 248
Employment agency, 213, 214
Employment agreement, 298–99
Employment application, 217–19
Employment interview, 219–21
Employment level, effect on real estate of, 46, 321, 325–26, 327, 345
Empty nester, 341
Entertainment expense. *See* Business expense
Entrepreneur, property manager as, 32, 34, 97
Environmental impact legislation, 353–54
Errors and omissions liability insurance, 286–87
Escalation clause, effect on management fee of, 179
Ethics, property management and, 12, 33, 128, 279
Executive property manager, job description of, 34–5
  marketing and, 151–52, 163, 165

  payroll of, 145
  responsibilities of, 17, 104, 111, 131, 147
Executive Consulting Services, Inc., 216
Extra-expense insurance, 287, 289

Faneuil Market, 358
Fayol, Henri, 7
Federal Civil Rights Act, 296
Federal Fair Housing Act, 296
Federal Home Loan Bank, 314, 356
Federal Home Loan Mortgage Corporation, 356
Federal Housing Administration, 318, 331, 339, 355
  Sections 68 and 603 of, 335
  Title VI of, 332
Federal Land Banks, 321
Federal National Mortgage Association, 356
Federal Tax Act of 1954, 340
Federal Urban Mortgage Bank, 314
Fee. *See* Management fee
Fidelity bond, 12, 284–85, 286, 290
Filing system, 251, 252
Financial accounting. *See* Accounting, financial
Financial statement. *See* Balance sheet; Operating report; Profit and loss statement
Financing, data concerning, 192
  history of practice of, 314–18, 328–31
Financing cost, 204, 205
Firm, partnership as, 89
Fiscal year, 134
Fixed expense, budgeting for, 206
Fixed management fee, 179
Flow chart, as internal control, 260
Foreclosures, 328, 329, 340
Foreign investment, in real estate, 350–52
Ford, Henry, 305
Forms, 193–94, 250, 275–77, 278
Fraud, 293–94, 295, 310
Fringe benefits. *See* Employee benefits

Rental market, effects on, 46–7, 340
Rental schedule, 201–02
Rent control, history of, 313, 333–36
Rent roll, 193, 259
Rescue mortgage, 330
Reserves, for management company, 136
for property expenses, 186, 190, 192, 206
Residential leasing, 121
Resident manager. *See* On-site manager
Resources, of management company, 153–55
of property manager, 69
Responsibility, as motivator, 27–8, 234, 235
organizational structure and, 122
Retail property, history of, 10, 17, 309–10, 322–24
Retained earnings, 133, 136
Risk, of management company, 281–82, 289
Risk management, 282
Rules, 60, 273–74

Sales presentation, 172–74
Satisfier, motivation theory and, 233–34
Savings and loan associations, 315
Say, J.B., 32
Schedule, as form of control, 54
Scheduled gross rent, 260
Schultz, Carlton, 11
Schwed, Fred, 325
Scientific management, 6–7, 12, 13–14
Sears, Roebuck and Company, 8
Second mortgage, 318, 328
Secretary, 145, 248–49
Service bureau, 265, 266–67
Shareholder, 92, 93
Sherman Antitrust Act, 176, 302
Shopping center, history of, 17, 337, 343–44
management of, 22, 23, 121
types of, 343–44

Short-term plan, 101
Signage, as marketing tool, 170
Situation analysis, 152, 155
Skyscraper, history of, 303–05, 321
Sleep, time management and, 82
Sloan, Alfred P. Jr., 8
Small business corporation, 95–6
Smith, Fred G., 306
Social responsibility, property management of, 17, 45, 361
Society of Industrial REALTORS®, 332
Software, computer technology and, 268
Sole proprietorship, 87–9
Solicitation, new business and, 164
Southern Pacific Railroad, 302
Span of control, 122
Speaking engagements, public relations and, 168–69
Specialty shopping center, 343
Staff size, marketing objectives and, 159
Standard operating procedure. *See* Procedure
Stockholder, 92
Stockholders' equity. *See* Owners' equity
Stock Market, corporate expansion and, 302
Depression and, 22, 324–27
as economic indicator, 302, 319
Stock option, as form of compensation, 63, 65–6
Statute of frauds, 181, 183
Statute of limitations, records management and, 252
Strategy, 101, 105–06
Strategic plan. *See* Long-range plan
Strip store, 344
Subchapter S corporation, 95–6
Suburban office building, 342
Suburbia, development of, 336–37, 339, 342
Supervision, 60, 110, 154
Supplier relations, 128, 165, 190, 191
Supply and demand, 46
Syndication, for real estate investment, 347, 349